Studies in Political Humour

Discourse Approaches to Politics, Society and Culture (DAPSAC)

The editors invite contributions that investigate political, social and cultural processes from a linguistic/discourse-analytic point of view. The aim is to publish monographs and edited volumes which combine language-based approaches with disciplines concerned essentially with human interaction – disciplines such as political science, international relations, social psychology, social anthropology, sociology, economics, and gender studies.

For an overview of all books published in this series, please see
http://benjamins.com/catalog/dapsac

General Editors

Ruth Wodak and Greg Myers
University of Lancaster

Editorial address: Lancaster University,
County College South, Department of
Linguistics and English Language,
Lancaster LA1 4YL, UK.
r.wodak@lancaster.ac.uk
and g.myers@lancaster.ac.uk

Associate Editor

Johann Unger
University of Lancaster
j.unger@lancaster.ac.uk

Advisory Board

Volume 46

Studies in Political Humour. In between political critique and public entertainment
Edited by Villy Tsakona and Diana Elena Popa

Studies in Political Humour

In between political critique
and public entertainment

Edited by

Villy Tsakona
Democritus University of Thrace, Greece

Diana Elena Popa
Dunarea de Jos University of Galati, Romania

John Benjamins Publishing Company
Amsterdam / Philadelphia

The paper used in this publication meets the minimum requirements of American National Standard for Information Sciences – Permanence of Paper for Printed Library Materials, ANSI z39.48-1984.

Library of Congress Cataloging-in-Publication Data

Studies in political humour : in between political critique and public entertainment / edited by Villy Tsakona, Diana Elena Popa.
      p. cm. (Discourse Approaches to Politics, Society and Culture, ISSN 1569-9463 ; v. 46)
Includes bibliographical references and index.
1. Political satire--History and criticism. 2. Wit and humor--Political aspects. 3. Political science--Humor. 4. Politics, Practical--Humor. I. Tsakona, Villy. II. Popa, Diana Elena. III. Title: Studies in political humor.
PN6149.P64S78   2011
809.7'93581--dc23   2011037699
ISBN 978 90 272 0637 4 (Hb ; alk. paper)
ISBN 978 90 272 8221 7 (Eb)

John Benjamins Publishing Co. · P.O. Box 36224 · 1020 ME Amsterdam · The Netherlands
John Benjamins North America · P.O. Box 27519 · Philadelphia PA 19118-0519 · USA

Table of contents

Acknowledgements

The point of departure for the present volume was the common interest in hu-mour and politics that the two editors shared as researchers in two relatively close European universities, Democritus University of Thrace, Greece and Dunărea de Jos University of Galați, Romania. While Villy Tsakona was mostly interested in humour *in* politics, Diana Elena Popa was intrigued by humour *on* politics. There-fore, they decided to devout their time and energy to present some recent trends in the study of political humour. It is worth pointing out here that this is not a book of proceedings inasmuch as it did not originate from any related colloquium or conference. Rather, the book project triggered the idea of organizing the 1st In-ternational Conference on Conventional and Unconventional Politics which was held at Dunărea de Jos University of Galați, Romania, in November 2009.

Shortly after both editors decided to embark on the project, other contributors were invited to join in to extend the areas covered by the present book. Conse-quently, the editors would like to acknowledge their gratitude to the contributors to this volume. Their hard work and commitment to the project has been crucial at every stage, first in response to our initial call to them as we began to develop the themes and overall vision of the volume, and second in response to the re-viewers' comments on the volume as a whole and its individual chapters. Ruth Wodak, Greg Myers, Johnny Unger, and Isja Conen from John Benjamins have shown great faith in this project and given us the time and feedback we needed to develop the volume. We have also greatly benefited from insightful remarks by the two anonymous reviewers of the volume. We naturally take responsibility for the remaining faults and imperfections. Warm thanks are also due to Maria Sifianou and Eleni Antonopoulou for their wholehearted support in our effort.

Finally, our thanks go to the dear ones for providing us with a warm and com-fortable environment we so needed to work happily and productively in order to get this project finished.

List of tables and figures

Tables

Figures

CHAPTER 1

Humour in politics and the politics of humour

An introduction

Villy Tsakona and Diana Elena Popa
Democritus University of Thrace, Greece /
Dunărea de Jos University of Galaţi, Romania

In this chapter, the authors offer a working definition of political humour and summarise its main aspects as discussed in the relevant literature: the genres where political humour surfaces or dominates; the reasons why political criticism is so often encoded in humorous terms; and the (side-)effects of political humour. They also discuss the so-called "inherent ambiguity of humour", thus explaining why political humour does not necessarily influence politics. Rather than provoking social and political change, political humour conveys criticism against the political status quo and recycles and reinforces dominant values and views on politics. The diverse sociopolitical conditions may influence who is allowed to participate in the creation and circulation of political humour and who may become its target.

1. Debunking myths on political humour

If politics is a serious matter and humour a funny one, the present volume investigates how and why the boundaries between the two are blurred: politics can be represented in a humorous manner and humour can have a serious intent. In particular, we set out to debunk two popular myths about political humour. First, political humour is considered to be subversive and leading to political change: by offering a different perspective on political issues, it not only leads the audience to question the effectiveness of political decisions and practices, but also serves as a means of resistance to, or even rebellion against, political oppression and social injustice. This view of political humour is directly related to a similar perspective on humour in general as a means of deconstructing social reality and, at the same time, creating and proposing an alternative one.

The second myth involves viewing political humour as a tradition of certain cultural communities. The relevant research often concentrates on humour as a prevailing and exclusive feature of specific sociocultural environments, mostly because it seems to be a highly valued practice therein. For instance, Fry (1976: 227) claims that

> [p]olitical humour is one of America's great national traditions. We have laughed and poked fun at our leaders and politicians from the earliest days of white men's inhabitation of this continent. Few public figures have been ignored by the spotlight of satire and comedy. [...] It becomes apparent that humour associated with public figures and public affairs plays a not insignificant part in shaping the destiny of the Nation.

In general, most monographs and volumes on political humour concentrate on its function and meaning in a specific sociocultural context (e.g. humour in US politics in Gardner 1994; Jones 2010; Lewis 2006; humour in former Socialist states in Krikmann and Laineste 2009) or adopt a diachronic or historical perspective (see among others Schutz 1976; Sauvy 1979; Corbeill 1996). Research has also focused on a particular type of political humour, namely ethnic jokes (see among others Apte 1985; Davies 1998, 2002; Brzozowska 2007), discussing mostly the socio-historical conditions of their production and circulation, but also their political dimension.

Our first aim is to show that, rather than provoking and inducing social and political change, humour serves mainly two functions: it conveys criticism against the political status quo and it recycles and reinforces dominant values and views on politics. Although the first – critical – function can easily be attested in political satire, political cartoons, etc., the latter may initially seem counterintuitive. However, recent research has claimed that, being a very popular communicative resource, humour sometimes manages to enhance commonsensical views on political affairs rather than to promote radical thinking.

To this end, the data analysed in the studies included in the present volume comes from different sociopolitical contexts in Europe and allows us to have a glimpse not only at contemporary political humour practices and genres, but also at how humour was used in the recent past. The case studies presented in this volume come from Estonia, Germany, Greece, Italy, Poland, and Romania, namely from European states with different sociopolitical histories and traditions. For instance, Estonia, Poland, and Romania are ex-Communist states in a rapid process of democratisation, while Germany, Greece, and Italy are more or less "older" democracies. Such diversity may influence – at least to a certain degree – not only the limits of political humour and the role of (official or other) censorship in setting these limits, but also the various functions political humour is expected to serve in each sociocultural community. The diverse sociopolitical conditions may also influence who is expected or allowed to participate in the creation and circulation of political humour and who may become its target. Hence, our second aim is to trace some similarities and differences in humour production, depending on the social and political particularities of each state or culture.

In what follows, we first define the basic concepts and terminology used in the present discussion, in order to clarify and account for the relation between humour and criticism (Section 2). We then offer a working definition of political humour and summarise its main aspects as discussed in the relevant literature: the genres where political humour surfaces or dominates; the reasons why political criticism is so often encoded in humorous terms (Section 3); and the (side-) effects of political humour (Section 4). In Section 5, we explore how the so-called "inherent ambiguity of humour" can help explain why political humour does not necessarily influence politics. The final section (Section 6) of this introduction is dedicated to the presentation of the volume chapters.

2.   Some basic concepts and terminology

One of the most debated issues in humour research is the very definition of the phenomenon under scrutiny: due to word borrowing, the term *humour* appears in many languages, where it seems to be used more or less differently. Moreover, the term is associated with, and differentiated from, other terms, such as the comic, irony, satire, ridicule, parody, mockery, scorn, funny, ludicrous, etc. This issue is further complicated by the fact that humour has attracted the attention of scholars coming from different disciplines (psychology, linguistics, literary studies, sociology, philosophy, anthropology, folklore studies, communication and media studies, translation studies, etc.; see Raskin 2008b) and focusing on different aspects and functions of what is generally called *humour*. In the present volume, following Ruch's (1998, 2002) studies on the content and use of the term *humour* in different cultures and languages, we use the word *humour* as an umbrella term covering *all* related phenomena.

The common denominator of all these phenomena seems to be incongruity, namely an unexpected element or event suddenly appearing in a given situation. The idea of incongruity[1] as the basis of humour dates back to philosophers such as Aristotle, James Beattie, Immanuel Kant, Søren Kierkegaard, Arthur

---

1.   On incongruity theories of humor, see among others Koestler (1964), Raskin (1985: 31–36), Davis (1993: 11–16), Attardo (1994: 47–49), Palmer (1994: 93–110), Popa (2003a), Critchley (2002: 3), Billig (2005: 57–85), Morreall (2009: 9–15).

Schopenhauer, and has been adopted and further developed by dominant contemporary theories of humour, such as the *General Theory of Verbal Humour* (Attardo and Raskin 1991; Attardo 1994, 2001). Adopting linguistic, and particularly pragmatic terminology, this theory describes incongruity as an opposition between two scripts, where a script is defined as a cognitive structure involving the semantic information associated with the words included in a text, representing a speaker's knowledge of the world, and providing information on the structure, components, functions, etc. of the entity or activity referred to. Based on the violation of what is expected or considered normal in given circumstances, humour emerges from two overlapping but opposed scripts.

Such violations, however, do not generate by default a humorous response: fear, agony, anxiety, panic, indignation, curiosity, disgust, etc. may also result from something deviating from the norms and disrupting social order. Thus, humour is further conceptualised as the *enjoyment of incongruity*: humorists and their audience have to feel safe and not threatened by the violation of their expectations (Morreall 1983, 2009; see also Dynel this volume). Disruption can be perceived as humorous only in "protected" environments and more or less "controlled" conditions, where participants do not feel in danger.

This view of humour as deviation from the norm brings to the surface its social function: humour constitutes a *social corrective* aiming at highlighting, eliminating, and even preventing any disruption from what is socially accepted and approved of. Hence, humour is often used as a means of criticism and social control, based on and projecting the (mostly implicit) norms and values of a specific community and heightening social boundaries between in-group and out-group members (Bergson 1901/1997; Archakis and Tsakona 2005, 2006, this volume; Billig 2005; Kuipers 2008b: 364–366). In other words, it simultaneously contributes to social bonding between interlocutors who agree on the content and targets of humour (the so called *inclusive* function of humour), and to enhancing the gap between speakers who do not adopt the same stance towards humorous themes and targets (the *exclusive* function of humour).

Finally, due to the relation between humour and enjoyment, as well as between humour and ridicule, humour is often associated (if not identified and confused) with laughter. Research on humour and laughter, however, tends to treat them as two separate phenomena: humour may not always result in laughter and laughter does not always indicate the presence of humour (see among others Glenn 2003; Greatbatch and Clark 2003; O'Connell and Kowal 2004, 2005). On the other hand, given that laughter is considered not only the most typical contextualisation cue for humour (Kotthoff 2000: 64), but also its desired effect (Norrick 2000: 172), it could be claimed that the co-presence of incongruity and laughter, whether in political or other kinds of humour, may help us define and account for humorous phenomena (Archakis and Tsakona 2005, 2006, this volume).

3.   Political humour: Definition, genres, and functions

Political humour is usually produced either by politicians, in order, for instance, to undermine their opponents, or by journalists, political commentators, artists, cartoonists, ordinary people, etc., in order to criticise politics and politicians (Raskin 1985: 222–246; Nilsen 1990; Paletz 1993; Speier 1998; Morreall 2005). It surfaces in political and non political settings. Politicians' humour prototypically occurs in settings where serious political discourse is expected to prevail, such as parliaments, political debates, party congresses, interviews, etc. Political humour produced by the media and ordinary people mostly occurs in the form of institutionalised humorous genres (Kuipers 2008b: 370), such as jokes, cartoons, TV or radio satirical shows, humorous websites, humorous festivals (as described in Abe 1998), etc. The latter kind of political humour may also spill over genres which are neither humorous by definition, such as news reports, graffiti, and political slogans, nor political, such as musicals (Colipcă 2009) and postmodern performances (Manteli this volume; see also Hariman 2008: 248).

Some humorous genres are more popular in certain sociocultural environments, while others are less common therein and this depends on the particularities of these contexts. For instance, at least before 1989, political humour referring to the Berlin Wall appeared in both East and West Berlin. In East Berlin, the Wall was (literally and metaphorically) invisible: it was inaccessible to citizens, thus it became a taboo subject generating a considerable amount of jokes circulating in private gatherings, as personal communication among intimates. On the contrary, in West Berlin, such humour was mostly cast in the form of graffiti on the Wall itself: for Western Berliners the Wall was visible and an integral part of the urban landscape. Hence, their Wall humour included statements or punch lines accessible to the public: they were (and still are) usually written by anonymous citizens on that part of the Wall that is in centre of the city (Stein 1989).

Political humour exhibits explicit coherence links to political discourse: without contextual knowledge on political issues, it cannot be processed and interpreted (Mulkay 1988: 210; Mascha 2008: 70, 2010; Tsakona 2008, 2009b, 2011a; Popa this volume). However, such links are not exactly intertextual, but rather contratextual. The difference between the two kinds of links could be summarised as follows: while intertextual links speak of the same things in more or less the same way and aim at building consensus by projecting certain views as "dominant" and "non negotiable", contratextual links are often realised by echoing the words and ideological stances of the opponent with a view to fulfilling a mocking and *discrediting* function, thereby constructing positive self-presentation and consensus on one's own stance.

(Vasta 2004: 112; our emphasis)

Since humour is by definition based on incongruity and serves as criticism, political humour could be defined as a communicative resource spotting, highlighting, and attacking incongruities originating in political discourse and action (cf. Chun 2004; Dodds 2007; Warner 2007; Georgalidou this volume).

More specifically, political humour brings to the surface the inconsistencies and inadequacy of political decisions and acts, and the incompetence, recklessness, and corruption of politicians and political leaders. It is usually based on how political reality is, while, at the same time, points out that this is in fact an incongruous reality: political affairs and politicians are not what they are expected to be (Dudden 1985; Raskin 1985: 222; Davies 1998: 77–88; Niven et al. 2003; Ancheta 2006; El Refaie 2009; Popa this volume; Watters this volume). On the other hand, political systems can manufacture a historical reality according to their view, values, and decisions on what is real or not, what is true or not, what is acceptable or not. Such an ideological stance may be adopted by other systems as well (i.e. the theatre system; see Manteli this volume). It could, therefore, be suggested that political humour is based on a (more often than not) *idealised* and/or *entrenched* view of politics: the criticism conveyed reveals the implicit, dominant, and often commonsensical views on how politics is to be conducted.

Needless to say, criticism against politics is not always cast in humorous terms – quite on the contrary. Being one of the main functions of political discourse, criticism is typically achieved in a most serious manner: politicians are expected to attack their opponents' decisions and delegitimise their policies, so as to discredit them and promote themselves. To this end, they usually employ serious – mostly logical and legal – argumentation, in order to convince their audience about their own credibility and sincerity. However, in many cultures and political systems, it is not uncommon for politicians to resort to humour to criticise and discredit their adversaries. Humour in such cases allows politicians to abide to politeness norms and to avoid rude behaviour (Martin 2004; Dynel this volume). It is not accidental that parliamentarians, for example, use humour in parliamentary settings, where institutional restrictions are imposed on their (verbal or other) behaviour (Harris 2001: 467; Ilie 2001: 255, 2004: 78; Miller 2004: 292; Meisel 2009: 228–231; Carranza Márquez 2010; Madzharova Bruteig 2010: 284–285; Ornatowski 2010: 256–259; Zima et al. 2010: 146–147, 151–160; Tsakona 2011b; Mueller this volume).

Humour is pervasive, positively evaluated, and eventually desired in most contemporary societies (Lockyer and Pickering 2001; Billig 2005; Pickering and Lockyer 2005). It is also deemed an important characteristic of good leadership enabling leaders to perform their role more effectively (Holmes and Marra 2006; Schnurr 2008). As a result, politicians attempt to enhance their popularity by adding a humorous tone or humorous remarks to their discourse whenever they are being watched by the wider audience: in political speeches broadcast by the media, in political interviews, etc. In doing so, they try to project a positive self-image and/or to attract prospective voters. At the same time, by focusing on the humorous performance of a politician, the attention of the audience is usually distracted from the important issues discussed (Martin 2004; Meisel 2009; Tsakona 2009a; Archakis and Tsakona this volume; Dynel this volume; Georgalidou this volume). Interestingly, politicians participate even in satirical TV shows to enhance their public and media persona, to increase their visibility, and to promote their political views and stances (Coleman et al. 2009).

The presence of humour renders political discourse memorable and attractive for the media: journalists often select humorous extracts for reproduction in their news articles, in order to appeal to their readership (Whaley and Holloway 1997). As humour is not considered a defining, prototypical feature of political and media discourse, it is argued that it contributes to the conversationalisation of public discourse (Fairclough 1995): originating in everyday interaction and colloquial discourse, humour offers a more trivialised view of political affairs and allows speakers to conceptualise politics in everyday terms (Gadavanij 2002; Alvarez-Cáccamo and Prego-Vásquez 2003; Morreall 2005: 76, 78; Tsakona 2009a; Georgalidou this volume). Hence, voters live by the illusion that politicians "speak the language of common people" and are "one of them". Humour is thus used to enhance audience involvement and engagement in politics, while it allows politicians and/or media people to promote specific standpoints and values and to persuade the audience on the "reasonableness" of political acts and decisions. In short, humour can contribute to the creation of a commonsensical view of political issues which is both attractive and deceptive for the audience.

An interesting interplay between politics, the media, and humour emerges in this context. On the one hand, the media are the main arena of political communication in modern societies: more than ever, political deliberation and confrontation take place "on air", "on paper", "on the web" and this is the main (if not the only) access citizens have to political discourse (Bayley 2004: 11; Craig 2004: 4; Fetzer and Lauerbach 2007). On the other, the media do not aim at encouraging political (or other) change: instead, their role in maintaining and reinforcing mainstream dominant values is crucial (Fairclough 1995). Hence, humour becomes a powerful tool in the hands of the media to simultaneously "criticize" political decisions and figures, and entertain the audience (Georgalidou this volume; Manteli this volume; Mascha this volume; Popa this volume; Watters this volume). In this light, humorous political criticism more often than not supports and recycles widespread views on politics rather than promotes radical ideas and changes:

> [H]umor is predominantly a conservative, rather than a liberating or construc-
> tive, force in society. [...] [A]lthough humour appears to be a radical alternative
> to serious discourse in the sense that it is socially separated from the serious
> mode and is organised in terms of contrary discursive practices, it seems in prac-
> tice overwhelmingly to support and reaffirm the established patterns of orderly,
> serious conduct.   (Mulkay 1988: 211–212; see also Billig 2005: 209, 212)

This is clearly illustrated, for instance, in Shelton Caswell's (2004) study on U.S. editorial cartoons published during more than two centuries of wars. Her analysis reveals that this kind of humour assumes "both opinion-moulding and opinion-reflecting roles" (Shelton Caswell 2004: 14): cartoonists are allowed to express their personal opinion and stance on current events, while at the same time respecting the values and traditions of their audience and eventually educating them on what is "right", "wrong", "fair", "unfair", etc. In other words, in political cartoons, popular ideas, stereotypes, and archetypes drawing on fundamental emotions, beliefs, and aspirations of the community are creatively exploited for political criticism and propaganda. Hence, editorial cartoons, as Shelton Caswell claims, offer valuable insight into the sociopolitical context of their production and circulation. Such findings are confirmed by several studies: not only political cartoons, but also satirical TV shows usually reflect popular political thought, thus naturalising and reinforcing the significance of certain beliefs (Morrison 1992; Landowski 1993; Morris 1993; Templin 1999; Edwards 2001; Louvi 2002; El Refaie 2003, 2004; Giarelli and Tulman 2003: 945-946; Niven et al. 2003; Santa Ana 2009; Tsakona 2008, 2009b; Mascha 2010).

Finally, the inclusive and exclusive functions of humour are most prominent in political humour. Since the latter targets an opponent on the basis of implicit or explicit norms and values, those who agree with these values belong to the political in-group, while those who disagree are outcast from the group. Via highlighting what is politically disapproved and indirectly projecting what is politically approved, humour can foster solidarity among people sharing specific political views. The political references employed for the production of humour can also alienate those who are not familiar with political affairs or those who have limited (or no) access to the political life of a state. Like all kinds of humour, political humour is built on contextual knowledge, hence it cannot be understood by people who are not informed on political issues. As a result, political humour usually does not inform the audience on political issues, but explicitly comments on them, and conveys critical stance towards certain political acts and figures (see above). To put it in Brown and Yule's (1983: 1–4) terms, political humour seems to have limited (or no) *transactional* function, in the sense that it does not transmit political information (see also Raskin 2008a: 27), but it fulfils a significant *interactional* one by establishing the boundaries between the different political parties and groups and between those who can communicate through it and those who cannot (Oring 2008: 39; Chłopicki 2009; Laineste 2009; Santa Ana 2009; Tsakona 2009b, 2011a; Ornatowski 2010: 256–259; Mueller this volume). If "at the heart of what we call 'politics' is the attempt to get others to 'share a common view' about what is useful-harmful, good-evil, just-unjust" (Chilton 2004: 199), humour can be called "political" not only because it refers to politics, but also because it achieves that goal.

In sum, political humour emerges in a variety of settings and genres, whether institutionalised or not, and its form and content are significantly influenced by the social, political, and cultural environment where it is produced. Furthermore, political humour helps politicians and media people to strike a balance between the criticism expected to be expressed by them towards political power, and the attractive and pleasant messages that are designed to be "consumed" by the wider audience. The outcome of this process could be called *politicotainment* (Riegert 2007), *polintertainment* (Panke 2009), or simply *entertaining politics* (Jones 2010), signifying the mixture of politics and entertainment aimed at eliciting an emotional response from the audience.

4. The (side-)effects of political humour

One of the most (and most hotly) debated issues in humour research relates to the impact of humour on politics and to its influence on public opinion as an integral part of public discourse. Some scholars suggest that humour reflects ideas and views already in circulation and is based on stereotypes which are already part of the audience's background knowledge (see among others Hodge and Mansfield 1985; Raskin 1985; Hanlon et al. 1997; Davies 1998; Marín-Arrese 2008), while others argue that humour targeting specific persons, ideas, or situations is capable of creating and establishing a negative impression or stereotype at their expense (see among others Billig 2001; Lockyer and Pickering 2005; Jones 2010). While in the first case any real implications of humour are downplayed or even ignored due to humorists' lack of serious intent, in the latter they are highlighted and become the centre of analytical attention, since humour is an integral part of the public and private spheres.

Between these two poles, Mulkay (1988) claims that the audience themselves decide to ignore or to capitalise on the "serious" implications and consequences of a humorous text. He thus distinguishes between *pure* humour, where participants ignore the "serious" potential of humorous utterances and texts, and *impure* or *applied* humour, where humour is considered a vehicle for serious meanings. More specifically, he claims that

> [b]ecause it is in principle unclear what precise combination of humour and reality work is being offered in any humorously signalled utterance, recipients are always faced with a choice in deciding how to respond.   (Mulkay 1988:67)

Generally, there is considerable doubt among researchers about the persuasive power of political humour. Given, however, that the discourse produced in political settings and especially in pre-election periods is believed to have an impact on public opinion and the election outcome, the *potential* effects of political humour have attracted the attention of some scholars.[2] For instance, Bippus (2007) performs an empirical test on audience perceptions of a politician's use of humour in a political debate, in order to identify and evaluate the factors affecting the effectiveness of political messages cast in humorous terms, and to assess receivers' attributions about politicians' motives in such cases. The results of her study reveal that politicians' humour is considered to be more effective if it is self-deprecating and of "high quality", which, in that context, is related to the timing of humour production and the amusement it caused. Interestingly, party affiliation does not appear to be a significant factor in assessing the effectiveness of political humour (although it would be expected to play a significant role in the degree of political humour's persuasiveness; see Mulkay 1988:209; Kuipers 2006:206).

Experimental research suggests that the effects of online political humour and satirical TV shows are both negative and positive (see Baumgartner and Morris 2006; Baumgartner 2007; and references therein). Such humour can foster cynicism towards politics and decrease support for politicians, political institutions, and leaders, especially among viewers who are not interested in politics. This could result from the incongruities and inconsistencies brought to the fore by political humour. Such unfavourable perceptions and lack of trust towards politicians may lead to (further) alienation from politics and to abstinence from elections. On the other hand, political humour increases viewers' confidence in their ability to understand politics, hence they are more likely to participate in the electoral process or to stay informed on political affairs (Foot and Schneider 2002;

---

2. To the best of our knowledge, such studies have been conducted mostly in the U.S., thus their findings reflect the (perceived) effectiveness of political humour in this particular socio-cultural environment.

Holbert 2005; Young and Tisinger 2006; see also Hart 1999). Furthermore, the relationship between political humour and the evaluation of politicians seems to be contingent on the type of humour: self-deprecating humour results in politicians' positive evaluation by the viewers (cf. above).

Experiments have also been conducted to investigate whether political humour, in the forms of irony and sarcasm, affects the audience's ability to scrutinize political arguments articulated in humorous terms. Polk et al. (2009) argue that humour could discourage the audience from scrutinizing and counterarguing a political message: humour recipients would either choose to dismiss the humorous political message as "mere joking" or would be reluctant to scrutinize the humorous message due to the complex inferential process required and to the distracting potential of humour. Significantly, the degree of recipients' political efficacy, namely their belief that they have the skills to participate in, and hence influence, the political system, seems to be directly analogous to their tendency to scrutinize and counterargue humorous political messages.

Although the effects of political humour on the audience's attitudes and stances towards politics and politicians have started being investigated, the question regarding its effects on the audience's *actual reactions* to political humour, namely their behaviour after being exposed to such humorous stimuli, remains unanswered, mostly because empirical research confirming any of the above hypotheses or experimental findings is scarce (see also Kuipers 2008a: 33; Polk et al. 2009: 203). However, it has been suggested that political humour can, for instance, backfire and be used at the expense of the humorist especially in settings where the serious mode prevails. In such cases, the humorist, most often a politician, is accused of lack of seriousness and integrity and of frivolous and irresponsible behaviour. Such accusations mar the positive self-image the humorist wishes to construct for him/herself (Tsakona 2009a; Archakis and Tsakona this volume; see also Nilsen 1990: 43–44).

Many scholars tend to agree that political humour contributes to the creation of a public space where political issues can be deliberated in a "pleasant" and quite "harmless" way, without usually posing any serious threat against the status quo, politicians, or the wider audience (Townsend 1997; Mascha 2008; Tsakona 2009b; cf. the enjoyment of incongruity and the conversationalisation of public discourse in Sections 2 and 3 respectively). This constitutes the "control function" of humour, where "resistance through joking provides mostly temporary relief but *stabilises* potentially conflictive situations" (Kuipers 2008b: 369, our emphasis, see also references therein; Santa Ana 2009; Laineste this volume; Manteli this volume; Watters this volume). In such public spaces, humorists (whether politicians or not) have the opportunity to enhance their popularity and make their opinions and evaluations widely known. The criticism expressed against political opponents may contribute to reinforcing mainstream political values and norms also projected by "serious" political discourse: for instance, political humour, to the best of our knowledge, does not usually project cooperation between opposed parties as an "incongruous" alternative to conflict – and the same holds for "serious" political discourse (see among others Beard 2000: 22; Chilton 2004: 1, 198).

The degree of openness of such public spaces and the potential function and dynamics of political humour therein depend on the political institutions of each state. Hence, one could suggest that the above mentioned *stabilisation of conflict* is achieved via different means in open, democratic states and in authoritative ones.

In open democracies, such spaces are normally not censored by the state, but are still controlled by media people, namely members of the ruling elite, who would be at least reluctant to contest the political status quo and challenge state institutions. Thus, political humour in such environments targets only specific political decisions and figures (Dudden 1985: 51; Giarelli and Tulman 2003: 948; Olson 2005: 264; Davies 2008: 31–32; Tsakona 2011a; Watters this volume). The media control over political humour can be illustrated in a – quite common nowadays – side-effect of political humour: its manipulation and reframing for political purposes (Laineste this volume). This is the case, for example, of the social and political repercussions that followed the publication of the so-called Muhammad cartoons in Denmark in September 2005. The relevant literature addresses a variety of issues such as the boundaries between humour and freedom of speech, the cartoons' degree of offensiveness depending on the religious sensibilities of their readership, their impact on international politics, and, more generally, the contextual parameters influencing their reception (see among others Sturges 2006; Harkness et al. 2007; Hussain 2007; Post 2007; Eide et al. 2008; Lewis 2008; Asad et al. 2009; Smith 2009).

The control and manipulation of political humour appears to be straightforward and highly institutionalised in oppressive regimes, where the state not only controls and censors the media and the public spaces, but may have access to private spaces as well. For example, in Eastern European Socialist states before 1989, political jokes circulating among citizens attacked politicians or state officials, but mostly protested against political authority, coercion, and the monopoly of political power. Such jokes functioned as a kind of passive resistance and an outlet for political resentment in contexts where alternative views on politics could not be openly voiced (Galateanu 1993; Davies 1998, 2009; Niculescu Grasso 1999; Laineste 2009; Stanoev 2009: 187; cf. the Franco jokes in Spain in Pi-Sunyer 1977). At the same time, in Romania and Poland, such jokes were circulated by state officials in everyday encounters to entrap the "enemies of the people" who dared to laugh at the sociopolitical system: their telling was considered a forbidden, illegal activity (Popa 2002, 2003b; Brzozowska 2009: 131, 152). It is at least equally in-teresting to note that, in Socialist East Germany, political jokes were even *created* by the regime itself. An ex-East German, later living in West Berlin, informant of Stein (1989: 95) states that

> [m]ost political jokes in the GDR do not originate with the folk, but are con-sciously developed at Party schools and institutions. They are then skilfully in-troduced to the folk, at beer tables and in small social gatherings, and from there they travel by word of mouth […]. In order to keep the people and popular senti-ment in control the Party creates political jokes, which allow the Party to develop the proper ideological stance and norms, in order to control the situation. And the jokes, which allow people to let off steam, also serve the purpose of quieting them.

Less often, but not less interestingly, it is suggested that political humour in op-pressive regimes may "be used both as a secondary reinforcement in the process of developing critical political consciousness necessary for challenge and resis-tance" and as "a *surrogate* for conflict that ultimately contributes to escapism and *acquiescence*" (Hong 2010: 27, our emphasis). In his study of Danish jokes against Nazi occupation (1940–1945), Hong (2010) convincingly argues that the rebellion content of political jokes and their retrospective analysis are not adequate criteria for determining their function: such criteria may even lead to the fetishisation of political humour by attributing to it more power than it actually carried/s. Rather than a powerful weapon against the Germans, Danish jokes at that time, being privately circulated and without bearing significant risk, deprecated the common enemy, established a clear boundary between the oppressors and the oppressed, and, most importantly, "provided the emotional satisfaction of attacking diaboli-cal power without any of the objective sequences, positive or negative, of actually doing so in the real world" (Hong 2010: 57). Thus, in his view, such humour was produced and circulated as a means of escapism and elusion and as a substitute for action against the Nazis (cf. Holdaway 1988).

Political humour may thus be a morale boosting strategy in the hands of the oppressed, but it may also become a mousetrap for dissidents or even a means of repression in the hands of the oppressors. In this light, the comparison of the uses and functions of political humour in diverse sociopolitical settings could be most revealing: the differences between such functions in the public spaces of open democracies and in those of (former) authoritative regimes could serve as an in-dicator for the degree of openness (or even democratisation) of a state (Lindstrom 1980; Abe 1998; Tunç 2001, 2002; Downie 2010; Ilie 2010: 210–211; Madzharova Bruteig 2010: 280; Mascha this volume; Popa this volume).

This is clearly illustrated in Ornatowski's diachronic study (2010) on the interactional norms in the Polish parliament. Among other discoursal phenomena, Ornatowski investigates the use of humour and laughter among Polish parliamentarians in the post-Communist era. Humour and laughter were strictly banned from the parliament under Communist rule, but they became a significant tool of deliberation after 1989. During the first months of the "new" parliament, humour and laughter emerged from the incongruities between the old and the new political reality, hence parliamentarians shared the same humorous targets and reasons to laugh. From this kind of humour, only parliamentarians from the former ruling coalition were excluded and this distinction gradually set the ground for the appearance of more aggressive and competitive types of humour. Subsequently, the increasing political fragmentation and instability led to the development of a different kind of humour, one that was clearly oriented towards the incongruities of the current political and economical reality and had an explicit entertaining function among parliamentarians. By the end of the 1990s and especially after 2001, humour in the Polish parliament had acquired a clear inclusive/exclusive function (see Section 3): parliamentarians employed humour to align with their political allies and to reject their political enemies. Fierce political attacks and denigration via humour became common practice, as the Polish parliamentary system became more competitive and political conflict escalated therein (cf. Tsakona 2009a; Archakis and Tsakona this volume; Georgalidou this volume; Mueller this volume). Hence, the evolution of the Polish parliamentary humour could be considered indicative of how the (more or less democratic) political context shapes the norms regulating humour usage.

To sum up, while the actual influence of political humour on citizens' (voting) behaviour remains largely unknown, the subversive nature of political humour appears to be challenged by research findings up to now: since most political humour is produced and/or circulated by the media or even by the state itself in some cases, it is not destined to promote radical thinking and rebellion. It appears more accurate to suggest that political humour brings to the surface common views on how politics should be conducted, and recycles popular political idea(l)s. As a result, it could be more productively exploited by scholars to unveil and investigate widespread assumptions and audience expectations regarding policies and politicians. Moreover, the sociopolitical conditions where political humour is created and interpreted plays a crucial role in shaping its function: it appears that political humour has been used and manipulated to silence, marginalise, and even eliminate political opponents, to divert audience attention from significant political issues, and for political branding.

5.   How "serious" can political humour be?

The present discussion has so far neglected, or deliberately overlooked, the inherent ambiguity of humour: by definition, humour is not meant to be taken seriously. The "serious" message of humour can be, and often is, ignored or denied (see Mulkay 1988 in Section 4). The final question raised from our discussion and the papers included in the present volume involves how and why political humour manages to "convince" the audience that it can convey "serious" criticism; more specifically, why it is widely considered to be a "powerful" means of criticism, although it is not actually as "powerful" as it is purported to be.

Drawing on Grice's (1975) cooperative principle, where *bona-fide communication* rules, Raskin (1985) suggests that humour and joke-telling in particular operate in the *non-bona-fide communication*, where no true, accurate, or relevant information is expected. In a similar vein, Mulkay (1988) distinguishes between the *serious* and the *humorous* mode. In the first one, the basic presuppositions, expectations, and procedures of social reality are maintained, while, in the latter one, the standards of feasibility, consistency, and coherence are much less restrictive; incongruity and contradiction rule. He aptly observes that there is *no a priori definition* of what is considered to be serious and what is not: it is up to the interlocutors to decide each time whether they wish to enter the humorous mode or not. In other words, it is interlocutors who define where the boundary between serious and humorous discourse is to be set.

Political humour by definition needs both modes to be processed: the serious one is related to information and background knowledge regarding political reality (see Section 3; cf. Mulkay 1988:197–204; Edwards 2001:2141; Marín-Arrese 2008:9ff.), while the humorous one reminds the audience that what is included in humour is not meant to be taken as accurate and abiding to the realm of reality. The distinction between pure and applied humour is relevant here: the audience has to decide whether they will ignore or capitalise on the serious implications and consequences of the humorous text (see Mulkay 1988 in Section 4; see also Holbert 2005:444; Polk et al. 2009:205–206). This combination of seriousness and humour could account, on the one hand, for political humour's conceptualisation as a means of criticism and, on the other, for its limited (if not nonexistent) influence on political affairs. Given that politics and political acts are deliberated and enforced exclusively and by default via the use of the serious mode, political humour seems to be devoid of "serious" content and consequences. As a result, political humour does not (and maybe cannot) induce political change.

Finally, the ambiguous nature of political humour can also account for its potential for reframing. Due to its ambiguity political humour can serve different (usually contrasting) political purposes: its content can be interpreted as "real" or "just fun" depending on the eye of the beholder. Especially

> mediated humour seriously complicates negotiations over the meaning of a joke, because mediated humour is not firmly located in one context anymore, making mediated jokes even more polysemic and ambiguous.
> (Kuipers 2008b: 388; see also Kuipers 2008a: 33; Dynel this volume; Georgalidou this volume; Laineste this volume)

The same, we suggest, holds for the academic investigation of humour: humour has to be interpreted as serious communication, namely as applied humour (in Mulkay's 1988 terms), to merit scholarly attention. Otherwise, it would be dismissed as trivial and unworthy of academic scrutiny.

6. A brief overview of this volume

The data analysed in the chapters of the present volume comes from different sociocultural contexts and languages. Their authors come from different disciplines, thus adopt a variety of methodological tools in their analyses. The chapters are classified in three parts: the first one (Chapters 2–5) involves humour produced by politicians usually as a means of attack against their adversaries, while the second one (Chapters 6–8) involves political humour produced by the media against politicians in power. The two chapters (9–10) constituting the third part of the volume involve public debates on and with political humour. Chapter 11 summarizes some main points of the volume and discusses further areas of inquiry. The function of political humour as a means of criticism seems to unite all the perspectives included here.

Chapters 2 and 3 investigate humour produced by politicians in parliamentary settings. Mueller examines parliamentary proceedings coming from the German Bundestag, which provide detailed recordings of audible reactions among the audience, including non-verbal reactions such as applause, *amusement* (so called *Heiterkeit*), and *laughing* (so called *Lachen*). The stenographers' differentiation between *laughing* and *amusement* is founded, on the one hand, on a historical understanding of "laughing at" in terms of hostile and satirical ridicule, and, on the other hand, on a concept of conciliatory "laughing with" which derives from the old concepts of *serenity* or *hilarity*. Laughing and amusement seems to indicate different attitudes of the laughers to their target. More specifically, *laughing* is always restricted to individuals or a political faction and constitutes a common form of rebuttal through which a parliamentarian's statement, claim, or request is rejected by a part of the audience. *Amusement*, on the other hand, is typically associated with the expression of a more positive attitude, and occurs among all members of the Bundestag. Such instances frequently co-occur with particular themes, such as the negotiation of time limits, the use of formal vs. informal language, teasing about parliamentary habits (absence during sessions, funny repartees, or linguistic lapses, etc.). The study highlights both aggressiveness/denigration and conciliation/consensus as functions of German parliamentary humour.

In Chapter 3, Archakis and Tsakona adopt a sociolinguistic, in particular a discourse analytic, perspective on parliamentary humour by viewing it as an informal communicative resource employed by politicians in a formal and highly institutionalised setting. In their study, humour highlights "unexpected" and politically "unacceptable" behaviour and defines the members of the political in-group. The data analysed consist of narratives told during a "no confidence" debate in the Greek parliament. Parliamentarians coming from both the government and the opposition narrate their personal everyday experiences as part of their argumentation against the opposed party. Humorous narratives allow them to criticise the adversary and to draw the attention of the audience to the opposed party's "incongruous" and hence "failed" policies and political acts. In the authors' view, the institutional particularities of the Greek political system and the publicity of such debates allow, or even encourage, parliamentarians to transfer common informal discursive practices in Greek society, namely story-telling and humour, into a formal setting where non narrative and serious discourse is expected to prevail. In doing so, Greek parliamentarians use the "language of common people" and their voters' views in support of their own argumentation. Even in critical political circumstances, such as "no confidence" debates, humour is employed to create a favourable impression on the wider audience watching the debate.

In Chapter 4, Georgalidou further investigates the use of humour by politicians inside and outside the parliament. Her data come from press conferences, media interviews, and the official proceedings of parliamentary sittings during a period of riots in Greece in December 2008. In her study, humour and metaphor are shown to be powerful weapons in the discourse of political adversaries. Furthermore, the role of the media in the formation of *dialogical networks* connecting utterances produced in different contexts (Leudar and Nekvapil 1998), as well as the parameter of audience design related to the publicisation of political discourse, are highlighted in her analysis for their impact on the linguistic choices of politicians. Via the analysis of (part of) an extensive dialogical network initiated by the statement of the leader of the Greek Communist Party as to *the caressing of the ears of the hooded*, she traces how the media contribute to the transformation of a specific wording into a sound bite that is being repeated in the discourse of politicians of all political parties and in a variety of contexts. The switching to the humorous mode, albeit in an aggressive and derogatory manner, the adoption or the rejection of the metaphor of the *caressing of the ears*, and the different meanings attributed to the term *hooded* are shown to contribute to the construction of various alignments which, in cases, can be considered incompatible with one's declared political ideology, but still form part of a highly competitive parliamentary system such as the Greek one. As in Archakis and Tsakona's chapter, political humour here seems to contribute to the formation of hybrid discourse modes which lead to the conversationalisation of political discourse.

In the last chapter dedicated to humour produced by politicians, Dynel discusses politicians' utterances which may be considered humorous from the wider audience's perspective, but stand very little chance of being regarded as such by their political adversaries. Dynel's paper is subscribing to linguistic media studies and is based on the premise that the viewer should be deemed as a special type of ratified participant. The discourse of TV debates is inherently anchored in two communicative levels, namely one between the interactants shown on the screen, and the other entailing the viewer, who interprets meanings generated by the global media product. While the two previous chapters merely recognize the importance of the wider audience in shaping politicians' (humorous or not) utterances in public debates, this one takes a step further by putting the audience into the spotlight: interlocutors in a political debate talk to each other *and simultaneously to the recipient* (i.e. audience in the studio and in front of the TV screen). In this context, verbal aggression, admittedly intrinsic to the discourse of political debates, is a strategic weapon deployed to assert one's power over the conversationalist. Dynel argues that such aggression is intended as a humorous stimulus to be appreciated by the recipients of such debates. The data examined comes from three electoral debates between potential Polish Prime Ministers. By employing verbal aggression, politicians aim to disaffiliate from each other and simultaneously to display their wit and sense of humour with a view to entertaining and fostering solidarity with the potential electorate.

The aggressive and affiliative functions of politicians' humour are the main focus of the first part of the volume. Although in Mueller's study these functions are identified in different instances of political humour, in the following ones both functions are simultaneously fulfilled: hostility and consensus are simultaneously directed at, and perceived by, different participants of the communicative event. Furthermore, while the cases analysed in Chapters 2–4 concentrate on utterances identified (and interpreted) as intended to be primarily humorous, the data examined in Dynel's study receive two (opposing) interpretations: an explicitly aggressive and a humorous one. The dual function of humour discussed here confirms one of the main points of incongruity theory, namely that incongruity may not always be perceived as humorous, especially if interlocutors (in the present case, politicians) feel threatened by it (see Section 2).

The second part of the volume refers to political humour targeting politicians and political views and practices. Popa's study brings forth the role that satire plays in a young post-Communist state, Romania. The data provided for analysis involves samples taken from the Romanian original satirical animated cartoon show *The Animat Planet Show*. Working as a mixture between satirical discourse and visual opinion representation, *The Animat Planet Show* enacted an active and sharp process of questioning and critique which managed to animate the democratic health of Romania until it was forced to close down. Relying on three main humour techniques, namely audio-visual, language-based, and a combination of the two above, political satire transmits current affairs messages, but also identifies and establishes connections between people and events in public life. Furthermore, via exaggeration and emphasis, TV satire draws attention on issues that might otherwise go unnoticed and helps the audience perceive and comprehend the implications of certain political acts performed by politicians. Consequently, political satire in the Romanian media offers the audience a tool for deliberating on current events and formulating opinions without, however, reforming or working as a corrective for poor political behaviour, a point previously addressed by humour researchers.

Watters investigates the work of Sabina Guzzanti, one of Italy's most well-known – but also most controversial – comedians, through an analysis of her impersonation of the current Prime Minister, Silvio Berlusconi. Sabina Guzzanti is a key player in Italian satire and the cultural opposition to Berlusconi. In her analysis, Watters discusses the performance techniques of Guzzanti, with reference to theories on impersonation and television comedy. Guzzanti's impersonation provides a continued counter-image to the mediated public image of Berlusconi and evolves not only over time, but also through Guzzanti's movement away from television, which leads her to focus further on satirical stage performance and to target Berlusconi more fervently. In this context, the problem of censorship is also highlighted, which has put pressure on the creators of Italian television satire since Berlusconi's arrival in the political arena. The current Italian situation, in which lawsuits against television companies and artists themselves have become commonplace, has meant that Guzzanti's style of satire has outgrown the confines that television impersonation can allow. The author concludes that, while impersonation is often thought of as skimming the surface of the political critique which other forms of satirical humour can provide, longstanding impersonations, such as that of Guzzanti's, are capable of exposing the media mask of the politician and reflecting their faults back at them throughout their political careers.

Both Popa and Watters are interested in contemporary media satire, as well as in the way this satire is received by both its targets and the wider audience. In both cases, the limits of satire are brought to the fore mostly by the actual reactions to it: in Romania, the satirical show is closed down almost without leaving any trace behind (e.g. the official webpage was removed from the web and recordings are no longer officially available to the public), while in Italy satire is controlled via lawsuits and pressure on its creators.

The issue of censorship also emerges in the following chapter on Mussolini's ascent to power. So, staying in Italy, but moving back in time, Mascha discusses Italian political satire of the 1920s as part of Italian popular culture, situated within a specific historical and cultural context and designed to create a mocking effect. In her analysis, she combines dominant historiography with oral history accounts, biographies, and caricatures, so as to paint a broad picture of the historical and cultural conditions which political satire picked up on. Her aim is to provide a reading of Italian history of the period 1919–1925 that will facilitate the reading of her primary sources, and to illustrate the cultural framework permitting or prohibiting political satire. The analysis of Italian popular culture and, in particular of its role of popular culture as counter-hegemony during the Fascist ascent, brings to the surface the limits of popular satire's action. These limits were directly related to the official and unofficial censorship that was imposed by the regime on the press during this period. In this context, Italian cartoonists produce and re-produce historical events through their designs reflecting on the politician's political image and practices in order to amuse their audience and to contribute to resistance, change, and the formation of political consciousness.

All the chapters included in the second part refer to the potential and limitations of political satire in the media. Humour targeting prominent political figures may be popular among the wider audience, but is also met with resistance from the political status quo. Such reactions appear to depend on the current sociopolitical particularities of each state and can even lead to silencing humorous opposition.

The third part of the volume concentrates on how political humour can become the object of serious political debates or the means for criticism which is not necessarily or entirely political. The two studies included here show that humour is sometimes exploited as part of an ongoing deliberation on issues that may or may not pertain to specific political actions or to politicians who may be responsible for them. Laineste takes us back to humour theory basics: jokes. Her study focuses on the manipulation of ethnic jokes circulating in Estonia for political purposes. Laineste explores how the joke content can be reframed and reinterpreted in the media. More specifically, she describes a polemics on jokes as humorous versus aggressive texts and investigates the question of taste at the service of political struggle. Her study relies on the culturally embedded analysis on different levels of cultural communication. Official and unofficial discourses appearing on the public (printed) media and internet forums are analysed. Four dimensions of discourses are detected in the material: *discourse of danger, official discourse, discourse of healthy reasoning,* and *discourse of self-criticism.* The results of her analysis show that the two modes of communication (officially regulated versus uncensored expressions of public opinion on internet forums) differ essentially in their choice of arguments and viewpoints, the latter strongly advocating the discourse of danger and referring to the need to strengthen the Estonian national integrity through forced assimilation. The unofficial discourse of nation-building is strong, radical, and often manipulated by the media and journalists. Laineste argues that it is the inherent nature of internet communication that allows such reframing of jokes, especially since they cannot be attributed to any particular author or creator, and that ideas about jokes are influenced by their social context, being continuously reformulated due to social change or political manipulation.

Last but not least, Manteli's study illustrates an a-typical, but not less interesting use of political humour: political humour as an integral part of a postmodern performance. This chapter applies a semiotic analysis to a Greek theatre performance and explores how humour functions in postmodern drama and theatre, thus bringing to the surface a fusion of different registers and highlighting the interaction between literary and non-literary conventions for the production of political humour and criticism. The author focuses on a postmodern Greek theatre performance entitled *Stalin: A Discussion about Greek Theatre* which explored Stalinism as a paradigm of power politics, suggested that Stalinism is comparable to Modern Greek theatre, and invited the audience to reflect on Modern Greek theatre symbols and mythologies. Manteli concentrates on verbal humour in toasts, politically allegorical episodes, parodied songs, and direct addresses in metatheatrical episodes. She also investigates parody on the performance level with reference to music, kinesics, proxemics, actors' appearance, and paralinguistic features, and considers intersemiotic parody signified as visual allusions to painting and films. It appears that humour and parody are activated not only verbally, but also through the interaction of visual, musical, paralinguistic and intersemiotic signs and codes. This kind of interaction of different active sources of humour on drama and performance level may be viewed as an extension to *hyperdetermined humour*, namely humour which may be interpreted in different ways (Attardo 2001: 100–101).

Both chapters offer invaluable insights into how humorous and meta-humorous discourse is constructed and exploited for more or less "serious" purposes. In Laineste's case study, ethnic jokes become the sparkle which managed to set on fire the intrastate conflict on national identity in Estonia and in particular the relations between the Estonian majority and the Russian minority. On the other hand, the analysis of the postmodern performance involving humour targeting the Modern Greek theatrical status quo via an analogy to Stalinism brings to the surface more creative and imaginative uses of political humour. Unlike the more or less typical uses of political humour examined in the first two parts of the volume, it is our contention that Manteli's chapter opens a window to a whole new world for the study of political humour. It appears that widely recognized political references and incongruities can be reframed to attack and undermine myths, practices, and standpoints which may not entirely be related to politics, but, in the case examined in Chapter 10, to art and theatre as well. In other words, the intertextual and in particular contratextual links political humour develops (see Section 3) seem to be expanding to other semiotic and social domains than politics.

Acknowledgments

The editors would like to thank Salvatore Attardo, Argiris Archakis, and Vicky Manteli for invaluable feedback on this introduction.

References

Abe, Goh. 1998. "Political and social satirical cartoons in Nepal." *A Collection of Treatises on Languages and Literature* 15: 53–70.

Alvarez-Cáccamo, Celso and Prego-Vásquez, Gabriela. 2003. "Political cross-discourse: Conversationalisation, imaginary networks, and social fields in Galiza." *Pragmatics* 13: 145–162.

Ancheta, Maria Rhodora G. 2006. "Reading Gloria-Garci jokes: The Semantic Script Theory of Humour/General Theory of Verbal Humour and Filipino political humour." Paper presented at the 9th Philippine Linguistics Congress, Department of Linguistics, University of the Philippines Diliman, January 25–27, Quezon City, Philippines. http://web.kssp.upd.edu.ph/linguistics/plc2006/papers/FullPapers/II-B-4_Ancheta.pdf (accessed December 5, 2009).

Apte, Mahadev L. 1985. *Humour and Laughter. An Anthropological Approach.* Ithaca/London: Cornell University Press.

Archakis, Argiris and Tsakona, Villy. 2005. "Analysing conversational data in GTVH terms: A new approach to the issue of identity construction via humour." *Humour: International Journal of Humour Research* 18: 41–68.

Archakis, Argiris and Tsakona, Villy. 2006. "Script oppositions and humorous targets: Promoting values and constructing identities via humour in Greek conversational data." *Stylistyka* XV: 119–134.

Asad, Talal, Brown, Wendy, Butler, Judith and Mahmood, Saba. 2009. *Is Critique Secular? Blasphemy, Injury and Free Speech* [The Townsend Papers in the Humanities 2]. Berkeley: The Townsend Center for the Humanities, University of California.

Attardo, Salvatore. 1994. *Linguistic Theories of Humour* [Humour Research 1]. Berlin/New York: Mouton de Gruyter.

Attardo, Salvatore. 2001. *Humorous Texts: A Semantic and Pragmatic Analysis* [Humour Research 6]. Berlin/New York: Mouton de Gruyter.

Attardo, Salvatore and Raskin, Victor. 1991. "Script theory revis(it)ed: Joke similarity and joke representation." *Humour: International Journal of Humour Research* 4: 293–347.

Baumgartner, Jody C. 2007. "Humour on the next frontier: Youth, online political humour and the JibJab effect." *Social Science Computer Review* 25: 319–338.

Baumgartner, Jody C. and Morris, Jonathan S. 2006. "The *Daily Show* effect: Candidate evaluation, efficacy, and American youth." *American Politics Research* 34: 341–367.

Bayley, Paul. 2004. "Introduction. The whys and wherefores of analysing parliamentary discourse." In *Cross Cultural Perspectives on Parliamentary Discourse* [Discourse Approaches to Politics, Society and Culture 10], Paul Bayley (ed.), 1–44. Amsterdam/Philadelphia: John Benjamins.

Beard, Andrian. 2000. *The Language of Politics* [Intertext]. London: Routledge.

Bergson, Henri. 1901/1997. *Le Rire. Essai sur la Signification du Comique.* Paris: Presses Universitaires de France.

Billig, Michael. 2001. "Humour and hatred: The racist jokes of the Ku Klux Klan." *Discourse and Society* 12: 267–289.

Billig, Michael. 2005. *Laughter and Ridicule. Towards a Social Critique of Humour* [Theory, Culture and Society]. London: Sage.

Bippus, Amy. 2007. "Factors predicting the perceived effectiveness of politicians' use of humour during a debate." *Humour: International Journal of Humour Research* 20: 105–121.

Brown, Gillian and Yule, George. 1983. *Discourse Analysis* [Cambridge Textbooks in Linguistics]. Cambridge: Cambridge University Press.

Brzozowska, Dorota. 2007. "Jokes, identity, and ethnicity." In *New Approaches to the Linguistics of Humour*, Diana Popa and Salvatore Attardo (eds), 88–96. Galați: Academica.

Brzozowska, Dorota. 2009. "Polish jokelore in the period of transition." In *Permitted Laughter. Socialist, Post-Socialist and Never-Socialist Humour*, Arvo Krikmann and Liisi Laineste (eds), 127–169. Tartu: ELM Scholarly Press.

Carranza Márquez, Aurelia. 2010. "The faces of humour: Humour as catalyst of face in the context of the British and the Spanish parliament." *Humour: International Journal of Humour Research* 23: 467–504.

Chilton, Paul A. 2004. *Analysing Political Discourse. Theory and Practice.* London: Routledge.

Chłopicki, Władysław. 2009. "The 'Szkło kontaktowe' show – A return to the old irrationality?" In *Permitted Laughter. Socialist, Post-Socialist and Never-Socialist Humour*, Arvo Krikmann and Liisi Laineste (eds), 171–181. Tartu: ELM Scholarly Press.

Chun, Elaine W. 2004. "Ideologies of legitimate mockery: Margaret Cho's revoicings of mock Asian." *Pragmatics* 14: 263–289.

Coleman, Stephen, Kuik, Anke and van Zoonen, Liesbet. 2009. "Laughter and liability: The politics of British and Dutch television satire." *The British Journal of Politics and International Relations* 11: 652–665.

Colipcă, Gabriela. 2009. "Shakespeare, the musical and political humour: Cole Porter's *Kiss me, Kate* revived." Paper presented at the 1st International Conference on Humour in Conventional and Unconventional Politics (ICHCUP), November 6–8, Dunărea de Jos University, Galați, Romania.

Corbeill, Anthony. 1996. *Controlling Laughter: Political Humour in the Late Roman Republic.* Princeton: Princeton University Press.

Craig, Geoffrey. 2004. *The Media, Politics and the Public Life.* Crows Nest: Allen and Unwin.

Critchley, Simon. 2002. *On Humour* [Thinking in Action]. London/New York: Routledge.

Davies, Christie. 1998. *Jokes and their Relation to Society* [Humour Research 4]. Berlin/New York: Mouton de Gruyter.

Davies, Christie. 2002. *The Mirth of Nations.* New Brunswick: Transaction Publishers.

Davies, Christie. 2008. "Response essays." In "The Muhammad cartoons and humour research: A collection of essays," Paul Lewis (ed.), 30–32. *Humour: International Journal of Humour Research* 21: 1–46.

Davies, Christie. 2009. "Post-socialist, socialist and never-socialist jokes and humour: Continuities and contrasts." In *Permitted Laughter. Socialist, Post-Socialist and Never-Socialist Humour*, Arvo Krikmann and Liisi Laineste (eds), 17–38. Tartu: ELM Scholarly Press.

Davis, Murray S. 1993. *What's So Funny? The Comic Conception of Culture and Society.* Chicago/London: The University of Chicago Press.

Dodds, Klaus. 2007. "Steve Bell's eye: Cartoons, geopolitics and the visualisation of the 'War on Terror.'" *Security Dialogue* 38: 157–177.

Downie, Andrew. 2010. "Banning political humour: No satire please, we're Brazilian." *Time*, August 26. http://www.time.com/time/world/article/0,8599,2013163,00.html (accessed April 3, 2011).

Dudden, Arthur Power. 1985. "The record of political humour." *American Quarterly* 37: 50–70.

Edwards, Janis L. 2001. "Running in the shadows in campaign 2000." *American Behavioural Scientist* 44: 2140–2151.

Eide, Elisabeth, Kunelius, Risto and Phillips, Angela (eds). 2008. *Transnational Media Events. The Mohammed Cartoons and the Imagined Clash of Civilizations.* Gothernburg: Nordicom.

El Refaie, Elisabeth. 2003. "Understanding visual metaphor: The example of newspaper cartoons." *Visual Communication* 2: 75–95.

El Refaie, Elisabeth. 2004. "'Our purebred ethnic compatriots': Irony in newspaper journalism." *Journal of Pragmatics* 37: 781–797.

El Refaie, Elisabeth. 2009. "Metaphor in political cartoons: Exploring audience responses." In *Multimodal Metaphor* [Applications of Cognitive Linguistics 11], Charles Forceville and Eduardo Urios-Aparisi (eds), 173–196. Berlin/New York: Mouton de Gruyter.

Fairclough, Norman. 1995. *Media Discourse.* London: Arnold.

Fetzer, Anita and Lauerbach, Gerda Eva (eds). 2007. *Political Discourse in the Media* [Pragmatics and Beyond New Series 160]. Amsterdam/Philadelphia: John Benjamins.

Foot, Kirsten A. and Schneider, Steven M. 2002. "Online action in campaign 2000: An exploratory analysis of the U.S. political web sphere." *Journal of Broadcasting and Electronic Media* 46: 222–244.

Fry, William F. 1976. "The power of political humour." *The Journal of Popular Culture* 10: 227–231.

Gadavanij, Savitri. 2002. "Intertextuality as discourse strategy: The case of no-confidence debates in Thailand." In *Leeds Working Papers in Linguistics and Phonetics* 9, Diane Nelson (ed.), 35–55.

Galateanu, Olga. 1993. "Discours de la dérision politique et la dérision du discourse politique." *Humoresque* 4: 69–79.

Gardner, Gerald C. 1994. *Campaign Comedy. Political Humour from Clinton to Kennedy* [Humour in Life and Letters]. Detroit: Wayne State University Press.

Giarelli, Ellen and Tulman, Lorraine. 2003. "Methodological issues in the use of published cartoons as data." *Qualitative Health Research* 13: 945–956.

Glenn, Phillip. 2003. *Laughter in Interaction* [Studies in Interactional Sociolinguistics 18]. Cambridge: Cambridge University Press.

Greatbatch, David and Clark, Timothy. 2003. "Displaying group cohesiveness: Humour and laughter in the public lectures of management gurus." *Human Relations* 56: 1515–1544.

Grice, H. Paul. 1975. "Logic and conversation." In *Syntax and Semantics*, vol. 3, Peter Cole and Jerry L. Morgan (eds), 41–58. London: Academic Press.

Hanlon, Heather, Farnsworth, Judy and Murray, Judy. 1997. "Ageing in American comic strips: 1972–1992." *Ageing and Society* 17: 293–304.

Hariman, Robert. 2008. "Political parody and public culture." *Quarterly Journal of Speech* 94: 247–272.

Harkness, S. Susan J., Magid, Mohamed, Roberts, Jameka and Richardson, Michael. 2007. "Crossing the line? Freedom of speech and religious sensibilities." *PS: Political Science and Politics* 40: 275–278.

Harris, Sandra. 2001. "Being politically impolite: Extending politeness theory to adversarial political discourse." *Discourse and Society* 12: 451–472.

Hart, Roderick P. 1999. *Seducing America: How Television Charms the Modern Voter* (revised edition). London: Sage.

Hodge, Bob and Mansfield, Alan. 1985. "'Nothing left to laugh at…': Humour as a tactic of resistance." In *Language and the Nuclear Arms Debate: Nukespeak Today* [Open Linguistics Series], Paul A. Chilton (ed.), 197–211. London/Dover: N. H. Frances Pinter.

Holbert, R. Lance. 2005. "A typology for the study of entertainment television and politics." *American Behavioural Scientist* 49: 436–453.

Holdaway, Simon. 1988. "Blue joke: Humour in police work." In *Humour in Society: Resistance and Control*, Chris Powell and George Paton (eds), 106–122. New York: St. Martin's.

Holmes, Janet, and Marra, Meredith. 2006. "Humour and leadership style." *Humour: International Journal of Humour Research* 19: 119–138.

Hong, Nathaniel. 2010. "Mow 'em all down grandma: The 'weapon' of humour in two Danish World War II occupation scrapbooks." *Humour: International Journal of Humour Research* 23: 27–64.

Hussain, Ali J. 2007. "The media's role in a clash of misconceptions: The case of the Danish Mohammad cartoons." *The Harvard International Journal of Press/Politics* 12: 112–130.

Ilie, Cornelia. 2001. "Unparliamentary language: Insults as cognitive forms of ideological confrontation." In *Language and Ideology. Volume II: Descriptive Cognitive Approaches* [Current Issues in Linguistic Theory 205], René Dirven, Roslyn Frank and Cornelia Ilie (eds), 235–263. Amsterdam/Philadelphia: John Benjamins.

Ilie, Cornelia. 2004. "Insulting as (un)parliamentary practice in the British and Swedish parliaments: A rhetorical approach." In *Cross Cultural Perspectives on Parliamentary Discourse* [Discourse Approaches to Politics, Society and Culture 10], Paul Bayley (ed.), 45–86. Amsterdam/Philadelphia: John Benjamins.

Ilie, Cornelia. 2010. "Managing dissent and interpersonal relations in the Romanian parliamentary discourse." In *European Parliaments under Scrutiny* [Discourse Approaches to Politics, Culture and Society 38], Cornelia Ilie (ed.), 193–221. Amsterdam/Philadelphia: John Benjamins.

Jones, Jeffrey P. 2010. *Entertaining Politics. Satiric Television and Political Engagement* (2nd edition) [Communication, Media and Politics]. New York/Toronto/Plymouth: Rowan and Littlefield.

Koestler, Arthur. 1964. *The Act of Creation*. London: Arcana, Penguin.

Kotthoff, Helga. 2000. "Gender and joking: On the complexities of women's image politics in humorous narratives." *Journal of Pragmatics* 32: 55–80.

Krikmann, Arvo and Laineste, Liisi (eds). 2009. *Permitted Laughter. Socialist, Post-Socialist and Never-Socialist Humour*. Tartu: ELM Scholarly Press.

Kuipers, Giselinde. 2006. *Good Humour, Bad Taste. A Sociology of the Joke* [Humour Research 7]. Berlin/New York: Mouton de Gruyter.

Kuipers, Giselinde. 2008a. "Response essays." In "The Muhammad cartoons and humour research: A collection of essays," Paul Lewis (ed.), 33–34. *Humour: International Journal of Humour Research* 21: 1–46.

Kuipers, Giselinde. 2008b. "The sociology of humour." In *The Primer of Humour Research* [Humour Research 8], Victor Raskin (ed.), 361–398. Berlin/New York: Mouton de Gruyter.

Laineste, Liisi. 2009. "Conclusion." In *Permitted Laughter. Socialist, Post-Socialist and Never-Socialist Humour*, Arvo Krikmann and Liisi Laineste (eds), 371–406. Tartu: ELM Scholarly Press.

Landowski, Eric. 1993. "On ne badine pas avec l'humour. La presse politique et ses petits dessins." *Humoresque* 4: 43–68.

Leudar, Ivan and Nekvapil, Jiří. 1998. "On the emergence of political identity in the Czech mass media: The case of the Democratic Party of Sudetenland." *Czech Sociological Review* 6: 43–58.

Lewis, Paul. 2006. *Cracking Up. American Humour in a Time of Conflict*. Chicago: University of Chicago Press.

Lewis, Paul (ed.). 2008. "The Muhammad cartoons and humour research: A collection of essays." *Humour: International Journal of Humour Research* 21: 1–46.

Lindstrom, Naomi. 1980. "Social commentary in Argentine cartooning: From description to questioning." *The Journal of Popular Culture* 14: 509–523.

Lockyer, Sharon and Pickering, Michael. 2001. "Dear shit-shovellers: Humour, censure and the discourse of complaint." *Discourse and Society* 12: 633–651.

Lockyer, Sharon, and Pickering, Michael (eds). 2005. *Beyond a Joke. The Limits of Humour*. Basingstoke: Palgrave Macmillan.

Louvi, Lina. 2002. *Περιγέλωτος Βασίλειον. Οι Σατιρικές Εφημερίδες και το Εθνικό Ζήτημα (1875–1886)* (The Kingdom of Ridicule. Satirical Newspapers and the [Greek] National Issue (1875–1886)). Athens: Estia. [in Greek]

Madzharova Bruteig, Yordanka. 2010. "Czech parliamentary discourse: Parliamentary inter-
   actions and the construction of the addressee." In *European Parliaments under Scrutiny*
   [Discourse Approaches to Politics, Culture and Society 38], Cornelia Ilie (ed.), 265–302.
   Amsterdam/Philadelphia: John Benjamins.
Marín-Arrese, Juana I. 2008. "Cognition and culture in political cartoons." *Intercultural Prag-
   matics* 5: 1–18.
Martin, Diane M. 2004. "Balancing on the political high wire: The role of humour in the rheto-
   ric of Ann Richards." *Southern Communication Journal* 69: 273–288.
Mascha, Efharis. 2008. "Political satire and hegemony: A case of 'passive revolution' during
   Mussolini's ascendance to power 1919–1925." *Humour: International Journal of Humour
   Research* 21: 69–98.
Mascha, Efharis. 2010. "Contradictions and the role of the 'floating signifier': Identity and the
   'New Woman' in Italian cartoons during Fascism." *Journal of International Women's Studies*
   11. http://www.bridgew.edu/SoAS/jiws/May10/FloatingSignifier.pdf (accessed March 20,
   2011).
Meisel, Joseph S. 2009. "Humour and insult in the House of Commons: The case of Palmer-
   stone and Disraeli." *Parliamentary History* 28: 228–245.
Miller, Donna R. 2004. "'Truth, justice and the American way': The APPRAISAL SYSTEM of
   JUDGEMENT in the U.S. House debate on the impeachment of the President, 1998." In
   Cross Cultural Perspectives on Parliamentary Discourse [Discourse Approaches to Poli-
   tics, Society and Culture 10], Paul Bayley (ed.), 271–300. Amsterdam/Philadelphia: John
   Benjamins.
Morreall, John. 1983. *Taking Laughter Seriously*. Albany: State University of New York Press.
Morreall, John. 2005. "Humour and the conduct of politics." In *Beyond the Joke. The Limits
   of Humour*, Sharon Lockyer and Michael Pickering (eds), 63–78. Basingstoke: Palgrave
   Macmillan.
Morreall, John. 2009. *Comic Relief. A Comprehensive Philosophy of Humour* [New Directions in
   Aesthetics 9]. Malden: Wiley-Blackwell.
Morris, Ray. 1993. "Visual rhetoric in political cartoons: A structuralist approach." *Metaphor
   and Symbolic Activity* 8: 195–210.
Morrison, Susan S. 1992. "The feminisation of the German Democratic Republic in political
   cartoons 1989–1990." *The Journal of Popular Culture* 25: 35–51.
Mulkay, Michael. 1988. *On Humour. Its Nature and Its Place in Modern Society*. Cambridge:
   Polity Press.
Niculescu Grasso, Dana Maria. 1999. *Bancurile Politice* (Political Jokes). Bucharest: Editura
   Fundației Culturale Române. [in Romanian]
Nilsen, Don L. F. 1990. "The social function of political humour." *The Journal of Popular Culture*
   24: 35–47.
Niven, David, Lichter, S. Robert and Amundson, Daniel. 2003. "The political content of late-
   night comedy." *The Harvard International Journal of Press/Politics* 8: 118–133.
Norrick, Neal R. 2000. *Conversational Narrative: Storytelling in Everyday Talk* [Current Issues
   in Linguistic Theory 203]. Amsterdam/Philadelphia: John Benjamins.
O'Connell, Daniel C. and Kowal, Sabine. 2004. "Hillary Clinton's laughter in media interviews."
   Pragmatics 14: 463–478.
O'Connell, Daniel C. and Kowal, Sabine. 2005. "Laughter in Bill Clinton's *My Life* (2004) inter-
   views." *Pragmatics* 15: 275–299.

Olson, Alison. 2005. "Political humour, deference, and the American revolution." *Early American Studies* 3: 363–382.

Oring, Elliott. 2008. "Response essays." In "The Muhammad cartoons and humour research: A collection of essays," Paul Lewis (ed.), 37–40. *Humour: International Journal of Humour Research* 21: 1–46.

Ornatowski, Cezar M. 2010. "Parliamentary discourse and political transition: Polish parliament after 1989." In *European Parliaments under Scrutiny* [Discourse Approaches to Politics, Culture and Society 38], Cornelia Ilie (ed.), 223–264. Amsterdam/Philadelphia: John Benjamins.

Paletz, David. 1990. "Political humour and authority: From support to subversion." *International Political Science Review* 11: 483–493.

Palmer, Jerry. 1994. *Taking Humour Seriously*. London/New York: Routledge.

Panke, Luciana. 2009. "The use of humour in the Brazilian campaign to raise voter awareness." Paper presented at the 1st International Conference on Humour in Conventional and Unconventional Politics (ICHCUP), November 6–8, Dunărea de Jos University, Galaţi, Romania.

Pickering, Michael and Lockyer, Sharon. 2005. "Introduction: The ethics and aesthetics of humour and comedy." In *Beyond the Joke. The Limits of Humour*, Sharon Lockyer and Michael Pickering (eds), 1–24. Basingstoke: Palgrave Macmillan.

Pi-Sunyer, Oriol. 1977. "Political humour in a dictatorial state: The case of Spain." *Ethnohistory* 24: 179–190.

Polk, Jeremy, Young, Dannagal G. and Holbert, R. Lance. 2009. "Humour complexity and political influence: An elaboration likelihood approach to the effects of humour type in *The Daily Show with Jon Stewart*." *Atlantic Journal of Communication* 17: 202–219.

Popa, Diana Elena. 2002. "The absence of reference in the Romanian joke translation." *Antares* V: 13.

Popa, Diana Elena. 2003a. "Humour and the concept of incongruity." In *Mélanges de Terminologie et de Sémantique*, Anca Gata (ed.), 136–146. Galaţi: Academica.

Popa, Diana Elena. 2003b. "The language of humour and the social context: English vs. Romanian." *Antares* VI: 53–60.

Post, Robert. 2007. "Religion and freedom of speech: Portraits of Muhammad." *Constellations* 14: 72–90.

Raskin, Victor. 1985. *Semantic Mechanisms of Humour* [Studies in Linguistics and Philosophy 24]. Dordrecht: D. Reidel.

Raskin, Victor. 2008a. "On the political impotence of humour". In "The Muhammad cartoons and humour research: A collection of essays," Paul Lewis (ed.), 26–30. *Humour: International Journal of Humour Research* 21: 1–46.

Raskin, Victor (ed.). 2008b. *The Primer of Humour Research* [Humour Research 8]. Berlin/New York: Mouton de Gruyter.

Riegert, Kristina (ed.). 2007. *Politicotainment: Television's Take on the Real* [Popular Culture and Everyday Life 13]. New York: Peter Lang.

Ruch, Willibald. 1998. "Foreword and overview. Sense of humour: A new look at an old concept." In *The Sense of Humour. Explorations of a Personality Characteristic* [Humour Research 3], Willibald Ruch (ed.), 3–14. Berlin/New York: Mouton De Gruyter.

Ruch, Willibald. 2002. "Humo(u)r research." Paper presented at the 14th Conference of the International Society for Humour Studies, July 3–7, Bertinoro, Italy. www.uni-duesseldorf.de/www/MathNat/Ruch/HumorSurvey.html (accessed July 10, 2002).

Santa Ana, Otto. 2009. "Did you call in Mexican? The racial politics of Jay Leno immigrant jokes." *Language in Society* 28: 23–45.

Sauvy, Alfred. 1979. *Humour et Politique.* Paris: Calmann-Lévy.

Schnurr, Stephanie. 2008. *Leadership Discourse at Work. Interactions of Humour, Gender and Workplace Culture.* Basingstoke: Palgrave Macmillan.

Schutz, Charles E. 1976. *Political Humour. From Aristophanes to Sam Ervin.* Rutherford: Faurleigh Dickinson University Press.

Shelton Caswell, Lucy. 2004. "Drawing swords: War in American editorial cartoons." *American Journalism* 21: 13–45.

Smith, Moira. 2009. "Humour, unlaughter and boundary maintenance." *Journal of American Folklore* 122: 148–171.

Speier, Hans. 1998. "Wit and politics: An essay on laughter and power." *American Journal of Sociology* 103: 1352–1401.

Stanoev, Stanoy. 2009. "Totalitarian political jokes in Bulgaria." In *Permitted Laughter. Socialist, Post-Socialist and Never-Socialist Humour,* Arvo Krikmann and Liisi Laineste (eds), 185–207. Tartu: ELM Scholarly Press.

Stein, Mary Beth. 1989. "The politics of humour: The Berlin Wall in jokes and graffiti." *Western Folklore* 48: 85–108.

Sturges, Paul. 2006. "Limits to freedom of expression? Considerations arising from the Danish cartoon affair." *IFLA Journal* 32: 181–188.

Templin, Charlotte. 1999. "Hillary Clinton as threat to gender norms: Cartoon images of the First Lady." *Journal of Communication Inquiry* 23: 20–36.

Townsend, Mary Lee. 1997. "Humour and the public sphere in 19th century Germany." In *A Cultural History of Humour. From Antiquity to the Present Day,* Jan Bremmer and Herman Roodenburg (eds), 200–221. Cambridge: Polity Press.

Tsakona, Villy. 2008. "Η χιουμοριστική αναπαράσταση της πολιτικής πραγματικότητας: Το παράδειγμα της σύγχρονης πολιτικής γελοιογραφίας" (The humorous representation of political reality: The example of contemporary political cartoons). In *Ο Λόγος της Μαζικής Επικοινωνίας: Το Ελληνικό Παράδειγμα* (The Discourse of Mass Communication: The Greek Example), Periklis Politis (ed.), 381–411. Thessaloniki: Institute for Modern Greek Studies, Manolis Triantafyllidis Foundation. [in Greek]

Tsakona, Villy. 2009a. "Humour and image politics in parliamentary discourse: A Greek case study." *Text and Talk* 29: 219–237.

Tsakona, Villy. 2009b. "Η κοινωνιογλωσσολογική προσέγγιση του χιούμορ στην πολιτική γελοιογραφία" (A sociolinguistic approach to political cartoon humour). In *8th International Conference on Greek Linguistics, Ioannina, 30 August–2 September 2007,* 1184–1194. Ioannina.   http://www.linguist-uoi.gr/cd_web/docs/greek/043_tsakonaICGL8_OK.pdf (accessed December 1, 2009). [in Greek]

Tsakona, Villy. 2011a. "Humour, religion, and politics in Greek cartoons: Symbiosis or conflict?" In *Humour and Religion: Challenges and Ambiguities,* Hans Geybels and Walter Van Herck (eds), 248–267. London: Continuum.

Tsakona, Villy. 2011b. "Irony beyond criticism: Evidence from Greek parliamentary discourse." *Pragmatics and Society* 2: 57–86.

Tunç, Asli. 2001. "*GIRGIR* as a sociological phenomenon in Turkey: The transformation of a humour magazine." *Humour: International Journal of Humour Research* 14: 243–254.

Tunç, Asli. 2002. "Pushing the limits of tolerance. Functions of political cartoonists in the democratisation process: The case of Turkey." *Gazette: The International Journal for Communication Studies* 64: 47–62.

Vasta, Nicoletta. 2004. "Consent and dissent in British and Italian parliamentary debates on the 1998 Gulf Crisis." In *Cross Cultural Perspectives on Parliamentary Discourse* [Discourse Approaches to Politics, Society and Culture 10], Paul Bayley (ed.), 111–149. Amsterdam/Philadelphia: John Benjamins.

Warner, Jamie. 2007. "Political culture jamming: The dissident humour of *The Daily Show with Jon Stewart.*" *Popular Communication* 5: 17–36.

Whaley, Bryan B. and Holloway, Rachel L. 1997. "Rebuttal analogy in political communication: Argument and attack in sound bite." *Political Communication* 14: 293–305.

Young, Dannagal G. and Tisinger, Russell M. 2006. "Dispelling late-night myths: News consumption among late-night comedy viewers and the predictors of exposure to various late-night shows." *The Harvard International Journal of Press/Politics* 11: 113–134.

Zima, Elisabeth, Brône, Geert and Feyarts, Kurt. 2010. "Patterns of interaction in Austrian parliamentary debates: On the pragmasemantics of unauthorised interruptive comments." In *European Parliaments under Scrutiny* [Discourse Approaches to Politics, Culture and Society 38], Cornelia Ilie (ed.), 135–164. Amsterdam/Philadelphia: John Benjamins.

PART I

Humour by politicians

CHAPTER 2

Fun in the German parliament?

Ralph Mueller
University of Fribourg, Switzerland

Based on a large digital corpus of political speeches from the parliamentary proceedings of the German Bundestag (German House of Representatives), this study provides an overview of situations in which amusement and laughing have been recorded. After explaining the differentiation between *Heiterkeit* "amusement" and *Lachen* "laughing", this study provides a typology of situations that trigger such responses. An analysis of corpus concordances shows that the category *Lachen* mostly indicates instances of scornful laughter, whereas amusement is generally less hostile. Moreover, the analysis demonstrates that most instances that provoked laughing do not display intentional humorous incongruity. Amusement, on the other hand, is typically motivated by some kind of intended humorous incongruity.

1.   Are German politicians funny?

Some people may seriously question whether there is sufficient material to write a full-length article about humour in the German parliament. It seems that humour in politics is associated primarily with funny anecdotes about statesmen or political satire, and that politicians themselves, and in particular German politicians, are not overly valued for their humour. However, the proceedings of the German House of Representatives (*Bundestag*) contain many references to events that are typically associated with humour, as they register a surprisingly high number of instances of laughing or amusement in the audience.

When analysing humour in parliamentary discourse, it is necessary to give an account of the formal constraints to which the production of humour is subject. Speaking in front of the Bundestag is regulated by various rules and implicit traditions; in such a situation a plenary speech takes on the character of formal discourse to a far greater extent than it does in a session of a parliamentary commission or a private conversation between parliamentarians. Constraints on the speech form in German plenary debates derive partly from official regulations, namely the *Geschäftsordnung des Bundestags* (Deutscher Bundestag 2006), which contain explicit rules concerning time limits or the form of interposed questions. However, many rules and customs are implicit, and in many cases even negotiable (e.g. the time limit). Consequently, the Chair supervises and exerts an influence on the formal aspects of speeches; s/he is entitled to interrupt speakers who speak too long or who are not speaking to the point. The Chair may also reprimand the use of certain expressions as *unparlamentarisch* "unparliamentary", although the exact definition of "unparliamentary" does not appear in the official regulations (Deutscher Bundestag 2006).

All these explicit and implicit rules lead to a distinct German style of political speech which favours unpretentious and straightforward communication with little in the way of rhetorical flourish such as unconventional metaphors or figures of speech (e.g. in contrast to Greek parliamentary speeches; see Archakis and Tsakona this volume). With the exception of a few less formal situations (e.g. the welcome address of the Chair at the beginning of a legislative period), speeches in the German Bundestag can be characterised as being of a serious nature. Overall, there is little use of humour, even though the data examined here reveal an interesting variety of humorous uses.

In this context, in Section 2, I take a closer look at the proceedings of the German Bundestag which provided the data for this study. Section 3 discusses the stenographer's differentiation between laughing (*Lachen*) and amusement (*Heiterkeit*), while Sections 4 and 5 provide a typological overview of the instances which have been recorded as laughing-provoking or amusement-provoking. Finally, Section 6 summarizes the findings of the present study.

2.   Corpus

This study is based on the proceedings of the German Bundestag from November 1994 to December 2006 (see Deutscher Bundestag 1994–2006). This time span includes three election periods and more than 750 parliamentary sessions.[1] The protocols represent spoken language in a written format; hence, they provide an edited reproduction of oral speech (Simmler 1978: 35–37). Usually, the protocols give a quite accurate account of the content, and even of the style of a speech. Moreover, the protocols also provide surprisingly meticulous records of the responses

---

1.   According to the *WordSmith* count, the data examined includes more than 53 million words (cf. Scott 2004). However, this number is only partly significant, as the protocols sometimes include extensive annexes which are irrelevant to the analysis of "amusement" or "laughing", which only occur in plenary speeches.

in the audience: they go so far as to record individual interjections (*Zwischenruf*), applause (*Beifall*), laughing (*Lachen*), and amusement (*Heiterkeit*).

German stenographers record amusement and laughing, in order to provide an overall impression of the audience response to the speeches. It appears that laughter is an important indicator of the audience's evaluation of a statement, even if it occurs significantly less frequently than applause (applause: 240,000 instances; laughter: 7,529; amusement: 7,424).

A short extract from a lively debate in the Bundestag may illustrate the meticulous recording of audience reactions in the protocols. In this example, Angela Merkel (at that time Leader of the Opposition) verbally attacks Gerhard Schröder, only a few months after her Christian Democratic Union had suffered a frustrating election defeat despite positive opinion polls:[2]

(1) Dr. Angela Merkel (CDU/CSU): Sie oder wir, Stillstand oder Fortschritt,
     (Lachen bei der SPD – Joachim Poß [SPD]: Koch oder Sie?)
     Staat oder Freiheit, Belastung oder Entlastung, Täuschung oder Verlässlichkeit, das sind die Alternativen in diesem Lande <, meine Damen und Herren>.
     (Lebhafter Beifall bei der CDU/CSU und der FDP – Joachim Poß [SPD]: Merkel oder Koch? – Weiterer Zuruf von der SPD: Das ist die größte Lachnummer, die ich je gehört habe!)
     <Und natürlich geht es um die Alternativen.>
     (Waltraud Lehn [SPD]: Sagen Sie mal was zum Fortschritt! – Weitere Zurufe von der SPD – Gegenruf des Abg. Volker Kauder [CDU/CSU]: Ruhe! – Lachen des Bundeskanzlers Gerhard Schröder)
     <Und jetzt sage ich Ihnen, dass wir uns in einem, in einem einig sind. Wir alle leben in einer Zeit, in der die Globalisierung> – Wissen Sie, was die Leute

---

2. Angle brackets indicate the author's adaptations of the protocol based on the video recording of some speeches. Dots in angle brackets indicate inaudible utterances. Citations from the proceedings of the Bundestag (appearing at the end of the original texts) should be read as follows:

XV	number of the election period
-013	number of the session
p. 897	page number in the proceedings
4/12/2002	date of speech delivery

German party initials stand for:

CDU	Christian Democratic Union
CSU	Christian Social Union
FDP	Free Democratic Party
PDS	Party of Democratic Socialism
SPD	Social Democratic Party of Germany

besonders gut leiden können? Das ist Ihr dauerndes Grinsen und Lachen auf der Regierungsbank.
(Heiterkeit und Beifall bei der CDU/CSU und der FDP – Johannes Kahrs [SPD]: Kommen Sie doch mal zur Sache! – Weitere Zurufe von der SPD)
(Bundestag, XV-013, p. 897, 04/12/2002)

Dr. Angela Merkel (CDU/CSU): You or us, progress or stagnation,
(Laughing among the SPD – Joachim Poß [SPD]: Koch[3] or you?)
government or freedom, burden or relief, deception or reliability, these are the alternatives of this country, <ladies and gentlemen>.
(Lively applause among the CDU/CSU and FDP – Joachim Poß [SPD]: Merkel or Koch? – […])
<And of course, this is about alternatives>
(Waltraud Lehn [SPD]: Say something about progress! Further interjection of the SPD – Counter-interjection by MP Volker Kauder [CDU/CSU]: Silence! – Laughing of Federal Chancellor Gerhard Schröder)
<And now I want to tell you that we agree on one thing, we agree on one thing. We all live in an era of globalisation> – You know what the people like in particular? It is your continuous grinning and laughter on the government front bench.
(Amusement and applause among the CDU/CSU and the FDP – Johannes Kahrs [SPD]: Get to the point! – Further interjections of the SPD)

Clearly, the wafer-thin majority gained by the coalition of SPD and the Green Party in the 2002 elections adds to the liveliness of this debate: SPD members and Chancellor G. Schröder respond with laughing to A. Merkel's protestations, the CDU/CSU express their solidarity with her and their rejection of G. Schröder's behaviour with applause and amusement. This short extract illustrates that protocols provide an interesting source of reactions to humorous instances in political speeches.

Of course, the appropriateness of parliamentary protocols as a source for investigating humour in the German parliament might be questioned, as the protocols rarely record the speaker's own laughing or non-verbal reactions such as facial responses and gestures. There are audio-visual recordings of speeches given after 1998 which provide additional contextual information and access to the exact word order used by a speaker. A comparison between the audio-visual recordings and the transcribed protocols reveals that stenographers suppress recurring discourse markers (e.g. *und* "and", *also* "so", *meine Damen und Herren* "ladies and gentlemen"). Furthermore, for the sake of readability, stenographers may slightly

---

3.   J. Poß alludes to Roland Koch, at that time Prime Minister of Hesse and A. Merkel's potential political rival within the CDU.

rearrange the order of the interjections, which is clearly shown in A. Merkel's responses in Example (1). Thus, the recordings provide more reliable evidence of the relation between word order and the occurrence of amusement or laughing. However, the recordings still provide – at best – only partial impressions of the verbal and non-verbal reactions in the audience. As a consequence, it is not advisable to rely solely on one source. The protocols have been used as primary source material, as they provide the most complete picture of the verbal interaction between speaker and audience, and because they allow for semi-automatic detection of humorous instances. Whenever necessary and possible, the accuracy of the protocols was checked against the audio-visual recordings.

3.   What are *Heiterkeit* and *Lachen*?

Making a differentiation between *Lachen* "laughing" and *Heiterkeit* "amusement" may not appear as the most elaborate typology of humorous responses, and – looking at the responses in Example (1) – it may not even appear as a particularly appropriate way of labelling responses to humour. However, it seems that stenographers follow the traditional differentiation between "laughing at" and "laughing with", as *Lachen* indicates scornful laughter and *Heiterkeit* a more general form of amusement.[4] The question is why "to laugh" should be semantically restricted to "laughing at". After all, laughter is considered to be the most typical reaction to humorous stimuli (Martin 2007). Moreover, laughter has frequently been considered to be *the* contextualisation cue for humour (see Archakis and Tsakona 2005: 44; Tsakona and Popa this volume, and references therein). It seems that this terminological differentiation has its foundation in the connection made in ancient rhetoric between laughter and the satirical, the ludicrous and the ridiculous. *Lachen*, as a consequence, indicates a different type of laughter from *Heiterkeit*.

   The term *Heiterkeit* in the sense of "amusement" has received very little attention in German humour research. This situation justifies a few detailed remarks about the concept of *Heiterkeit*. The abstract noun *Heiterkeit* does not appear until the mid 18th century. It is a derivative of the adjective *heiter* "clear", indicating clear colours, distinct shapes, beautifying things (Kiedaisch and Bär 1997: 13–17),[5] and – as a meteorological term – clear weather. In the history of ideas we can differentiate two major concepts of *Heiterkeit*: one is associated with serenity

---

4.   Based on information provided by Wolfgang Behm, Head of the stenographic service of the Bundestag (personal communication 27/10/2009).

5.   Even at the beginning of the 18th century we also find the verb *erheitern* as an equivalent of *enlighten*: "Das wird aber das aufgeklärete, das durch Künste und Wissenschaften *erheiterte*

and the other with hilarity. German literary scholars have mostly focused on the serenity concept (Kiedaisch and Bär 1997; Schöttker 1998; Weinrich 2001), which is in some respects similar to the poetic concept of humour and constitutes a positive attitude in the face of an imperfect and often tragic reality. However, in the context of the 18th century literary anacreontic tradition, there are documents which establish a connection between the mood of *Heiterkeit* and *esprit* or wit (Schöttker 1998).[6] As a consequence, it is not always clear whether the attribute *heiter* in descriptions of facial expressions or moods in the 18th century should be understood as hilarity or rather as serenity.

In sum, both concepts of *Heiterkeit* seem to be associated with a positive mood, which facilitates the production and reception of humour (in particular *esprit*). The term *serene* as an equivalent of *Heiterkeit* may appear as an obsolete concept, especially when it comes to marking audible reactions from the audience in the Bundestag. Nevertheless, it could still be used to evaluate the attitude of top leaders, as the calm placidity associated with serenity used to be considered an appropriate attitude for emperors and princes to adopt (cf. Weinrich 2001). Therefore it can be said that *Heiterkeit* in the Bundestag (henceforth amusement) is an audible response of the audience representing a generally positive attitude to a person or the person's statements.

4. Laughing – *Lachen*

The protocols in the corpus record slightly more laughing (7529 instances) than amusement (7424 instances). Whereas amusement was in some instances recorded among all members of the Bundestag, laughing was always restricted to individuals or a political faction (e.g. the Christian Democrats CDU/CSU, or the Social Democrats SPD).

Typically, laughing is a simple form of rebuttal through which a speaker's statement, claim, or request is rejected by a part of the audience. This model of rebuttal is illustrated by G. Schröder's laughing at A. Merkel's objections (in Example (1); see Section 2). In the protocols, the function of laughing as an expres-

---

Germanien nicht leiden!" ("The enlightened and – by the influence of Arts and Sciences – *brightened* Germany will not accept that"; Gottsched 1752:674, my emphasis).

6. For example, "Ein ehrlicher Mann […] kann zwar fast immer aufgelegt seyn, etwas ernsthaftes zu arbeiten […], aber nicht immer etwas witziges, welches eine gewisse Heiterkeit des Geistes verlangt […]" ("An honourable man may almost always be in the mood to write something serious, but not always something funny, which requires a certain hilarity/serenity? of mind"; Lessing 1867:120).

sion of disagreement is explicitly signalled in almost 300 instances by the phrase *Lachen und Widerspruch* or *Lachen und Zurufe* "laughing and objections/protests [among members of ...]". In the following example, it is a single parliamentarian, the Minister of Foreign Affairs Joschka Fischer, who rebuts a speaker's claim:

(2)   Ursula Lietz (CDU/CSU): Wir haben <– und das müssen Sie zur Kenntnis nehmen, Herr Außenminister> – <zu beklagen>, dass zwar <...> ein erfolg-reicher NATO-Gipfel <in Prag> stattgefunden hat, dass <aber> die deutsche Delegation <...> einen recht jämmerlichen Eindruck <gemacht> hat.
([...] – Lachen des Bundesministers Joseph Fischer)

(Bundestag, XV-014, p. 1018, 5/12/2002)

Ursula Lietz (CDU/CSU): We have <to complain> <– and you should acknowledge this, Minister of Foreign Affairs> – that although there was <...> a successful NATO summit <in Prague>, the German delegation <...> <made> a miserable impression.
([...] – Laughing of the Federal Minister of Foreign Affairs Joseph Fischer)

There is nothing particularly funny or ironic about U. Lietz's statement. It is rather Fischer's response that imposes the interpretation that U. Lietz's accusation is not to be taken seriously. J. Fischer's laughter appears as strategic, as it allows a rebuttal without actually entering into an argument with U. Lietz.

Example (3) suggests that in the protocols laughing indicates a kind of reaction which seeks to impose humour onto a statement contrary to the intention of the speaker, in order to undermine the effect of what is said. In this respect, the category "laughing and applause" (*Lachen und Beifall*) constitutes an interesting category which involves deliberate misunderstanding, as the following Example (3) demonstrates: the speaker, Peter Struck, wanted to point out that the budgetary policy of the SPD was an improvement in comparison to that of the previous conservative government. His words, however, could also be interpreted the opposite way:

(3)   Peter Struck (SPD): Die Menschen spüren inzwischen, daß es zwischen Waigelscher Haushaltspolitik und unserer einen gravierenden Unterschied gibt:
(Lachen und Beifall bei Abgeordneten der CDU/CSU – Wilhelm Schmidt [Salzgitter] [SPD]: Einen guten!)

(Bundestag, XIV-072, p. 6512, 24/11/1999)

Peter Struck (SPD): People feel that there is a serious difference between the budgetary policy of [the former Minister of Finance] Waigel and ours.
(Laughing and applause among CDU/CSU – Wilhelm Schidt [Salzgitter] [SPD]: A good difference!)

Through the combination of laughing and applause members of the CDU/CSU can demonstrate that they understand the phrase "serious difference" in the opposite way to that intended by P. Struck of SPD.

Finally, laughing sometimes marks a humorous response to inappropriate behaviour. This may be illustrated in the speech that was given by Detlef Kleinert, where the (slow) rhythm, the content of his speech, and his frequent pauses suggested that he had consumed alcohol before speaking:

> (4)   Vizepräsident Dr. Burkhard Hirsch: Herr Kollege Kleinert, Ihre Redezeit ist abgelaufen. Sie müssen zum Schluß kommen.
> Detlef Kleinert (Hannover) (FDP): Herr Präsident Hirsch, ich bedaure das zutiefst.
> (Lachen bei der SPD, dem BÜNDNIS 90/DIE GRÜNEN und der PDS)
> Aber im Hinblick darauf, daß die Aufnahmefähigkeit
> (Lachen bei der SPD, dem BÜNDNIS 90/DIE GRÜNEN und der PDS)
> eines Teils der Mitglieder des Hauses offenbar nachhaltig eingeschränkt ist,
> (Lachen bei der SPD, dem BÜNDNIS 90/DIE GRÜNEN und der PDS)
> bin ich durchaus der Meinung, daß wir eine Unterhaltung über die rechts- und innenpolitischen Fragen, die hier entschieden werden müssen, bei nächster Gelegenheit in einer etwas verständigeren Atmosphäre fortsetzen sollten.
> (Beifall bei der F.D.P. – Lachen und Beifall bei der SPD, dem BÜNDNIS 90/ DIE GRÜNEN und der PDS – Rainder Steenblock [BÜNDNIS 90/DIE GRÜNEN]: Eine nüchterne Rede!)
>
> (Bundestag, XIII-005, p. 150, 23/11/1994)
>
> Deputy Chair Dr. Burkhard Hirsch: Dear colleague Kleinert, your speaking time is over. You need to finish.
> Detlef Kleinert (Hannover) (FDP): Your Honour Mr. Hirsch, I deeply regret this.
> (Laughing among SPD, Green Party, and PDS)
> But given the fact, that the receptiveness
> (Laughing among SPD, Green Party, and PDS)
> of some members of the House is apparently irreversibly impaired,
> (Laughing among SPD, Green Party, and PDS)
> I maintain that we should continue the debate on internal and legal policy issues, which need to be decided here, on another occasion in a more rational atmosphere.
> (Applause among FDP – Laughing and applause among SPD, Green Party, and PDS – Rainder Steenblock [Green Party]: A sober speech!)

In this case, there are strong indications that laughing amongst SPD, Green Party, and PDS parliamentarians is indeed scornful. Nevertheless, there is also a funny incongruity between the speaker's critical remark about the "receptiveness of the House" and his own state. In this context, it is noteworthy that D. Kleinert's speech is still a popular clip on the internet (*Detlef Kleinert alkoholisiert im Bundestag* 1994).

In sum, laughing may fulfil a range of different communicative and social functions, even if these functions occasionally overlap:

a. Rebuttal: laughing may be used as a plain rebuttal of a statement or as a comment without engaging in a serious discussion (Examples (1) and (2)).

b. Ironic *applause*: laughing may mark an ironic interpretation of a statement or comment (Example (3)).

c. Denigration: laughing may serve as a reaction to denigrate or infer criticism of out-group members, and, hence, strengthen in-group relations (Example (1); see also Dynel this volume).

d. *Social control*: laughing may be used to mark behaviour which is considered inappropriate (Example (4)).

5. Amusement – *Heiterkeit*

In almost 80% of all occurrences amusement was assigned to a single faction or an individual (see Table 1). This partisan nature of amusement appears, for instance, in the Example (1), where conservative factions supported a comment by A. Merkel with "amusement and applause". Nevertheless, as amusement generally marks a more positive attitude to humorous stimulus than laughing, it does also

Table 1. Distribution of types of amusement in the German *Bundestag*

Category	Tokens	Rate %
All parliamentarians: Amusement	174	2.3%
All parliamentarians: Amusement and applause	47	0.6%
Without specification of laughter: Amusement	1358	18.3%
Without specification: Amusement and applause	61	0.8%
Parties: Amusement	3125	42.1%
Parties: Amusement and applause	2554	34.4%
Parties: Amusement and expression of agreement	10	0.1%
Parties: Amusement and expression of disagreement	2	0.02%
Individual parliamentarians: Amusement	80	1.1%
Individual parliamentarians: Amusement and applause	10	0.1%
Total	7421	100%

indicate situations which stenographers considered as being "genuinely funny". Moreover, in 22% of all occurrences, amusement was not associated with a specific faction: 221 instances recorded mirthful amusement among all parliamentarians (i.e. *Heiterkeit [und Beifall] im ganzen Hause*, "amusement [and applause] among all parliamentarians").

Even if there are relatively few instances of amusement among all parliamentarians, they deserve particular attention as they seem to constitute instances of humour that were appreciated despite political affiliation. Many instances of amusement among all parliamentarians occurred in situations which concerned expectations about the form of parliamentary speeches. The following themes or situations triggering amusement can be identified in the corpus examined:

a. Negotiation of time limits
b. Violation of expectations and regulations concerning the form of parliamentary discourse
c. Use of formal language vs. informal language; in particular, use of Standard German vs. Non-Standard German
d. Teasing about parliamentary habits such as absence during sessions
e. Inappropriate behaviour and linguistic lapses
f. Verbal humour
g. Reactions to funny repartee

5.1   Time limits as a source of amusement

In parliamentary discourse, time is one of the most important issues and, despite strict time planning, parliamentary sessions may last until very late at night.

According to the *Geschäftsordnung* (Deutscher Bundestag 2006), there are strict time limits which are expected to be enforced by the Chair. Nevertheless, speaking time remains a contentious issue for several reasons: first of all, time limits may be negotiated, for example, beforehand in the Commission for Internal Procedures (*Ältestenrat*). In addition, an individual's speaking time may be extended due to an interposed question. Finally, it is a matter of judgement on the part of the Chair to decide when s/he should signal to parliamentarians that they need to end their speech. This situation poses a communicative challenge, as interrupting a speaker is a potentially face-threatening act:

(5)   Vizepräsident Dr. Norbert Lammert: Frau Kollegin Lehn.
      Waltraud Lehn (SPD): Ich überziehe erst um 31 Sekunden.
      (Heiterkeit im ganzen Hause – [...])

      (Bundestag, XV-134, p. 12262, 27/10/2004)

Deputy Chair Dr. Norbert Lammert: Dear colleague Lehn.
Waltraud Lehn (SPD): So far I have exceeded my speaking time by only 31 seconds.
(Amusement among all parliamentarians – [...])

Such discussions show that parliamentarians expect the Chair to exercise a certain degree of discretion when deciding at what point to interrupt. In addition, the Chair may also have to justify exceptional prolongation:

(6)   Vizepräsident Dr. h. c. Rudolf Seiters: Weil Sie heute Namenstag haben, habe ich Sie etwas länger reden lassen.
(Heiterkeit im ganzen Hause)

(Bundestag, XIV-201, p. 19759, 15/11/2001)

Deputy Chair Dr. h.c. Rudolf Seiters: As it is your nameday, I allowed you to speak a little longer.
(Amusement among all parliamentarians)

General amusement about the negotiation of time limits constitutes the largest category of instances of amusement. The emerging question involves why this issue has so much humorous potential for parliamentarians. Such amusement seems to express some kind of solidarity among parliamentarians in the face of the difficulties of keeping up with the formal requirements of parliamentary speeches. Parliamentarians sometimes also respond with amusement when the Chair demands that the time limit be observed:

(7)   Vizepräsident Hans Klein: Alle haben ein bisschen überzogen. Ich bin zwar nicht sofort eingeschritten, aber ich bitte Sie doch, sich an die Redezeit zu halten. Bringen Sie mich doch bitte nicht immer in diese Schulmeisterrolle.
(Heiterkeit im ganzen Hause)

(Bundestag, XII-040, p. 3169, 31/05/1995)

Deputy Chair Hans Klein: Everybody has overrun the time limit. I did not intervene immediately, but I would like to ask you to abide by the time limit for the speech. Please do not push me into the role of the schoolmaster.
(Amusement among all parliamentarians)

The schoolmaster metaphor bears negative connotations, as it can be associated with pedantic and arrogant behaviour. Apparently, Chairpersons prefer not to interfere too much during parliamentary speeches. In many cases they also look for indirect ways to indicate that a speaker has to terminate his/her speech. In such cases, humour plays an important role, as it allows for a less serious way of interrupting somebody:

(8)   Vizepräsident Dr. Hermann Otto Solms: Das war ein schöner Schlusssatz.
(Heiterkeit und Beifall im ganzen Hause)
Annette Widmann-Mauz (CDU/CSU): Okay. – Ich bedanke mich, Herr
Präsident.

(Bundestag, XV-079, p. 6947, 27/11/2003)

Deputy Chair Dr Hermann Otto Solms: That was an excellent closing
sentence.
(Amusement and applause among all parliamentarians)
Anntette Widmann-Mauz (CDU/CSU): Okay. – Thank you, your Honour.

A Chair does not need to make a polite request; s/he could simply turn off the
microphone. Hence, a momentary lapse of power, such as the one illustrated in
Example (8), may trigger amusement in the audience. In this respect, it seems that
the many instances of amusement in relation to time limits are partly triggered by
the fact that complying with time limits is a challenge for every parliamentarian.

5.2   Amusement about the form and content of speeches

There are specific conventions in parliamentary interaction. For instance, it is the
Chair who makes sure that interposed questions are indeed formulated in the
form of a question. In the heat of the debate, however, such regulations are often
forgotten, as in the following interposed question of Georg Girisch:

(9)   Georg Girisch (CDU/CSU): Herr Bollmann, ich <will> Ihnen <...> – <und
der> Herr Minister Trittin kennt <ganz genau> meine Meinung –, <ich
will Ihnen ganz genau sagen,> was mich persönlich an der Verpackungs-
verordnung stört.
(Zurufe von der SPD: Frage!)
– <und da frage ich Sie,> Sind Sie bereit, dies zur Kenntnis zu nehmen?
(Heiterkeit im ganzen Hause)

(Bundestag, XV-142, p. 131275, 25/11/2004)

Georg Girisch (CDU/CSU): Mr. Bollmann, I <want> to tell you <...> –
Minister Trittin knows <exactly> my opinion – <I want to tell you exactly>,
what I do not like about the packing act.
(Interjection from the SPD: Question!)
– <and I ask you> Will you acknowledge that?
(Amusement among all parliamentarians)

The statement is in this case only superficially turned into the form of a question
initiating an apparent incongruity between what is expected (i.e. a genuine question) and what actually occurs. But there are also more sophisticated questions,

which humorously play with the fine line between real questions and rhetorical questions:

(10)　Birgit Homburger (FDP): Herr Kollege Loske, würden Sie mir zustimmen, dass Sie eigentlich ein ganz intelligenter Bursche sind
(Heiterkeit im ganzen Hause – […])
und dass Sie deshalb wissen, dass all das, was Sie eben gesagt haben, nicht stimmt […].
(Bundestag, XIV-204, p. 20177, 28/11/2001)

Birgit Homburger (FDP): Dear colleague Loske, would you agree that you are actually a rather smart guy
(Amusement among all parliamentarians – […])
and that you should, therefore, know that everything you have just said is incorrect […].

This kind of amusement seems to confirm a shared attitude that the conventions of parliamentary interaction may – at least sometimes – be manipulated to serve different purposes than the ones they are actually intended to serve. This sometimes lax handling of parliamentary conventions is apparent in the form of the interposed questions which do not necessarily carry their original function of demanding clarification on a certain subject. In fact, interposed questions may also extend a speaker's speaking time. In some cases, amusement arises from the fact that the Chair jokingly refers to this additional function of an interposed question:

(11)　Vizepräsident Dr. Norbert Lammert: Herr Kollege Manzewski, möchten Sie kurz vor Ende Ihrer Redezeit
(Heiterkeit im ganzen Hause)
dieselbe durch eine Zusatzfrage des Kollegen Funke verlängern lassen?
(Bundestag, XV-053, p. 4439, 26/06/2003)

Deputy Chair Dr. Norbert Lammert: Dear colleague Manzewski, would you like – just before the end of your speaking time –
(Amusement among all parliamentarians)
to extend your speaking time by accepting an additional question from colleague Funke?

In fact, Dirk Manzewski will, at the end of his response, ask Reiner Funke to stay a little longer in front of the microphone, so that he also can talk for a little longer. The negotiations between D. Manzewski on the rostrum, R. Funke (waiting in front of the microphone), and Deputy Chair N. Lammert (who repeatedly urges an end to Manzewski's speech) trigger three more instances of "amusement among all parliamentarians" in the corpus examined.

5.3   Formal vs. informal style

There are a few instances of amusement which seem to revolve around the choice of appropriate register. Particularly colloquial, informal, or even rude use of language is apparently perceived as a funny deviation:

(12)   Vizepräsidentin Anke Fuchs: […] Bevor ich abstimmen lasse, möchte ich jeden bitten, darüber nachzudenken, was er von dem Wort „Schnarchhahn“ hält. Ich halte diesen Ausdruck zwar nicht für parlamentarisch; aber ich weiß nicht genau, was ich mir darunter vorstellen soll.
(Heiterkeit im ganzen Hause)
(Bundestag, XIV-144, p. 14149, 19/01/2001)

Deputy Chair Anke Fuchs: […] Before we proceed to the voting, I would like to ask everyone to think about the word "snore cock". I do not think this expression is parliamentary; but I do not know what I should make of it.
(Amusement among all parliamentarians)

The expression *Schnarchhahn* "snore cock" did not trigger any humour when it was used earlier in the debate to insult a parliamentarian (see XIV-144, p. 14144). It seems that amusement in this context is triggered by the fact that such expressions are not compatible with the formality of parliament, as the next example also illustrates:

(13)   Ulrike Höfken (BÜNDNIS 90/DIE GRÜNEN): <da geben> Sie mit der einen Hand, <was> Sie mit dem <ich sage mal> „Arsch“ <in Anführungsstrichen> wieder ein <reißen>.
(Zurufe von der CDU/CSU, der SPD und der FDP: Oh! Pfui!) […]
Vizepräsident Wolfgang Thierse: Kollegin Höfken, ich unterstelle, dass Sie jenes Wort ohne Zweifel als ein Zitat unseres größten Klassikers verwendet haben.
(Heiterkeit im ganzen Hause)
Insofern geht es unbeanstandet durch.
(Bundestag, XVI-025, p. 1962, 16/03/2006)

Ulrike Höfken (Green Party): Whatever you give with one hand, you take back with your <quote-unquote> "arse".
(Interjections from CDU/CSU, SPD and FDP: Oh! Tut!) […]
Deputy Chair Wolfgang Thierse: Dear colleague Höfken, I suppose that you certainly used that word as a citation from our greatest classic.[7]

---

7.   Goethe is famous for using the expression "er kann mich am Arsch lecken" ("he can lick me in the ass") in his play *Goetz von Berlichingen* (Goethe 1773/1979).

(Amusement among all parliamentarians)
As such it is accepted without complaints.

This contrast between formal and informal or rude expressions can be found in many insults (Pursch 2009), in particular in J. Fischer's famous insult "Mit Verlaub, Herr Präsident, Sie sind ein Arschloch" ("If you pardon the expression, your Honour, you are an arsehole").[8]

Moreover, the contrast between formal and informal expressions is sometimes exploited to create parallelisms. For instance, Wilhelm Schmidt provoked amusement among all parliamentarians by contrasting his informal remark "Wir wollen, dass der Laden hier besser läuft" ("The Bundestag should run more smoothly"), with the very formal expression "Das Hohe Haus soll besser funktionieren" ("The 'High House' – i.e. the parliament – should function more efficiently"; Bundestag, XIII-47, p. 3856, 29/06/1996). A particular example of this kind of contrasting parallelism has been provided by Wolfgang Börnsen who contrasted the informal Low German version *een schöön Schiet mit de Schippsbu* "nice shit in the shipbuilding industry" with the more formal Standard German version *eine kritische Lage mit dem Schiffbau* "critical situation" (Bundestag, XIV-81, p. 7514, 20/01/2000).

The Example (14) draws attention to the fact that the use of Non-Standard German in parliament is another rare, but nevertheless distinct, source of amusement. Longer official communications in Low German or in other dialects have elicited a lot of amusement. The following conversation between Peter Harry Carstensen and Lisa Peters is, for instance, entirely in Low German:

(14)   Peter Harry Carstensen (CDU/CSU): [...] – Fru Kollegin Peters, besteiht nich ook de Möglichkeit, dat de Red op plattdüütsch holen warden, damit de Gruppen, [...] ut Nordfriesland un ut Dithmarschen, dat en beten better verstohn kann?
(Heiterkeit)
Lisa Peters (FDP): Jo, Peter Harry, ik weet nich, ob de bi jo in Dithmarschen nu überhaupt kein Hochdüütsch verstoht. Ik wür dat jo giern moken. [...], aver ik glöv, dann komm wi mit de Stenographen und mit all de annern in Ruum nich klor, weil wi dat jo hüde nich besonners anmeld hebbt.
(Heiterkeit und Beifall im ganzen Hause)
                              (Bundestag, XIII-044, p. 3617, 22/06/1995)

---

8. This interjection occurred in the Bundestag on October 18, 1984; it was, however, not recorded in the protocols, as the session had been officially adjourned a few seconds before.

> Peter Harry Carstensen (CDU/CSU): [...] Dear colleague Peters, could you hold your speech in Low German, so that the groups from Northern Frisia and Dithmarschen [...] may understand a little better?
> (Amusement)
> Lisa Peters (FDP): Well, Peter Harry, I can't believe that they do not understand any Standard German at all in Dithmarschen. I would like to do that. [...] but I believe that the stenographers and all the others in this room may have difficulties, since we have not announced that in advance.
> (Amusement and applause among all parliamentarians)

First of all, hearing Low German or dialect in the Bundestag is an uncommon experience and may – due to the contrast with typical political discourse – trigger amusement. At the same time, parliamentarians involved in this kind of conversation frequently mention that Non-Standard German may pose some problems for the stenographers.

Even if speaking non-standard variations of German may be sometimes associated with the lower social classes, it also suggests solidarity among people who originate in the same geographical area. This is clearly illustrated in the following example where Cem Özdemir, a son of Turkish immigrants, speaks in Swabian dialect immediately after a speech in Low German:

(15)   Manfred Carstens [CDU]: Dat is nu wirklich in use Land un in Europa wichtig, [...], sondern dat dei Lüer dat ook schnacket.
(Beifall bei der CDU/CSU, der F.D.P. und der SPD)
Vizepräsident Dr. Antje Vollmer: Das Wort hat jetzt der Abgeordnete Cem Özdemir.
(Heiterkeit und Beifall im ganzen Hause)
Cem Özdemir (BÜNDNIS 90/DIE GRÜNEN): Frau Präsidentin! Liebe Kolleginne und Kollege! Koi Sorg, i schwätz net Türkisch; [...] Bevor i aber afang, [...], möcht i mi glei bei de Stenographe quasi entschuldige. I woiß, daß die es heut oabend net grad leicht hend, ond i hoff, daß se trotzdem oinigermaße zstroich kommet damit.
(Heiterkeit und Beifall im ganzen Hause)
(Bundestag, XIII-235, p. 21638, 07/05/1998)

Manfred Carstens [CDU]: This is really important in our country and in Europe [...] that the people speak their own [minority] language.
(Applause among CDU/CSU, FDP, and SPD)
Deputy Chair Dr. Antje Vollmer: Next speaker is MP Cem Özdemir.
(Amusement and applause among all parliamentarians)
Cem Özdemir (Green Party): Your Honour, dear colleagues. Don't worry, I will not speak Turkish; [...] before I begin my speech [...] I would like to

apologise to the stenographers. I know it is not easy for them tonight, and I hope that they will get along with it.

(Amusement and applause among all parliamentarians)

The amusement is explainable by the contrast between Özdemir's migrant background and the debate about regional and minority languages. Özdemir triggers additional amusement by apologising to the stenographers in his Swabian dialect (including a characteristic expression such as *zstroich komme* "to get along with something"). As Özdemir is one of the most prominent politicians with a migrant background, we may also wonder what kind of social function the amusement fulfils: it seems that Özdemir's migrant background and his address in the context of the debate on a law supporting European regional languages provide the basis for humorous incongruity. In this respect, amusement seems to have the double edged quality of being both friendly and hostile.

5.4   Teasing about parliamentary habits and behaviour

Some teaching material provided by the Bundestag for schools includes explanations justifying the poor attendance of parliamentarians during plenary sessions and their lack of attention whilst in the plenum itself (see among others Deutscher Bundestag 2009: 17). In fact, visual recordings of the German Bundestag demonstrate that the plenum is sometimes rather empty during the sessions. Moreover, those parliamentarians who are present do not necessarily focus on the speaker, but may read newspapers or chat with their neighbours. Of course, such behaviour should be seen in the larger context of the tight timetables of parliamentarians. It is, therefore, a common practice that parliamentarians only need to attend those debates which are related to their own specialist fields, and to participate in voting. As a result, discussions about parliamentarians' presence and expected behaviour occasionally take place, which frequently trigger amusement, for example, when late-arrivals are welcomed ironically by the Chair (cf. Bundestag, XIII-241, p. 22370, 16/06/1998). In fact, the issue of presence/absence and attention/inattention are recurring themes of amusement:

(16)   Präsident Dr. Norbert Lammert: Herzlichen Glückwunsch, Herr Kollege Hofreiter, zu Ihrer ersten Rede im Deutschen Bundestag,
(Beifall)
aus deren Anlass die eigene Fraktion nahezu vollzählig angetreten ist, was festgehalten zu werden verdient.
(Heiterkeit im ganzen Hause)

(Bundestag, XVI-17, p. 1249, 10/02/2006)

> Chair Dr. Norbert Lammert: My congratulations, dear colleague Hofreiter, on your first speech in the Deutsche Bundestag
> (Applause)
> on the occasion of which your own faction has appeared almost in its entirety, something well worth being recorded.
> (Amusement among all parliamentarians)

In sum, despite lax regulations concerning the attendance and attention of parliamentarians, it seems that the issue of participating or not (and how) in debates is a contentious one. Moreover, remarks about attendance or attention during the session are potentially face-threatening acts, hence they are frequently accompanied by mirth. In this respect, many verbal exchanges concerning attendance and attention may be understood in terms of teasing. Teasing encompasses the double edged nature of humour of being both (potentially) prosocial and aggressive (Martin 2007: 124).

5.5   Inappropriate behaviour and lapses

The double edged nature of humour is also apparent in the amused reaction to inappropriate behaviour or linguistic lapses. In the following example, a parliamentarian speaks without a manuscript and starts moving away from the speaker's desk in such a way that he leaves the coverage area of the microphone:

(17)   (Der Redner verlässt das Pult in Richtung Regierungsbank)
Vizepräsident Dr. h. c. Rudolf Seiters: Herr Kollege Riesenhuber, bleiben Sie bitte am Rednerpult stehen!
(Heiterkeit und Beifall im ganzen Hause)
(Bundestag, XIV-190, p. 18536, 27/09/2001)

(The speaker leaves the rostrum and walks towards the government's front bench)
Deputy Chair Dr. h.c. Rudolf Seiters: Dear colleague Riesenhuber, please stay on the rostrum!
(Amusement and applause among all parliamentarians)

The amusement in this instance is probably enhanced by the fact that this behaviour is typical of Heinz Riesenhuber (cf. Bundestag, XV-048, p. 4045, 05/06/2003). He is known for an impromptu style of speech, academic extravagances (e.g. bow ties), and complicated sentences (stenographers tend to simplify his sentences). Subsequently, Rudolf Seiters teases Riesenhuber for his academic style of speech:

(18)   Dr. Heinz Riesenhuber (CDU/CSU): Ich bitte um Nachsicht, Herr
       Präsident.
       Vizepräsident Dr. h. c. Rudolf Seiters: Die Kommilitonen sitzen direkt vor
       Ihnen.
       (Heiterkeit im ganzen Hause)
       Dr. Heinz Riesenhuber (CDU/CSU): Ich kann leider keinen Dialog mit dem
       Präsidenten führen. Die Ehrfurcht vor deinem Amt, lieber Rudi, hindert
       mich daran.
       (Heiterkeit im ganzen Hause)
                                              (Bundestag, XIV-190, p. 18536, 27/09/2001)

       Dr. Heinz Riesenhuber (CDU/CSU): I ask for indulgence, your Honour.
       Deputy Chair Dr. h.c. Rudolf Seiters: The fellow students are sitting in front
       of you.
       (Amusement among all parliamentarians)
       Dr. Heinz Riesenhuber (CDU/CSU): Unfortunately, I cannot conduct a dia-
       logue with the Chair. My respect for your office, dear Rudi, deters me from
       that.

Amused reactions have also been elicited by simple slips of the tongue such as
Überweisungsanschlag "assault of petition" instead of *Überweisungsvorschlag*
"proposal of petition" (Bundestag, XIII-177, p. 15939, 04/06/1997) and *Gastster-*
begewerbe "guest dying industry" instead of *Gastgewerbe* "hotel industry" (Bundestag, XIII-021, p. 1489, 16/02/1995).

   A particular category of slips consists of unintended ambiguities. The Bundestag is a demanding audience. Parliamentarians are ready to criticise any form
of imprecise use of words via interjections, but also via laughter or amusement.
For instance, one speaker triggered amused responses for naively saying that she
would like to say something before speaking ("Am Anfang möchte ich ein paar
Worte loswerden"; Bundestag, XV-078, p. 6853, 26/11/2003). Similar ambiguities
have been observed in the context of laughing which marks ironic applause. Of
course, we need to bear in mind that this classification is made by stenographers.
It seems that they differentiate between ambiguities which are based on deliberate
misinterpretation (hence, scornful laughing) or ambiguities which are more easily apprehensible (hence, amusement). In the following extract, the Chair, Wolfgang Thierse, announces the wrong order of speakers and attributes his mistake to
misinformation given to him from the Left/his left, thus unintentionally suggesting that left-wingers had (deliberately?) passed him the wrong list:

(19)   Präsident Wolfgang Thierse (SPD): Das Wort hat der Bundeskanzler der
       Bundesrepublik Deutschland, Gerhard Schröder.
       (Michael Glos [CDU/CSU]: Nein, das ist nicht ausgemacht! […])

<Ist nicht … Mir ist dieser Zettel gereicht worden … Was ist los? … Also [laughs]> – Ich bitte um Entschuldigung. <Das ist eine> Fehlinformation, die mir von links gegeben worden ist.
(Heiterkeit im ganzen Hause – Walter Hirche [FDP]: Natürlich von links! – Friedrich Merz [CDU/CSU]: Ich würde mich auf links nicht verlassen!)
– <Also, von hinten … Von meinem Nachbarn links und der hat sie von hinten>.
(Heiterkeit im ganzen Hause)
Ich erteile also das Wort dem Vorsitzenden der CDU/CSU-Fraktion [=Friedrich Merz]. <Also wiederum nicht.>
(Heiterkeit im ganzen Hause)
<Also, das wird jetzt allmählich ärgerlich …> Lieber Kollege Glos, nachdem die Verwirrungen nunmehr vorbei sind, erteile ich Ihnen mit Vergnügen das Wort.
(Heiterkeit und Beifall bei der CDU/CSU und der FDP)
(Bundestag, XIV-189, p. 18366, 26/09/2001)

Chair Wolfgang Thierse (SPD): The next speaker is the Chancellor of the Federal Republic Germany, Gerhard Schröder.
(Michael Glos [CDU/CSU]: No, this is not what we agreed upon […])
<Is not … I received this … What's the matter here? … Well> I am sorry. <This [mistake]> was based on misinformation given to me from the left.
(Amusement among all parliamentarians - Walter Hirche [FDP]: Of course, from the left – Friedrich Merz [CDU/CSU]: I would never trust the left!)
– <Well, from behind … from my neighbour on the left who got it from behind.>
(Amusement among all parliamentarians)
Our next speaker is then the chairman of the CDU/CSU faction [Friedrich Merz] <Again wrong.>
(Amusement among all parliamentarians)
<Now, this is getting annoying …> Dear colleague Glos, since all the disorder is over now, I am happy to welcome you to the rostrum.
(Amusement and applause among CDU/CSU and FDP)

In this particular instance, it takes W. Thierse a little longer before he comes up with the correct speaker, which leads to further amusement among the audience. At first sight, it is not clear why this instance is evaluated as "amusement" and not as "laughing". The allusion to unreliable leftists provides a clear target for humour. Moreover, the Chair, W. Thierse, is a member of SPD, hence his lapse embarrasses himself. However, the audio-visual recordings show that the mood of parliamentarians is generally humorous: it is clear that members of the leftist government laugh, and even W. Thierse laughs occasionally.

5.6   Verbal humour

Example (19) exhibited qualities of humorous wordplay, as *left* was interpreted in an incongruous way, that is to say, not in terms of spatial deixis, but in terms of political orientation. However, there were, in general, only a few instances in which the audience or parts of the audience responded with amusement to a pun evoking two (or more) opposed scripts (cf. Hempelmann 2004: 384ff.):

(20)   Heiner Geißler (CDU/CSU): Wir können dann gemeinsam zur Gruft schrei-
        ten. Konform, uniform, Chloroform.
        (Heiterkeit bei der CDU/CSU)
                                        (Bundestag, XIII-131, p. 11803, 17/10/1996)

        Heiner Geißler (CDU/CSU): We can then walk together to the grave.
        Conform, uniform, chloroform.
        (Amusement among CDU/CSU and FDP)

There are also instances which prove that it is possible to amuse parliamentarians with an anecdote (e.g. Bundestag, XVI-074, p. 7401, 15/12/2006). These are – as is Example (20) – instances which show that speakers may integrate verbal humour into their speeches.
    The following example consists of an ironic use of an extended metaphor:

(21)   Joschka Fischer (BÜNDNIS 90/DIE GRÜNEN): Es ist in der Tat ein überzeu-
        gendes Bild: In Niedersachsen breitet sich die Wüste Sahara aus.
        (Michael Glos [CDU/CSU]: Nein, die Nordsee!)
        Die Menschen fliehen; sie fliehen gen Süden.
        (Heiterkeit im ganzen Hause)
        Große Karawanen machen sich auf den Weg, dem verheißenen Glück zu fol-
        gen, von dem sie hier gehört haben. Das Paradies hat einen Namen: Bayern.
        (Heiterkeit im ganzen Hause – Beifall bei Abgeordneten der CDU/CSU)
        Dort herrschen paradiesische Zustände; denn die CSU regiert seit anno
        dunnemals. Der Hausmeister im Paradies heißt selbstverständlich Michael
        Glos.
        (Heiterkeit im ganzen Hause)
                                        (Bundestag, XIII-247, p. 23035, 03/09/1998)

        Joschka Fischer (Green Party): It is indeed a persuasive picture. The Sahara is
        spreading throughout Lower Saxony.
        (Michael Glos [CDU/CSU]: No, the North Sea!)
        The people are fleeing; they are fleeing to the South.
        (Amusement among all parliamentarians)
        Great caravans are on the move, driven by the promise of good fortune here
        which they have heard about. This paradise has got a name: Bavaria.

(Amusement among all parliamentarians – Applause among parliamentarians of the CDU/CSU)
There conditions are like paradise, because CSU have been ruling since the year dot. The caretaker's name in this paradise is, of course, Michael Glos.
(Amusement among all parliamentarians)

J. Fischer's ironic passage elaborates the metaphorical comparison between Bavaria and paradise. However, J. Fischer does not stick to the conventional use of paradise as a metaphor, but he elaborates on this metaphorical imagery by suggesting that Michael Glos will assume the role of St. Peter's as the keeper of the Pearly Gates.

5.7   Repartee: Joking as collaboration or challenge

In general, there are only a few instances of amusement which are triggered by the form and content of a single speaker's statement. In most instances of amusement, verbal humour is embedded in verbal interaction involving several participants. The examples so far have demonstrated that German parliamentary discourse allows for interjections or interposed questions, and that such interventions are clearly recorded in the protocols. These dialogic parts are a characteristic element of political discourse in the Bundestag, and most instances of humour in the Bundestag occur within such interactions. At the same time, it is the dialogic nature of the speeches that enhances humour. Even if there are instances in which amusement is triggered by a speaker's pun or anecdote, it seems that the following verbal interactions are much more efficient in provoking amusement.

It is difficult to provide a systematic typology of these instances where humour is a joint product, as they always involve a variety of dimensions. Nonetheless, it is possible to identify recurring functions such as responding to a challenge or correcting a statement. And it can also be said that there are three prominent patterns in amusing interaction: slightly modified repetition of words or gestures, climactic arrangement, and allusion to common knowledge. In the following example, Franz Müntefering (SPD) challenges Guido Westerwelle (FDP):

(22)   Franz Müntefering (SPD): Wenn ich Herrn Westerwelle höre, dann sehe ich Frau Thatcher schon ihr Handtäschchen schwingen.
(Heiterkeit und Beifall bei der SPD und dem BÜNDNIS 90/DIE GRÜNEN)
[...]
(Abg. Dr. Guido Westerwelle [FDP] hält eine Damenhandtasche hoch – Heiterkeit im ganzen Hause)
– Herr Westerwelle, das habe ich doch vermutet.
(Bundestag, XV-032, p. 2510, 14/03/2003)

> Franz Müntefering (SPD): When I hear Mr. Westerwelle, I can already see
> Mrs. Thatcher swinging her handbag.
> (Amusement and applause among SPD and Green Party)
> [...]
> (MP Dr. Guido Westerwelle [FDP] lifts a handbag – Amusement among all
> parliamentarians.)
> – Mr. Westerwelle, I thought that might be the case.

This instance of amusement relies heavily on common knowledge among parliamentarians. On one level, F. Müntefering reminds the audience of Margaret
Thatcher's handbag episodes in the meetings of the European Council. However,
there is more going on here: a year after F. Müntefering's speech, G. Westerwelle
publicly admitted his homosexuality, but it seems that parliamentarians already
knew about it.[9] Outsiders not aware of G. Westerwelle's homosexuality may have
faced difficulty in understanding the presuppositions behind this amusing statement. By appealing to common knowledge, F. Müntefering's hostile banter also
contributes to the creation of a shared identity among parliamentarians.

Correction also leads to the joint production of humour through dialogue,
as in the following example where Chair N. Lammert rectifies a remark by Thea
Dückert (Green Party):

(23) Dr. Thea Dückert (BÜNDNIS 90/DIE GRÜNEN): <Sie hätten sich vielleicht
      mal orientieren können an einem> Ratschlag von Weihbischof Hengsbach
      [...] <...>, der Folgendes kundgetan hat – ich zitiere mit der Erlaubnis des
      Präsidenten –:
      Habe ich ohne wichtigen Grund durch eine Wortmeldung [...] eine Sitzung
      verlängert und somit mich und andere von der Familie ferngehalten? Lieber
      Gott, hilf mir, meinen Mund zu halten, bis ich weiß, worüber ich rede!
      (Heiterkeit und Beifall beim BÜNDNIS 90/DIE GRÜNEN und bei der
      SPD)
      Vizepräsident Dr. Norbert Lammert: Frau Kollegin, darf ich nur der
      Vollständigkeit halber hinzufügen, dass es sich bei dem zitierten Herrn
      Hengsbach nicht um einen Weihbischof, sondern einen leibhaftigen Kardinal
      gehandelt hat, was man an der Qualität des Zitats auch mühelos erken-
      nen kann. (Heiterkeit im ganzen Hause – Beifall beim BÜNDNIS 90/DIE
      GRÜNEN und bei der SPD)

---

9. Cf. the amusement about Rainder Steenblock's Freudian slip, when he said that he would
take note of G. Westerwelle's FDP with "joyful excitation/arousal" (*freudiger Erregung*; Bundestag, XV-72, p. 6172, 6/11/2003).

Dr. Thea Dückert (BÜNDNIS 90/DIE GRÜNEN): Ich danke, Herr Präsident. Ich weiß, dass ich Ihnen nicht widersprechen darf, obwohl es natürlich <auf den Zeitpunkt> ankommt, wann er diese Worte gesagt hat.
(Heiterkeit und Beifall beim BÜNDNIS 90/ DIE GRÜNEN und bei der SPD)
(Bundestag, XV-135, p. 12361, 28/10/2004)

Dr. Thea Dückert (Green Party): <You should have followed the> advice of auxiliary bishop Hengsbach […] <…> who said – I cite with the Chair's permission –:
Have I ever kept me or somebody else away from our families by prolonging a meeting with an unnecessary statement? God, help me to shut up until I know what I am talking about!
(Amusement and applause among the Green Party and SPD)
Deputy Chair Dr. Norbert Lammert: Dear colleague, may I just add for the sake of completeness that Mr. Hengsbach whom you cited is not an auxiliary bishop, but a veritable cardinal, which you can easily tell from the quality of the citation.
(Amusement among all parliamentarians – Applause among the Green Party and SPD)
Dr. Thea Dückert (Green Party): Thank you, your Honour. I know, I am not allowed to contradict, although it might be relevant <at what stage of his career> he made that remark.
(Amusement and applause among the Green Party and SPD)

There are, as previously mentioned, also recurring formal elements in jointly produced humour which might be labelled as climactic arrangement and modified repetition:

(24)   Dr. Manuel Kipper (BÜNDNIS 90/DIE GRÜNEN): Wir brauchen Preistransparenz, wir brauchen Rechtssicherheit für Kunden, wir brauchen […], wir brauchen […], wir brauchen […], wir brauchen […], wir brauchen eine intensivere Forschung an Verschlüsselungsverfahren.
(Zuruf von der CDU/CSU: Sagen Sie doch, was wir nicht brauchen!)
Präsidentin Dr. Rita Süssmuth: Jetzt brauchen wir die Einhaltung der Redezeit.
(Heiterkeit im ganzen Hause)
(Bundestag, XIII-138, p. 12330, 14/11/1996)

Dr. Manuel Kipper (Green Party): We need price transparency, we need legal security for clients, we need […], we need […], we need […], we need […], we need intensive research on cryptographic technique.
(Interjection from the CDU/CSU: Tell us what we do not need!)
Chair Dr. Rita Süssmuth: We need compliance with speaking time now!
(Amusement among all parliamentarians)

Rita Süssmuth asks Manuel Kipper to finish by replicating the syntactic structure of his speech. In this context it should be kept in mind that exaggerated use figures of speech is unpopular in the Bundestag, and the laughing in the audience provoked by R. Süssmuth's structural echoing seems to support this.

Climactic arrangements provide additional possibilities, as they may extend to a remarkable length, as Example (25) illustrates. During a session of questions about the support of tourism development in Germany, the Parliamentary State Secretary Siegmar Mosdorf deliberates on potential holiday destinations in Germany and the audience assists with many additional suggestions:

(25)   Siegmar Mosdorf (Parl. Staatssekretär beim Bundesminister für Wirtschaft und Technologie): Ich sage bloß: Einmal weniger Mallorca und dafür ein Aufenthalt bei uns, am Schwäbischen Meer, am Bodensee, im Schwarzwald oder in der Sächsischen Schweiz, wo es besonders schön ist.
(Dirk Niebel [F.D.P.]: Oder in Heidelberg!)
– Oder in Heidelberg; das ist ganz wichtig.
(Zuruf von der CDU/CSU: Oder in Bayern!)
– Oder in Bayern. Einmal weniger Mallorca und sich einmal zu Hause umschauen.
(Zurufe von der CDU/CSU: Oder Schleswig-Holstein! – Oder Wilhelmshaven!)
– Ja, natürlich, Wilhelmshaven.
Vizepräsidentin Anke Fuchs: Die Nordsee vergessen Sie immer, Herr Kollege. Das ist unglaublich.
(Heiterkeit im ganzen Hause […])
                                        (Bundestag, XIV-152, p. 14924, 15/02/2001)

Siegmar Mosdorf (Parliamentary State Secretary): All I want to say is: One visit less to Mallorca, and instead a holiday with us at Lake Constance, in the Black Forest, or in Saxon Switzerland, where it is particularly beautiful.
(Dirk Niebel [FDP]: Or in Heidelberg!)
Or in Heidelberg, this is important.
(Interjection from the CDU/CSU: Or in Bavaria!)
Or in Bavaria. One visit less to Mallorca and have a look at your home country instead.
(Interjection from the CDU/CSU: Or Schleswig-Holstein! Or Wilhelmshaven!)
Yes, of course, Wilhelmshaven.
Deputy Chair Anke Fuchs: The North Sea, you always forget it, dear colleague. This is unbelievable.
(Amusement among all parliamentarians […])

It is interesting to see how several parliamentarians engage in a collaborative game of mentioning additional holiday destinations, even though such interjections do not add anything new to S. Mosdorf's statement.

6. Conclusion

The present analysis and the proposed categorisation of different types of laughing and amusement in the German parliament confirm the stenographers' differentiation between the hostile – *laughing at* – behaviour (i.e. laughing/*Lachen*) and the conciliatory – *laughing with* – behaviour (i.e. amusement/*Heiterkeit*). In German parliamentary debates, laughing typically indicates a condescending attitude: most instances carried no apparent humorous element (or *script opposition*; see Attardo and Raskin 1991) which would help to interpret the responses as expressions of genuine humour. As a consequence, laughing is frequently associated with mere rebuttal of statements, ironic applause, and denigration. Laughter is in this respect a means by which to rebuff a serious statement without entering into a serious debate by dismissing it as non-serious. At the same time, laughter is distributed according to party and coalition alliances; hence, it signals criticism of the opposing faction and serves as a marker of in-groups and out-groups.

Amusement, on the other hand, is typically associated with the expression of a more positive attitude. It expresses some kind of basic consensus between the speaker and (part of) the audience, as revealed by their common preoccupation with limits on speaking time or with the choice of the appropriate register. Moreover, there are also some instances of amusement which seem to be grounded in a generally shared appreciation of humorous incongruity among all parliamentarians regardless their ideological affiliation. Nevertheless, amusement is not a harmless form of humour. Even amusement is typically linked with a humorous target and is associated with forms of teasing.

In sum, both amusement and laughter contain aggressiveness and conciliation in different degrees. The fundamental difference between laughing and amusement can be illustrated by the contrast between "laughing and applause" and "amusement and applause": whereas applause with laughter can be reliably interpreted as ironic and denigrating, the latter expresses consensus between the speaker and (at least a part of) the audience.

References

Archakis, Argiris and Tsakona, Villy. 2005. "Analyzing conversational data in GTVH terms: A new approach to the issue of identity construction via humour." *Humour: International Journal of Humour Research* 18: 41–68.

Attardo, Salvatore and Raskin, Victor. 1991. "Script theory revis(it)ed. Joke similarity and joke representation model." *Humour: International Journal of Humour Research* 4: 293–347.

Detlef Kleinert alkoholisiert im Bundestag. 1994. http://www.youtube.com/watch?v=siw-MAiKVtA (accessed November 8, 2009).

Deutscher Bundestag. 1994–2006. In *Verhandlungen des deutschen Bundestages.* XII. Periode, 1. Sitzung – XVI. Periode, 74. Sitzung.

Deutscher Bundestag. 2006. *Geschäftsordnung des deutschen Bundestages in der Fassung der Bekanntmachung vom 2. Juli 1980 (BGBl. I S. 1237), zuletzt geändert laut Bekanntmachung vom 26. September 2006 (BGBl. I. S. 2210).* http://www.bundestag.de/parlament/funktion/gesetze/go.pdf (accessed October 20, 2008).

Deutscher Bundestag (ed.). 2009. *Fakten. Der Bundestag auf einen Blick.* Berlin.

Goethe, Johann Wolfgang von. 1773/1979. *Frühe Dramen: Goetz von Berlichingen, Clavigo.* München: Dtv.

Gottsched, Johann Christoph. 1752. *Grundlegung einer Deutschen Sprachkunst nach dem Muster der besten Schriftsteller des vorigen und jetzigen Jahrunderts [1725]* (3rd edition). Leipzig: Breitkopf.

Hempelmann, Christian F. 2004. "Script opposition and logical mechanism in punning." *Humour: International Journal of Humour Research* 17: 381–392.

Kiedaisch, Petra and Bär, Jochen A. 1997. "Heiterkeitskonzeptionen in der europäische Literatur und Phiosophie. Einführung in die Geschichte eines Begriffs und seine Erforschung." In *Heiterkeit. Konzepte in Literatur und Geistesgeschichte*, Petra Kiedaisch and Jochen A. Bär (eds), 7–30. München: Fink.

Lessing, Gotthold Ephraim. 1867. "Vorrede zum dritten und vierten Theile der Schriften [1754]." In *Lessing's Werke*, Karl Goedeke (ed.), 116–120. Leipzig: Göschen'sche Verlagshandlung.

Martin, Rod A. 2007. *The Psychology of Humour. An Integrative Approach.* Burlington: Elsevier.

Pursch, Günter. 2009. *Das parlamentarische Schimpfbuch. Stilblüten und Geistesblitze unserer Volksvertreter in 60 Jahren Bundestag* (2nd edition). München: Herbig.

Schöttker, Detlev. 1998. "Metamorphosen der Freude. Darstellung und Reflexion der Heiterkeit in der Literatur des 18. Jahrhunderts." *Deutsche Vierteljahresschrift für Literaturwissenschaft und Geistesgeschichte* 72: 354–375.

Scott, Mike. 2004. *WordSmith Tools. Version 4.0.0.* Oxford: Oxford University Press.

Simmler, Franz. 1978. *Die politische Rede im Deutschen Bundestag. Bestimmung ihrer Textsorten und Redesorten* [Göppinger Arbeiten zur Germanistik 245]. Göppingen: Kümmerle.

Weinrich, Harald. 2001. *Kleine Literaturgeschichte der Heiterkeit* (extended edition). München: Beck.

CHAPTER 3

Informal talk in formal settings

Humorous narratives
in Greek parliamentary debates

Argiris Archakis and Villy Tsakona
University of Patras, Greece / Democritus University of Thrace, Greece

Rather than a one-to-one correspondence between varieties and contexts, hybridity is often observed in communicative settings due to the plurality of sociolinguistic resources speakers draw upon to shape the particular style of talk which will best serve their communicative intent. This seems to be the case with Greek parliamentary discourse: although the parliament constitutes a highly institutionalised, formal setting, where logical and legal argumentation is expected to prevail, Greek parliamentarians employ oral humorous narratives to persuade the voting audience and create and maintain bonds with them. The wider cultural and political context plays a significant role in determining parliamentarians' stylistic choices: orality and respective practices are highly valued in Greek culture, where story-telling in particular is often used for argumentative purposes.

1. Introduction: Can formal settings "afford" informal talk?

Drawing upon Labov's (1966, 1972) influential approach to style, sociolinguists usually consider stylistic variation to be organised according to the degree of attention speakers pay to their own speech. Thus, sociolinguists assume a continuum with "more formal, careful speech" on the one end, and "more casual, unmonitored speech" on the other (Rickford and Eckert 2001: 2). Moreover, they acknowledge the existence of links between social situations and stylistic clusters, with prestigious and serious talk appearing in the course of formal and attended speech activities (Coupland 2007: 218–219; see also Coupland 2001: 187).

However, more recent approaches to stylistic variation coming from critical discourse analysis and interactional sociolinguistics challenge the above assumptions. Fairclough (1995: 241) points out that "the matching of language to context is characterised by indeterminacy, heterogeneity and struggle", whereas Coupland (2001:196), based on and quoting Bakhtin (1981), points out that "all discourse 'lives on the boundary of its own context and another, *alien* context'" (our emphasis). In line with these observations our approach to style variation does not presuppose a one-to-one correspondence between linguistic varieties, registers, text types, etc. and particular contexts, but rather goes beyond the well-known distinction between formality and informality. More specifically, we assume that there is a plurality of sociolinguistic resources that participants draw upon to shape their styles of talk in relation to their specific communicative intent (Fairclough 1995; Coupland 2001, 2007; Giles 2001:211).

This plurality and mixture of sociolinguistic resources is attested in what Fairclough (1995) defines as the *conversationalisation* of public discourse, namely the strategic use of informal conversational resources and themes coming from everyday interaction in political and media discourse. In particular, *political cross-discourse* refers to politicians' tendency to often cross the boundaries of their official role, social status, and language by switching towards a more conversational, informal, and personalised style and by drawing on discourse resources which are not considered compatible with their social status. Political cross-discourse involves the use of metaphor, metonymy, polyphonic and dialectal speech, humour, narratives, and direct speech.[1] Such informal conversational resources and themes originating in local social networks and entering political discourse and oratory are strategically employed by politicians in their attempt to create a more personalised view of political affairs, hide the unequal distribution of discursive resources along different social groups, and avoid political argumentation (Alvarez-Cáccamo and Prego-Vásquez 2003; see also Gadavanij 2002; Marquez 2010:84).

In this context, our central research question concerns why informal discursive practices occur in "alien" formal contexts such as parliamentary debates, namely in a communicative setting where the serious mode is expected to prevail and which are considered highly formal in most cultures and states (van Dijk 2000; Bayley 2004a; Ilie 2006, 2010a, b). Parliaments are responsible for preparing, discussing, and passing or rejecting bills, criticising government policies, electing the President of the Republic, revising the Constitution, etc. Hence, the

---

1.   The concept of *political cross-discourse* draws on that of *crossing* which involves

> code alternation by people who are not accepted members of the group associated with the second language they employ. It is concerned with switching into languages that are not generally thought to belong to you. This kind of switching, in which there is a distinct sense of movement across social or ethnic boundaries, raises issues of social legitimacy that participants need to negotiate.   (Rampton 1995:280)

discourse produced therein is typically formal and predominantly argumentative (van Dijk 2002: 229; van der Valk 2003: 314, 316; Steiner et al. 2004). Among the different kinds of political cross-discourse identified above, we intend to focus on humour and narratives, in particular in their combination in the form of *humorous narratives*.

Even though parliamentary humour has not been extensively discussed in the literature of parliamentary discourse analysis, its use and function have been briefly commented on in several studies. Parliamentary humour is usually described as a means of expressing criticism and aggression in a mitigated and socially acceptable manner, namely without violating parliamentary rules of conduct (Harris 2001: 467; Ilie 2004: 78; Miller 2004: 292; Meisel 2009: 228–231; Carranza Márquez 2010; Madzharova Bruteig 2010: 284–285); or as a means of identity construction: politicians present themselves as humorists so as to enhance their popularity, while, at the same time, they divert the attention of the audience from the important issues discussed (Meisel 2009; Tsakona 2009a). In general, humour seems to be significant in political communication, as it is considered to be a particularly effective means of conveying influential political messages and of rendering such messages memorable and persuasive, in part by distracting from counterarguments (see Niven et al. 2003: 120, and references therein).

Given the above, the aim of the present study is to explore the function of humorous narratives occurring in Greek parliamentary debates. To this end, first, we present the key concepts of our analysis: we offer a working definition of humour and of the main tools used for its analysis, namely the punch line and the jab line, as well as a brief description of (humorous) oral narratives (Section 2). In Section 3, we present some relevant aspects of the wider political and cultural context in which Greek parliamentary discourse is produced: it seems that the institutional design of the Greek parliament, as well as the preference of Greek speakers for positive politeness strategies and their tendency to use story-telling for argumentative purposes, all constitute significant parameters for the interpretation of our data. Based on the analysis of our corpus, we will argue that politicians tell humorous narratives, in order, on the one hand, to negatively evaluate their adversary(ies) and, on the other, to present themselves as politicians who understand people's problems and needs and can talk the "language of common people", thus satisfying the expectations of the (voting) audience and enhancing their involvement (Section 4). In the same section, we also discuss what happens when the constructed nature of a humorous narrative comes to the surface and humour backfires. Section 5 summarises the findings of the present study and explores areas for further research.

2.   Humour, narratives, and humorous narratives

Humour is based on incongruity, namely on the incompatibility between two co-occurring meanings or ideas. In linguistic, and particularly in pragmatic terms, incongruity is described as an opposition between two *scripts* evoked in a single text, where a script is defined as a cognitive structure involving the semantic information associated with the meanings included in a text, representing speaker's knowledge of the world, and providing information on the structure, components, functions, etc. of the entity or activity referred to (Raskin 1985; Attardo 2001; see also Tsakona and Popa this volume).

For analytical purposes two kinds of humorous lines are identified by the *General Theory of Verbal Humour* (Attardo 2001). They are both based on incongruous meanings, namely they are fully or partially compatible with two different and opposed scripts, but they are differentiated by their position: the *punch line* is the final utterance of a text and marks its unexpected ending, while the *jab line* can occur in any part of a text before its ending and marks its content as humorous. Both may consist of a word, a phrase, or even a sentence causing a script opposition (Attardo 2001: 82–83; Tsakona 2007).

Another important aspect in the analysis of humour is its *target*. Since humour is based on script opposition, a humorous event has to deviate from the norm, namely to contradict what is expected or normal in given circumstances. Therefore, humour is directly related to and results from evaluation or criticism procedures and can actually be used as a means of criticism: it aims at correcting our way of behaving, whenever this behaviour deviates from what is socially expected or approved. In this sense, the target of humour is directly related to the social function of humour and may be a person, an institution or, generally, whatever causes an incongruity (see among others Attardo 2001: 23–24; Archakis and Tsakona 2005: 47–48).

Humour occurs in a variety of social settings and genres. One of the most common genres including humorous instances is everyday *oral narratives*. As to their structure and content, Labov (1972: 360–361) suggests that oral narratives consist of a sequence of at least "two clauses which are temporally ordered". This narrative skeleton, namely the *complicating action*, can be surrounded by other components, such as *orientation* (i.e. the identification of time, place, persons, and their activities) and *evaluation* (revealing the narrator's attitudes and emotions towards the point of the story). Oral narratives are normally completed by a *resolution* component presenting the outcome or consequences of the complicating action. More specifically, Labov (1972: 360) defines narratives as "one method of recapitulating past experience by matching a verbal sequence of clauses to the sequence of events which actually occurred".

We characterise a narrative as *humorous* if it contains a punch line and/or jab lines, namely one or more utterances including a semantic/pragmatic incongruity between what is expected to happen and what actually happens (Archakis and Tsakona 2005, 2006). Humorous oral narratives are typically told among peers in casual interaction (family gatherings, parties, over coffee, etc.) and contribute not only to the amusement of the interlocutors, but also to bonding and building in-group identity. Via humorous stories interlocutors share experiences and negotiate what is accepted or not among group members, thus defining, reinforcing, and confirming common views, values, and norms (see also Norrick 1993:44–59, 2004).

Canned narrative jokes, namely fictional stories circulating with more or less the same content, belonging to the folklore, and typically exchanged in peer groups for amusement, can also be considered humorous narratives in the sense described above. Narrative jokes share the same structure with oral narratives. Their only difference lies in that, instead of a resolution, narrative jokes end up with a punch line which *implies* rather than explicitly describes the outcomes of the complicating action.[2] A detailed and explicit description of the outcomes would kill the joke (Tsakona 2000).

Finally, we suggest that a clear distinction should be made at this point between the parliamentary narratives examined here as a means of the conversationalisation of political discourse (see Section 1), and the "grand", "cultural", or "national" narratives frequently occurring in political settings and hence attracting scholarly attention (see among others de Cillia et al. 1999; Stapleton and Wilson 2003; Shenhav 2005, 2008). "Grand" narratives with a national significance aim at constructing the political and/or national identity and history of a nation or state and are circulated and consolidated via political discourse, the media, and education systems. By containing national, historical, and cultural materials known to the majority of the audience, "national" narratives allow politicians to legitimise the policies advocated and to create a sense of continuity between present day politics and the collective national experience. Our focus, however, is on parliamentarians' tendency to reproduce their *everyday experiences with ordinary people* as well as *fictional stories belonging to the folklore* as part of their argumentation, namely in support of their claims or of their criticism against their opponents. The narratives examined here resemble to what Ilie (2003:258) calls a "narrative digression" introduced for exemplification purposes (see also Schubert 2010:150–151). Such oral narratives are not common in parliamentary settings and do not usually attract scholarly attention, hence research on them is scarce

---

2.   On the implicitness of the punch line in jokes, see among others Dolitsky (1983), Oring (1992:87–90), and Attardo (1994:289–290).

(see, however, Fetzer 2010). What is more, sometimes when oral narratives occur in parliamentary or political debates, their use is negatively evaluated by politicians themselves, since they are considered a means of suppressing evidence and avoiding argumentation (Komlósi and Tarrósy 2010: 964–965).

In the following section, we discuss the particularities of the Greek political and cultural context which favour, and could account for, narrative performances in the Greek parliament.

3.   Parliamentary discourse in the Greek context

In modern democracies, parliament is considered one of the most serious institutional settings, where issues of utmost political and national importance are deliberated. Institutional discursive features and ritualised forms of interaction (e.g. address forms, politeness norms, turn-taking procedures) are important in this setting, where parliamentarians are expected to express, negotiate, and justify their political positions and policies, as well as to evaluate, attack, and delegitimise those of the opponent. Given that persuasion is considered to be one of the most important goals parliamentarians have to attain, they usually resort to logical, legal, and political argumentation. As a result, parliamentary discourse analysis has so far focused mainly on the argumentative strategies employed by parliamentarians to persuade their audience (see among others Bayley 2004a; Ilie 2006, 2010a, b).

Furthermore, the particular institutional design of each parliament and its political history and culture also play a significant role in shaping the discourse produced therein. For example, parliamentary discourse is sensitive to the institutional differences between parliamentary and presidential political systems, or between consensus and competitive democracies (van der Valk 2003: 316; Bayley 2004b: 2–7; Steiner et al. 2004; Ilie 2010b). The Greek political system is a competitive, unicameral parliamentary one. There are no party coalitions; instead, the ruling party has the majority of votes, practically controls the legislative process, and can quite safely ignore the opposition, since there is no second chamber to object to or counter a bill approved of by the majority. This combination strengthens the competition between the government and the opposition (in recent years, usually the two major parties, the conservative Nea Dimocratia and the socialist PASOK), so the possibility that parliamentary debates may consist of pure argumentation turns out to be rather weak. In addition, in Greece, as in many Western democracies, parliamentary deliberation and confrontation take place "on air": the Greek parliament runs its own TV channel for publicising its work, whereas TV or radio news from other channels or stations often refer to parliamentary debates and reproduce extracts coming from the official recordings of the Greek parliament.

In this context, and in contrast to common expectations for parliamentary settings, the main interest of Greek politicians is not to provide political and legal arguments on the issues discussed in parliament. When they do so, their arguments are "presumptive", namely they are intended "to create a unique pragmatic effect" rather than provide evidence in support of the stated claims (Komlósi & Tarrósy 2010: 971). More often than not, Greek parliamentarians wish to address a wider audience using a familiar (i.e. everyday and conversational) mode in order to attract the attention of the public and persuade them that their policies are right, that their criticism is justified, and that they have something better to propose than their opponents. Thus, Greek politicians have the opportunity to project not their work and policies, but rather themselves as friendly and trustworthy persons, working hard for the public benefit, using the "language of common people", and, ultimately, understanding the public's desires and needs (Tsakona 2008a, 2009b).[3]

This communicative orientation of Greek parliamentarians is not irrelevant to the importance attached by the Greek culture to the (verbal and interactional) maintenance and enhancement of in-group relations. In politeness theory terms (Brown and Levinson 1987), Greek society exhibits a positive politeness orientation: Greek speakers tend to treat their addressee "as a member of an in-group, a friend, a person whose desires and personality are known and liked" (Sifianou 2006: 110; see also Archakis and Tzanne 2009).

Closely connected to the positive politeness orientation of the Greek culture is "the orality bias of contemporary Greek society" which is manifested "in the preponderance of features associated with oral texts" (Georgakopoulou 2004: 52; see also Tziovas 2001). This is due to the fact that "speaking and spoken texts have been found to be prototypically more immediate, animated, dramatised" (Georgakopoulou 2004: 51). As a result, oral features are very often transferred from their prototypical contexts to more formal and institutionalised ones, such as academic writing (Koutsantoni 2005) and parliamentary discourse (Bakakou-Orfanou 2008; Tsakona 2008b, 2009b). In the latter case, Greek politicians employ a variety of informal conversational resources (everyday lexis, repetition, parallelism, alliteration, rhyme, punning, neologisms, hyperbole, metaphor, idioms,

---

3. The same holds for politicians in other states and sociocultural contexts, where "symbiotic relations" between political discourse and the media exists (Fetzer and Weizman 2006: 143; see also Fetzer and Lauerbach 2007; Ilie 2010c; and Section 1 in the present paper, on the conversationalisation of political discourse).

proverbs, etc.) to enact their speeches in parliamentary debates and to project themselves as eloquent orators and as "one of the people" at the same time.

In such an orality-oriented cultural context, one of the main rhetorical strategies for argumentation seems to be story-telling. As Georgakopoulou (2004: 53) aptly points out, Greek interactants prefer "to base their evidence for the views expressed on hearsay and the anecdotal, experiential knowledge conveyed through stories, as opposed to more abstract, deductive process of reasoning". Thus, Greek interactants perform dramatised and animated story-tellings, where events appear to speak for themselves. Their goal is to increase participants' emotional and experiential involvement in the narrated events.

In the following section, we discuss the function of humorous narratives in Greek parliamentary discourse. Greek parliamentarians seem to switch towards more conversational stylistic choices for expressing their alignment with the audience (cf. Fetzer 2010: 181) even in critical circumstances, such as "no confidence" debates which actually constitute a threat to the government and a chance for the opposition to lead the country to early elections.

4.   Data analysis

The data of the present study comes from the written proceedings available in the official website of the Greek Parliament (*Hellenic Parliament* 2011). They include the speeches delivered during a "no confidence" debate which took place on February 2–4, 2007 (226,939 words). In this corpus, 89 humorous extracts were isolated; 9 of them included a humorous narrative and 2 of them a narrative joke.

In parliamentary democracies, "no confidence" debates can be launched anytime by the opposition, who accuse the government of inadequacy and incompetence in handling one or more important issues. Their aim is to vote the government out of office and lead the country to elections. Hence, the government is expected to present and support their work and to defend themselves against the opposition's criticism. Consequently, such debates attract the attention of the media and the wider audience.

The "no confidence" debate under examination was initiated by PASOK to question the way the government of Nea Dimocratia handled several parliamentary and state issues and to arouse the attention of the media and the wider audience. Although the 3-day-debate gave them the chance to scrutinise governmental work, it was clear from the beginning that their chances of overthrowing the government were practically non-existent due to the strong party loyalty of the members of Nea Dimocratia (see also Tsakona 2009a).

In the first example, PASOK parliamentarian Sylvana Rapti aims at criticising the Minister of Economy, George Alogoskoufis:[4]

(1) Συλβάνα Ράπτη (ΠΑΣΟΚ): Ευχαριστώ, κύριε Πρόεδρε.

Κυρίες και κύριοι συνάδελφοι, *το βλέπουμε και το νιώθουμε όλοι ότι η οικο-*
νομία πηγαίνει καλύτερα, πηγαίνει πολύ καλύτερα (1). Δεν το λέω εγώ αυτό,
το είπε χθες ο Υπουργός επί των Οικονομικών, ο κ. Αλογοσκούφης.

Ομολογώ ότι μόλις το άκουσα έμεινα αμήχανη. Λέω «εδώ κάτι χάνω, κάτι δεν
καταλαβαίνω καλά» και μου φαίνεται ότι δεν είμαι μόνο εγώ, είναι και άλλοι
πολλοί που δεν το καταλαβαίνουν. Γιατί αυτό; Γιατί ξέρετε μόλις προχθές,
των Τριών Ιεραρχών, βρισκόμουν στα Πετράλωνα. Τα Πετράλωνα είναι μια
πολύ ωραία συνοικία, αλλά πονεμένη, υποβαθμισμένη, στην Α΄ Περιφέρεια
της Αθήνας όπου εκλέγομαι και όπου στην ίδια περιφέρεια εκλέγεται και ο
Υπουργός Οικονομίας, ο κ. Αλογοσκούφης.

Στα Πετράλωνα, λοιπόν, που πήγα οι άνδρες και οι γυναίκες, ανεξαρτήτως
ηλικίας, *δεν κατάλαβαν τίποτα από αυτήν τη βελτίωση της οικονομίας (2).*
Γινόταν εκεί ένα πανηγύρι. *Το πανηγύρι δεν είχε στηθεί γιατί πάει καλύτερα η*
οικονομία, είχε στηθεί για να γιορτασθούν οι Τρεις Ιεράρχες στην περιοχή (3).
Όλοι έλεγαν λοιπόν ότι υποφέρουν. Όλοι έλεγαν ότι τα βγάζουν δύσκολα
πέρα. *Πώς είναι δυνατόν όμως ο κ. Αλογοσκούφης να μην μπορεί να πείσει*
τους ψηφοφόρους της περιφέρειάς του ότι πάει καλύτερα η οικονομία, αλλά να
το ισχυρίζεται από αυτό εδώ το Βήμα (4), είναι ένα ερώτημα το οποίο αναζητά
απάντηση και πιστεύω ότι θα τη λάβουμε.

Βέβαια, ο Υπουργός είχε στοιχεία, παρέθεσε αριθμούς […].

(February 3, 2007)

Sylvana Rapti (PASOK): Thank you, Your Honour [addressing the Chair].

Dear colleagues, *it is perfectly clear to everybody that the economy is picking*
up, very much so (1). It is not me who says that, it is the Minister of Economy,
Mr. Alogoskoufis, who told us so yesterday.

I must admit that, upon hearing it, I was baffled. I thought to myself "I am
missing out on something here, I don't get it" and I think that I am not alone in
that. There are a lot of people who don't get it. Why is that? Because, you know,
only two days ago, on the day of the Three Holy Hierarchs, I was at Petralona.
Petralona is a very nice district, but also a troubled, underprivileged district

---

4. Greek parliamentary discourse extracts are translated into English by the authors. Needless
to say that the interlingual transference of humour is never a simple task and may have had
undesirable stylistic effects in the target version. All humorous lines (punch lines and jab lines)
are marked in italics and numbered. Square brackets include additional contextual information
and square brackets including dots in both versions indicate omissions of text which was not
considered necessary for the present discussion.

in the 1st Constituency of Athens, which happens to be both my constituency and that of the Minister of Economy Mr. Alogoskoufis.

Well, in Petralona, *nobody seemed to realise that we are in the middle of an economy picking up* (2) irrespective of their gender or age. A festival was taking place on that day, *not to celebrate the economic boom, but to celebrate the Three Holy Hierarchs* (3).

Well, everybody said that they suffer. Everybody said that they cannot make ends meet. *But how is it possible for Mr. Alogoskoufis to be unable to convince the voters in his own constituency that the economy is picking up, while at the same time claiming that much on this forum?* (4) This is a question demanding an answer and I believe that we will get the answer.

Of course, the Minister [of Economy] has provided evidence, he produced figures […].

S. Rapti narrates what she witnessed during her visit to a religious festival organised in a district belonging to her constituency. Her narrative is produced in support of her humorous opening statement (jab line 1)[5] and, simultaneously, constitutes evidence for her claim that the only person who actually detects any improvement in the economy is the Minister of Economy in his figures. More specifically, there is a script opposition between the (well-known and implied here) "serious" economic problems which, among other things, led the opposition to launch a "no confidence" debate, and the economic improvement suggested by the Minister of Economy in his speech.

In her narrative (*Γιατί ξέρετε… θα τη λάβουμε* "Because, you know… the answer"), she uses 3 jab lines to attack the Minister of Economy for his (supposedly) unsuccessful measures and the inconsistency between what he said in his parliamentary speech and what ordinary people experience in their everyday lives. The first script opposition (jab lines 2–3) lies in the fact that the Greek people do not actually experience any economic improvement (hence, they can celebrate only for religious reasons), while the Minister of Economy has provided evidence to the contrary. The second script opposition (jab line 4) is based on the fact that, despite the evidence G. Alogoskoufis has produced, he has not managed to convince his (prospective) voters. In other words, the Minister of Economy becomes the target of S. Rapti's humour for his ineffective policies and his unreliable data.

---

5. This utterance can also be considered *ironic*. The distinction between irony and humour lies beyond the scope of the present study. Suffice to say here that both phenomena are based on incongruity (see among others Attardo 1994, 2001; Barbe 1995) and that contemporary approaches to humour view it as an umbrella term including a variety of phenomena, such as irony, parody, satire, comedy, etc. (Ruch 2002; see also Tsakona and Popa this volume).

In the following example, Panos Panagiotopoulos, a parliamentarian of the ruling party, expresses his certainty that PASOK's motion of "no confidence" will not result in early elections and that, in the next elections (whenever they may be), Nea Dimocratia will be the winner:

(2) Πάνος Παναγιωτόπουλος (Νέα Δημοκρατία): [...] Το τι θα κάνει ο Κώστας Καραμανλής και το αν θα σηκώσει το γάντι, όπως ακούσαμε έτσι προκλητικά να μας καλούν αγορητές του ΠΑ.ΣΟ.Κ., αυτό θα το σταθμίσει ο Πρωθυπουργός της χώρας και επικεφαλής της κυβερνώσας Πλειοψηφίας όχι με κριτήριο τα μικροκομματικά παίγνια του ιερού κομματικού παλατιού της Χαριλάου Τρικούπη αλλά με κριτήριο το δημόσιο συμφέρον, με κριτήριο το συμφέρον του ελληνικού λαού.

Σήμερα, πριν έρθω στην Αίθουσα του Κοινοβουλίου, είχα την ευκαιρία μέσα σε ένα ταξί να συνομιλήσω λίγο με το θυμόσοφο οδηγό του, έναν χαρακτηριστικό εκπρόσωπο του μέσου Έλληνα και της μέσης Ελληνίδας. Ξέρετε τι μου είπε, εντελώς επιγραμματικά, έχοντας ακούσει από τις ειδήσεις την περιβόητη πρόταση του ΠΑ.ΣΟ.Κ. και την παρέμβασή του, για να οδηγήσει τη χώρα σε πρόωρες εκλογές; Μου είπε θυμόσοφα, όπως μόνο ο απλός Έλληνας ξέρει να διατυπώνει: *πρώτη φορά βλέπω αρνί να ζητάει να έρθει το Πάσχα πιο γρήγορα!* (5)

Ευχαριστώ πολύ.

(Χειροκροτήματα από την πτέρυγα της Νέας Δημοκρατίας)

Μάρκος Μπόλαρης (ΠΑΣΟΚ): Μας το ξαναείπατε.

Κωνσταντίνος Καϊσερλής (ΠΑΣΟΚ): Είναι η τρίτη φορά που το λέτε.

[...]

Πέτρος Ευθυμίου (ΠΑΣΟΚ): Και έρχεστε σήμερα [απευθύνεται στα μέλη του κυβερνώντος κόμματος] να απαξιώσετε [την πρόταση μομφής του ΠΑΣΟΚ] ο καθένας με τον τρόπο του και με τα παραδείγματά του, [για παράδειγμα φέρνω] τον ταξιτζή του κ. Παναγιωτόπουλου, που κατά σατανική σύμπτωση τρεις φορές τον πετυχαίνει να του πει το ίδιο πράγμα. Είναι εκπληκτική αυτή η συνθήκη. Αλλά δεν σκέπτεστε τον πραγματικό Έλληνα πέραν από τον κατασκευασμένο ταξιτζή.

(February 2, 2007)

Panos Panagiotopoulos (Nea Dimocratia): [...] What Costas Karamanlis will do [i.e. whether he will go to elections or not] and whether he will pick up the gauntlet, as we heard speakers from PASOK say in such a provocative manner, this is up to the Prime Minister of the country and Head of the ruling majority to decide, based not on the petty politics games of the "sacred palace" at Harilaou Trikoupi street [i.e. where the headquarters of PASOK used to be at that time], but on the public benefit, on what is best for the Greek people.

Today, before coming to the Parliamentary Chamber, while riding a taxi, I had the chance to speak for a couple of minutes to a shrewd taxi-driver, a typical representative of ordinary Greek men and women. Do you know what he told me most succinctly, after having heard on the news PASOK's notorious motion of "no confidence" and their intervention, in order to lead the country to early elections? He told me rather shrewdly, in a manner only ordinary Greeks express themselves: *for the first time ever, I see a lamb asking for Easter to come earlier!* (5)
Thank you very much [end of his speech].
(Applause coming from Nea Dimocratia's wing)
Markos Bolaris (PASOK): You have told that [story] before.
Constantinos Kaiserlis (PASOK): It's the third time you tell that [same story].
[...]
Petros Efthymiou (PASOK): [addressing the members of the ruling party] And here you are today devaluating [PASOK's motion of "no confidence"], each of you in their own way and their own pet-stories, [for instance] Mr. Panagiotopoulos' taxi-driver, who, by evil coincidence, happens to say the same thing three times over. It's truly amazing. But you do not care for real Greek people, only for the imaginary taxi-driver.

P. Panagiotopoulos narrates an incident with a humorous punch line (5), in order to attack the opposition for their expressed wish for early elections, which led them to launch this "no confidence" debate. This humorous narrative (*Today... come earlier!*) rounds up his speech underlining the fact that it is the Prime Minister alone who will decide on the date of the next elections and that he will not yield to any pressure from the opposition.

More specifically, P. Panagiotopoulos reproduces the words he (supposedly) heard from a taxi-driver who used a metaphor to ridicule PASOK's motion of "no confidence". This metaphor evokes the well-known Greek tradition of roasting lamb on a spit on Easter day: members of PASOK asking for early elections are metaphorically represented as lambs which are in a hurry to be roasted and consumed on Easter day and, thus, become the humorous target. The clear implication is that early elections will result in PASOK's downfall, hence the punch line of the narrative elicits the applause of the parliamentarians of Nea Dimocratia. Humour is used here to attack and ridicule the opponent for their choices and policies.

The response of members of the (targeted) opposition to this humorous narrative should not go unnoticed, since it seems to reveal the constructed nature of (at least) the second narrative example and its frequent use as a weapon of attack. More specifically, three parliamentarians coming from PASOK (M. Bolaris,

C. Kaiserlis, and P. Efthymiou) claim that P. Panagiotopoulos has used the same narrative before, most probably to make the same (or a similar) point, thus undermining both his credibility and his effort to create a humorous effect at the expense of the opposition. Moreover, P. Efthymiou's reaction indicates how the humour produced by one parliamentarian can backfire and, hence, be used at his/her own expense: he accuses P. Panagiotopoulos and his party that they do not care for the needs of the Greek people (cf. Tsakona 2009a).

Our last example involves the telling of a narrative joke in parliament. Elias Kallioras, a parliamentarian of the ruling party, rounds up his speech by telling the following joke:

(3) Ηλίας Καλλιόρας (Νέα Δημοκρατία): Και κλείνω με ένα ανέκδοτο: «Δύο άνθρωποι» – δεν λέω ότι είναι ο κ. Παπανδρέου και το νούμερο δύο του ΠΑ.ΣΟ.Κ. [μάλλον εννοεί τον Ευάγγελο Βενιζέλο] – «πέφτουν στο κενό από τον τεσσαρακοστό όγδοο όροφο [ενός ουρανοξύστη]». Να πω ότι σαράντα οκτώ είναι οι μήνες της εκάστοτε κυβερνητικής θητείας. «Όταν πέφτουν προς το κενό και φτάνουν στον δέκατο τρίτο όροφο» – τόσοι μήνες έχουν μείνει μέχρι το τέλος της κυβερνητικής θητείας – «γυρνάει ο ένας στον άλλον και λέει: 'Μέχρι εδώ καλά πάμε'» (6).
Ευχαριστώ, κύριε Πρόεδρε.
(Χειροκροτήματα από την πτέρυγα της Νέας Δημοκρατίας)
(February 4, 2007)

Elias Kallioras (Nea Dimocratia): And I end up with a joke: "Two people" – I don't mean to say that it is Mr. Papandreou and the second in the hierarchy of PASOK [most probably he refers to Evangelos Venizelos] – "are falling off from the forty-eighth floor [of a skyscraper]". Let me say that forty-eight is the number of months of each government's term of office. "While falling down and reaching the thirteen floor" – so many months are left until the end of this government's term of office – "one of the two turns to the other and says: 'So far, so good'" (6).
Thank you, Your Honour [addressing the Chair].
(Applause coming from Nea Dimocratia's wing)

This joke is an adapted version of a quite popular joke ridiculing excessive optimism and naiveté. It is reappropriated to suit the political purposes of the parliamentarian.[6] In his version, E. Kallioras refers to two PASOK leading politicians,

---

6. The original joke is part of the jokelore of both Greek and English:

Πέφτει ένας από τον εκατοστό όροφο ουρανοξύστη. Καθώς περνάει από τον πεντηκοστό, τον ρωτάνε: Πώς πάει; Κι αυτός με πλήρη αισιοδοξία: Ως εδώ, καλά!
(Σκόρπιες Σκέψεις 2011)

namely George Papandreou and most probably Evangelos Venizelos, by presenting them as two people falling down from a high building, which metaphorically
represents the ruling party's term of office. The two men are under the impression
that everything is fine, although they are facing imminent death, namely their
political defeat in the upcoming elections. In other words, the punch line (6) of
the joke is based on two opposed scripts: in the first one, everything seems to go
well for the leading politicians of the opposition, while, in the second one, they
are about to crash on the pavement: their ultimate end is closer than they think.

E. Kallioras employs this joke to negatively evaluate PASOK and their decision to launch the "no confidence" debate. In particular, he emphasizes the fact
that they are out of touch with reality: they do not realise that their party is not
as popular as they think, thus they should not expect a victory in next elections
(cf. Example (2)). This adapted version of the joke and its appropriate positioning
at the end of E. Kallioras' speech trigger the applause of the parliamentarians of
his party.

In sum, parliamentarians switch to the humorous narrative mode to support
their argumentation. Significantly, in the first two narratives, the main protagonists
are Greek people expressing their views on politics. To this end, parliamentarians
not only address the wider audience by using a more familiar and conversational
mode, but also represent ordinary people's discourse in a formal setting where
argumentation is expected to prevail and everyday narratives are not very common. Example (3) consists of a well-known narrative joke which is adapted to suit
the political agenda of the speaker. A popular genre is transferred from everyday, informal contexts to the parliament, thus constituting a typical case of political cross-discourse (see Section 1). Parliamentarians resort to ordinary people's
discursive practices, namely story-telling and joke-telling, and use "the animation of characters' speech as a source of agency, responsibility and knowledge"
(Georgakopoulou 1997: 144). In so doing, they secure the attention of the wider
audience and present themselves as "one of them". They also show that they are in
constant contact with the citizens whose views they promote rather than speaking for themselves: it is the members of their constituencies (Example (1)) and
ordinary working people (Example (2)) that count. Finally, they implicitly suggest
that the jokes ordinary people exchange for entertainment could provide valuable
insight into political affairs and be used for political critique.

A man jumps off the top of a skyscraper. As he falls past a fifth floor window, he's heard
to mutter, "So far, so good". (*The Red Book Where Writers Are* 2011)

5. Discussion and concluding remarks

Humorous narratives prototypically occur in casual conversations among peers. Their appearance in a highly institutionalised and formal setting, such as the parliamentary one, merits scholarly attention.

The data under examination shows that politicians tend to adopt sociolinguistic resources coming from informal interaction and to adjust them to their particular needs and purposes, in the present case, persuasion and criticism. Hence, they address their colleagues and, most importantly, the wider audience, in a familiar tone and relate their everyday personal experiences. The humorous targets in their stories serve the purpose of drawing the boundaries between "accepted" and "non accepted" behaviour, thus defining the members of the in-group. The criticism expressed in a humorous manner is based on, and simultaneously highlights, the political values and standpoints that bring together politicians and their voters.

The use of narratives as a means of argumentation is not accidental here: parliamentarians transfer a very common discursive practice in Greek culture from its prototypical (oral and informal) context to a communicative setting where non narrative and serious discourse prevails. In their narratives, ordinary people become the main protagonists and their views are reproduced and put into wider circulation. In narrative joke-telling in particular, popular texts are reappropriated to fit the current political context. Thus, parliamentarians show that they do not distance themselves either from how ordinary people evaluate political practice or from the way they express their views in their everyday encounters.

Interestingly, our data reveals that humorous narratives produced in parliamentary debates may consist of artificially constructed events to serve the purposes of the narrator, and that their repetition may bring their constructed nature to the surface. In such cases, humour backfires: it can actually be used by the adversary to undermine the humorist's integrity and, eventually, his/her attempt at creating a humorous effect.

As to style variation, the present study confirms that the well-known, but rather rigid distinction between formal and informal talk and settings cannot capture the heterogeneity and hybridity of (at least) some communicative settings. The degree of speakers' attention to their speech cannot account for the stylistic switches from informal to formal modes of communication – and vice versa. Rather, the communicative ethos and orientation of the interactants, in the present case the importance Greek speakers attach to the maintenance and enhancement of in-group relations, should be taken into serious consideration. In our view, this is the key to understanding the occurrence of conversational discursive practices in "alien", namely formal and highly institutionalised, settings.

In this light, diachronic, cross-genre, and cross-cultural studies would be most interesting. Contemporary Greek parliamentary speeches could be compared to earlier ones, when parliamentary debates were not broadcast on television or the radio and the wider audience did not have easy access to them. Alternatively, such data could be compared to other political genres, such as political interviews, political speeches in official ceremonies or in open-air political rallies, to confirm or revise the findings of the present study and to further explore the function of humour and humorous narratives in Greek political culture.

Finally, a cross-cultural perspective would also be revealing as to whether cultural and institutional parameters influence the occurrence of humour and humorous narratives in political and parliamentary discourse. Given that humour is considered one of the central strategies in political debates and campaigns in some states (e.g. in the U.S.; see among others Gardner 1994; Jones 2005), a comparative study could bring to the surface common traits and developments. The institutional differences may also play a significant role in the presence or absence of humour and humorous narratives in politics. Hence, in presidential political systems and in consensus democracies (as in France or Germany), where party coalitions are common political practice and party discipline is not so strong, humorous digressions may not occur as often as, or in the same form as, in parliamentary political systems and competitive democracies, where the majority is in control of the legislative process and parliamentary deliberation does not necessarily influence political decisions and acts.

For example, the use of humour both in the German parliament (see Mueller this volume) and in the Greek one is not frequent, despite the different institutional and sociocultural environment these two operate in. Nevertheless, there seems to be an intriguing difference in the functions of parliamentary humour, which could be related to the different political practices and norms attested therein. More specifically, the distinction between laughing and amusement investigated by Mueller (this volume) reveals that humour in the German parliament can be more or less aggressive, in the sense that sometimes it is more critical and aims at denigrating and ridiculing the political adversary (laughing), while in other cases it relates to issues that do not involve political confrontation, but rather comments on parliamentary procedures and interaction (amusement). More than that, the quantitative analysis of Mueller's data clearly shows an equal distribution of these two kinds of parliamentary humour. Such findings could indicate that, unlike the Greek case examined here, where humour predominantly constitutes a weapon of political attack (see also Tsakona 2009a, 2011), German parliamentary humour does not first and foremost contribute to political polarisation between opposing parties; it is equally often used as an important means of negotiating parliamentary roles and rules, and of entertaining parliamentarians. Needless to say, more research along these lines is expected to bring to the surface more similarities and/or differences in the ways politicians employ humour in different parliaments.

Acknowledgements

The authors wish to thank Eleni Antonopoulou and the audience of the 1st International Conference on Humor in Conventional and Unconventional Politics (Dunarea de Jos University, Galati, Romania, 6–8 November 2009) for insightful comments on an earlier version of this paper.

References

Alvarez-Cáccamo, Celso and Prego-Vásquez, Gabriela. 2003. "Political cross-discourse: Conversationalisation, imaginary networks, and social fields in Galiza." *Pragmatics* 13: 145–162.
Archakis, Argiris and Tsakona, Villy. 2005. "Analysing conversational data in GTVH terms: A new approach to the issue of identity construction via humour." *Humour: International Journal of Humour Research* 18: 41–68.
Archakis, Argiris and Tsakona, Villy. 2006. "Script oppositions and humorous targets: Promoting values and constructing identities via humour in Greek conversational data." *Stylistika* XV: 119–134.
Archakis, Argiris and Tzanne, Angeliki. 2009. "Constructing social identities through storytelling: Tracing Greekness in Greek narratives." *Pragmatics* 19: 341–360.
Attardo, Salvatore. 1994. *Linguistic Theories of Humour* [Humour Research 1]. Berlin/New York: Mouton de Gruyter.
Attardo, Salvatore. 2001. *Humorous Texts: A Semantic and Pragmatic Analysis* [Humour Research 6]. Berlin/New York: Mouton de Gruyter.
Bakakou-Orfanou, Ekaterini. 2008. "Προφορικότητα και πολιτικός λόγος" (Orality and political discourse). In Γλώσσης χάριν. Τόμος αφιερωμένος από τον Τομέα Γλωσσολογίας στον καθηγητή Γεώργιο Μπαμπινιώτη (For Language. Festschrift for Professor George Babiniotis by the Department of Linguistics), Amalia Moser, Ekaterini Bakakou-Orfanou, Christoforos Charalambakis and Despina Chila-Markopoulou (eds), 389–401. Athens: Ellinika Grammata. [in Greek]
Bakhtin, Mikhail. 1981. *The Dialogic Imagination: Four Essays* [University of Texas Press Slavic Series 1]. Ed. Michael Holquist. Transl. Caryl Emerson and Michael Holquist. Austin: University of Texas Press.
Barbe, Katharina. 1995. *Irony in Context* [Pragmatics and Beyond New Series 34]. Amsterdam/Philadelphia: John Benjamins.
Bayley, Paul (ed.). 2004a. *Cross Cultural Perspectives on Parliamentary Discourse* [Discourse Approaches to Politics, Society and Culture 10]. Amsterdam/Philadelphia: John Benjamins.

Bayley, Paul. 2004b. "Introduction: The whys and wherefores of analysing parliamentary discourse." In *Cross Cultural Perspectives on Parliamentary Discourse* [Discourse Approaches to Politics, Society and Culture 10], Paul Bayley (ed.), 1–44. Amsterdam/Philadelphia: John Benjamins.

Brown, Penelope and Levinson, Stephen C. 1987. *Politeness. Some Universals in Language Usage* [Studies in Interactional Sociolinguistics 4]. Cambridge: Cambridge University Press.

Carranza Márquez, Aurelia. 2010. "The faces of humour: Humour as catalyst of face in the context of the British and the Spanish parliament." *Humour: International Journal of Humour Research* 23: 467–504.

Coupland, Nikolas. 2001. "Language, situation, and the relational self: Theorising dialect-style in sociolinguistics." In *Style and Sociolinguistic Variation*, Penelope Eckert and John R. Rickford (eds), 185–210. Cambridge: Cambridge University Press.

Coupland, Nikolas. 2007. "Aneurin Bevan, class wars and the styling of political antagonism." In *Style and Social Identities: Alternative Approaches to Linguistic Heterogeneity* [Language, Power and Social Process 18], Peter Auer (ed.), 214–245. Berlin/New York: Mouton de Gruyter.

de Cillia, Rudolf, Reisigl, Martin and Wodak, Ruth. 1999. "The discursive construction of national identities." *Discourse and Society* 10: 149–173.

Dolitsky, Marlene. "Humour and the unsaid." *Journal of Pragmatics* 7: 39–48.

Fairclough, Norman. 1995. *Critical Discourse Analysis: The Critical Study of Language* [Language in Social Life]. London: Longman.

Fetzer, Anita. 2010. "Small stories in political discourse: The public self goes private." In *Narrative Revisited: Telling a Story in the Age of New Media*, Christian R. Hoffmann (ed.), 163–183. Amsterdam/Philadelphia: John Benjamins.

Fetzer, Anita and Lauerbach, Gerda Eva (eds). 2007. *Political Discourse in the Media* [Pragmatics and Beyond New Series 160]. Amsterdam/Philadelphia: John Benjamins.

Fetzer, Anita and Weizman, Elda. 2006. "Political discourse as mediated and public discourse." *Journal of Pragmatics* 38: 143–153.

Gadavanij, Savitri. 2002. "Intertextuality as discourse strategy: The case of no-confidence debates in Thailand." In *Leeds Working Papers in Linguistics and Phonetics* 9, Diane Nelson (ed.), 35–55.

Gardner, Gerald. 1994. *Campaign Comedy. Political Humour from Clinton to Kennedy* [Humour in Life and Letters]. Detroit: Wayne State University Press.

Georgakopoulou, Alexandra. 1997. *Narrative Performances. A Study of Modern Greek Storytelling* [Pragmatics and Beyond New Series 46]. Amsterdam/Philadelphia: John Benjamins.

Georgakopoulou, Alexandra. 2004. "Reflections on language-centred approaches on Modern Greek society and culture." *ΚΑΜΠΟΣ: Cambridge Papers in Modern Greek* 12: 45–68.

Giles, Howard. 2001. "Couplandia and beyond." In *Style and Sociolinguistic Variation*, Penelope Eckert and John R. Rickford (eds), 211–219. Cambridge: Cambridge University Press.

Harris, Sandra. 2001. "Being politically impolite: Extending politeness theory to adversarial political discourse." *Discourse and Society* 12: 451–472.

Hellenic Parliament. 2011. The official website. http://www.hellenicparliament.gr/en (accessed February 24, 2011).

Ilie, Cornelia. 2003. "Parenthetically speaking: Parliamentary parentheticals as rhetorical strategies." In *Dialogue Analysis 2000. Selected Papers from the 10th IADA Anniversary Conference, Bologna 2000*, Marina Bondi and Sorin Stati (eds), 253–264. Tübingen: Max Niemeyer Verlag.

Ilie, Cornelia. 2004. "Insulting as (un)parliamentary practice in the British and Swedish parliaments: A rhetorical approach." In *Cross Cultural Perspectives on Parliamentary Discourse* [Discourse Approaches to Politics, Society and Culture 10], Paul Bayley (ed.), 45–86. Amsterdam/Philadelphia: John Benjamins.

Ilie, Cornelia. 2006. "Parliamentary discourse." In *Encyclopedia of Language and Linguistics* (2nd edition), Keith Brown (ed.), 188–197. Oxford: Elsevier.

Ilie, Cornelia. 2010a. "Analytical perspectives on parliamentary and extra-parliamentary discourses." *Journal of Pragmatics* 42: 879–884.

Ilie, Cornelia (ed.). 2010b. *European Parliaments under Scrutiny* [Discourse Approaches to Politics, Culture and Society 38]. Amsterdam/Philadelphia: John Benjamins.

Ilie, Cornelia. 2010c. "Identity co-construction in parliamentary discourse practices." In *European Parliaments under Scrutiny* [Discourse Approaches to Politics, Culture and Society 38], Cornelia Ilie (ed.), 57–78. Amsterdam/Philadelphia: John Benjamins.

Jones, Jeffrey P. 2005. *Entertaining Politics. New Political Television and Civic Culture* [Communication, Media and Politics]. Lanhan: Rowman and Littlefield.

Komlósi, László I. and Tarrósy, István. 2010. Presumptive arguments turned into a fallacy of presumptuousness: Pre-election debates in a democracy of promises. *Journal of Pragmatics* 42: 957–972.

Koutsantoni, Dimitra. 2005. Greek cultural characteristics and academic writing. *Journal of Modern Greek Studies* 23: 97–138.

Labov, William. 1966. *The Social Stratification of English in New York City*. Washington: Centre for Applied Linguistics.

Labov, William. 1972. *Language in the Inner City. Studies in the Black English Vernacular* [Conduct and Communication]. Philadelphia: University of Pennsylvania Press.

Madzharova Bruteig, Yordanka. 2010. "Czech parliamentary discourse: Parliamentary interactions and the construction of the addressee." In *European Parliaments under Scrutiny* [Discourse Approaches to Politics, Culture and Society 38], Cornelia Ilie (ed.), 265–302. Amsterdam/Philadelphia: John Benjamins.

Marquez, Maria Aldina. 2010. "The public and private sphere in parliamentary debate: The construction of the addresser in the Portuguese parliament." In *European Parliaments under Scrutiny* [Discourse Approaches to Politics, Culture and Society 38], Cornelia Ilie (ed.), 79–107. Amsterdam/Philadelphia: John Benjamins.

Meisel, Joseph S. 2009. Humour and insult in the House of Commons: The case of Palmerston and Disraeli. *Parliamentary History* 28: 228–245.

Miller, Donna R. 2004. "'Truth, justice and the American way': The APPRAISAL SYSTEM of JUDGEMENT in the U.S. House on the impeachment of the President, 1998." In *Cross Cultural Perspectives on Parliamentary Discourse* [Discourse Approaches to Politics, Society and Culture 10], Paul Bayley (ed.), 271–300. Amsterdam/Philadelphia: John Benjamins.

Niven, David, Lichter, S. Robert and Amundson, Daniel. 2003. "The political content of late night comedy." *The Harvard International Journal of Press/Politics* 8: 118–133.

Norrick, Neal R. 1993. *Conversational Joking. Humour in Everyday Talk*. Bloomington: Indiana University Press.

Norrick, Neal R. 2004. "Humour, tellability and conarration in conversational storytelling." *Text* 24: 79–111.

Oring, Elliott. 1992. *Jokes and Their Relations*. Lexington: The University Press of Kentucky.

Rampton, Ben. 1995. *Crossing: Language and Ethnicity among Adolescents* [Real Language Series]. London/New York: Longman.

Raskin, Victor. 1985. *Semantic Mechanisms of Humour* [Studies in Linguistics and Philosophy 24]. Dordrecht: D. Reidel.

Rickford, John R. and Eckert, Penelope. 2001. "Introduction." In *Style and Sociolinguistic Variation*, Penelope Eckert and John R. Rickford (eds), 1–18. Cambridge: Cambridge University Press.

Ruch, Willibald. 2002. "Humo(u)r Research." Paper presented at the 14th Conference of the International Society for Humour Studies, Bertinoro, Italy, 3–7 July 2002. www.uni-duesseldorf.de/www/MathNat/Ruch/HumorSurvey.html (accessed July 10, 2002).

Schubert, Christofer. 2010. "Narrative sequence in political discourse: Forms and functions in speeches and hypertext frameworks". In *Narrative Revisited: Telling a Story in the Age of New Media*, Christian R. Hoffmann (ed.), 143–162. Amsterdam/Philadelphia: John Benjamins.

Shenhav, Shaul R. 2005. "Concise narratives: A structural analysis of political discourse." *Discourse Studies* 7: 315–335.

Shenhav, Shaul R. 2008. "Showing and telling in parliamentary discourse: The case of repeated interjections to Rabin's speeches in the Israeli parliament." *Discourse and Society* 19: 223–255.

Sifianou, Maria. 2006. *Discourse Analysis: An Introduction* (2nd edition). London: Hillside Press.

Σκόρπιες Σκέψεις (Scattered Thoughts). 2011. http://atakataka.blogspot.com/2010/12/16.html (accessed January 19, 2011). [in Greek]

Stapleton, Karyn and Wilson, John. 2003. "A discursive approach to cultural identity: The case of Ulster Scots." *Belfast Working Papers in Language and Linguistics* 16: 55–71.

Steiner, Jürg, Bächtiger, André, Spörndli, Markus and Steenberger, Marco R. 2004. *Deliberative Politics in Action. Analysing Parliamentary Discourse* [Theories of Institutional Design]. Cambridge: Cambridge University Press.

The Red Book Where Writers Are. 2011. http://www.redroom.com/publishedwork/the-comic-toolbox-how-be-funny-even-if-youre-not (accessed January 19, 2011).

Tsakona, Villy. 2000. *Το ανέκδοτο στην επικοινωνία: Πραγματολογική ανάλυση* (Jokes in communication: A pragmatic analysis). Unpublished MA thesis. University of Athens, Greece. [in Greek]

Tsakona, Villy. 2007. "Towards a revised typology of humorous texts and humorous lines." In *New Approaches to the Linguistics of Humour*, Diana Popa and Salvatore Attardo (eds), 35–43. Galaţi: Academica.

Tsakona, Villy. 2008a. "Creativity in parliamentary discourse: Pragmatic goals and institutional affordances." Paper presented at the Sociolinguistics Symposium 17, Amsterdam, The Netherlands, 3–5 April 2008.

Tsakona, Villy. 2008b. "Κοινοβουλευτικός λόγος: Μια πρώτη προσέγγιση" (Parliamentary discourse: A linguistic analysis). In *Μελέτες για την ελληνική γλώσσα. Πρακτικά της 28ης ετήσιας συνάντησης του Τομέα Γλωσσολογίας του τμήματος Φιλολογίας της Φιλοσοφικής Σχολής του Αριστοτελείου Πανεπιστημίου Θεσσαλονίκης, 21–22 Απριλίου 2007, «Γλώσσα και κοινωνία»* (Studies in Greek Linguistics. Proceedings of the 28th Annual Meeting of the Department of Linguistics, School of Philology, Faculty of Philosophy, Aristotle University of Thessaloniki. 21–22 April 2007, "Language and Society"). Thessaloniki: Institute for Modern Greek Studies, 391–401. [in Greek]

Tsakona, Villy. 2009a. "Humour and image politics in parliamentary discourse: A Greek case study." *Text and Talk* 29: 219–237.

Tsakona, Villy. 2009b. "Linguistic creativity, secondary orality, and political discourse: The Modern Greek myth of the 'eloquent orator.'" *Journal of Modern Greek Studies* 27: 81–106.

Tsakona, Villy. 2011. "Irony beyond criticism: Evidence from Greek parliamentary discourse." *Pragmatics and Society* 2: 57–86.

Tziovas, Dimitris. 2001. "Residual orality and belated textuality in Greek literature and culture." In *A Reader in Greek Sociolinguistics. Studies in Modern Greek Language, Culture and Communication*, Alexandra Georgakopoulou and Marianna Spanaki (eds), 119–134. Bern: Peter Lang.

van der Valk, Ineke. 2003. "Right-wing parliamentary discourse on immigration in France." *Discourse and Society* 14: 309–348.

van Dijk, Teun A. 2000. "Parliamentary debates." In *Parliamentary Discourses on Ethnic Issues in Six European States*, Ruth Wodak and Teun A. van Dijk (eds), 45–78. Austria: Drava, Austrian Federal Ministry of Education, Science and Culture.

van Dijk, Teun A. 2002. "Political discourse and political cognition." In *Politics as Text and Talk. Analytic Approaches to Political Discourse* [Discourse Approaches to Politics Society and Culture 4], Paul A. Chilton and Christina Schäffner (eds), 203–237. Amsterdam/Philadelphia: John Benjamins.

CHAPTER 4

"Stop caressing the ears of the hooded"
Political humour in times of conflict

Marianthi Georgalidou
University of the Aegean, Greece

Based on data coming from media and parliamentary settings, the purpose of this study is to examine instances of humour in the discourse of politicians during a period of social turmoil in Greece. The analysis confirms the impact of humorous contributions, as well as other forms of linguistic creativity, in constructing, and resisting the construction of, damaging political identities in the discourse of political opponents. It also confirms the symbiotic relations among politics and media, via the formation of dialogical networks, which are shown to contribute to the blurring of ideological boundaries and identities in politics.

1. Introduction

The present study investigates functions of humour in the discourse of Greek politicians. The data under examination come from press conferences, media interviews, and the official proceedings of parliamentary sittings during a period of riots in December 2008. Following the shooting of Alexandros Grigoropoulos, a fifteen year old student, by a policeman, a great number of young people, mainly high school and university students, demonstrated in the centre of all major Greek cities for several days. Incidents of violence were quite common during those protests. The discourse of politicians and political analysts at the time revolves around demonstrators who covered their faces using hoods and are therefore called *κουκουλοφόροι* "hood-bearers, the hooded".

In this context, the subject matter of most press conferences and public discussions at the time concerned accusations made by Alexandra Papariga, the leader of the Greek Communist Party (henceforth KKE), against the leadership of another left wing party, the Coalition of the Left Radicals (henceforth SYRIZA), that they "caress the ears of the hooded", implying that, via their public statements, they wish to "please" the hooded individuals and attract their votes. In so doing, A. Papariga also accused them of contributing to uncontrollable violence.

Extensive reference to the events and the allegations was also made during the budget debate which took place days after the shooting, while turmoil was still prevailing on the streets and in the educational institutions of all major Greek cities. Derivatives of the term κουκούλα "hood" were used in discourse produced or reproduced by the media and in the discourse of parliamentarians during the budget debate sittings. Different connotations were attributed to the various derivatives that were used in such discourse.

More specifically, the term κουκουλοφόροι, namely the people bearing hoods or else "the hooded", has been used by conservative politicians to describe groups of rioters that are considered to be affiliated with extremist political groups of the Left. It has also been used by the left opposition to refer to groups of debatable political affiliations that were considered to be unofficially collaborating with the riot police forces. The verb derivative of the noun κουκούλα "hood", namely κουκουλώνω "to hood, to cover up", has been used to metaphorically refer to the alleged covering up of economic and political scandals on the part of the government. Also, the past participle κουκουλωμένη "hooded (fem.)", has been used to describe the situation the country was supposed to be in, whereas the proposed budget was also presented as if wearing "a peculiar hood" in order not to face the problems in the economy.

The analysis of the data is intended to show how mostly aggressive and derogatory humour as well as other means of linguistic creativity are used as a means for constructing, and resisting the construction of, damaging political identities in the discourse of political opponents (see also Mulkay 1988; Ilie 2001; Harris 2001; Morreall 2005; Bippus 2007; Hobbs 2007; Tsakona 2008, 2009; Dynel this volume). On the part of the accusers, humour is used to cover up the lack of adequate sociopolitical analysis of the groups and the identities of the hooded individuals participating in the riots. It is also used to construct damaging political identities of the accused party, portraying its leadership and representatives as irresponsible supporters of violent deeds. On the part of the accused, humour is used to resist the construction of such identities and counterbalance the effects of opposing propaganda. At the same time, it is used to attribute different meanings to the terms κουκούλα "hood" and κουκουλοφόροι "hooded", as well as to counterattack political opponents and challenge their credibility by highlighting unexpected coalitions among what are perceived as incompatible political ideologies. Similarly, humour is used by all parliamentary parties of the left opposition to attack the government: first, they accuse them of making use of non-institutional alliances in order to trigger off violent deeds and thus justify their switching to restrictive legislative measures over security issues; secondly, they introduce a different use of the term(s) *hood(ed)* to refer to the covering up of numerous economic scandals that were extensively discussed in the press at the time.

Based on the analysis of the data, the theoretical issues that will be addressed concern the structures and functions of humour in political discourse. In accordance with numerous studies highlighting aspects of political and parliamentary discourse that concern the rhetoric of political combat (see among others Mulkay 1988; Lakoff 1995; Harris 2001; Ilie 2001; Morreall 2005; Tsakona 2008, 2009), humour and metaphor are shown to be powerful weapons in the discourse of political adversaries. Moreover, the role of the media, as well as parameters of audience design connected to the publicisation of political discourse are highlighted for their impact on the linguistic choices of politicians (see Bell 1984; Leudar and Nekvapil 1998; Niven et al. 2003; Fetzer and Weizman 2006). What is more, the present study suggests that different kinds of incongruity, the humorous target, and the various ways in which these are exploited within dialogical networks (see Leudar and Nekvapil 1998; Nekvapil and Leudar 2002; Archakis and Tsakona 2010) constitute key analytical tools to explore the social consequences and real implications of humour in politics.

In what follows, after a brief overview of the literature concerning political humour (Section 2), I provide information on the political conditions that led to the activation of the dialogical network under analysis (Section 3). In Section 4, I present the sources of the data (i.e. press conferences, interviews, and the official proceedings of the Greek parliament), as well as the excerpts that are scrutinized in Section 5. Finally, Section 6 summarizes the findings of the present study.

2.   Research on political humour

Humour has recently become a major issue in the analysis of the discourse produced by politicians (see Bippus 2007; Tsakona and Popa this volume, and references therein). Focusing on political humour produced within institutionalised humorous genres, such as political satire and political cartoons, research has mainly explored the close relations among modes of discourse that could have been considered as incompatible. Humorous texts concerning politics are constructed to display incongruities and contradictions that directly parallel those to be found in the world of serious politics (Mulkay 1988: 203). At the same time, the perceived incompatibility[1] among institutional political debate and the use of humour has proven not to be the case, as politicians frequently employ humour of a rather aggressive nature (as opposed to the so-called *pure* and *playful* humour, in

---

1.   Whereas political discourse pertains to the serious mode, namely to discourse which is meant to be well-documented and informative, the serious message of humorous contributions can be ignored or denied (Mulkay 1988; Tsakona and Popa this volume).

Mulkay 1988:204) to attack political opponents and/or defend their own stances and identities. Political discourse, therefore, pertaining to the sphere of serious discourse, is shown to interact with the humorous mode in various ways (Mulkay 1988; Morreall 2005; Dynel this volume).

Political humour produced by politicians can be indicative of the different ways in which politics is organised in various sociocultural and political systems. Humour in competitive democracies, such as the Greek one, is proven particularly aggressive, mainly promoting polarisation and the discrediting of the opponent (Tsakona 2009; Archakis and Tsakona this volume), while in consensus democracies, such as the German one, humour is equally often employed to foster solidarity among parliamentarians (Mueller this volume). At times, self-denigrating humour can also function as a defensive strategy, contributing to anxiety relief and mood improvement (Bippus 2007). As Mulkay (1988:120) puts it, in an us/them framework, approval of one's own political grouping and denigration of other's views and actions is a basic structural principle within political language. In such a framework, humour serves as a deconstructive strategy, representing some other speaker's version of the world as unreliable (Mulkay 1988:207). What is more, instances of political verbal combat via the humorous mode, metaphors, and other forms of linguistic creativity are entertained by the media: extracts chosen for their creativity are being reproduced and distributed to large audiences through the media (Archakis and Tsakona 2010).

Political and even parliamentary discourse is thus produced within a context of addressing divergent audiences. Despite the fact that parliamentarians' primary addressees seem to be their fellow parliamentarians, the fact of the matter is that their speeches are monitored by voters and the press, as they are accessible through the parliament television channel and the internet. Publications of the proceedings are available at the official site of the parliament on the internet, where transcripts of speeches are publicised within days after the sittings. However, the public mainly gets information on the work of the parliament through the media, where highly mediated extracts of debates are reproduced based on their potential to arouse the interest of the readership not only as important instances of parliamentary work, but also due to their switching to conversational genres and their potential to serve as sound bites. This process can be shown to lead to the conversationalisation and, in cases, to what has been referred to as the *de-ideologisation of politics* (Fairclough 1998; Archakis and Tsakona 2010). Nevertheless, as ideological stances and agendas are in the background of all political action, the term *de-ideologisation* does not accurately describe the outcome of political discourse adjusting to the expectations and (perceived) needs of the wider audience. What seems to be the case is the crossing of ideological boundaries and the blurring of political identities since ambiguity serves as a means of simultaneously addressing variable audiences. Within this context, humour, as well as other means of linguistic creativity, contribute to the commonsensical viewing of political issues, which can be both attractive – via the conversationalisation of discursive practices – and deceptive – via the lack of well-documented political analysis. It can also contribute to the recycling and reinforcing of dominant values and views on politics (Tsakona and Popa this volume).

Intertextuality and the formation of extensive *dialogical networks* are also connected to the mediation of politics through the media. Reference to previously produced texts and the formation of sequential structures among interlocutors who do not directly recognise each other as valid communicative partners, are linked to the distribution of contributions of individual actors in time and space (Leudar and Nekvapil 1998). As media and parliamentary events become part of the same dialogical network, topically relevant contributions of different actors acquire the status of linked events, despite the fact that responses by independent participants can be mutually contradictory (Nekvapil and Leudar 2002).

In this context, the focus of analysis of this study is a dialogical network initiated by statements of politicians in the media, which was later transferred to parliamentary settings. All the extracts – humorous as well as serious – analysed subsequently refer to the Greek riots of December 2008.

3. The aftermath of December 2008 riots

Following the shooting of the fifteen year old student Alexandros Grigoropoulos by a police officer, Athens and other major Greek cities went through a period of extensive rioting that caused commercial transactions and other activities to cease for more than a week. Most high schools all over the country remained closed as a result of the students' decision to proceed with the sit-in of the school units. Students of all ages, as well as civilians were protesting against police arbitrariness and against oncoming political and economic crises which not only had its roots in the much discussed global economic recession, but also in incidents that indicated extensive phenomena of corruption within domestic political life. Things escalated when excuses were made on the part of the political leadership of the Ministry of Public Order as to the accidental nature of the so-called "incident". Demonstrations, therefore, acquired a quite explosive nature as the people participating in them were aware of cases involving the loss of human life during encounters with the police forces in the past, and the minimal sentences that policemen who were found guilty had faced. Statements made by the attorney of the defendant as to the ricochet of the bullet that had killed the student, contributed to the continuation of the protests, as it was suspected that the defence of the accused party was trying to establish the accidental nature of the shooting, so that the defendant would face a minor sentence.

As is often the case in periods of turbulence and rioting, groups of debatable political identities also found the opportunity to pursue their own agendas by contributing to the escalation of violence. As a result, various groups wearing hoods, scarves, or helmets were monitored in the streets at the time. A number of them covered their faces to protect themselves from the extensive use of chemicals on the part of the police. Others exploited the opportunity to act illegally either by destroying public and private property and looting, or by provoking the escalation of violence in the encounters of the demonstrators with the police. Numerous videos were uploaded on the internet or projected during news and other television programmes depicting people wearing hoods who appeared to be part of the riot police forces, as they were moving and acting very close to, or even inside, police patrols.

As a result, the press and the media devoted abundant time presenting the incidents and commenting on them. Politicians of all political parties were invited to contribute their analyses of the protesting and the rioting. Establishing who the culprits for this rather uncontrollable situation were proved a unique opportunity for politicians to attack opponents and cause damage to the image of rival political parties. What is more, the announcement of the decision of the opposition not to consent to the re-election of the President of the Greek Republic initiated discussions over possible dates for the then imminent early elections, and rivalry among parties became even more intense. In this context, the statement of the leader of one of the minor opposition parties, namely KKE, as to the "caressing of the ears of the hooded" by another minor opposition party SYRIZA, triggered a number of reactions by all parliamentary parties. Interviews, public statements, and parliamentary speeches referred to the accusations: humour and other means of linguistic creativity were employed to both attack and defend the accused and counterattack the accusers. Extracts of this extensive dialogical network are presented and analysed in the following sections.

4.   The data under analysis

The data under scrutiny come from two sources: from interviews of prominent politicians in the media and the press, and from the official proceedings of the Greek parliament available at its official website (*Hellenic Parliament* 2009). I analyse four extracts of statements made during press conferences and interviews by politicians in the media and the press. Examples (1)–(3) were recorded and transcribed by the researcher, whereas Example (4) was published in the newspaper *Kyriakatiki Eleftherotypia* (Pappas 2008). I also analyse extracts of speeches of parliamentarians of all political wings that were delivered during five full sittings of the Greek parliament in the 2009 budget debate. Examples (5)–(14) come from the official proceedings of the Greek parliament.

More specifically, Example (1) is part of a press conference which took place immediately after a formal meeting of the leader of KKE, A. Papariga, with the then Prime Minister of Greece, Constantinos Karamanlis. The two leaders met two days after the shooting of A. Grigoropoulos, in the midst of ongoing violent riots. The reporters, who were waiting for A. Papariga outside the Maximou Mansion, namely the Prime Minister's official residence, kept asking questions about her conversation with the Prime Minister focusing on the possibility of early elections. A. Papariga, however, seized the opportunity to directly address the leadership of the other parliamentary party of the Left, namely SYRIZA, and ask them to quit supporting the rioters. The statement was repeatedly broadcasted by all news and political commentary programmes. Furthermore, party leaders and representatives were asked to comment on it and state whether they agreed with the accusations levelled against SYRIZA. Example (2) is part of a television interview that took place two days later in the morning soft news programme of MEGA channel, *Κοινωνία Ώρα Mega* ("Society Mega Hour"). The leader of SYRIZA, Alexis Tsipras, who was not a parliamentarian at the time, was invited to discuss the insinuations made by A. Papariga as to the party's so called support of the rioters. Example (3) originates in a statement made by George Karatzaferis, the leader of Popular Orthodox Rally (henceforth LAOS), a conservative right wing political party. Example (4) comes from a published interview of Theodoros Pangalos, one of the most prominent members of the Greek Socialist Party (henceforth PASOK) that was then the major opposition party.

The rest of the Examples (5)–(14) come from the budget debate in the Greek parliament which took place on December 17–21, 2008. Despite the fact that parliamentary debates over fiscal issues and financial resources are of crucial importance as far as the governmental policies are concerned, most speakers of all political parties made either short or extensive reference to the events and the riots that were the major issue of public interest at the time. The criteria for the selection of the extracts presented here are (a) their reference to the current events via dialogical networks that were formed through the mediation of television news programmes and the press; (b) their relevance to the theme of the rioting; and (c) the use of the terms *hooded* and *hood(s)* with a number of different connotations (see Section 1). The extracts will be discussed as indicative of the political stance adopted by all five parliamentary parties towards the events, their attempt to exploit them for political gain, and the linguistic means that were used to this end. Analysis will focus on incongruity and humour within the context of political conflict.

5.   The analysis of the data

5.1   Statements in the media and the press

The first example is the above mentioned extract by the leader of KKE, A. Papariga, during the press conference that immediately followed her meeting with the then Prime Minister, C. Karamanlis. A. Papariga chose to attack SYRIZA, a rival left party, by directly inviting its leadership to stop "caressing the ears of the hooded". She went on using the metonymy of *κάλπη, ψήφους, καρέκλα, μαξιλάρια* "ballot-boxes, votes, chairs, and pillows" that SYRIZA was supposed to be looking forward to, to make the connection between its alleged affiliation with groups of rioters and the possibility of acquiring positions of power in a hypothetical future governmental coalition with the then major opposition party, namely PASOK:

(1)   Αλεξάνδρα Παπαρήγα (KKE): Καλούμε από αυτή τη θέση την ηγεσία του ΣΥΡΙΖΑ να σταματήσει *να χαϊδεύει τα αφτιά των κουκουλοφόρων* – εε δε λέμε ότι ταυτίζεται με αυτούς αλλά ωστόσο πιστεύουμε ότι *χαϊδεύει τ' αφτιά* βλέποντας μπροστά του την *κάλπη, ψήφους, καρέκλα, μαξιλάρια* δε ξέρω τι. Να σταματήσει.   (December 9, 2008)

Alexandra Papariga (KKE): From this position we invite the leadership of SYRIZA to stop *caressing the ears of the hooded* – eh we are not saying that they identify with them, but nevertheless we believe that *they are caressing the ears* looking forward to *the ballot-box, votes, chair, pillows* I don't know what. They should stop.

The discoursal choices made by A. Papariga, namely the use of metaphor and metonymy rather than the straightforward reference to facts proving the alleged support of violent deeds on the part of her political opponents, triggered a number of reactions by politicians and the media, as well as bloggers on the internet and ordinary people in private interactions. Her very successful – in terms of reportability – wording became a sound bite and was immediately broadcast and extensively discussed in all media news programmes and political discussion panels. Moreover, other politicians, political analysts, and reporters were asked to comment on it and state whether they agreed with the accusations or not. All of the extracts that will be discussed subsequently are connected to this statement/

request for immediate action, as they either directly or indirectly refer to the allegations made, in an attempt to further elaborate on them or to rebut their content.

Example (2) is a transcribed extract of the interview of A. Tsipras, the leader of SYRIZA, in the morning political commentary news programme, two days after the previous statement:[2]

(2) 1. Γιώργος Οικονομέας (δημοσιογράφος): Ο κύριος Αλέξης Τσίπρας λοιπόν είναι εδώ μαζί μας. Καλημέρα σας κύριε πρόεδρε.
     2. Αλέξης Τσίπρας (ΣΥΡΙΖΑ): Καλημέρα.
     3. Δημήτρης Καμπουράκης (δημοσιογράφος): Καλημέρα.
     4. Γιώργος Οικονομέας (δημοσιογράφος):   [Τελικά χαϊδεύετε τ' α//]
     5. Αλέξης Τσίπρας (ΣΥΡΙΖΑ): ((χαμόγελο)) *[Έχω αφήσει την κουκούλα]* έξω. *Ήρθα χωρίς την κουκούλα όμως σήμερα.*
     6. Γιώργος Οικονομέας (δημοσιογράφος): ((γέλιο)) Ναι. Τώρα η αλήθεια βέβαια είναι ότι ορισμένα στελέχη σας κάνουν κάποιες δηλώσεις οι οποίες θα μπορούσαν και να [παρεξηγηθούνε//]
     7. Αλέξης Τσίπρας (ΣΥΡΙΖΑ): [Εντάξει. Να- καταρχάς] να πω δυο λόγια γι' αυτά που άκουσα εισαγωγικά που είπατε.

                                        (*Society Mega Hour*, December 11, 2008)

     1. George Oikonomeas (journalist): Well, Mr. Alexis Tsipras is here with us. Good morning to you, Mr. President.
     2. Alexis Tsipras (SYRIZA): Good morning.
     3. Dimitris Kambourakis (journalist): Good morning.
     4. George Oikonomeas (journalist):   [After all, do you caress the e//]
     5. Alexis Tsipras (SYRIZA): ((smiling)) [*I have left the hood outside.*] *Today I came without the hood.*
     6. George Oikonomeas (journalist): ((laughter)) Yes. Now the truth of course is that some of your party cadres make some statements that could even be   [misinterpreted//]
     7. Alexis Tsipras (SYRIZA): [Right. To- to begin with] I want to say a few words concerning the introduction that I heard you making.

In an effort to control the damage (cf. Morreall 2005) provoked by the attribution of responsibility for the chaotic situation in Greece to the leadership of his party, as well as to rebut the alleged coalition with the groups of the "hooded" that are

---

2. Symbols used in the transcription:

    -       self-repair
    //   interruption
    (( ))   extralinguistic information
    [ ]   simultaneous speech

repulsive to the public, A. Tsipras employs humour directed to himself (cf. Bippus 2007). Bypassing the attempt of G. Oikonomeas to immediately pose a yes/no question as to the "caressing of the ears of the hooded" by SYRIZA (turn 4), he initiates a humorous exchange by stating that he came to the programme "without his hood", which he has "left outside" the television studio (turn 5). Humour is produced by means of the incongruous image of a serious politician and leader of a parliamentary party wearing a hood during a television interview. Laughter by all interlocutors is a further marker of the humorous mode established. Despite the fact that they all switch back to the serious mode immediately afterwards (turns 6 and 7), the humorous jab line[3] contributes to the relief of tension produced by both the ongoing violent events and the party's alleged promoting of the rioting. It also counts as an attempt to ridicule claims and neutralise arguments of political adversaries (cf. Hobbs 2007) by the framing of himself and the political party he is representing as incompatible with people who proclaim the use of violence. Nevertheless, as it will be discussed subsequently (see Examples (3) and (4)), political adversaries exhibited no intention of abandoning a rather successful attempt to further traumatise the public image of the accused party and cause a dramatic decrease of its percentages that had appeared to be impressively high in various opinion polls before the events (5% in the 2007 national elections, up to 18% a couple of months before the riots).

Following the statement by the leader of the KKE and the extensive discussions it generated, the leader of LAOS, a conservative opposition party, which had recently castigated the lack of a dynamic intervention on the part of the government and the police against the rioters, aligned with A. Papariga in the framing of SYRIZA as the political culprit for the escalation of violence:

(3)   Γιώργος Καρατζαφέρης: Δε γνωρίζω αν υπάρχει σύνδεση, αυτό όμως που πιστεύω είναι ότι *εάν υπήρχε εκλογικό τμήμα των κουκουλοφόρων ο ΣΥΡΙΖΑ θα έπιανε ποσοστό Τσαουσέσκου.*   (December 12, 2008)

George Karatzaferis: I don't know whether there is a connection, but what I believe is that *if there was a polling station of the hooded, SYRIZA would get Ceauşescu percentages.*

G. Karatzaferis chooses aggressive humour produced by the incongruity of a supposedly "polling station of the hooded" in which SYRIZA would acquire the near 100% "percentages of Ceauşescu", the notorious dictator of Romania, before the collapse of his regime. What is more, the stated lack of knowledge as to the

---

3. For the definitions of jab lines and punch lines, see Attardo (2001) and Archakis and Tsakona (this volume). In the examples presented here they are marked in italics.

connection with the "hooded" (*Δε γνωρίζω αν υπάρχει σύνδεση* "I don't know whether there is a connection") is immediately refuted, as the speaker expresses the strong belief that SYRIZA would come first in their preferences, had there been a "polling station of the hooded". Therefore, the first part of the utterance does not function as redressive action, but it further reinforces the derogatory force of the statement via pragmatic incongruity of the speaker's lack of knowledge and his subsequent belief in the alleged "connection".

Despite the fact that LAOS and KKE represent opposing parliamentary wings, their alignment is easily explained by their common goal to absorb as much as possible of the public resentment towards anybody who could be held responsible for the ongoing turbulence, thus maximising their influence on future voters. SYRIZA's claiming of a large proportion of voters in the previous months, at least according to polls, called for an aggressive opposition among smaller rival parliamentary parties. *Instrumental* or else *applied* humour (Mulkay 1988; Morreall 2005) as a communicative strategy in political discourse contributes to the framing of political adversaries as dangerous for the society, as they are metaphorically identified with violent groups and non-democratic regimes. In a "gladiatorial combat" among opposing parties, humorous insults constitute a powerful weapon in a confrontational political process (Ilie 2001; Dynel this volume).

A couple of days later, in the midst of the parliamentary sessions over the budget, T. Pangalos, one of the most prominent parliamentarians of PASOK, also chooses to align with both minor left and right wing opposition in framing SYRIZA as the political leadership of "the hooded":

(4) Θεόδωρος Πάγκαλος: Σήμερα όμως έχουμε να κάνουμε με πενήντα άτομα στο ένα σημείο, εκατό στο άλλο, δηλαδή μιλάμε για ένα φαινόμενο πολιτικής αλητείας. Ε αυτό το φαινόμενο πολιτικής αλητείας το καθοδηγεί η πολιτική ηγεσία του ΣΥΡΙΖΑ.   (Pappas 2008)

Theodoros Pangalos: Today we have to deal with fifty people here, one hundred there; therefore, we are talking about a phenomenon of political vagrancy. Well, this phenomenon of political vagrancy is directed by the political leadership of SYRIZA.

Despite the fact that his statement, actually a bald-on-record insult, is far from humorous, it forms part of the dialogical network that was initiated by the statement of the leader of KKE, as it indirectly endorses its content. It is thus indicative of the strategically ambivalent attitude of PASOK towards SYRIZA. In contrast to the seemingly non-confrontational attitude of his party (see Section 5.2), T. Pangalos straightforwardly points at SYRIZA as the political culprit of the rioting. Although this line of action is not followed by other parliamentarians of PASOK

during the budget debate, it nevertheless adds to the force of the attack against
SYRIZA. T. Pangalos made no reference to this statement of his in his next day's
speech in the parliament, despite the fact that considerable time was devoted to
the discussion of the recent events.

5.2   "Hooded" in the Greek parliament: The budget debate

The budget debate is considered one of the most important parliamentary sittings as it deals with major fiscal issues. Nevertheless, much of the parliamentary
discussion time in December 2008 was devoted to the events that had recently
taken place. Humour of a rather bitter and aggressive nature is indicative of the
different attitudes acquired by political adversaries, as well as subject to the overall frame that was established through public discussions on television and the
press concerning the recent events. The formation of dialogical networks (Leudar
and Nekvapil 1998; Nekvapil and Leudar 2002; Archakis and Tsakona 2010) is,
therefore, at work, as parliamentarians and party leaders take the opportunity
to address multiple audiences, both inside and outside the parliament, in order
to further elaborate on statements made in the press and on television, or rebut
charges levelled against them by political adversaries. In this context, I examine
various instances of parliamentary discourse produced by speakers of all parliamentary wings either for their contribution to the framing of the discussion or for
their strategic use of humour to attack political adversaries.

Greek Communist Party (KKE)
In her closing speech in the budget debate, A. Papariga, the leader of KKE, re-
frained from repeating her widely quoted accusation as to the "caressing of the
ears of the hooded". Yet, in line with both her public statement in the media (Example (1)) and with that of the leader of the conservative right wing opposition
(Example (3)), Nikolaos Moraitis, a KKE parliamentarian, chooses to launch one
more attack against SYRIZA, repeating the accusation of nurturing the "hooded"
for political gain:

(5)   Νικόλαος Μωραΐτης (KKE): [Τ]α ηγετικά τους στελέχη *χαϊδεύουν τα αφτιά*
των κουκουλοφόρων, για να ψαρέψουν στα θολά νερά, με καιροσκοπισμό και
διγλωσσία.   (December 20, 2008)

Nikolaos Moraitis (KKE): [T]heir leadership [i.e. the leadership of SYRIZA] is
caressing the ears of the hooded, in order to fish in unclear waters with oppor-
tunism and hypocrisy.

He refers to the alleged affiliation of SYRIZA with the rioting groups reintroducing the same metaphor used by his party leader, namely "the caressing of the ears" (Example (1)), together with another popular saying, which is also metaphorical, as to their effort "to fish in unclear waters" for more voters in the forthcoming elections.[4] Such creative linguistic choices which infringe expectations of formality and argumentation, are nonetheless compatible with a highly competitive parliamentary system and are here employed to damage the public image of the adversary party (cf. Tsakona 2008; see also "the pragmatics of aggression" in Dynel this volume).

At a different part of his speech, however, N. Moraitis realigns with the rest of the left opposition parties by accusing the government of playing "dirty games with the hooded" (Example (6)) in order to distract public attention from the death of the boy, as well as from economic and other scandals:

(6) Νικόλαος Μωραΐτης (ΚΚΕ): Οπότε ας αφήσετε, κύριοι της Κυβέρνησης, τα βρώμικα παιχνίδια με τους κουκουλοφόρους. Αποκαλυφθήκατε και τα είδε όλη η Ελλάδα στην τηλεόραση. Δεν τους είδε όμως η Κυβέρνηση παρόλο που βλέπει πολύ-πολύ τηλεόραση! Πόλεις παραδόθηκαν στις φλόγες. Αφήσατε να καεί το εμπορικό κέντρο της Αθήνας για να ξεχαστεί η δολοφονία του δεκαπεντάχρονου Αλέξη.   (December 20, 2008)

Nikolaos Moraitis (KKE): Therefore, *let go, you gentlemen of the government, of the dirty games with the hooded.* You have been revealed and the whole of Greece has seen it on television. The government, however, has not seen it, *despite the fact that they spend such a long time watching television!* Cities were left to flames. You let the city centre burn in order for the murder of fifteen year old Alexis to be forgotten.

Realigning with the left opposition, he also attacks the government by means of a humorous jab line insinuating the excessive amount of time the members of government supposedly spend watching television instead of trying to stop the riots. His humour is based on the incongruous image of governmental officials watching television, when they should be dealing with politics. N. Moraitis further elaborates on the theme of incompetence on the part of the government by insinuating that, despite the fact that they watch television, they cannot actually see what the whole of Greece has seen, namely the government's alleged manipulation of the "hooded".

---

4. Similarly, another KKE parliamentarian, Ioannis Protoulis, in his budget speech, refers to SYRIZA as the party which supports the rise of a so-called social movement "for reasons of canvass, in order to coax one or two votes" (*για ψηφοθηρικούς λόγους, για να αρπάξει καμία ψήφο*).

Popular Orthodox Rally (LAOS)
In his concluding speech, G. Karatzaferis, the leader of LAOS, makes no direct reference to neither his initial statement (Example (3)), nor SYRIZA's alleged involvement with the so called "hooded". Via a series of jab lines, he accuses PASOK of not adopting a clear position towards the events, anticipating political gain from the wear of the ruling party. At the same time, he congratulates KKE for their "stout-hearted attitude" and "clear talk" against the rioters and addresses the government with a request for immediate legal action against any person wearing a hood:

(7)   Γιώργος Καρατζαφέρης (ΛΑΟΣ): Δεν πρόκειται κανείς να μας βγάλει από την κρίση, εάν δεν σταματήσουμε αυτό το οποίο συμβαίνει έξω. Και ερωτώ: Είμαστε έτοιμοι να το αντιμετωπίσουμε ή *ο καθένας περιμένει το κάτι τι του απ' αυτήν την κρίση;* Ή *ο κ. Παπανδρέου περιμένει την τρικλοποδιά της Νέας Δημοκρατίας* για να δει τι θα γίνει; Και ξέρετε, το είπα και το επαναλαμβάνω: Η πιο παλικαρίσια στάση ήταν απ' αυτόν που βρίσκεται ακριβώς απέναντί μου, από το Κομμουνιστικό Κόμμα Ελλάδας. Ξεκάθαρες κουβέντες. Εσείς τι είπατε; Θέλω να ακούσω τι είπε το ΠΑ.ΣΟ.Κ. αυτές τις μέρες. Δεν ψελλίζετε τίποτα, ούτε καν μιλάτε, για να δείτε *πού θα πάει η ζυγαριά.*
Εμείς έχουμε συγκεκριμένες προτάσεις και όποιος θέλει τις ακούει. Πρώτον, ιδιώνυμον η κουκούλα. *Όποιος φοράει κουκούλα, κατευθείαν από το αφτί στον Εισαγγελέα, ανεξαρτήτως γιατί τη φοράει.* Η κουκούλα πρέπει να είναι ιδιώνυμο. Και μην φοβάστε τη λέξη ιδιώνυμο.   (December 21, 2008)

George Karatzaferis (LAOS): Nobody is going to get us out of the crisis, if we don't stop what is going on outside. And I am asking you: are we ready to face it or *is each one of us expecting their little something*? Or *is Mr. Papandreou waiting for Nea Dimocratia's trip-up* to see what is going to happen? And, you know, I said it before and I am repeating it now: the most stout-hearted attitude came from the party that is in the exact opposite side, the Greek Communist Party [KKE]. Clear talk. What have you said? I want to hear what PASOK has said these days. You do not whisper, you do not even talk, waiting to see *where the scale will tip.*
We have specific proposals and whoever wants to can listen to them. First of all, wearing a hood should be considered a *delictum sui generis. Whoever is wearing a hood should be tweaked by the ear and taken to the district attorney right away, no matter why they are wearing it.* Wearing a hood should become a *delictum sui generis.* And do not be afraid of the term *delictum sui generis.*

The jab line portraying anybody wearing a hood as *tweaked by the ear and* immediately *taken to the district attorney* is based on the fact that this idiom is normally used in the context of child rearing for children that are caught misbehaving. It seems that G. Karatzaferis actually addresses the wider audience watching parliamentary sittings mainly on television, both by means of the familiar and rather funny image[5] of caring parents or strict teachers reacting to the frivolity of their children and pupils respectively by tweaking them by the ear, as well as linguistic choices pertaining to the vernacular. By invoking such an association, he actually conceals the seriousness of the demand for the penalisation of *intention* to act illegally rather than the criminal act itself. It also portrays the judiciary system as a caring guardian who would see to the correction of imminent offensive behaviour, further concealing the political implicatures of such a wording concerning respect for basic human rights (cf. the metaphors in conservative discourse discussed in Lakoff 1995). The conversationalisation of political discourse, therefore, is further elaborated by the humorous mode that is evoked by reference to the act of "tweaking" a supposedly naughty child "by the ear".

In sum, as damage was already at work as far as the targeting of SYRIZA is concerned, both G. Karatzaferis and A. Papariga refrain from repeating their statements in the media and choose to align and realign with different parties of the opposition in order to attack other targets, namely the two major parties, PASOK and Nea Dimocratia.

Nea Dimocratia
Interestingly, parliamentarians of the ruling party Nea Dimocratia, neither straightforwardly accuse adversary political parties for the escalation of violence in major Greek cities nor use humorous or creative language in this context. They choose to request the condemnation of the episodes by the rest of the parliamentary parties and only imply that, at least on the part of SYRIZA, this is not the case. The alignment of Nea Dimocratia with the rest of the opposition against SYRIZA, can be implied by Theodora Bakoyanni's (Minister of Foreign Affairs) reference to the "caressing of the young children" (χαϊδεύοντας τα νέα παιδιά) on the last day of the budget debate. This is a wording that echoes the first part of A. Papariga's well-known statement as to "the caressing of the ears of the hooded" and can therefore be considered part of the dialogical network sustained by repetitive reference to it (see Examples (1) and (13)). Both Prokopis Pavlopoulos, the Minister of Internal Affairs, and C. Karamanlis, the Prime Minister, in their speeches refer

---

5.   There is no *a priori* definition of what is considered to be serious and what is not; it is the interlocutors who decide where the boundary between the two is to be set (Mulkay 1988; Tsakona and Popa this volume). In the case of Example (7), reference to the imaginary *tweaking by the ear* can activate the humorous mode, at least in the context of Greek culture, as it recalls scenes of teacher-pupil and father-son reprimanding, even depicted, for example, in popular comedies.

to the need for straightforward condemnation of the "hooded" – again insinuating that this has not been the case for all parliamentary parties.

Greek Socialist Party (PASOK)

PASOK seems to adopt a different stance towards the events, as well as a different alignment as far as the direction of criticism is concerned. They choose to frame the government as the culprit for all tribulations and make reference to the term *hooded* mainly to attribute different meanings to the word. In Example (8), Alexandros Papadopoulos, a former minister of PASOK, via a jab line based on punning, presents the country as if wearing a hood, thus suggesting a different meaning of the term *hooded* from the one "established" so far:

(8)   Αλέξανδρος Παπαδόπουλος (ΠΑΣΟΚ): *[Η χώρα μας] τώρα έχει βάλει και την κουκούλα, είναι κουκουλωμένη η χώρα. Απευθυνόμενος σε εσάς, κύριοι της Κυβέρνησης, θέλω να εκφράσω μια παραδοξολογία. Δεν μπορώ να αντιληφθώ πώς, άνευ ιδίας ικανότητας, πραγματικά εξακολουθείτε να είστε Κυβέρνηση. Ευχαριστώ.*
(Χειροκροτήματα από την πτέρυγα του ΠΑ.ΣΟ.Κ.)

(December 20, 2008)

Alexandros Papadopoulos (PASOK): *[N]ow [the country] has also put on the hood, the country is hooded.* And addressing you, gentlemen of the government, I want to highlight an absurdity. *I cannot understand how you, having no proven competence, are actually still in power.* Thank you [he terminates his speech].
(Applause from PASOK's wing)

A. Papadopoulos counterattacks the government by implying incompetence that is not yet fully perceived, since the country is incongruously depicted as a person wearing a hood that inhibits her/his ability to see. The repetition of the word *hood* via its derivative *hooded* further contributes to the humorous effect of the jab line.

A. Papadopoulos' speech is concluded with a punch line in the form of an indirect rhetorical question introduced as an already established absurdity. The first part of the rhetorical question (*πώς, άνευ ιδίας ικανότητας* "how you, having no proven competence") asserts the supposedly widely recognised lack of exhibited competence on the part of the government, whereas the second (*πραγματικά εξακολουθείτε να είστε Κυβέρνηση* "are actually still in power") rhetorically questions their still being in power. As parliamentarians extensively use intertextual references to discredit the opponent (Antaki and Leudar 2001), A. Papadopoulos's punch line alludes to the discourse produced on the previous day by Sotiris

Hatzigakis, the Minister of Justice. After accusing PASOK and SYRIZA for making similar mistakes, hence addressing both parties as being in alignment concerning important issues, S. Hatzigakis concluded his speech with the following punch line: *Κυρίες και κύριοι του ΠΑ.ΣΟ.Κ., κυβερνήσατε σαν τραγωδία, θέλετε να επανέλθετε σαν φάρσα* ("Ladies and Gentlemen of PASOK, you have governed as a tragedy and you want to return to power as a farce"). This utterance is actually a punning distortion of the well-known quote by Karl Marx: *History repeats itself, first as tragedy, second as farce*. Both wordings, namely the "hooded country" and the punning allusion to S. Hatzidakis' earlier statement, are instances of verbal aggression via the disaffiliative use of humour (cf. Dynel this volume).

Two more PASOK parliamentarians refer to the *hood(ed)* to attack the government in a similar way as SYRIZA does (see Example (12)). Firstly, the verb derivative of the noun *hood* is used by Ioannis Dimaras to refer to the covering up of the real estate scandal involving monasterial communities in Mount Athos (the Monastic State of Hagion Oros). More specifically, I. Dimaras asked:

(9) Ποιος πήγε, λοιπόν, το θέμα του Βατοπεδίου σε Εξεταστική Επιτροπή; Αυτός
     που θέλει να το κουκουλώσει;   (December 20, 2008)

     Who then took the issue of Batopedi to a Commission of Inquiry? Is it the
     same person who intends to hood it [i.e. to cover it up]?

alluding to the Prime Minister C. Karamanlis who had previously stated that "[politicians] go to Commissions of Inquiry to hood [i.e. cover up] scandals" (*πηγαίνει κάποιος σε Εξεταστική Επιτροπή για να κουκουλώσει το θέμα*).

In the sitting of the following day, Apostolos Kaklamanis also refers to the "hooded" as *οι γνωστοί άγνωστοι* [i gností ágnosti] "the known unknown", thus making use of the popular pun to insinuate the covering up of groups of "the hooded" by the police, and the political manipulation of the rioting by the government in order to both distract public attention from scandals and justify imminent strict security policies. A. Kaklamanis further abstains from criticism against SYRIZA by concluding his speech with a punch line depicting societies that exhibit no social mobility as "resembling a graveyard", indirectly justifying young protesters:

(10) Διότι χωρίς κινητικότητα, φίλες και φίλοι, ιδιαίτερα των ηλικιών στις οποίες
      ανήκω και εγώ πια, νοείται κοινωνία σύγχρονη, δημιουργική κοινωνία; Είναι
      ένα σκέτο νεκροταφείο.   (December 21, 2008)

      Because without social mobility, dear friends, especially at the age group I
      myself belong to, is there such a thing as a modern, creative society? It [i.e.
      society] is a plain graveyard.

Along the same lines, George Papandreou, the leader of PASOK and the opposition, chooses to direct his criticism against the government and only refers to "the various groups of the hooded" (... *και των διάφορων κουκουλοφόρων*), thus implying the existence of groups of debatable political affiliations.

Coalition of the Left Radicals (SYRIZA)

The first extract (Example (11)) of the discourse strategies adopted by SYRIZA is an extract from Panagiotis Lafazanis' speech. It should be reminded that SYRIZA had not only faced criticism for what was perceived as non-damnatory discourse against the rioting groups, but had also been straightforwardly accused of nurturing the so called "hooded":

(11)   Παναγιώτης Λαφαζάνης (ΣΥΡΙΖΑ): Μην ψάχνετε, λοιπόν, να βρείτε πολιτικές δυνάμεις της Αριστεράς, οι οποίες τάχα δείχνουν μία ανοχή, ή καλύπτουν κουκουλοφόρους. Γιατί αυτό που θα έλεγα εγώ και θα έχει μία πραγματική αξία είναι ότι ο προϋπολογισμός *που καταθέσατε φοράει μία ιδιόμορφη κουκούλα, μία κουκούλα για να μη βλέπει τα πραγματικά προβλήματα και τις πραγματικές ανάγκες της κοινωνίας, ιδιαίτερα της νεολαίας.*

(December 17, 2008)

Panagiotis Lafazanis (SYRIZA): So, do not look for political affiliations of the Left which exhibit a so called tolerance, or cover up the hooded. Because what I would say, which would have a real value, is that *the budget you have submitted is wearing a peculiar hood, a hood so as not to see the real problems and the real needs of the society, and especially of the youth.*

After denying political affiliation with extremist groups, P. Lafazanis is chronologically the first speaker in the budget debate to introduce an alternative use of the term *hooded* via punning (cf. Example (8)). His jab line, based on metaphor, presents the proposed budget as "wearing a hood" in order not to deal with the problems the society is facing. P. Lafazanis proposes a different perception of "the wearing of a hood": this time it is not used for the covering up of identities, but for the voluntary blindness that would allow the government not to face unpleasant realities. He also reverses the roles of the accuser/defendant by challenging the government to defend the proposed budget. His choice is in accordance with his institutional role as a representative of the opposition in a confrontational parliamentary procedure.

Alexandros Alavanos, the head of the parliamentary group of SYRIZA, is the last speaker on the part of SYRIZA in the budget debate. During the final session, his speech, as well as the speeches of prominent parliamentarians and party leaders, is watched by numerous audiences both inside the parliament and on television. Larger audiences are addressed on this final day as the debate reaches a

climactic point, with political adversaries having the chance to repair damage that
had been caused by adversaries on the previous sessions, and also strike back in
an attempt to score points for their own (see also Tsakona 2009). In this context,
A. Alavanos makes use of numerous jab lines to identify and highlight incongruities in the discourse of political adversaries. He attacks the government and the
Prime Minister personally by portraying him as spending his time playing play
station instead of working out problems, an image reminiscent of the government
watching television evoked by N. Moraitis (see Example (5)):

(12)   Αλέξανδρος Αλαβάνος (ΣΥΡΙΖΑ): Τι κάνει η Κυβέρνηση; Έχει την εντύπωση
       κανείς ότι *αντί να λύνει ένα πολιτικό πρόβλημα έχουμε έναν Πρωθυπουργό ο
       οποίος παίζει playstation με τους αστυνομικούς με την επίσημη στολή από τη
       μια μεριά και με τους αστυνομικούς με τις κουκούλες από την άλλη.*
       (Θόρυβος – Διαμαρτυρίες από την πτέρυγα της Νέας Δημοκρατίας).
                                                              (December 21, 2008)

       Alexandros Alavanos (SYRIZA): And what does the government do? One
       has the impression that *we are having a Prime Minister who, instead of work-
       ing out a political problem, plays play station* [as a playmate] *with policemen
       wearing the official uniform on the one side and policemen wearing hoods on
       the other.*
       (Noise – Protests from Nea Dimocratia's wing)

Together with the construction of the incongruous image of the Prime Minister as
a frivolous politician who does not realise the gravity of the situation, A. Alavanos
also insinuates deliberate provocation of violent episodes that the Prime Minister
is well aware of. He portrays the Prime Minister not only as an irresponsible politician who, in the middle of a crisis, spends his time playing, but also as somebody
who is the playmate of the very groups that are thought to have been causing
major turmoil. Similar insinuations as to the affiliation of groups of "hooded"
individuals with the riot police are also made by parliamentarians of the other left
opposition parties.

    In the following extract of his speech, A. Alavanos produces more jab lines
describing the parliament as "unbelievable" and the much repeated metaphor of
"the caressing of the ears" as the "headline". He lists phrases that had been used
to attack Socialist and Communist political parties in the past, and he repeats
statements made by representatives of adversary political parties to highlight incongruities among political ideologies and discoursal choices:

(13)   Αλέξανδρος Αλαβάνος (ΣΥΡΙΖΑ): Και να σας πω κάτι; *Είναι απίστευτη η
       σημερινή Βουλή. Είναι απίστευτη η σημερινή συνεδρίαση και όλη η συνεδρίαση
       αυτή που εξέφρασε πολιτικές κρίσεις σε σχέση μ' αυτό το ζήτημα.* Ακούσαμε

την κυρία Μπακογιάννη – περιγραφή θα κάνω – να χρησιμοποιεί ακριβώς τις ίδιες εκφράσεις με την κυρία Παπαρήγα: «Χαϊδεύουμε» τους κουκουλοφόρους. *Αυτό το «χάιδεμα των αφτιών» είναι ο τίτλος!*
(Θόρυβος, διαμαρτυρίες από την πτέρυγα της Νέας Δημοκρατίας)
Όπως από παλιά λέγατε, κύριοι συνάδελφοι, «από Βορράν κίνδυνος» ή «εσωτερικοί εχθροί», τώρα είναι το «χάιδεμα των αφτιών». Ακούμε από το Κ.Κ.Ε. ότι είμαστε οπορτουνιστές και ακούμε από τη Νέα Δημοκρατία ότι είμαστε καιροσκόποι, επί το ελληνικότερον. *Ακούμε από τον κ. Καρατζαφέρη να δίνει συγχαρητήρια στο Κομμουνιστικό Κόμμα για τον τρόπο που λειτουργεί στις διαδηλώσεις και την ίδια στιγμή να προτείνει ιδιώνυμο και να κόψουμε τις κουκούλες και να καταργηθεί το άσυλο.*   (December 21, 2008)

Alexandros Alavanos (SYRIZA): And let me tell you something. *Today's parliament is unbelievable. Today's session is unbelievable as well as all the sessions that expressed political judgment on this issue.* We heard Mrs. Bakoyanni – I am just making a description – using the exact same expressions as Mrs. Papariga. We "caress" the hooded. *This "caressing of the ears" has become the headline!* (Protests from Nea Dimocratia's wing)
As in the old days dear colleagues, when you would talk about the "danger from the North" or the "internal enemies", now it is the "caressing of the ears". On the part of KKE we hear that we are opportunists, and on the part of Nea Dimocratia that we are speculating, to make use of Greek.[6] *And we hear Mr. Karatzaferis congratulate the Communist Party [i.e. KKE] for the way they do their protesting and at the same time suggest [that wearing a hood become] a delictum sui generis, to cut the hoods and abolish the asylum.*

The jab lines in Example (13) are meant to challenge and devalue adversary discourse by proposing an alternative arrangement of extracts of speeches produced by representatives of political ideologies which are to be perceived as incompatible. While reversing the attacked/attacker roles, A. Alavanos repeatedly uses the vernacular expression *απίστευτη* "unbelievable (fem.)" to describe parliamentary procedures as far as the accusations of unparliamentary action on the part of his party are concerned. He uses a jab line to contrast A. Papariga's wording to the discourse used by oppressive regimes in the past, which insinuated a coalition among the then illegal left wing parties with the former Communist states of Eastern Europe and the so called "danger from the North". He thus makes reference to a period of dictatorial regimes in the recent political history of Greece (1967–1974).

---

6. The term *οπορτουνιστές* "opportunists" is a loan word in Greek, whereas the equivalent Greek term *καιροσκόποι* is here translated as "those who speculate".

A. Alavanos also makes indirect reference to the role of the media in the reproduction of A. Papariga's statement as a sound bite (see Example (1)), by referring to it as the "headline", and he further highlights the fact that the same
wording has also been used by a prominent member of the right wing government T. Bakoyanni (see above). He, therefore, contrasts supposedly adversarial
political discourse to bring incongruous similarities to the surface. The speaker
also contrasts the act of congratulating KKE for their orderly protesting by the
leader of LAOS to his proposed *delictum sui generis* for the penalisation of hoods
(see Example (7)). By depicting incongruous alignments of rival politicians who
attack the party he represents, A. Alavanos counterattacks political adversaries by
making use of aggressive and confrontational applied humour (cf. Mulkay 1988;
Morreall 2005).

By means of the same mode, he attacks the leadership of PASOK by depicting
this party as "a member of this club" (Example (14)), namely the so-called club of
the parties attributing responsibility for the rioting to SYRIZA:

(14) Αλέξανδρος Αλαβάνος (ΣΥΡΙΖΑ): Μας έκανε εντύπωση το γεγονός ότι τελικά
και το ΠΑ.ΣΟ.Κ. *προσχώρησε σ' αυτή τη λέσχη.* [...] Ο Κοινοβουλευτικός
Εκπρόσωπος του ΠΑ.ΣΟ.Κ. βγήκε και βγαίνει και λέει όχι μόνο ότι [ο
ΣΥΡΙΖΑ] έχει ευθύνες, όχι ότι «χαϊδεύει αφτιά», αλλά ότι ηγείται των ομά-
δων βίας. Κύριε Παπανδρέου, απευθύνομαι σ' εσάς, να μας πείτε τώρα εδώ,
αν αυτή είναι θέση του ΠΑ.ΣΟ.Κ.. Γιατί μας δημιουργεί ανησυχία. *Γιατί τότε
φοβόμαστε ότι αν έχει μέλλον το ΠΑ.ΣΟ.Κ. δεν έχει μέλλον η ίδια η χώρα.*

(December 21, 2008)

Alexandros Alavanos (SYRIZA): We were impressed by the fact that *PASOK
became a member of this club.* [...] The spokesman of PASOK claimed and
still claims that not only [SYRIZA] is responsible [for the riots], not only
they "caress the ears" [of the "hooded"], but they are the leaders of violent
groups. Mr. Papandreou, I am addressing you, you should tell us here and
now whether this is the official position of PASOK. Because we are worried.
*Because we are afraid that if PASOK does have a future, the country does not
have a future.*

By means of the metaphorical expression of describing an adversary political party as a member of an imaginary club whose members have rather debatable bonds
(*το ΠΑ.ΣΟ.Κ. προσχώρησε σ' αυτή τη λέσχη* "PASOK became a member of this
club"), A. Alavanos depicts what he perceives to be an incongruous alignment of
PASOK with the rest of the parliamentary wings. He then proceeds with a direct
request for confirmation as to the official position of PASOK towards his party,
which is concluded by a punch line in the form of a pun stating that "if PASOK
has a future [i.e. is popular enough to win next elections and become the ruling

party], the country does not have a future" (αν έχει μέλλον το ΠΑ.ΣΟ.Κ. δεν έχει μέλλον η ίδια η χώρα). The future of the country and the future of PASOK (which may, in his view, become the next ruling party) are represented as mutually exclusive, therefore incongruous, facts. It is the perceived incongruity of the possible scenarios that produces the ironic or humorous[7] effect of the statement.

To sum up, taking into consideration bits of an extensive dialogical network that was initiated by the public statement of the leader of the KKE as to "the caressing of the ears of the hooded", I have examined various aspects of the organisation of rival political discourse at work. First, I have tried to show how media contribute to the transformation of a specific wording (Example (1)) into a sound bite, which is being repeated in the discourse of politicians of all parties both inside and outside the parliament. Secondly, the switching to the humorous mode (albeit in an aggressive and derogatory manner), the adoption or the rejection of the metaphor of the "caressing of the ears", and the different meanings attributed to the term *hood(ed)* are shown to contribute to the construction of various alignments that, in cases, can be considered incompatible with one's declared political ideology, but still form part of a highly competitive parliamentary system. Finally, I have tried to show how the symbiotic relations among media and parliamentary institutions contribute to the formation of hybrid discourse modes that lead to the conversationalisation and consequent neutralization of dominant values (Fairclough 1995), as well as the blurring of boundaries among allegedly opposing political ideologies.

6.   Discussion and conclusions

The present study investigated functions of humour in the discourse of Greek politicians. The data under examination came from press conferences, media interviews, and the official proceedings of parliamentary sittings during a period of riots in Greece, in December 2008. They were selected so as to depict the overall context created by an extensive dialogical network which included both humorous and non-humorous references to "the hooded", around which adversary political discourse evolved.

On the part of the accusers, humour was used to cover up the lack of adequate sociopolitical analysis of the groups and the identities of the individuals bearing

---

7.   Despite the fact that irony and humor are considered different phenomena (Attardo 2001), they quite often overlap. Interpretation of statements as either entertaining (i.e. stereotypically humorous) or offensive (i.e. possibly ironic) is mostly a matter of the different interpretive perspectives acquired by speakers, addressees, and audiences.

hoods and participating in the riots. It was also used to construct damaging political identities of one of the parties of the left opposition, namely SYRIZA, portraying its leadership and its representatives as irresponsible supporters of violent
deeds (Examples (1), (3), and (5)). The analysis of extracts of political discourse
both within and outside the parliament exhibited alignments of politicians affiliated to adversary political parties, mainly KKE and LAOS (Example (7)). It
also exhibited ambivalent discourse on the part of PASOK: after launching a non-
humorous attack against SYRIZA (Example 4), thus aligning with the rest of the
opposition, PASOK appeared to realign with SYRIZA in the sharing of similar attributions to the terms *hood* and *hooded* and in directing criticism to the government (Examples (8)–(11)). At the same time, all the parties of the left opposition,
namely PASOK, KKE, and SYRIZA, again realigned to attack Nea Dimocratia
via aggressively humorous jab lines insinuating manipulation of the rioting and
unacceptable affiliations with groups of hooded that had been contributing to the
escalation of violence (Examples (6) and (12)).

On the part of the accused, humour was used to resist the construction of
such identities and counterbalance the effects of opposing propaganda. Self-denigrating humour (Example (2)), as well as aggressive humour depicting incongruities in the discourse of political adversaries (Examples (11)–(14)) were meant
to relieve tension and discredit the opponents. At the same time, humour was
used to attribute different connotations to the terms *hood* and *hooded*, so as to
challenge the credibility of the opponents and cancel their trustworthiness, by
highlighting temporary alignments among what were perceived as incompatible
political ideologies.

In other words, the data under scrutiny illustrate how humour is used as a
means for constructing, and resisting the construction of, damaging political
identities in the discourse of political opponents. It confirms the impact of humour, as well as other forms of linguistic creativity, in the construction of political discourse and political identities. Despite the fact that humour produced by
politicians themselves has only recently become the focus of political discourse
analysis, a number of important studies exhibit its impact on the organisation of
political debate (see among others Mulkay 1988; Lakoff 1995; Ilie 2001; Harris
2001; Morreall 2005; Tsakona 2008, 2009; Dynel this volume; Mueller this volume). Humour seems to be a powerful weapon in adversary political discourse
as it allows participants to become implicitly aggressive. It also allows for the organisation of defending one's stances and actions either by relieving accumulated
tension and/or by launching counterattacks in an effort to reverse the roles of
the accused/accuser. The humorous mode is also connected to the highly mediated transmission and reproduction of instances of political discourse and
their distribution to large audiences through the media. As a result, the media

and institutional settings for the production of politics, such as the parliament, sustain symbiotic relations, with the latter showing signs of adjustment in order to accommodate divergent audiences (see among others Bell 1984; Leudar and Nekvapil 1998; Fetzer and Weizman 2006; Archakis and Tsakona 2010).

Based on the above findings, aggressive humour as well as the adoption of related metaphors by rival political parties are shown to be compatible with the Greek parliamentary system that does not encourage cooperation in the form of party coalitions (Tsakona 2008, 2009), but nevertheless allows the crossing of the boundaries among contrastive ideologies, especially when it comes to temporary benefits in the struggle for higher percentages in (upcoming) national elections. The present study shows how the use of humour and the sharing of variable metaphors contribute to the construction of unstable alignments aiming at the destruction of the political image of different opponents. Discoursal choices, as the ones discussed here, thus, show how politicians addressing multiple audiences and targets at the same time, resort to humour, metaphors, puns, and popular sayings which constitute conversationalised and, hence, more easily accessible forms of talk. They also show that the local organisation of the political system together with the role of the media in the formation of mediated dialogical networks that are based on the reproduction and distribution of such linguistic forms, contribute to the blurring of ideological boundaries and possibly to the neutralization and reinforcement of beliefs that form part of ideological biases.

References

Antaki, Charles and Leudar, Ivan. 2001."Recruiting the record: Using opponents' exact words in parliamentary argumentation." *Text* 21: 467–488.
Archakis, Argiris and Tsakona, Villy. 2010. "'The wolf wakes up inside them, grows werewolf hair and reveals all their bullying': The representation of parliamentary discourse in Greek newspapers." *Journal of Pragmatics* 42: 912–923.
Attardo, Salvatore. 2001. *Humorous Texts: A Semantic and Pragmatic Analysis* [Humour Research 6]. Berlin/New York: Mouton de Gruyter.
Bell, Allan. 1984. "Language style as audience design." *Language in Society* 13: 145–204.
Bippus, Amy. 2007. "Factors predicting the perceived effectiveness of politician's use of humour during a debate." *Humour: International Journal of Humour Research* 20: 105–121.
Fairclough, Norman. 1995. *Media Discourse*. London: Arnold.
Fairclough, Norman. 1998. "Political discourse in the media: An analytical framework." In *Approaches to Media Discourse*, Allan Bell and Peter Garret (eds), 142–162. Oxford: Blackwell.
Fetzer, Anita and Weizman, Elda. 2006. "Political discourse as mediated and public discourse." *Journal of Pragmatics* 38: 143–153.

Harris, Sandra. 2001. "Being politically impolite: Extending politeness theory to adversarial political discourse." *Discourse in Society* 12: 451–472.

Hellenic Parliament. 2009. The official website. www.hellenicparliament.gr (accessed March 10, 2011).

Hobbs, Pamela. 2007. "Lawyers' use of humour as persuasion." *Humour: International Journal of Humour Research* 20: 123–156.

Ilie, Cornelia. 2001. "Unparliamentary language: Insults as cognitive forms of ideological confrontation." In *Language and Ideology. Volume II: Descriptive Cognitive Approaches* [Current Issues in Linguistic Theory 205], René Dirven, Roslyn M. Frank and Cornelia Ilie (eds), 235–263. Amsterdam/Philadelphia: John Benjamins.

Lakoff, George. 1995. "Metaphor, morality, and politics, or why Conservatives have left Liberals in the dust." *Social Research* 62: 177–214.

Leudar, Ivan and Nekvapil, Jiří. 1998. "On the emergence of political identity in the Czech mass media: The case of the Democratic Party of Sudetenland." *Czech Sociological Review* 6: 43–58.

Morreall, John. 2005. "Humour and the conduct of politics." In *Beyond the Joke. The Limits of Humour*, Sharon Lockyer and Michael Pickering (eds), 63–78. Basingstoke: Palgrave Macmillan.

Mulkay, Michael. 1988. *On Humour. Its Nature and its Place in Modern Society.* Cambridge: Polity Press.

Nekvapil, Jiří and Leudar, Ivan. 2002. "Sekvenční struktury v mediálních dialogických sítích" (Sequential structures in media dialogical networks). *Czech Sociological Review* 38: 483–500. [in Czech]

Niven, David, Lichter, S. Robert and Amundson, Daniel. 2003. "The political content of late-night comedy." *The Harvard International Journal of Press/Politics* 8: 118–133.

Pappas, Tasos. 2008. "Ο ΣΥΡΙΖΑ καθοδηγεί την πολιτική αλητεία" (SYRIZA is the leader of political vagrancy). *Kyriakatiki Eleftherotypia*, December 21. http://www.enet.gr/?i=issue.el.home&date=21/12/2008&id=1972 (accessed March 10, 2011). [in Greek]

Tsakona, Villy. 2008. "Creativity in parliamentary discourse: Pragmatic goals and institutional affordances." Paper presented at the Sociolinguistics Symposium 17, Amsterdam, The Netherlands, 3–5 April 2008.

Tsakona, Villy. 2009. "Humour and image politics in parliamentary discourse: A Greek case study." *Text and Talk* 29: 219–237.

CHAPTER 5

Entertaining and enraging

The functions of verbal violence
in broadcast political debates

Marta Dynel
University of Łódź, Poland

This article formulates a theoretical proposal on the pragmatics of verbal violence which promotes humour in televised political debates. Its underlying objective is to contest the well-entrenched assumption that the viewer should be conceptualised as an overhearer, in favour of a new theoretical construct, namely the recipient. Interlocutors in a political debate not only talk with each other, but also, if not primarily, communicate meanings to the recipient. By employing verbal aggression, a politician may have a twofold communicative intention with regard to two different ratified hearers: s/he aims to disaffiliate from the conversationalist, thereby entertaining, and fostering solidarity with, recipients. The theses put forward are illustrated with examples from Polish pre-election debates televised in October 2007.

1. Introduction

Humour, in its various manifestations, fulfils a wide range of functions in interpersonal communication, its primary role being interlocutors' expression of solidarity, coupled with common ground signalling. This role stands vis-à-vis a power-based function, namely originating conflict and disaffiliation between the parties involved. This is achieved via what is here called *disaffiliative conversational humour*, namely inherently aggressive humorous chunks of texts occurring in verbal interactions. It is here argued that such disaffiliative humour is genuinely meant to disparage one hearer, while its humorous potential is usually observed only by a listener/hearer who is not the *target/butt*. It can then be posited that analysing interpersonal consequences of disaffiliative humour necessitates extending the classic dyadic model constituted by the speaker and the hearer, and allowing for subtypes of the latter category. The problem is further complicated in the case of televised programmes.

The discourse of TV programmes, such as political debates, operates on two distinct, albeit mutually dependent, levels, namely the interlocutors' level and the higher level at which the audience interprets communicative interchanges shown on the screen. Each utterance is then interpreted by a number of hearers. Hearer/listener types can be divided into ratified ones and unratified ones, namely overhearers. Although the TV viewer is sometimes conceptualised as an overhearer, it is here postulated that a separate category of a ratified participant should be introduced instead. Thus, the viewer is regarded as yet another hearer type captured under the term *recipient* (understood as a theoretical concept), whilst the term *metarecipient* is employed in reference to a special recipient category focused on the two communicative levels, namely the interlocutors' level and the higher one which involves the viewer's participation and inferring meanings communicated for him/her on the screen.

The main objective of this article is to discuss the workings of aggressive utterances in political debates in the context of their twofold pragmatic import: an attack against the interlocutor, and humour to be appreciated by the viewer. The theoretical postulates are illustrated with interactions constructed by three Polish Prime Minister candidates in three debates televised in October 2007. Aggressive/humorous utterances prevail in the discourse of each candidate, who is claimed to deploy them to disparage the conversationalist, as well as to entertain, and forge solidarity with, the recipient (see also Archakis and Tsakona this volume).

To this end, Section 2 introduces the notion of verbal violence/aggression, shedding light on its characteristics and functions in media discourse, notably its potential to engender humorous effects. Thus, the concept of disaffiliative humour is discussed. The focus of attention in Section 3 is the typology of hearers participating in televised debates on two communicative levels, with interlocutors on the screen and the TV viewer being accounted for. Section 4 brings all these strands together and teases out the workings of aggression in televised political debates, exemplified by Polish pre-election debates. In Section 5, general conclusions are presented.

2.   Verbal aggression and humour in the media

The central point of attention here is *verbal violence/aggression* in televised political debates. verbal aggression, also referred to as verbal violence, is here defined as a set of linguistic strategies by means of which the speaker attacks/abuses (e.g.

denigrates or ridicules) the interlocutor and/or infringes the latter's conversational rights, for example by means of invectives, interruptions, or too high a pitch of voice.[1]

Verbal aggression in televised programmes, including political ones, has recently garnered some scholarly interest. For instance, Luginbühl (2007) expounds on conversational violence in political debates, while Archer (2008) conceives of impoliteness as a subtype of verbal aggression, which need not be the effect of "personal sense of spite" (Archer 2008: 189). The methodological underpinnings of this distinction are of importance to (im)politeness researchers. Specifically, verbal violence in media discourse is conceptualised as *impoliteness* (see among others Culpeper 2005; Lorenzo-Dus 2007, 2009). Nonetheless, the perspective assumed here contributes to humour studies, insofar as aggression which politicians manifest against one another may be deemed as engendering humorous effects. The issue of entertainment potential residing in impoliteness/aggression also tends to be raised, albeit intermittently (Culpeper 2005; Lorenzo-Dus 2007, 2009). A statement may then be ventured that verbal violence tends to coincide with humour, specifically aggressive humour. It must be stressed here that the focus of interest is verbal aggression carrying potential for humorousness, but not necessarily *funniness*. Humorousness is a binary category representing a stimulus' theoretical capacity to induce a humorous response, while funniness is a gradable category indicating the degrees of appreciation of a humorous text, which is differently perceived by individuals (Carrell 1997). Essentially, a hypothesis is put forward that verbal violence in televised discourse promotes humorous effects from the viewer's perspective, whilst s/he need not invariably consider such aggressive humour funny, depending on his/her sense of humour and attitude towards the speaker and the attacked hearer.

Aggressive humour is widely recognised as a power-based verbal tool, geared towards controlling the target and fostering conflict (see among others Martineau 1972; Rodrigues and Collinson 1995; Holmes and Marra 2002a, 2002b), which stands in stark contrast to the solidarity-building, affiliative function of humour (see among others Martineau 1972; Ervin-Tripp and Lampert 1992; Graham et al. 1992; Norrick 1993; Attardo 1994; Collinson 1988; Hay 1995, 2000; Cann et al. 1997; Martin 2007). Nevertheless, in both theoretical and empirical discussions on conversational humour, authors frequently omit to expound on the fact that

---

1. Kuipers (2008) rightly notes that frequently terms, such as hostility, aggression, superiority or rivalry, are used interchangeably, which she considers untenable. Superiority (this use of the term is not directly related to superiority theories of humour addressed later in this chapter) or rivalry need not entail hostility and willingness to hurt the other party, which is the case of conflict and hostility promotion, the focal point of this article.

in the case of *multi-party conversations*, the speaker's utterance may bear a two-fold meaning, namely humour and genuinely derogatory force to be recognised by respective hearers, who may appreciate the effect a given utterance has (or should have) on other parties, all being in accordance with the speaker's intent (see Ziv 1984; Eder 1993; Kotthoff 1996, 2007; Dynel 2008, 2010a). A similar assumption can be found in Freud's (1905/1960) discussion of tendentious jokes. The act of joke-telling involves a tripartite arrangement of people, namely the coalition of the joke teller and the hearer/audience against the butt. The same can be endorsed for aggressive conversational humour, whereby the speaker builds an in-group with the hearer, for whose enjoyment an utterance is produced, and an out-group with the individual, a hearer or a non-hearer, who is lambasted or even humiliated.

The term *disaffiliative humour* (cf. Martin et al. 2003; Dynel 2010a) is here used in reference to aggressive utterances which the speaker means to be truly abusive and demeaning to one hearer but humorous to another. Disaffiliative humour can also be targeted at an absent party, namely a non-participant, but such cases are immaterial here. This blanket category of humour is associated with such phenomena as *sarcasm* (Partington 2006; Dynel 2009b), *disparagement* (Zillmann 1983; Ford and Ferguson 2004; Ferguson and Ford 2008), *putdowns* (Zillmann and Stocking 1976; Dynel 2009b), *ridicule* (Ziv 1984; Billig 2005), or *mocking* (Ziv 1984; Norrick 1993; Everts 2003).[2]

Regardless of its form, an unequivocally aggressive utterance is non-humorous from the perspective of the listener to whose detriment it is produced, although the latter may appreciate that the offensive utterance is simultaneously a humorous stimulus for another hearer and the speaker. One may venture to claim that, in the absence of another listener beside the one attacked, an aggressive utterance may be devoid of any humorous capacity, given that there is nobody the speaker can aim to entertain and affiliate with, at the expense of the target. Disaffiliation and aggression may hence give rise to humour only when there is at least one non-targeted hearer, who may enjoy the humorous utterance, together with the speaker. Consequently, disaffiliative humour is simultaneously in a way affiliative, because it demonstrates camaraderie and strengthens bonds of solidarity between those who laugh (or display other signs of enjoyment), distancing the amused individuals from the target (Eder 1993; Kotthoff 1996, 2007). In other words, disaffiliative humour is based on forming out-groups and in-groups, being humorous solely

---

2.   A few of the authors listed in the references above consider the humour categories to be affiliative by nature. However, here all the phenomena are perceived only as genuinely aggressive, disaffiliative humour, distinct from friendly *teasing*, which captures pretended aggression (see Dynel 2008, 2009b, 2010a, and references therein).

to the latter (cf. LaFave et al. 1973, 1974; Priest and Wilhelm 1974; Stocking and Zillmann 1976; McCauley et al. 1983; Duncan 1985; Decker 1986). Essentially, the humorous potential of an aggressive remark is pivoted, to a large extent, on the act of disaffiliation. In the context of the present article, the in-group member with whom the speaker affiliates and builds solidarity is the viewer, while the target is the disaffiliated party, namely a member of the out-group (and so must be his/her supporters who do not find the remark amusing).

That humour can carry aggression, and thus disaffiliation, is reflected by superiority theories (see among others Keith-Spiegel 1972; Morreall 1983, 1987; Raskin 1985; Attardo 1994; Billig 2005), which enjoy a long philosophical tradition, going back to the writings by Plato and Aristotle (Morreall 1983, 1987), while the first full-fledged superiority theory is credited to Hobbes (1651/1957), later developed by Bergson (1900/1911). Superiority theories are premised on the assumption that central to humour experience are the feeling of superiority, mockery, and amusement at the expense of the butt/target of humour (not necessarily in the form of jokes; see also Tsakona and Popa this volume).[3] All the same, it must be emphasised that superiority theories are not capable of capturing all humour, irrespective of claims to the contrary (see Gruner 1978), for there are humour manifestations which are perfectly benevolent and free from any underlying aggression or hostility (Martin 2007; Davies 2008; Morreall 2008).

Aggressive conversational humour (see Coates 2007; Dynel 2009a, 2009b), which can be captured by superiority theories, is prevalent in media discourse, both fictional (series and films) and TV programmes, carrying entertainment values for wide audiences. Humour also occurs in televised political debates, a genre usually not geared towards entertainment. Furthermore, research shows that humour of various types is by no means absent from political discourse (see among others Meyer 1990; Moore 1992; Levasseur and Dean 1996; Martin 2004; Partington 2006, 2008; Bippus 2007; Yarwood 2007; Archakis and Tsakona this volume; Georgalidou this volume; Mueller this volume). It is reported to be a rhetorical tool in political debates (Kuipers 2008), and to display aggressive potential

---

3. The state-of-the-art picture of humour research within the superiority perspective alone is multifarious. There have been numerous accounts of humour which victimises the target via disparagement, belittlement, debasement, degradation, humiliation, and the like (see Berlyne 1969; Keith-Spiegel 1972; LaFave 1972; Gruner 1978; Zillmann 1983; Morreall 1987; Martin 2007). The most recent development of the approach focuses on the attitudinal account. Accordingly, the hearer experiences merriment based on the disparagement of others when feeling unaffiliated with, or having a negative attitude to, the "object of repulsion" (LaFave 1972; Zillmann and Cantor 1976). Another refinement of the theory (Zillmann and Cantor 1976; Zillmann 1983) transcends the notion of reference groups, focusing on the disposition, either negative or positive, to the disparaging and the disparaged.

between political adversaries, their global aim being to wittily entertain the public (Speier 1998). However, no generalisations can be made about the success of humour as a rhetorical strategy, on the grounds that viewers' humour perception is contingent on a number of factors. Audiences respond to humour depending on their personalities and socio-demographic backgrounds (Prerost 1993; Lowis 2003), and on their political preferences (Priest 1966; Priest and Abrahams 1970; Weise 1999). It is rational to assume that respondents will favour humour of politicians whom they support and will be unwilling to enjoy the humour of a politician of whom they are not supportive. Yet another factor is the category of humour. For example, Bippus (2007) adduces evidence that self-denigrating humour is regarded as a most effective rhetorical strategy in political discourse.

Culpeper (2005) attempts to explain the interface between impoliteness and entertainment, which corresponds to the interdependence between verbal aggression and humour. Culpeper's (2005:45) arguments are: "intrinsic pleasure" (impoliteness being engaging), "voyeuristic pleasure", "the audience is superior" (related to superiority theories of humour), and "the audience is safe". These four criteria, however, can be reduced to the superiority theory which holds for disaffiliative humour and embraces the factors listed by Culpeper. In order to appreciate a humorous stimulus, hearers must feel safe, namely they must know that the attack is not launched against them, which is the case of media audiences interpreting one interlocutor's aggressive barbs against another. The safety factor is the subordinate *sine qua non* for disaffiliative humour perception. The notion of intrinsic pleasure appears to be somewhat elusive and so is that of voyeuristic pleasure. In essence, any pleasure, which is closely related to humour experience, may derive from observing the inferiority (even if only momentary, consequent upon a single utterance) of the butt. What appears to be of even greater importance in generating humour is the speaker's intellectual victory over the interlocutor. Additionally, it can be hypothesised that it is the speaker's wit manifesting itself in an aggressive act that is a vehicle for aggressive humour. By producing an aggressive utterance, the speaker testifies to, or appropriates his/her power over (cf. Watts 1991), the conversationalist.

Elaborating on rudeness (immediately relevant to aggression), Beebe (1995) posits that a speaker asserts his/her power over an interactant with a view to appearing superior, having control over someone's actions, and winning power in the interaction. Even though at the outset of each debate, both candidates (are expected to) enjoy equal power, this will change as they co-construct discourse in a power struggle. This conforms to the contemporary view of power as a negotiable phenomenon enacted within discourse (see among others Eelen 2001; Mills 2003; Locher 2004; Mullany 2008).

In the case of televised debates, interlocutors (performing the roles of speakers and hearers alternately) enact and negotiate power, thereby performing their identity in front of audiences. The speaker, here a politician participating in a debate, strives to achieve these goals, relying on an assumption that his utterance is directed not only to the interlocutor but also to another hearer, namely the viewer, who keeps assessing his verbal performance. The pertinent question concerns the hearer role which the TV viewer performs in media discourse.

3.   Hearer types in televised debates

Several authors have propounded extensions of the canonical *dyadic* (speaker/ sender – hearer/recipient) model, proposing classifications of *participant roles* (Hymes 1972, 1974; Goffman 1976/1981a, 1979/1981a, 1981b; Clark and Carlson 1982; Bell 1984, 1991; Thomas 1986; Clark and Schaefer 1987, 1992; Levinson 1988; Schober and Clark 1989; Clark 1996). Based on a careful analysis of the competitive postulates and their methodological problems (which cannot be discussed for reasons of space), another classification is championed here (see also Dynel 2010a, 2010b, 2010c, 2011a, 2011b, 2011c). Participants are divided into *unratified participants* and *ratified participants*. The latter term is used synonymously with *interlocutors*, *conversationalists* and *interactants*, who embrace the *speaker* and *ratified hearers/listeners*. Hearers are dichotomised into ratified and unratified subtypes. The former, most important in the present study, further bifurcate into the *addressee*, and another interactant, for lack of a better term, called the *third party*.[4] The third party is a participant who is entitled to listen to the speaker and draw inferences, even though s/he is not the primary party, namely the addressee. The distinction between the addressee and the third party is drawn primarily in the light of verbal and non-verbal cues, such as terms of address, second person verbs and pronouns, or eye contact. By contrast, *unratified hearers*, also referred to as *overhearers*, divided into *bystanders* and *eavesdroppers*, are participants who listen to a conversation without the speaker's authorisation (and usually without ratified hearers' authorisation). Whilst interlocutors are oblivious to eavesdroppers, they are aware of bystanders' presence.

In the light of the above, three ratified participants, specifically interlocutors, of a political debate (two politicians and a journalist) partaking in each turn conflate (a) the speaker, (b) the addressee, namely the party who is overtly addressed,

---

4.   Levinson's (1988) term *target* is avoided here, due to its use in humour research in reference to the butt of aggressive humour, while the term *recipient* recurrent in literature, is reserved for yet another participant discussed later.

and (c) the third party, namely another interlocutor to whom a particular utterance is not addressed. Given that a debate is a form of discourse which is constructed in front of audiences, two more types of hearers must be distinguished, namely two types of *recipients*: audience in the studio (recipients 1) and TV viewers (recipients 2).

Media discourse is, by nature, communicatively twofold inasmuch as it is rooted in interlocutors' face-to-face interactions and their communication with audiences. There is an interactional relationship between journalists, guests, and the audience, the central idea being that broadcast talk is produced for the audience. Several authors have addressed this issue, deploying a range of different terms. For instance, Scannell (1991) argues in favour of several *communicative circuits* inherent in televised programmes, which hold simultaneously, such as a host and an interviewee, an interviewee and an audience, as well as a host and TV viewers. Taken together, such circuits constitute participation framework holding for broadcast talk (cf. Bell 1984; O'Keeffe 2006). On the other hand, Burger (1984, 1991) pictures media communication as two concentric *communication circles*, namely the *inner circle* representing the interactants on the screen forming the *primary situation*, and the *outer circle* concerning the audience's decoding of discourse constructed in the former circle, namely the *secondary situation*. An intermediate level is also in operation in the case of a studio audience's presence. Regrettably, the status of the studio audience remains somewhat vague.[5]

Overall, media talk intrinsically rests on what is here called *levels of communication* or *communicative levels*, entailing different hearers dichotomised into listening interlocutors and audiences, for whose benefit televised interactions take place. In other words, broadcast talk, inclusive of the discourse of political debates, is rooted in interlocutors' interactions in the studio, which are transmitted to wide audiences. The term *level of communication* is seen as preferable to concepts proposed by other authors, since it facilitates differentiation between participation frameworks in the studio, the distinction between studio and TV audiences, and the collective sender's impact on the media product.

---

5.   Similar to Burger's (1984, 1991) postulate is Fetzer's (2006) conceptualisation of a media political interview as a *dual frame of reference*, conflating the *first-frame interaction* of interviewer and interviewee, and the *second-frame* or *media-frame* interaction comprised of the first-frame interacting with the media frame. This notion is very broad and combines participants' interaction in the studio with and an array of elements peculiar to the nature of mass-mediated interaction, including features of the broadcasting format. For the sake of clarity, these concepts should be dissociated and discussed separately, which is why Fetzer's parlance is not followed here.

Audiences' comprehension is facilitated by the participants in media talk (Hutchby 2006; see also Goffman 1981b; Heritage 1985; Bell 1991; Scannell 1991; Clayman and Heritage 2002). Politicians (and their spin doctors) take into account viewers' cognitive resources (e.g. background knowledge and intelligence), when communicating meanings to the latter. In other words, speakers need to ensure that they are understood by their target audience and that they come over as persuasive. Whether and how they are understood depends on the audiences' actual perception, which is idiosyncratic and reliant on numerous factors. For instance, the most knowledgeable and intelligent audience members will not only infer messages intentionally relayed by a politician, but also appreciate meanings that speakers wish to hide, hence recognising their manipulative strategies. On the other hand, viewers may be lacking in requisite resources and fail to fully grasp the meaning of a politician's utterance. Variation in comprehension levels regardless, the focus of attention here is the ideal picture of comprehension as intended by the speaker.

Authors tend to dub media audiences *overhearers* or *overhearing audience* (see among others Heritage 1985; Heritage and Greatbatch 1991; Clayman and Heritage 2002; Bubel 2006, 2008; Tolson 2006; Weizman 2008; Garces-Conejos Blitvich 2009). This well-entrenched conceptualisation appears to be ill-advised, for the TV (together with studio) audiences are the primary, presupposed receivers of the talk. The standpoint assumed here is best summarised by Scannell (1991:1):

> The effect of listening to radio and TV output is not that of overhearing talk not intended to be overheard. All talk on radio and TV is public discourse, is meant to be accessible to the audience for whom it is intended. Thus broadcast talk minimally has a double articulation: it is a communicative interaction between those participating in discussion, interview, game show or whatever and, at the same time, is designed to be heard by absent audiences. The talk that takes place on radio and television has listenable properties intentionally built into it.

Interlocutors (here, in the case of electoral debates, a journalist and two Prime Minister candidates) produce *polylogues* (Kerbrat-Orecchioni 1997, 2004), with the presumption that the discourse is to be interpreted (and understood) by the general public, namely the potential electorate. It may even be argued that alternating between the roles of the speaker, the addressee, and the third party, interlocutors construct discourse by directing their utterances not (or at least not only) to one another but to the viewer, even if tacitly. In other words, the focus on the audience is what interacting participants orient themselves to and what they display in co-constructing their talk. TV and studio audiences can thus be conceived of as active listeners, whose interaction is largely restricted to active interpretation (Tolson 2006).[6]

Consequently, the postulate that a viewer should be conceptualised as an overhearer is not given support here (see also Dynel 2011c). By contrast, viewers are the most important hearers to whom the speaker (here, politician) talks, intending them to infer meanings, which is why they should be regarded as ratified participants. On the other hand, due to the two levels of communication (and viewers' inability to be interlocutors), viewers can hardly be deemed as addressees or the third party in the debate. On rare occasions, however, a politician may address viewers, talking straight into the camera eye. Due to this, a distinct category has been proposed, namely the *recipient*, used as a technical term (Dynel 2001a, 2011c).

A special type of the recipient is the *metarecipient*, an informed viewer who watches a debate as if from a superior position, analysing it consciously and making more insightful observations about meanings conveyed and methods employed to this end. The metarecipient is a recipient who is not only familiar with chosen communicative processes, but also consciously scrutinises them. The metarecipient is then an academic who, rather than watching a debate as a regular recipient and a voter, will interpret chosen aspects of discourse or media techniques (e.g. camera angle), appreciating the means by which certain effects are engendered upon regular viewers. Here, the present author and the reader of the article are metarecipients, both of whom investigate the twofold meaning of aggressive utterances conveyed to distinct hearers.

Figure 1 represents the stage of production of a single turn by the speaker at a particular moment. A political debate displays two main communicative levels, the recipient's level, affording a bird's-eye view of the other one, namely the level of interlocutors, embracing the speaker, the addressee, and the third party. The three interlocutors' level displays a participatory format resembling that of everyday conversations.

In casual conversations, manifesting themselves in dialogues or polylogues, participant roles are constantly negotiated among interlocutors, according to regular *turn-taking* procedures (see among others Schegloff and Sacks 1973; Sacks et

---

6. In face-to-face interaction, the speaker does not intend that the overhearer, an unratified participant in everyday encounters, should glean any meanings (Clark and Carlson 1982). Therefore, the speaker is not responsible for making him/herself understood (Schober and Clark 1989), and even employs strategies to hinder any potential overhearing or comprehension on the part of the unratified listener (Clark and Schaefer 1987). In other words, speakers will employ the strategies of *concealment* or, at least, *indifference* to overhearers (cf. Clark and Schaefer 1987).

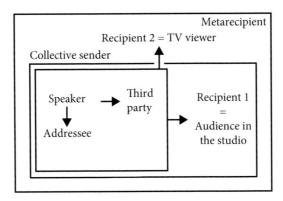

Figure 1. Participants in each turn of a televised debate held by two politicians and a journalist

al. 1974/1978; Goodwin 1981; Levinson 1983).[7] Furthermore, the status of each hearer may be changed halfway through an utterance, since "a single turn may consist of multiple utterance events" (Levinson 1988: 216). Participants are thus expected to be alert to constant changes in their participation statuses in a conversation, while propositions can be produced across different speakers' turns. Each utterance/turn partaking in an interaction is produced by the speaker and directed towards the addressee, and the third party. The performance of the interlocutors' roles, namely the speaker, the addressee and the third party, can change swiftly between the two politicians and the journalist, albeit in conformity with the debate format. Here, emphasis is placed primarily on aggressive utterances produced by one politician and addressed towards the other, with the journalist performing the role of the third party.

Each utterance is directed at the higher-order hearer, namely the recipient (a member of the studio audience or TV audience), including the metarecipient. The metarecipient, albeit technically a subtype of the recipient, assumes a better informed position, consciously analysing (chosen elements of) the form and content of the collective sender's product and the discourse at the interlocutors' level. As already indicated, the recipient may be either a member of the audience in the studio (recipient 1) or a TV viewer (recipient 2). Although a debate is held for the benefit of recipients, they cannot legitimately participate in it as speakers. Of course, studio audience can provide feedback by applause or other non-verbal cues, such as cheering or booing, but they are not allowed to contribute any utterances to the

---

7.   Put simply, "[t]he talk of one party bounded by the talk of others constitutes a turn, with turn-taking being the process through which the party doing the talk of the moment is changed" (Goodwin 1981: 2).

debate *per se*. On the other hand, TV viewers may comment verbally upon what they hear, but this would not count as a contribution to the exchange between the ratified participants. In essence, the recipient of either type is only an active listener and conducts inferential processes on the basis of the meanings communicated and their background knowledge (Clark and Carlson 1982; Clark 1996).

Additionally, the recipient 2's uptake is affected by media rendition (e.g. camera movement and angle or editing). A televised debate is the product of the *collective sender*, embracing not only the interlocutors but also the director, camera operators, or sound technicians. Meanings are conveyed by both the interlocutors' discourse (in focus here) and by dint of an array of TV ploys, which can be interpreted in the context of Bell's (1991) *embedding*, which involves intermediate levels of news production, starting from the crude version of a programme to the edited version shown to the mass audience.

4. Aggression in electoral debates

It is here argued that the speaker, namely one politician in a debate, intends an aggressive utterance addressed to his/her opponent to be a source of witty aggressive humour to be appreciated by a recipient who is not in sympathy with the target, namely the addressee (and rarely the third party). In other words, an aggressive utterance produced by a participant in a debate carries a twofold pragmatic meaning: one to be inferred by the addressee, the political opponent, and the other by the recipient. When producing such a verbalisation, a politician expects the recipient not to be a zealous supporter of the outwitted or disparaged interlocutor. Such a viewer stands a stronger chance of reinforcing his/her negative attitude towards the speaker, rather than appreciate his/her wit and the disaffiliative humour targeted at the butt, as do the aggressive speaker's supporters.

The two meanings of an aggressive remark are by no means mutually exclusive and one is contingent on the other. Accordingly, the speaker coveys an aggressive meaning towards the addressee, and thereby displays his/her wit and rhetorical skills to the viewer, which appears to be his/her ultimate objective. The viewer is thus meant to appreciate the emerging humorous effect and, consequently, to find the speaker witty and rhetorically victorious over the belittled opponent. On the other hand, being verbally attacked, the opponent will either concede defeat, even if only for a moment, or attempt to take retribution by a verbal counterattack. Additionally, the attacked party realises that, in accordance with the speaker's plan, the recipient should interpret the aggressive utterance as amusing.

The examples presented below come from three Polish Prime Minister pre-election debates televised in October 2007. Those were held consecutively at irregular intervals in the climate of political discontent, after an early dissolution of the government led by Jarosław Kaczyński (the late President's twin brother). He ran for Prime Minister again, representing Prawo i Sprawiedliwość ("Law and Justice"; henceforth PiS), the right-wing party. One of his competitors was Aleksander Kwaśniewski, the left-wing (Lewica i Demokracja, i.e. "Left Wing and Democracy"; henceforth LiD) candidate and former President of Poland. By 2007 he had gained notoriety for his inapt public appearances made in the state of alcohol intoxication. The third candidate, who was ultimately elected, was Donald Tusk, the representative of Platforma Obywatelska (Civic Platform).

The three debates held by each pair of politicians conformed to the same format. The debates were divided into topical sections mediated by different journalists. Each section embraced a few questions posed to both candidates, who were alternately given the floor to answer. The candidates had earlier been familiarised with the queries and could, therefore, prepare their answers in advance. Some time was also allotted to pre-prepared questions political opponents posed to one another. Although the debate format presupposed few interactions, the politicians frequently would not refrain from interrupting the legitimate speaker at a given moment, which was the most striking and prevalent manifestation of aggression (cf. Hutchby 1992; Beebe 1995; Bilmes 1997).

Irrespective of differences in their policies and discursive strategies, all the three candidates resorted to verbal aggression. The journalist could contribute and intervene if the politicians' exchange went adrift, but had to strive to remain overtly impartial. It may be conjectured that the inferences they made concerning the speakers' aggressive turns were (meant to be) similar to those made by the recipients.

The following discussion is conducted from the metarecipient's perspective and accounts for the interactive processes at the two communicative levels and the conjectured communicative goals the interlocutors have when displaying verbal aggression. In other words, the metarecipient's analysis sheds light on what interactants aim to achieve and the linguistic strategies they employ to this end, as well as what regular viewers, namely recipients, ideally infer when witnessing their talk.

The instances cited and succinctly discussed below are a representative sample of verbal aggression with which the three debates were replete. The first example below illustrates an aggressive but witty response reminiscent of what Veale et al. (2006) and Brône (2008) call *trumping*:[8]

---

8. The examples were transcribed from the three debates and translated into English by the author. Discourse analytic conventions (e.g. the indication of pauses) are not followed here, inasmuch as non-verbal aspects of speech are not germane to the present analysis. What must be

(1)   1.   Aleksander Kwaśniewski: Jak Pan, jako przyszły premier i Platforma, która będzie kierować Polską, chce tą politykę zagraniczna prowadzić?
      2.   Donald Tusk: Obawiam się o Pana. Jak Pan wróci do swoich towarzyszy z LiD-u to wie Pan, co Panu powiedzą za to, że Pan trzeci raz mówi: „Platforma wygra wybory a Tusk będzie premierem"? Oczekiwali od Pana więcej wiary.

      1.   Aleksander Kwaśniewski: How will you, as the future Prime Minister, and Civic Platform, which will lead the country, handle international affairs?
      2.   Donald Tusk: I'm worried about you. When you face your LiD party members, do you know what they will tell you about the fact that for the third time you're saying, "Civic Platform will win the election and Tusk will be the Prime Minister"? They have expected more faith on your part.

Metarecipients can gather that, rather than respond to the interlocutor's query (1), D. Tusk resorts to a clever rhetorical ploy (2) by capitalising on the premise A. Kwaśniewski has introduced to pose his question, namely D. Tusks's being elected. D. Tusk makes use of the opponent's failure to employ the hypothetical mood and hence issues an accusation of A. Kwaśniewski's disloyalty towards his party. This accusation is unfounded, of which both the interlocutors and the recipient are cognisant, perceiving it only as a means of engendering a rhetorical effect, not conveying propositional, truth-value content. It can be conjectured that D. Tusk's response is aimed at procrastination, owing to his incapability of providing a spontaneous answer to the thorny question. Irrespective of his rational for this turn, he comes across to the recipient as a very witty speaker who does not lose his bearings in this anxiety-provoking conversational situation. A. Kwaśniewski, on the other hand, must feel thrown off balance, as his question, aimed to challenge D. Tusk's standpoint, is not met with a relevant response and, more importantly, he is outwitted.

In another example, two candidates engage in an act of reciprocal aggression which resembles friendly teasing (see among others Norrick 1993; Partington 2006; Martin 2007; Dynel 2008, 2009b) focused on an irrelevant topic. However, since the interlocutors presuppose the presence of the recipient, the interaction must be viewed as a genuine verbal power struggle orientated towards outdoing each other:

---

highlighted, though, is that none of the candidates raised his voice considerably, which would have been a pronounced manifestation of conversational violence and would have overtly breached the default decorum principle typical of political debates.

(2) 1. Donald Tusk: Chciałbym żeby Pan wreszcie zrozumiał, że dobra polityka zagraniczna nie polega na nieustannym grymaszeniu, strojeniu groźnych min, dla przykładu…
2. Jarosław Kaczyński: Mam groźną minę zrobić?
3. Donald Tusk: Nie, no mnie Pan nie przestraszy. I wie Pan, problem polega na tym, że…
4. Jarosław Kaczyński: A ja się cieszę, że Pan nie ma tych wilczych oczu co zwykle.
5. Donald Tusk: Ale niech Pan się zdecyduje, czy ja mam wilcze oczy, czy wilcze zęby.
6. Jarosław Kaczyński: Dotąd zwykle oczy.
7. Monika Olejnik (journalist): Nie wiem czy to było merytoryczne i zagraniczne, ale proszę bardzo, ma Pan jeszcze czas.
8. Donald Tusk: Ze strony Pana Kaczyńskiego nie było to merytoryczne, raczej zoologiczne. Ale o zwierzętach nie będziemy gadać, bo byśmy mogli tutaj parę dowcipów tak zadysponować, że raczej nie byłby Pan zadowolony.

1. Donald Tusk: I'd like you to understand finally that handling foreign affairs does not entail continuous sulking and making angry faces, for instance.
2. Jarosław Kaczyński: Shall I make an angry face?
3. Donald Tusk: No, you won't scare me. And you know, the problem resides in the fact that…
4. Jarosław Kaczyński: And I'm happy you don't have these wolf-like eyes, as usual.
5. Donald Tusk: Would you please decide if I have wolf-like eyes or teeth?
6. Jarosław Kaczyński: So far usually teeth.
7. Monika Olejnik (journalist): I don't know whether this was substantial and related to foreign affairs, but you still have time.
8. Donald Tusk: On the part of Mr. Kaczyński, this wasn't substantial, rather zoological. But it is not animals that we will talk about, because we could deploy a few jokes, so that you wouldn't be pleased.

The interaction cited above occurs during D. Tusk's time slot, with the presentation of his viewpoint on foreign affairs being illegitimately interrupted by his opponent. The exchange devoid of political arguments is unintentionally prompted by D. Tusk's implicit criticism of J. Kaczyński's mishandling of foreign affairs (1), to which the latter replies with a comment neither particularly witty nor relevant but aggressive (2). D. Tusk gives this interruption short shrift via humour and attempts to return to the topical talk (3), only to be interrupted by J. Kaczyński, who brings up the irrelevant topic of appearance, which constitutes another aggressive act on his part (4). To recognise the import of this comment, the recipient is expected to be aware of the fact that, in his various TV appearances, J. Kaczyński compared D. Tusk's facial features to wolf's, thus indirectly attributing some unidentified wolf-like characteristics (possibly vileness) to his character and/or actions. D. Tusk lets himself be involved in the idle metaphorical talk, yet rationalises and questions the attack in the light of similar ones (5), which J. Kaczyński welcomes with a straightforward reply, rather than creatively turn the tables to his favour (6). At this point, the journalist takes the speaking role, giving floor to the legitimate speaker (7). D. Tusk resumes his position but again raises the irrelevant topic (8). It is worth noting that he first treats J. Kaczyński as the third party and it is only halfway through the turn that he addresses him. D. Tusk cleverly exploits the topic, winning the verbal battle with the adversary, admittedly much to recipients' amusement. The jokes he refers to are an abundant group proliferating in Poland as a result of events on the political arena and are couched in allusions to his opponent's surname, which (roughly translated) means "related to a duck". Most recipients, perhaps save those unequivocally supportive of J. Kaczyński, will appreciate D. Tusk's wit and conversational victory, while regarding the former's turns superfluous and thus rude, as well as aggressive, albeit hardly scintillating or amusing.

Yet another instance displays the speaker's overt attack against the addressee rendered by means of butting in and disrupting the flow of the legitimate speaker's answer, and thus blocking the latter's linguistically with interruptions in a much more vehement than in the example above. Moreover, the illegitimately intertwined text is a demeaning parody of the interlocutor, specifically his tendency towards using a stylistically awkward, pleonastic expression "obvious obviousness":

(3) 1. Aleksander Kwaśniewski: Pan Kaczyński jest mistrzem dwóch rzeczy: formułuje tezę, wierzy w nią i sam sobie udowadnia. No i używa sformułowania oczywista oczywistość. Nie ma porozumienia LiD-PO.

2. Jarosław Kaczyński: Dyskusja była pożyteczna, bo pokazała niezmienność pewnych postaw. Pan jest całkowicie nieuleczalny. Broni pan tego, czego obronić się nie da. [...] Ale sądzę, że po tych dwóch latach dla bardzo wielu Polaków będzie zupełnie oczywiste...

3. Aleksander Kwaśniewski: ...oczywista oczywistość...

4. Jarosław Kaczyński: ...że opcja, która jest reprezentowana przez PiS, to jest ta opcja na rzeczywistą zmianę. To, że Pan nie chce nic zmienić, to jest oczywiste, tak, oczywiste...

5. Aleksander Kwaśniewski: ...oczywista oczywistość...

6. Jarosław Kaczyński: ...obawiam się, że PO też nie chce nic zmienić...
7. Aleksander Kwaśniewski: ...i to też jest oczywiste
8. Jarosław Kaczyński: Proszę się nie przedrzeźniać!

1. Aleksander Kwaśniewski: Mr. Kaczyński is an expert on two things: he formulates a thesis, believes in it, and proves it; and he uses the term "obvious obviousness". There is no such thing as LiD-PO coalition.
2. Jarosław Kaczyński: The discussion was useful as it showed the rigidity of some views. You are incurable. You defend what cannot be defended. [...] But I believe that after these two years, for many Poles this will be perfectly obvious...
3. Aleksander Kwaśniewski: ...obvious obviousness...
4. Jarosław Kaczyński: ...that what PiS supports is orientated towards actual change. That you don't want to change anything is obvious, yes obvious...
5. Aleksander Kwaśniewski: ...obvious obviousness...
6. Jarosław Kaczyński: I'm afraid that the Civic Platform doesn't want to change anything either...
7. Aleksander Kwaśniewski: ...and this is also obvious...
8. Jarosław Kaczyński: Don't imitate me please!

The aggressive interchange opens with a sarcastic comment on the part of A. Kwaśniewski (1), who disrupts J. Kaczyński's answer. By means of a set-them-up-knock-them-down technique, A. Kwaśniewski ridicules J. Kaczyński's argumentative skills and verbal propensity. The term *expert*, by default, conveys positive connotations, which are cancelled in view of the following part of the utterance. It is interesting that in A. Kwaśniewski's first utterance quoted above, J. Kaczyński performs the role of a third party not the addressee, given that he is referred to in the third person form. J. Kaczyński strikes back with voicing his criticism of the addressee and using the word *obvious* (2), part of the infamous phrase, which his conversationalist further exploits with relish (3, 5, 7). Cognisant of the audience's potential enjoyment of his verbal aggression, A. Kwaśniewski keeps parodying and trying to distract J. Kaczyński, who reacts defensively (8) only after A. Kwaśniewski's third attempt. J. Kaczyński's ultimate reaction in the form of an imperative, power-based as it may be, is no patch on his interlocutor's aggressive utterances. Admittedly, as long as not in favour of J. Kaczyński, recipients will take delight in the spectacle of humiliation staged by A. Kwaśniewski.

More successful retribution is epitomised by A. Kwaśniewski's response to J. Kaczyński's overt criticism of his policies:

(4)   1.   Aleksander Kwaśniewski (do Jarosława Kaczyńskiego): Panie Prezydencie, jeżeli Pan mówi, że ja załatwiłem wszystko to, co każdy by załatwił, to to jest brutalna ocena, z którą się nie zgadzam, ale mógłbym równie brutalnie powiedzieć: Pan za to zepsuje to, co tylko Pan potrafi zepsuć na tym świecie.

  1.   Aleksander Kwaśniewski (to Jarosławm Kaczyński): Mr. President, if you're saying that I handled only what everybody else could handle, this is a very cruel assessment I disagree with, but I could equally cruelly say that you will bungle what only you in the whole world can bungle.

Following the rhetorical pattern used by his opponent earlier in the debate now alluded to, Kwaśniewski deploys verbal violence, admittedly voicing even more virulent criticism of the conversationalist, and outwitting the latter. Again, recipients stand a strong chance of finding this utterance wittily aggressive and entertaining at the expense of the targeted addressee of the turn.

5.   Conclusions and final comments

Premised on a postulate that the viewer should be conceptualised as a special ratified hearer, called *recipient*, the article aimed to corroborate that aggressive utterances deployed in TV programmes, such as electoral debates, convey two distinct meanings to two ratified hearers. Aggressive utterances frequently emerge as being humorous and testify to the speaker's quick-wittedness and verbal skill from the recipient's perspective, but simultaneously attack and belittle another interlocutor. Specifically, a belief was espoused that the three politicians have resorted to verbal aggression with a view to achieving two, seemingly contradictory but mutually dependent, objectives. On the one hand, each speaker performs aggressive acts, attacking and/or denigrating the conversationalist, namely the butt, and indirectly his advocates. On the other hand, acts of verbal aggression have an affiliative facet, since the speaker aims to amuse, and forge solidarity with, other ratified hearers, primarily recipients in the studio and in front of the TV screen. Aiming to attain these two goals, each politician, frequently displays his wit and discursive victory over the interlocutor. On the whole, "acts of conversational violence are a combined strategy of dominance, defamation and of enhancing their own image" (Luginbühl 2007: 1385).

Interestingly, with the exception of a few verbal lapses, which may be regarded as unintentional humour (e.g. J. Kaczyński's statement "Nawet największy autorytet mnie nie przekona, bo ja mam swój własny rozum"; "Even the greatest authority cannot convince me, as I have my own common sense"), all humorous utterances are manifestations of the speaker's aggression towards the other politician and subscribe the category of disaffiliative, power-building humour. Contrary to the thesis that self-denigrating humour benefits politicians in their self-presentation, no such can be found in the three Polish debates. Nor can any other forms of benign humour. The emerging conclusion concerning the exemplifying data, therefore, is that humour in the three political debates is disaffiliative in character and employed as a subversive rhetorical strategy. Nevertheless, it is also noteworthy that verbal aggression in which political discourse abounds, is not amenable to unequivocal verbal abuse, which would be most inappropriate in this type of discourse. Most of the aggressive utterances which are produced serve as a testament to the speaker's wit and humour.

It would be wrong to assume that being profuse in verbal violence, which bears humorous potential for the recipient, is a guarantee of a candidate's victory in a debate, let alone an election. It is only argued that humour, inclusive of its disaffiliative type targeted at the opponent, is one of multitudinous factors constituting a candidate's image politics. Nevertheless, verbal aggression is a provocative strategy geared towards amusing the audience and it may turn out to be a two-edged sword, detrimental not only to the individual attacked but also to the speaker (see also Archakis and Tsakona this volume). A politician may come over as being uncouth rather than witty and rhetorically skilful. Incidentally, opinion polls conducted after the debates indicated that such was the majority of Poles' perception of A. Kwaśniewski. verbal aggression is a dangerous weapon of destruction and distraction, which may enrage the butt, as well as entertain or enrage the viewer, and which should thus be handled with utmost care.

References

Archer, Dawn. 2008. "Verbal aggression and impoliteness: Related or synonymous?" In *Impoliteness in Language: Studies on its Interplay with Power in Theory and Practice* [Language, Power and Social Process 21], Derek Bousfield and Miriam Locher (eds), 181–207. Berlin/New York: Mouton de Gruyter.

Attardo, Salvatore. 1994. *Linguistic Theories of Humour* [Humour Research 1]. Berlin/New York: Mouton de Gruyter.

Beebe, Leslie. 1995. "Polite fictions: Instrumental rudeness as pragmatic competence." In *Linguistics and the Education of Language Teachers: Ethnolinguistic, Psycholinguistics and Sociolinguistic Aspects. Georgetown Round Table on Languages and Linguistics*, James Alatis, Carolyn A. Straehle, Brent Gallenberger and Maggie Ronkin (eds), 154–168. Georgetown: Georgetown University Press.

Bell, Allan. 1984. "Language style as audience design." *Language and Society* 13: 145–204.

Bell, Allan. 1991. *The Language of News Media* [Language in Society 17]. Oxford: Blackwell.

Bergson, Henri. 1900/1911. *Laughter: An Essay on the Meaning of the Comic*. London: Macmillan.

Berlyne, Daniel. 1969. "Laughter, humour, and play." In *The Handbook of Social Psychology*, vol. 3, Gardner Lindzey and Elliot Aronson (eds), 795–852. Reading: Addison-Wesley.

Billig, Michael. 2005. *Laughter and Ridicule: Towards a Social Critique of Humour* [Theory, Culture and Society]. London: Sage.

Bilmes, Jack. 1997. "Being interrupted." *Language in Society* 26: 507–531.

Bippus, Amy. 2007. "Factors predicting the perceived effectiveness of politicians' use of humour during a debate." *Humour: International Journal of Humour Research* 20: 105–121.

Brône, Geert. 2008. "Hyper- and misunderstanding in interactional humour." *Journal of Pragmatics* 40: 2027–2061.

Bubel, Claudia. 2008. "Film audiences as overhearers." *Journal of Pragmatics* 40: 55–71.

Bubel, Claudia. 2006. *The Linguistic Construction of Character Relations in TV Drama: Doing Friendship in* Sex and the City. PhD thesis, Universitat des Saarlandes, Saarbrucken, Germany. http://scidok.sulb.uni-saarland.de/volltexte/2006/598/pdf/Diss_Bubel_publ.pdf (accessed February 9, 2011).

Burger, Harald. 1984. *Sprache der Massenmedien*. Berlin: de Gruyter.

Burger, Harald. 1991. *Das Gesprach in den Massenmedien*. Berlin: de Gruyter.

Cann, Arnie, Calhoun, Lawrence and Banks, Janet. 1997. "On the role of humour appreciation in interpersonal attraction: It's no joking matter." *Humour: International Journal of Humour Research* 10: 77–89.

Carrell, Amy. 1997. "Joke competence and humour competence." *Humour: International Journal of Humour Research* 10: 173–185.

Clark, Herbert. 1996. *Using Language*. Cambridge: Cambridge University Press.

Clark, Herbert and Carlson, Thomas. 1982. "Hearers and speech acts." *Language* 58: 332–372.

Clark, Herbert and Schaefer, Edward. 1987. "Concealing one's meaning from overhearers." *Journal of Memory and Language* 26: 209–225.

Clark, Herbert and Schaefer, Edward. 1992. "Dealing with overhearers." In *Arenas of Language Use*, Herbert Clark (ed.), 248–273. Chicago: University of Chicago Press, Center for the Study of Language and Information.

Clayman, Steven and Heritage, John. 2002. *The News Interview: Journalists and Public Figures on the Air* [Studies in Interactional Sociolinguistics 16]. Cambridge: Cambridge University Press.

Coates, Jennifer 2007. "Talk in a play frame: More on laughter and intimacy." *Journal of Pragmatics* 39: 29–49.

Collinson, David. 1988. "Engineering humour: Masculinity, joking and conflict in shop-floor relations." *Organisation Studies* 9: 181–199.

Culpeper, Jonathan. 2005. "Impoliteness and entertainment in the television quiz show: *The Weakest Link*." *Journal of Politeness Research* 1: 35–72.

Decker, Wayne. 1986. "Sex conflict and impressions of managers' aggressive humour." *Psychological Record* 36: 483–490.

Duncan, Jack. 1985. "The superiority theory of humour at work: Joking relationships as indicators of formal and informal status patterns in small, task-oriented groups." *Small Group Behaviour* 16: 556–564.

Dynel, Marta. 2008. "No aggression, only teasing." *Lodz Papers in Pragmatics* 4: 241–261.

Dynel, Marta. 2009a. *Humorous Garden-Paths: A Pragmatic-Cognitive Study*. Newcastle: Cambridge Scholars Publishing.

Dynel, Marta. 2009b. "Beyond a joke: Types of conversational humour." *Language and Linguistics Compass* 3: 1284–1299.

Dynel, Marta. 2010a. "Friend or foe? Chandler's humour from the metarecipient's perspective." In *Pragmatic Perspectives on Language and Linguistics, Vol. II: Pragmatics of Semantically Restricted Domains*, Iwona Witczak-Plisiecka (ed.), 175–205. Newcastle: Cambridge Scholars Publishing.

Dynel, Marta. 2010b. "Not hearing things – Hearer/listener categories in polylogues." *mediAzioni* 9. http://mediazioni.sitlec.unibo.it/images/stories/PDF_folder/document-pdf/2010/dynel_2010.pdf (accessed February 9, 2011).

Dynel, Marta. 2010c. "On 'Revolutionary Road': A proposal for extending the Gricean model of communication to cover multiple hearers." *Lodz Papers in Pragmatics* 6: 283–304.

Dynel, Marta. 2011a. "I'll be there for you: On participation-based sitcom humour." In *The Pragmatics of Humour across Discourse Domains* [Pragmatics and Beyond New Series 210], Marta Dynel (ed.), 311–333. Amsterdam/Philadelphia: John Benjamins.

Dynel, Marta. 2011b. "Two communicative levels and twofold illocutionary force in televised political debates." *Poznań Studies in Contemporary Linguistics* 47: 283–307.

Dynel, Marta. 2011c. "'You talking to me?' The viewer as a ratified listener to film discourse." *Journal of Pragmatics* 43: 1628–1644.

Eder, Donna. 1993. "'Go get ya a French!': Romantic and sexual teasing among adolescent girls." In *Gender and Conversational Interaction* [Oxford Studies in Sociolinguistics], Deborah Tannen (ed.), 17–30. New York: Oxford University Press

Eelen, Gino. 2001. *A Critique of Politeness Theories* [Encounters 1]. Manchester: St. Jerome Publishing.

Ervin-Tripp, Susan and Lampert, Martin. 1992. "Gender differences in the construction of humorous talk." In *Locating Power: Proceedings of the Second Berkeley Women and Language Conference,* Kira Hall, Mary Buchholtz and Birch Moonwoman (eds), 108–117. Berkeley: Berkeley Women and Language Group, Linguistics Department, University of California.

Everts, Elisa. 2003. "Identifying a particular family humour style: A sociolinguistic discourse analysis." *Humour: International Journal of Humour Research* 16: 369–412.

Ferguson, Mark A. and Ford, Thomas E. 2008. "Disparagement humour: A theoretical and empirical review of psychoanalytic, superiority and social identity theories." *Humour: International Journal of Humour Research* 21: 283–312.

Fetzer, Anita. 2006. "'Minister, we will see how the public judges you': Media references in political interviews." *Journal of Pragmatics* 38: 180–195.

Ford, Thomas E. and Ferguson, Mark A. 2004. "Social consequences of disparagement humour: A prejudiced norm theory." *Personality and Social Psychology Review* 8: 79–94.

Freud, Sigmund. 1905. *Der Witz und seine Beziehung zum Unbewussten,* Leipzig: Deutucke. Translated as Freud, Sigmund. 1960. *Jokes and Their Relation to the Unconscious.* Transl. James Strachey. New York: Norton.

Garces-Conejos Blitvich, Pilar. 2009. "Impoliteness and identity in the American news media: The 'Culture Wars'". *Journal of Politeness Research* 5: 273–303.

Goffman, Erving. 1976. "Replies and responses." *Language in Society* 5: 257–313. Reprinted in *Forms of Talk*, Erving Goffman, 1981, 5–77. Philadelphia: University of Pennsylvania Press.

Goffman, Erving. 1979. "Footing." *Semiotica* 25: 1–29. Reprinted in *Forms of Talk*, Erving Goffman, 1981, 124–159. Philadelphia: University of Pennsylvania Press.

Goffman, Erving. 1981a. *Forms of Talk.* Philadelphia: University of Pennsylvania Press.

Goffman, Erving. 1981b. "Radio talk: A study of the ways of our errors." In *Forms of Talk*, Erving Goffman, 197–330. Philadelphia: University Pennsylvania Press.

Goodwin, Charles. 1981. *Conversational Organisation: Interaction between Speakers and Hearers*. New York: Academic Press.

Graham, Elizabeth, Papa, Michael J. and Brooks, Gordon P. 1992. "Functions of humour in conversation: Conceptualisation and measurement." *Western Journal of Communication* 56: 161–183.

Gruner, Charles. 1978. *Understanding Laughter: The Workings of Wit and Humour*. Chicago: Nelson-Hall.

Hay, Jennifer. 1995. *Gender and Humour: Beyond a Joke*. Unpublished MA thesis, Victoria University of Wellington, Wellington, New Zealand.

Hay, Jennifer. 2000. "Functions of humour in the conversations of men and women." *Journal of Pragmatics* 32: 709–742.

Heritage, John. 1985. "Analyzing news interviews: Aspects of the production of talk for an overhearing audience." In *Handbook of Discourse Analysis*, vol. 3, Teun A. van Dijk (ed.), 95–119. New York: Academic Press.

Heritage, John and Greatbatch, David. 1991. "On the institutional character of institutional talk: The case of news interviews." In *Talk and Social Structure: Studies in Ethnomethodology and Conversation Analysis*, Don Boden and Deirdre H. Zimmerman (eds), 95–129. Berkeley/Los Angeles: University of California Press.

Hobbes, Thomas. 1651/1957. *Leviathan*. Oxford: Claredon Press.

Holmes, Janet and Marra, Meredith. 2002a. "Having a laugh at work: How humour contributes to workplace culture." *Journal of Pragmatics* 34: 1683–1710.

Holmes, Janet and Marra, Meredith. 2002b. "Over the edge? Subversive humour between colleagues and friends." *Humour: International Journal of Humour Research* 15: 65–87.

Hutchby, Ian. 1992. "Confrontation talk: Aspects of 'interruption' in argument sequences on talk radio." *Text* 12: 343–371.

Hutchby, Ian. 2006. *Media Talk: Conversation Analysis and the Study of Broadcasting* [Issues in Cultural and Media Studies]. Maidenhead: Open University Press.

Hymes, Dell. 1972. "Models of the interaction of language and social life." In *Directions in Sociolinguistics: The Ethnography of Communication*, John Gumperz and Dell Hymes (eds), 35–71. New York: Holt, Rinehart and Winston.

Hymes, Dell. 1974. *Foundations in Sociolinguistics: An Ethnographic Approach* [Conduct and Communication]. Philadelphia: University of Pennsylvania Press.

Keith-Spiegel, Patricia. 1972. "Early conceptions of humour: Varieties and issues." In *The Psychology of Humour*, Jerry Goldstein and Paul McGhee (eds), 3–39. New York: Academic Press.

Kerbrat-Orecchioni, Catherine. 1997. "A multilevel approach in the study of talk-in-interaction." *Pragmatics* 7: 1–20.

Kerbrat-Orecchioni, Catherine (ed.), 2004. "Polylogue." *Journal of Pragmatics* 36 (Special Issue): 1–146.

Kotthoff, Helga. 1996. "Impoliteness and conversational humour." *Folia Linguistica* 30: 299–327.

Kotthoff, Helga. 2007. "Oral genres of humour. On the dialectic of genre knowledge and creative authoring." *Pragmatics* 12: 263–296.

Kozloff, Sarah. 2000. *Overhearing Film Dialogue*. Berkeley/Los Angeles: University of California Press.

Kuipers, Giselinde. 2008. "The sociology of humour." In *The Primer of Humour Research* [Humour Research 8], Victor Raskin (ed.), 361–398. Berlin/New York: Mouton de Gruyter.

LaFave, Lawrence. 1972. "Humour judgments as a function of reference groups and identification classes." In *The Psychology of Humour*, Jerry Goldstein and Paul McGhee (eds), 195–210. New York: Academic Press.

LaFave, Lawrence, Haddad, Jay and Marshall, Nancy. 1974. "Humour judgments as a function of identification classes." *Sociology and Social Research* 58: 184–194.

LaFave, Lawrence, McCarthy, Kevin and Haddad, Jay. 1973. "Humour judgments as a function of identification classes: Canadian vs. American." *Journal of Psychology: Interdisciplinary and Applied* 85: 53–59.

Levasseur, David and Dean, Kevin. 1996. "The Dole humour myth and the risks of recontextualizing rhetoric." *Southern Communication Journal* 62: 56–72.

Levinson, Stephen C. 1983. *Pragmatics* [Cambridge Textbooks in Linguistics]. Cambridge: Cambridge University Press.

Levinson, Stephen C. 1988. "Putting linguistics on a proper footing: Explorations in Goffman's participation framework." In *Erving Goffman: Exploring the Interaction Order* [Northeastern Series on Feminist Theory], Paul Drew and Anthony Wootton (eds), 161–227. Boston: Northeastern University Press.

Locher, Miriam. 2004. *Power and Politeness in Action: Disagreements in Oral Communication* [Language, Power and Social Process 12]. Berlin/New York: Mouton de Gruyter.

Lorenzo-Dus, Nuria. 2007. "(Im)politeness and the Spanish media: The case of audience participation debates." In *Research on Politeness in the Spanish Speaking World*, Maria Placencia and Carmen García-Fernández (eds), 145–166. London: Lawrence Erlbaum Associates.

Lorenzo-Dus, Nuria. 2009. "'You're barking mad – I'm out': Impoliteness and broadcast talk." *Journal of Politeness Research* 5: 159–187.

Lowis, Michael. 2003. "Cartoon humour: Do demographic variables and political correctness influence perceptions of cartoon funniness?" *Mankind Quarterly* 43: 273–289.

Luginbühl, Martin. 2007. "Conversational violence in political TV debates: Forms and functions." *Journal of Pragmatics* 39: 1371–1387.

Martin, Diane M. 2004. "Balancing on the political high wire: The role of humour in the rhetoric of Ann Richards." *Southern Communication Journal* 69: 273–285.

Martin, Rod A. 2007. *The Psychology of Humour. An Integrative Approach*. Burlington: Elsevier.

Martin, Rod, Puhlik-Doris, Patricia, Larsen, Gwen, Gray, Jeanette and Weir, Kelly. 2003. "Individual differences in uses of humour and their relation to psychological well-being: Development of the Humour Styles Questionnaire." *Journal of Research in Personality* 37: 48–75.

Martineau, William. 1972. "A model for the social function of humour." In *The Psychology of Humour*, Jerry Goldstein and Paul McGhee (eds), 101–125. New York: Academic Press.

McCauley, Clark, Woods, Kathryn and Coolidge, Christopher. 1983. "More aggressive cartoons are funnier." *Journal of Personality and Social Psychology* 44: 817–823.

Meyer, John. 1990. "Ronald Reagan and humour: A politician's velvet weapon." *Communication Studies* 41: 76–88.

Mills, Sarah. 2003. *Gender and Politeness* [Studies in Interactional Sociolinguistics 17]. Cambridge: Cambridge University Press.

Moore, Mark. 1992. "'They Quayle Quagmire': Political campaigns in the poetic form of burlesque." *Western Journal of Communication* 56: 108–124.

Morreall, John. 1983. *Taking Laughter Seriously*. Albany: State University of New York Press.

Morreall, John. 1987. *The Philosophy of Laughter and Humour*. Albany, NY: State University of New York Press.

Morreall, John. 2008. "Philosophy and religion." In *The Primer of Humour Research* [Humour Research 8], Victor Raskin (ed.), 211–242. Berlin/New York: Mouton de Gryuter.

Mullany, Louise. 2008. "'Stop hassling me!': Impoliteness, power and gender identity in the professional workplace." In *Impoliteness in Language: Studies on its Interplay with Power in Theory and Practice* [Language, Power and Social Process 21], Derek Bousfield and Miriam Locher (eds), 231–251. Berlin/New York: Mouton de Gruyter.

Norrick, Neal. 1993. *Conversational Joking: Humour in Everyday Talk*. Bloomington: Indiana University Press.

O'Keeffe, Anne. 2006. *Investigating Media Discourse* [Domains of Discourse]. London: Routledge.

Partington, Alan. 2006. *The Linguistics of Laughter. A Corpus-Assisted Study of Laughter-Talk* [Routledge Studies in Linguistics 5]. London/New York: Routledge.

Partington, Alan. 2008. "From Wodehouse to the White House: A Corpus-assisted study of play, fantasy and dramatic incongruity in comic writing and laughter-talk." *Lodz Papers in Pragmatics* 4: 189–213.

Prerost, Frank. 1993. "Locus of control as a factor in the appreciation of election year political cartoons." *Psychological Reports* 72: 217–218.

Priest, Robert. 1966. "Election jokes: The effects of reference group membership." *Psychological Reports* 18: 600–602.

Priest, Robert and Abrahams, Joel. 1970. "Candidate preference and hostile humour in the 1968 elections." *Psychological Reports* 26: 779–783.

Priest, Robert and Wilhelm, Paul G. 1974. "Sex, marital status, and self-actualisation as factors in the appreciation of sexist jokes." *Journal of Social Psychology* 92: 245–249.

Raskin, Victor. 1985. *Semantic Mechanisms of Humour* [Studies in Linguistics and Philosophy 24]. Dordrecht: D. Reidel.

Rodrigues, Suzana and Collinson, David. 1995. "'Having fun?': Humour as resistance in Brazil." *Organisation Studies* 16: 739–768.

Sacks, Harvey, Schegloff, Emanuel and Jefferson, Gail. 1974. "A simplest systematics for the organisation of turn-taking for conversation." *Language* 50: 696–735.

Scannell, Paddy. 1991. "Introduction: The relevance of talk." In *Broadcast Talk*, Paddy Scannell (ed.), 1–13. London: Sage.

Schegloff, Emanuel and Sacks, Harvey. 1973. "Opening up closings." *Semiotica* 8: 289–327.

Schober, Michael and Clark, Herbert. 1989. "Understanding by addressees and overhearers." *Cognitive Psychology* 21: 211–232.

Speier, Hans. 1998. "Wit and politics: An essay on laughter and power." Transl. Robert Jackall. *American Journal of Sociology* 103: 1352–1401.

Stocking, Holly and Zillmann, Dolf. 1976. "Effects of humorous disparagement of self, friend and enemy." *Psychological Reports* 39: 455–461.

Thomas, Jenny. 1986. *The Dynamics of Discourse: A Pragmatic Analysis of Confrontational Interaction*. Unpublished PhD thesis, Lancaster University, Lancaster, United Kingdom.

Tolson, Andrew. 2006. *Media Talk: Spoken Discourse on TV and Radio*. Edinburgh: Edinburgh University Press.

Veale, Tony, Feyaerts, Kurt and Brône, Geert. 2006. "The cognitive mechanisms of adversarial humour." *Humour: International Journal of Humour Research* 19: 305–340.

Watts, Richard. 1991. *Power in Family Discourse* [Contributions to the Sociology of Language 63]. New York/Berlin: Mouton de Gruyter.

Weise, Richard. 1999. "Partisan perception of political humour." *Humour: International Journal of Humour Research* 9: 199–207.

Weizman, Elda. 2008. *Positioning in Media Dialogue Negotiating Roles in the News Interview* [Dialogue Studies 3]. Amsterdam/Philadephia: John Benjamins.

Yarwood, Dean. 2001. "When Congress makes a joke: Congressional humour as serious and purposeful communication." *Humour: International Journal of Humour Research* 14: 359–394.

Zillmann, Dolf. 1983. "Disparagement humour." In *Handbook of Humour Research*, vol. 1, Paul McGhee and Jeffrey Goldstein (eds), 85–107. New York: Springer-Verlag.

Zillmann, Dolf and Cantor, Joanne. 1976. "A disposition theory of humour and mirth." In *Humour and Laughter: Theory, Research, and Applications*, Andrew Chapman and Hugh Foot (eds), 93–116. New Brunswick, NJ: Transaction.

Zillmann, Dolf and Stocking, Holly. 1976. "Putdown humour." *Journal of Communication* 26: 154–163.

Ziv, Avner. 1984. *Personality and Sense of Humour*. New York: Springer.

PART II

Political humour in the media

CHAPTER 6

Political satire dies last

A study on democracy, opinion formation, and political satire

Diana Elena Popa
Dunărea de Jos University of Galați, Romania

The present study reinforces the claim that humour can hardly work as a corrective for poor political behaviour and cannot inspire reform. Subsequently, it can merely function as a medium for protest and critique, which are incontestable inherent elements for a democratic society. Therefore, the study would like to bring forth the role of political satire in the media, which can be overtly or covertly expressed, and argue that its disappearance is dangerous, potentially leading to lack of public participation and political apathy, which, in turn, could erode the democratic health of a fairly young post-Communist society, such as Romania. The data under analysis is extracted from an original Romanian satirical animated cartoon sitcom *The Animated Planet Show*.

> Prime ministers and politicians can be hurt by cartoons, but they should remember the cartoonist's role is not to couch favour or approval. [...] The reputations of the real political giants have not been impaired by the images created by the cartoonists. [...] Great politicians rise above the invective [...].   (Baker 2007: 26)

1. Introduction

Romanians have a long history of using political humour to their advantage. In Communist times, humour was for Romanians, as for other neighbouring Socialist countries, a mode for expressing their passive resistance and, to some extent, acts of tacit rebellion. The huge anti-Communist jokelore had no other means of transmission and circulation than individual, private performance of jokes at home or anywhere else that qualified as a "safe", Securitate-free environment.[1]

After 1989, there was, for a few years, an obvious and fairly abrupt decrease in the number of political jokes as a natural consequence of the fact that political humour had become legitimate. When people stopped telling jokes against the Communist regime, the processes of political joke transmission and circulation were disrupted. In recent years, the media has successfully undertaken the role of transmitting political humour. The status of such humour has changed; from a resistance tool, it has turned into a commercial mass market product as Romania has quickly changed from a totalitarian regime to a competitive market economy and a parliamentary democracy. In fact, the situation was similar for all former Communist countries that had to switch from Communism to capitalism in a very short period of time (see Strukov 2007: 135) and to learn how to redefine the relation between citizens, representatives, and the government (see also Bennett 2003).

The media is currently the most significant channel for message transmission: it constitutes "the sites where politics and public life are played out, the sites where the meanings of public life are generated, debated and evaluated" (Craig 2004: 4). Moreover, we live in a mediated world; the "mediated public life" indicates the kind of social relationships between public figures and the public, as the public does not often directly encounter politicians and public issues, but rather media images, representations, and stories about those politicians and public issues. When working to reproduce dominant understanding of issues and events, the media as a "knowledge or knowledge-processing" institution (Cottle 1998: 8) succeeds in making social problems visible to the public. In other words, the meaning of politics is partly determined by the everyday situations in which political issues and debates are interpreted. Furthermore, the communicative forms of the media have often blurred the distinction between private and public, and between factual and fictional representation.

The use of political humour in the media, and in television in particular, enacts an active and sharp process of questioning and critique, an "ongoing scrutiny of public life" (Craig 2004: 4) that manages to animate the democratic health of post-Communist contemporary Romanian society. In fact, satire is no longer simply an occasional style, it is its own genre[2] and today's class of satire TV forms a key part of televised political culture (Gray et al. 2009). Moreover, the use of

---

1.   See Speier (1998) and Popa (2002, 2003). For a more extensive study, see Davies (2007) and Krikmann and Laineste (2009).

2.   The democratic tradition of ridiculing and teasing politicians enjoys a long and honourable heritage (see among others Müller 1995; Rose 2001; Lockyer 2006; Watters this volume).

entertainment techniques to reach the popular voter is not a corruption of previously pure political communication but rather constitutionally required by the very form of modern representative democracy (Hartley 2007: 25).

Consequently, the current study is based on the premises that popular culture and in this case specifically entertainment television can be a forum for political activity (Street 1997, 2001), where citizen engagement with politics is more frequently textual than organizational or participatory in the traditional sense (Jones 2010). Television entertainment formats, satire TV included, perform a public function representing and teaching aspects of contemporary citizenship to vast cross-demographic populations, which Hartley (1999, 2007) identified as *democratainment*. *Democratainment*, *politicotainment* (Riegert 2007), or *entertaining politics* (Jones 2010), all articulate and direct emotions and stimulate people to describe, reflect, and fantasize about politics thereby providing tools, if not motivation, for citizenship (van Zoonen 2005). In other words, the present study is another privileged example in understanding the function of satire in contemporary democratic societies (see also Watters this volume).

More specifically, this chapter will examine satirical political animations, a media form that combines verbal satirical discourse with a type of visual opinion representation. According to Maggio (2007), 20th and 21st century versions of cartoons help create a subversive way of understanding the world because "cartooning has an inherent element of democracy to it: democracy based on cognitive freedom forms a basis of democratic individualism" (2007: 238). The field of politics is complex and bewildering, and cartoons offer a way of explaining the significance of real life events and characters through the means of an imaginary scenario (El Refaie 2009: 176). More than that, animated cartoons as a form of multimodal metaphor, in Forceville's (2009) acceptance of the term, are employed to pursue a range of communicative goals: to explain things to people, to persuade people, and to propagate a critical stance towards a certain topic. The working hypothesis for the present paper is that political satirical animations, as semiotic domain (Tsakona 2009: 1171), perform four distinct yet equally important functions in the contemporary democratic Romanian political setting or any other liberal democracy, for that matter:[3]

---

3. The political as subject matter in the service of entertainment is nothing new for politics as drama (Jones 2010: 14), and as such it has always had entertainment value for individuals, communities, and the nation. Such examples range from ancient times to contemporary world (see Riegert 2007). However, the content and form of political satire have only relatively recently aroused academic interest and mostly in the United States (see among others Baym 2005; Brewer and Marquardt 2007; Gaines 2007; Warner 2007; Gray et al. 2009; Jones 2010). The British *Spitting Image*, for instance, has been scarcely looked into (Wagg and Strinati 1992).

a. They offer the public a tool for deliberating on present conditions, as they provide metalanguage for discourse about the social and political order (Greenberg 2002:1).
b. They become a potential source of political information acquisition by bringing forth what no other medium could openly transmit or is "too timid to say" (Gray et al. 2009:4).
c. They constitute an ongoing scrutiny of public life, and thus could possibly work as a corrective for the poor social and political behaviour; they might also inspire reform (Nilsen and Nilsen 2000).
d. If nothing else, they at least function as a medium for protest and critique (Terdiman 1985:152) against such inappropriate "public behaviour" through their evaluative communicative function.

In what follows, Section 2 will take a closer look at the structure and content of *The Animated Planet Show* bringing forth its original yet internationally acknowledged format of animated satirical political cartoons. Further on, Sections 3 and 4 will test the working hypothesis of the present study, which relates to the functions of political satirical animations in liberal democracies. While Section 3 illustrates the main targets of political humour, Section 4 deals, in more detail, with political humour mechanisms in multimodal contexts. Finally, Section 5 includes an outline of the main concluding remarks regarding the potential impact and the role played by political satirical shows in today's democratic societies.

2. *The Animated Planet Show*'s structure and content: A brief overview

The corpus of the present study consists of 14 episodes of the 2007–2008 season of *The Animated Planet Show* (original title *Animat Planet Show*; see Figure 2).

This sitcom is unique both in form and content: it is the only Romanian political parody that utilises 2D computer animations. The show was first broadcast in 2005. The team that worked on the project was made up of the *Divertis* group, a very popular and extremely successful political satirical group that was founded in 1981,[4] and a few external collaborators that helped with both the cartoons and the scripts (for a detailed list of producers, script writers, and characters, see *The Animat Planet Show* 2008). During its run, the show received record

---

4. The fact that *Divertis* was founded in 1981 is highly relevant because it means that they started their stage performances in Communist times, under Ceauşescu. Their work has ever since been identified as an act of protest against the ruling political system and a form of rebellion against politicians' foibles and abuses.

Figure 2. *The Animated Planet Show* icon for the 2007–2008 season

ratings ranging from 7.2 to 8.9 (according to *Divertis audienţa-record* 2006; see also Lazăr 008).

Perhaps the first internationally acknowledged show of the genre is the British *Spitting Image* (1984–1996). Although not running for such a long time, the Australian *Rubbery Figures* (1984–1990) and the German *Hurra Deutschland* (1987–1991) were equally popular in their countries of origin. France had *Le Bébête Show* and *Les Guignols de l'Info*, Italy *Teste di Gomma*, Portugal *Contra Informação*, Spain *Las Noticias del Guiñol*, Switzerland *Les Bouffons de la Confédération* and Sweden *Riksorganet*. A certain number of countries adopted the very same format of the British *Spitting Image* such as New Zealand with *Public Eye* (1980s), Chile with *Los Toppins* and *31 Minutos* which satirized national politicians. In the case of Japan, *Spitting Image Japan* was a direct copy of the British show both in terms of format and name, and again targeting national politics. In some other countries though, such as the United States and Greece, the local versions of *Spitting Image*, *Spitting Image: Down and Out in the White House* and *ΦΤΥΣΤΟΥΣ* respectively, were not so popular. In South Africa, *Za News* was banned due to controversial content. So was the Russian *Kukly*, which had to close down in 2002 after pressure from the Kremlin. Other former Communist East European countries which have similar satirical national shows are Bulgaria, Czech Republic, Hungary, Poland, and Serbia. Finally, even closer to the Romanian version are the 2D and 3D computer animations shows in Britain *2DTV*, Canada *Et Dieu Créa… Laflaque*, and Finland *The Autocrats*.

When speaking about the name of the sitcom, Toni Grecu, the founder of *Divertis* and the initiator of *The Animated Planet Show* project, expressed his strong belief that the show was the cartoon animated version of what Romania stands for (see Păduraru 2008). What the sitcom set out to accomplish was a parody of today's Romania and its public life, in which politics plays a major part. Interestingly, *The Animated Planet Show* managed to perfectly illustrate the present mediated public life that contemporary societies experience and in which the public generally do not directly encounter politicians and public issues but rather representations and stories about them.

This "mediated" social relationship between the public and public figures is illustrated in the cartoon at two distinct levels: fictional and factual. The fictional level refers to the story level involving both characters and the plot. The Meşteru family, the main characters of the sitcom, all have the same hobby, namely watching television. For them, watching TV is not merely a way of relaxing or spending their spare time, but is literally a means of escaping reality, since the TV set allows them to experience whichever reality best suits them, be it a football match, a political reunion, or a talk-show. Hence they become active participants in a TV-mediated reality. The factual level is related to what the audience feels while watching this satirical cartoon. The cartoon heroes reflect the values and convictions of the Romanian common people, thus allowing them to identify themselves with the presented types, situations, or background. The image of reality reflected in the cartoons, however, "is not always exclusively anchored in the actual reality but often transmits instead an idealised and incisive image of everyday life" (Ginman and von Ungern-Sternberg 2003:71). Furthermore, by constructing idealisations of the world, *The Animated Planet Show* reframes political issues, thus offering a tool for deliberating on present socialpolitical conditions.

The 2007–2008 season which was broadcast weekly was made up of 14 episodes consisting of more than 230 minutes of animations that were stored and archived. As mentioned above, the show presented the stories of a fictional, yet supposedly authentic, Romanian working class family. The very names Ana and Manole Meşteru are symbolic in that they evoke two characters in one of the oldest Romanian ballads, *Meşterul Manole* ("Manole, the Master Builder"). *Meşteru*, which means "master builder", is the family name used for the main characters. The parody is innocuous though, as the ballad itself is not the object of ridicule.

Figure 3. Version of *The Animated Planet Show*

The family is made up of Manole Meşteru, the ever drunk couch potato father that works as a house painter, his wife Ana, who is unemployed and spends all her time watching TV, Vicky, the 16-year-old daughter who must deal with teenage problems, and Matilda, Manole's mother-in-law who also loves drinking and watching TV. Last but not least, there is the family pet, Gina, a white hen that lives with the family and shares their passion for watching TV (see Figure 3).

All other characters that are considered episodic are contemporary public figures ranging from politicians to artists, and from TV stars and journalists to sports personalities. The 2007–2008 season introduces 86 Romanian contemporary public figures, three famous national historical figures, and five international politicians, as shown in Table 2.

The fact that over half (55.2%) of the episodic characters are (national and international) politicians comes as no surprise since *The Animated Planet Show* has been conceived as a primarily political satirical show from its inception.

It is also worth noting that while the Manoles and all the bit-part characters are fully drawn cartoons, all public figures are a complex mixture of real images

Table 2. List of episodic characters

Public figures	Categories	No.	%
International	Politicians	5	5.3
Historical	Former rulers of historical Romania or ancient Dacia	3	3.1
Contemporary	Politicians	44	46.8
	Media persons (TV stars and journalists)	25	26.5
	Athletes	11	11.7
	Artists	6	6.3
Total		94	100

and drawings: real pictures of those characters' faces come attached to caricatural representations of their bodies. The voices of the cartoon characters are either those of the *Divertis* group, who imitate the original voices, or the public figures' actual voices, which are further processed and "attached" to the cartoons. The projected political personhood is hence achieved at three distinct yet interrelated levels, such as they were identified by Corner (2003: 68):

a. iconically – which displays the demeanour, posture, and associative contexts of the political self;
b. vocally – voice identification;
c. kinetically – relating to the political self in action.

The Animated Planet Show belongs to the sitcom genre, since it is a fictional narrative series in which an impossible and insoluble situation reveals new comic possibilities in each episode (Holland 2000: 115). Although the comedy may be resolved in each episode, the situation is never resolved (Fiske 1987: 144). As a satirical political show, it is meant to be funny, yet the purpose is not solely humour in itself, but also the intent to bring about improvement or change to the corrupt and dishonest political life. In fact, as Teng (2009: 207) points out, a generic convention of cartooning is to include a critical stance towards a particular sociopolitical situation, event or person. Even so, satire "is not obliged to solve what is perceived as a problem or replace what is satirically disassembled or unmasked with a solution" (Quintero 2007: 4).

Usually, there was a delay between the actual time of writing the script – including all the latest political and public life events – and the time of broadcasting, between which the contents of the show need to be kept well hidden. This was due to the hard work required to produce such political cartoons. Davidson (2003: 5) notes that

> certainly the daily effort first to abstract the gist of separate political slips, shocks and staggers as they happen; then to correlate these to the larger global

disturbances; and finally to comment satirically upon their significance before they have passed from "topicality" altogether, makes what would otherwise be a pleasant profession into an exacting one.

It is also pointed out that political cartoons "must of necessity cultivate foresight, learn to measure events and anticipate their consequences in time to meet them punctually when they happen" (Davidson 2003:5), or even be cautionary prophetic and idealistically visionary (see Quintero 2007:2). Davidson's comments are confirmed by the people who work on *The Animated Planet Show*. T. Grecu reveals that, while the writing of the script takes a few days, the process of drawing the cartoons may take up to three weeks (see Rădulescu 2008). If, however, the creators of such shows fail to comply with timeliness and topicality, their shows will fail in offering the tool for deliberation on current sociopolitical conditions.

3.   Political satire, parody, and "pasquinaded" politicians

In what follows, I will focus on the content of *The Animated Planet Show* and attempt to test the working hypothesis. Since political satirical shows are public media entertainment, they may work as a pasquinade in which political figures are publicly lampooned and mocked. As Paletz (1990:483) rightly points out,

> offering abundant targets to laugh at and about, authority is a perpetual source of humour. Some of the subjects are perennial: ruler's foibles, self-importance, chicanery, corruption, scandals and blunders. Then there are policies: these may be inept from the start, or be made so through incompetent execution.

Humorist T. Grecu acknowledges that "politics is the most important source of inspiration for humorists" (Rădulescu 2008). His statement is confirmed by the empirical data which indicates that 55.31% of the total number of characters in the 2007–2008 season of the show under examination target politicians (see Table 2).

The *Animated Planet Show* resorts to two distinct satirical strategies: an *overt* and a *covert* strategy. What I call here an *overt satirical strategy* is an instant process that is easily acknowledged as such by the public: the Manole family strongly and openly criticises various other characters and phenomena in politics, the media, or public life in general. Concomitantly, the show makes use of a *covert satirical strategy* that conjoins the private and the public: on the one hand, *The Animated Planet* parodies modern family life by taking its assumptions to the extreme; and, on the other hand, it exposes the ridicule of the actions of politicians and other public figures by taking all their statements and purported beliefs to their furthest supposedly logical conclusion, revealing their hypocrisy and stupidity.

Figure 4. Manole and Vicky, his daughter, trying to study in the kitchen
(*Animat Planet Show* 2007b)

The following example parodies the ideal traditional life, hence it can be considered an overt satirical strategy (see Figure 4):[5]

(1)   Acasă la Manole. În bucătărie Vicky încearcă din greu să-şi facă temele. În
      spatele ei este televizorul. Manole intră şi se aşează la masa din bucătărie.
      Deschide televizorul. Fata se încruntă:
      – Băi, nene! Mă deranjezi! Lasa-mă să învăţ! Mă pregătesc pentru Olimpiadă!
      Faza pe clasă.
      – Olimpiadă? Manole se îneacă. Adică înveţi pentru educaţie fizică?
      Fata se încruntă la el.
      – Nu, băi nene! Bate cu pumnii în masă. Auzi?! Educaţie fizică! Băi tată, tare
      incult mai eşti! Olipiadele sunt de tot felul! Sunt întreceri din alea cum erau
      pe vremuri, pe muntele Olimp!
      – Alpinism, adică?!
      – Aoleu, nimic nu ştii! Muntele Olimp e ăla pe care trăiau zeii, băi nene, şi
      conduceau lumea de sus de-acolo! Nu ştii? Zeus?! Gagiul care trăznea pe toţi!
      Trosc! Începe să bată cu pumnii în masă.
      – Prostii dintr-astea vă învaţă pe voi la şcoală? Ăia care conduc lumea sunt
      politicienii, nu zeii! Ha! Ha! Zei?! Na! Uite, să mă trăznească dacă există! Râde
      şi se maimuţăreşte când deodată, din televizor, îl trăzneşte un fulger. Cade la
      pământ.
      (Example 1 taken from the episode on December 2nd, 2007;
      see *Animat Planet Show* 2007b)

---

5.   All transcripts together with their translation into English were done by the author.

Manole's house. In the kitchen, Manole's daughter, Vicky, is trying hard to do her homework. Behind her there is a TV set. Manole enters and sits down. He turns on the TV. The girl frowns at him:

Vicky: "Hey, old champ! You're disturbing me! Let me do my homework! I'm preparing for the Olympiad! It's the class competition!"

Manole: "The Olympiad?" he chokes. "So, you're preparing for the P.E. [i.e. physical education] course?"

The girl frowns at him.

Vicky: "No!" She gets angry and starts hitting the kitchen table with her fists. "What P.E. course? Dad, you're completely backward! Olympiads are of all sorts! They all involve that ancient concept of competition, like those held on Mount Olympus!"

Manole: "You mean mountaineering?!"

Vicky: "You know nothing of this! Mount Olympus is where the Greek Gods were supposed to live, man! And they ruled the world from up there! You don't know Zeus? It's that guy who struck down everybody! Bang! Bang! Bang!" she starts hitting the kitchen table again.

Manole: "Is this what they teach you at school, all this rubbish? The ones that rule the world are the politicians, not gods!" He laughs. "Imagine, gods! Let them strike me down now if they really exist!" He laughs and makes faces when all of a sudden he falls down, struck by lightening coming from the TV set.

In Example (1), Vicky would like to study and prepare her school tasks, whereas her father, contrary to normal behaviour, disturbs her. Moreover, the father is shown as lacking the knowledge and consciousness of elementary information gained through school education. Thus, the show parodies the traditional parent model in which the parent is normally more knowledgeable than his/her children and is able to meet the children's thirst for knowledge. Instead, Manole starts criticizing the school system for not teaching students about "real life" and, most importantly, for not providing the young with the ability to meet the challenges of real life.

The parody of the traditional family takes a sudden turn: it becomes a covert satirical strategy that relies on the unstated, yet context-emerging verbo-pictorial simile "politicians are like gods". This will further develop in the rest of the show into a thoroughly drawn analogy between specific contemporary Romanian political figures (e.g. the President of Romania, the Prime Minister, the leaders of opposing parties) and the Greek Gods, all acting naturally in an imaginary make-believe scenario.

Figure 5. Ana, Gina, and Ion Iliescu in the Romanian Parliament
(*Animat Planet Show* 2007a)

In the next example, the ridicule of the actions of politicians[6] arises as their statements are taken to the furthest logical conclusion, revealing their hypocrisy (see Figure 5):

(2)   Ana, care lucrează ca femeie de serviciu la Parlament, se întâlneşte cu Ion Iliescu.
– Domnule Iliescu! Chiar voiam sa vorbesc cu dvs. Că sunteţi mai apropriat de oamenii din popor. N-aţi putea să-l angajaţi si pe bărbate-meu, Manole, aici? Zidar, zugrav, şofer..orice?! Orice!
– Să vedem! Să vedem! răspunde Iliescu ezitînd. E un moment dificil! Noi parlamentarii am decis să ne reducem cheltuielile să ducem o viaţă spartană. Se întoarce şi pleacă. Mai vorbim că sunt grăbit!

(Example 2 taken from the episode on October 7th, 2007;
see Animat Planet Show 2007a)

Ana who is working as a cleaning lady in the House of Parliament meets Ion Iliescu.
Ana: "Oh, I'm so glad to see you! I meant to talk to you about something! You have always been closer to the people! Could you please hire my husband, Manole, to work here? He could be a builder, house painter, driver, or anything you want him to be! Anything at all?!"
Iliescu hesitating: "We'll see! We'll see!" hesitating again. "Rough times for us, too! We, parliamentarians, have decided to cut down on our expenses and

---

6. For information on the politicians and political parties appearing in the examples discussed, see Appendix I at the end of the chapter.

live a Spartan life", he states as he turns his back and leaves. "We'll talk about it some other time! I'm in a hurry now!"

The mere juxtaposition of the words *parlamentarii* "parliamentarians" and *viață spartană* "Spartan life" in the same sentence produces a hilarious effect. Moreover, a politician who is supposedly closer to the people, Ion Iliescu, proves to be no better than the others, and symbolically turns his back, indifferent to ordinary people and their requests.

Pastiche, another important satirical component, in its postmodernist sense is also used for satirical purposes in the show (Rose 1983, 1991). In *The Animated Planet Show*, we can easily identify the skeletal form of well-known (fairy) tales (e.g. *The Three Little Piglets, Cinderella, Little Red Riding Hood, The Goods of Greece* previously illustrated), novels and plays (e.g. *The Jungle Book* and *Robinson Crusoe, The King Lear*), or movies (e.g. *300, Rocky, The Matrix Trilogy, Titanic, How the Grinch Stole Christmas*). Although placed in a new context, they are not the object of the ridicule. Instead, the pastiche creates the context for the target of the satirical show, namely contemporary political life.

In sum, whether overtly or covertly expressed, political satire in the show has political authority as its main target. The former level is represented by the individual seeking or occupying a position of authority (e.g. I. Iliescu in Example (2)). The latter pertains to:

a. The authority position itself (e.g. the President of Romania in the *Gods of Greece* episode, see the discussion of Example (1)).

b. The institution housing the position, such as the parliament (e.g. Example (2)).

c. The policies that a person promotes or is identified with (e.g. humouring voters with false promises or lying to their faces, as in Example (2); see also the *Robinson Crusoe* episode, *Three Little Piglets,* or *300*).

d. The political system as a whole (e.g. Examples (1)–(3); see also the *300* episode).

The next section of the present chapter will deal with what I consider to be the primary humour[7] techniques used in The Animated Planet Show to achieve political satire.

---

7. Humour, in the present study, is to be perceived as an umbrella term covering all related phenomena (including parody and satire) and incongruity is the common denominator of all these phenomena (see Tsakona and Popa this volume).

4. Humour techniques in *The Animated Planet Show*

In the data under examination, three general categories of humour techniques could be identified: audio-visual techniques, language-based techniques, and the category where audio-visual and language-based techniques interact (see Table 3; for a general list of humour techniques, see Berger 1998; Buijzen and Valkenburg 2004).

The following Example (3) shows how these techniques are combined and function in this political satirical animation. When analyzing and discussing the function of such techniques, it is necessary to take both a cognitive and a pragmatic point of view. In particular, we intend to focus on the multimodal metaphorical conceptualization and critical stance in terms of what is actually shown in the animated cartoon show, as well as in terms of the cultural and general discourse context. The factual pragmatic knowledge is an essential condition in trying to decode the fine grained interpretations of the animated cartoons.

At the beginning of the episode, where Example (3) is taken from, there is a glamorous atmosphere of an awards ceremony conducted by *The Animated Planet Show* for all politicians who ran in the 2007 elections. All pictorial details (the stage, the red carpet, the big audience, etc.) trigger the awards ceremony scenario which will further involve prototypical relations between objects and members. However, once the title of the awards is announced, the "Cocoa Awards", the satirical show starts to unveil the cluster of humour techniques upon which this

Table 3. List of humour techniques

Audio-visual techniques	Common techniques	Linguistic techniques
chase	absurdity	bombast
clownish behaviour	eccentricity	conceptual surprise
clumsiness	embarrassment	cliché
coincidence	conceptual surprise	frame incongruity
fight	imitation	polysemy
grotesque appearance	infantilism	play on words
ignorance	irreverent behaviour	distorted proverbs/sayings
impersonation	malicious pleasure	sarcasm
peculiar sound	metaphor	witticism
peculiar voice	misunderstanding	
reversed anthropomorphism	repetition	
ridicule	ridicule	
slapstick	rigidity	
sudden appearance/disappearance	sexual allusions	
visual surprise	speed	
	stereotype	

particular show relies. The title of the awards has a scatological connotation that ridicules the election process as well as the same old political figures that ran in the elections. The prize, a golden carrot, which perceptually resembles an authentic awards statue and which is offered to the politicians is ridiculous and constitutes a satirical indicator of what they deserve to be awarded for their personal contributions. The scene under examination develops as follows:

(3) (taken from the episode on December 2nd, 2007; see *Animat Planet Show* 2007b; the original Romanian text appears in Appendix II)
   A voice: "Animated Planet awards a prize to the most animated cartoon-like elections in Romania; here are the nominees for 'These are the people, for them we should vote!' category..."
   The prize is shown as a golden carrot.
   Iliescu and Hrebenciuc come onto the scene. Iliescu is dressed in all red and Hrebenciuc in pink.
   Iliescu: "The results we got are the worst from all elections in which the Social Democratic Party ran. I feel like crying! Hrebe, what are we to do to save our party?" Iliescu nudges Hrebenciuc and Hrebenciuc yawns.
   Hrebenciuc: "If I succeed in getting my boy to marry Băsescu's daughter, the problem is solved. There's going to be a wedding and we will form a coalition with the Democratic Party. We're re-uniting the old NSF [i.e. National Salvation Front] boss!"
   Iliescu: "If you succeed, I'll stand witness! I want to be there for them!"
   Hrebenciuc: "And who will lead the new coalition?"
   Suddenly Geoană appears from nowhere riding a green winged horse.
   Geoană: "Me, of course! I am the leader of the Social Democratic Party! I'm high up!" He pretends to be flying with his hands high up above his head.
   Iliescu: "You are high all right!" Iliescu hits the horse that neighs and disappears. "Poor him! He's talking nonsense!"
   Prizes begin to be awarded:
   A voice: "On number three, the Bronze Medal goes to the National Liberal Party because they are still running in the elections, although they get chicks for being members of the government!"
   The audience shouts: "The Social Democratic Party isn't dead yet!"
   Tăriceanu enters the stage, on his motorcycle. He's all dressed up. "We have 13% of the total votes and we still rule, and the Democrat Party has 30% but do not. That feels good! Only the Democratic Liberal Party got on my nerves because they stole our votes!"
   Flutur comes in hopping and with his ears in the shape of butterfly wings.
   Flutur: "Hm... you wanted us to wait and see? You made us, loser! We all thank you!" He starts laughing scornfully.

The audience members applaud.

A voice: "The next winner is the Social Democratic Party, who should be happy to receive the Silver Medal!"

Geoană comes in on his green winged horse.

Geoană: "Listen, I have a confession to make! We're going to merge with the Democratic Party and I will be the leader of the Democratic Social Democratic Party! He raises his hands up showing the victory sign. Hrebe is planning the wedding!"

Iliescu: "Look at that fool! He blabs out our secret! Viorel, we need to meet for an extraordinary congress. He is ruining the Romanian left wing!"

Geoană: "I am the engine of this party! Come on now, let's go!" speaking to his horse. "I'll show them all to my party! Come on now, old rip!"

The horse: "Oh, don't you dare call me an old rip!" The horse makes Geoană fall off his back and says: "Enough! The political campaign is over! Green horses are now free to rest until the next elections. The horse neighs and takes off from the stage".

[…]

Băsescu enters the stage pumping up the orange logo of the Democratic Party.

A voice: "First Prize goes to the Democratic Party! The Party that rocks!" Meanwhile the logo blows up.

Videanu enters the stage dressed up as a construction worker. He holds a shovel in his hands.

Videanu: "I'm sorry I came dressed up like this, but we've started working on the tunnel that will clear away the traffic in Bucharest!"

Someone from the audience shouts:

"Where are you digging, Mr. Mayor?"

"Under the Tăriceanu government, where else if not there? That's where it got stuck. Thank you for the medal! We deserve to win! We are the best!"

"Băse is the best, uncle Videanu!" Someone from the audience starts shouting.

"Without Băse, the engine, you are nothing!"

Videanu: "You are wrong! Mr. President is not the engine of our Party!"

In the audience, someone says: "You're right! He's the entire train!"

A steam engine comes onto the stage and runs over Videanu. Băsescu is in the steam engine dressed up as the ticket inspector.

Băsescu: "All aboard! The passenger train for Cotroceni – the House of Parliament – Victoria Square leaves the station! All other parties are required to wait for us to go". He laughs. "I love to be the engine! I will run over everybody!" He laughs scornfully and mimics a train whistle with his lips.

[…]

Elena Udrea is also on the train.

Udrea: "Hmmm, Traian! I love when you are steaming! Go on, steam some more! Hmmm!"

Băsescu: "Hold on to your seat, Elena!"

The train leaves the station.

The first scene opens with Ion Iliescu and Victor Hrebenciuc talking. They have been identified as the two most important political figures in the Social Democratic Party, even though, officially, Mircea Geoană is the leader. I. Iliescu is all dressed up in red, an evocative colour for his former Communist identity. V. Hrebenciuc is dressed in pink, which is meant to illustrate his eccentric nature. The two characters start talking about the poor results the Social Democratic Party scored in the 2007 elections. Nonetheless, they seem to find the right solution for getting out of trouble: to get V. Hrebenciuc's son to marry President Traian Băsescu's daughter. Their wedding is possible, but not yet probable. The wedding is then metaphorically used for a significant political act, namely the coalition between I. Iliescu's Social Democratic Party and T. Băsescu's favourite party, the Democratic Party. The wedding metaphor is not visually represented in the cartoon but rather used to address the pressing issue of a conceptually incongruous political coalition between the right and the left wing. In fact, it seems that the opposition has been toying with the idea of such a coalition as a long-term solution, since it would give them the opportunity to exercise greater control over those in power. When it comes to who will be the leader of such a coalition, another humour technique is used, namely the sudden appearance. M. Geoană comes out of nowhere, clumsy and infantile, and makes a bombast remark that he is the only one entitled to lead the coalition. The surprise works at the audio-visual level, as he appears riding a green winged horse (see Figure 6). He talks nonsense and

Figure 6. Ion Iliescu and Mircea Geona riding the green horse
(*Animat Planet Show* 2007b)

behaves foolishly, an attitude which in Romanian is rendered by the phrase *cai verzi pe pereți* "green horses on the wall". At the same time, the dialogue exchange that M. Geoană has with I. Iliescu is a play on words using the very same phrase.

The next part of the show dealing with the National Liberal Party uses several humour techniques: teasing, ridicule, and absurdity. Speed, as a technique, plays its own part in the present show. The frames move quickly, and whenever one stingy remark targets a certain politician or group/party, another remark is made to target a different politician or group. This happens when someone from the public shouts out loud that the Social Democratic Party is not dead.

The Prime Minister Călin Popescu Tăriceanu will not be forgotten. He comes on stage on his motorcycle, wearing a top hat. He is considered to be a gentleman in politics and to possess eccentric hobbies. The stereotypical image of the top hat is symbolic of what Romanians perceived of C. P. Tăriceanu's not too firm, yet accurate, political acts. However, his passion for motorcycles has often brought him both physical and ethical[8] problems. C. P. Tăriceanu's discourse is sprinkled with elements that indicate absurdity and malicious pleasure, as well as a touch of infantilism when talking about his political colleagues.

Gheorghe Flutur is graphically represented as a human being that has butterfly ears coincident with his name Flutur, which means "butterfly". In the present study, I shall call this humour technique *reversed anthropomorphism*, that is to say, humans acquire animal features. However, the characters' faces are left human and even though they have animal bodies, they preserve all their human features.[9] G. Flutur's lines include irreverent behaviour, sarcasm, and hostility. His malicious humour[10] is rendered through audio-visual techniques – the peculiar sound of scornful laughter and the gestures accompanying his words.

The Social Democratic Party is called on stage to receive the Silver Medal. Here again, M. Geoană makes his unexpected appearance on the same green horse. Visually, M. Geoană's movements are clownish. He is being ridiculed in the show for his clumsiness and inappropriate behaviour in the political world. M. Geoană reintroduces, in a fairly ambiguous yet relevant manner, the wedding metaphor.

---

8. The former Prime Minister C. P. Tăriceanu had a motorcycle accident in July 2006 which triggered intense public debates at that time.

9. The visual context of this creature reminds us of Forceville's (2002) hybrid metaphors that cue both animal and human elements.

10. The use of malicious or aggressive humour by politicians is – in Dynel's (this volume) words – a provocative strategy geared towards amusing the audience.

On the other hand, I. Iliescu's comments emphasise his open embarrassment and disappointment. I. Iliescu's words are meant to ridicule his own spontaneous reaction to any political act: as a former Communist leader, he knows that he needs to organise an extraordinary congress of the Social Democratic Party. I. Iliescu also exaggerates when saying that M. Geoană will ruin the entire Romanian left wing.

M. Geoană's bombastic discourse is ridiculed. He also manifests malicious pleasure when speaking about what he might do to his party colleagues. M. Geoană is showed as being full of pent-up anger and he gives vent to his frustration by calling his imaginary horse names. However, the green winged horse disapproves with M. Geoană's gruffness and upset by its rider's ungratefulness decides to go on vacation until the next elections begin.

T. Băsescu's presence on the stage pumping up the Democrat's logo is also a visual metaphor. Here the political act implied is the unofficial and illegal help that the Democratic Party received from President T. Băsescu, hence emphasizing an issue that might otherwise go unnoticed.

Next, Andriean Videanu's entrance onto the stage is visually dominated by his construction worker outfit. He is being ridiculed here for having succeeded in creating chaotic traffic in Bucharest. The mayorship and traffic in Bucharest were equally considered to be the worst under A. Videanu. Exaggeration is used here as a humour technique meant to achieve the satirical effect. The shovel is definitely too small to be used for digging a tunnel in order to "clear out" the traffic in Bucharest. Furthermore, A. Videanu's discourse is bombastic, yet he seems to completely ignore the magnitude of the disaster created by his incompetence. Through the technique of frame opposition, the show then reveals another "quality" possessed by A. Videanu: that of the usurper of C. P. Tăriceanu's government. A pun is created here relying on the polysemous word *a săpa* "to dig", which can be used, depending on the context, for "digging", as well as for "undermining someone's position". Last but not least, the use of the familiar *nea* "uncle" as a form of address instead of *domnul* "mister" targets A. Videanu, as an individual seeking to occupy a position of authority for which he was not ready or right.

The use of the nickname *Băse* for President T. Băsescu also targets him as an individual: one of T. Băsescu's most typical political campaign strategies aimed at showing that he was not like other politicians who spoke *to* the people, but not *with* the people. Therefore, he enjoyed going to public places and pretending to be "a nice fellow" whom all could come to and speak with about what was bothering them.

At this point in the show, another multimodal metaphor is introduced, namely President T. Băsescu as an engine. He is identified as an engine for two distinct reasons: he is the engine of the Democratic Party that keeps the party alive, and he is also the engine that runs over anybody and everybody. Here, T. Băsescu is ridiculed for being a president that does not comply with any regulations and who does only what he wants. The metaphor is intrinsically supported by the naming of the three main destinations that the Băsescu engine never fails to reach: Cotroceni, namely the presidential residence, the House of Parliament, and Victoria Square, where the government residence is.

The example ends with an open sexual allusion from Elena Udrea to President T. Băsescu and a hint at the supposed relationship between the President and E. Udrea, a fervent member of the Liberal Democratic Party.

As illustrated by Example (3), *The Animat Planet Show* is undeniably a rich source of entertainment. However, the internal mechanisms ranging from incongruity and surprise to satire and pastiche, from teasing and ridicule to sarcasm and hostility, activate a whole gamut of emotions on the part of the audience towards the political self and political engagement. Situational themes, such as the awards ceremony presented above, make the connection to a non-political event which is used by cartoonists to domesticate the political world (Conners 2005). The rhetorical fantasia (Edwards 2001) advanced by the cartoonists in their metaphors about the Romanian political life is meant to keep the audience on their toes regarding weighty political matters in a way that allows them to withstand pressure, but which also stimulates them to reflect and fantasize about politics. This is highly relevant in the context of a young post-Communist society, such as Romania, where there was a need for an institutionalized humorous genre which should be able to debunk politicians for their glaring errors, open hostility, empty promises, feeble excuses, and harebrained schemes.

5.   The end of the show and some concluding remarks

All in all, *The Animated Planet*, as illustrated by the Examples (1)–(3), provides valuable evidence that the first two hypotheses stated in the present study are valid: the show does offer the public a tool for deliberating on present conditions, as it provides metalanguage for discourse about the social and political order in the Romanian private (Examples (1)–(2)) and public life (Example (3)). The show also provides information about political issues, events, and players, and offers the audience the mental maps of the political and social world outside their direct experience.

More specifically, the animations constitute a means for the transmission of messages that no other medium could openly transmit at that time: the facts that I. Iliescu and V. Hrebenciuc are the ones who are pulling the strings in the Social Democratic Party; that the Social Democrats were secretly planning to form a conceptually incongruous coalition with the Democrats; that President T. Băsescu, although not legally and ethically, was indeed the engine of a political party (the Democratic Party); that A. Videanu had been an incompetent Mayor of Bucharest, etc. It is worth noting here that no matter how hilarious, exaggerated, and fictitious the information provided by the animation show appeared to be at that time, it proved to be politically accurate as the coalition between the two parties did form almost two years later. More importantly, politicians on both sides did acknowledge that the talks between the two sides had started two years before it happen, which is precisely when the satirical show first mentioned it. In other words, the show produced a "centrifugal push of political information" (Jones 2010: 4) and the broadcasting channel has demonstrated that they were willing to take programming risks that other channels never would, and thus expand the audience's understanding of how democracy can be viewed and understood through alternative narratives about politics.

In spite of its entertainment qualities, the political satirical show *Animated Planet* informed its audience and elicited participation (see the ratings in Section 2) and debate (mostly on blogs and forums): the show worked as a true source of political information and knowledge that no other media formats were at that time able to provide, in the form of reliable, referential cognizance of the sociopolitical world (Dahlgren 2003), and performed successfully as a powerful formulator of opinions. Nevertheless, given the acerbity of the political class and perhaps the lack of a Romanian tradition in satirical lampooning, the show could only temporarily function as an institutionalized humorous genre, such as it is identified by Kuipers (2008), where cartoonists are permitted, and actually expected, to articulate truths that would be degrading for politicians and their actions (see also Tsakona 2011).

In short, the functions performed by the satire TV genre could be reduced to the following:

a. It facilitates message transmission for current affairs.
b. It recalls and identifies potential errors in political life, thus facilitating the process of establishing connections between people and events in public life.
c. It draws attention through exaggeration and emphasis on issues that may otherwise go unnoticed.
d. It identifies and acknowledges the actors in certain political issues.
e. It helps the audience perceive and comprehend the implications of certain political acts performed by the politicians.

Although the satirical show turned out to be an ongoing scrutiny of contemporary public life, as time has shown, it was unable to work as a corrective for poor social and political behaviour. It was also unable to inspire reform. In contrast, politicians were the ones who tried to reform the show. In early 2008, when E. Udrea was represented as Eve and drawn naked by the cartoonists of the show, she considered the show to have gone too far. Consequently, she expressed her indignation electronically on her blog, where she also threatened the show's producers with a lawsuit if they did not stop "misrepresenting" her. The producers' response was prompt and firm: they would rather stop working on the show than reform it.

On October 2008, at the very beginning of their 2008-2009 season, and one month before the 2008 Romanian parliamentary elections, the producers of the show were officially informed that due to the economic crisis *The Animated Planet Show* would no longer be broadcast on Antena 1. The real reason for the ending of the show was revealed a bit later (cf. Calen and Nicoleanu 2008) when the Social Democratic Party admitted that the episode on October 12th, in which the members were depicted as shadowy politicians in a King Lear parody, was too much during the pre-election period. Therefore, they asked that the show be suspended until after the elections. When the show began to broadcast again, after parliamentary elections in November 2008, it did not run until January 2009, as it was supposed to, but stopped in December 2008. It had functioned as a vivid medium for protest and critique, but it had to end. The show had been *reformed*. If the show had not been closed down in 2008, it would have been interesting to see to what extent, in election times, *The Animated Planet Show* could still preserve its reliability as a source of political information and, on the other hand, to what extent it could still construct images of political candidates which established parameters for their campaign messages.

T. Grecu, the initiator of the project, declared during an interview to a national newspaper (Rădulescu 2008) that the show needed to stop because one could not possibly parody a parody. In his opinion, politicians' words and actions were at that time the best purveyors of involuntary humour and was thus something with which *The Animated Planet Show* could not compete. Moreover, he bitterly remarked that due to the trivialisation of politics, entertainment television had eventually passed in the hands of politicians themselves.

Acknowledgments

The author wishes to thank Elisavet Vlachaki for helping with the preparation of the figures included in this chapter.

Primary sources

Animat Planet Show. 2007a. Episode of October 7th, part 1 of 4. http://www.youtube.com/ watch?v=U3FuRti_hz0 (accessed March 17, 2011).

Animat Planet Show. 2007b. Episode of December 2nd, part 1 of 4. http://www.youtube.com/ watch?v=9ZJY8KN2zLg (accessed March 17, 2011).

Animat Planet Show. 2008. The official website. www.animatplanet.ro; http://www.antena1.ro/ index.php?page=showandid=7 (accessed January 8, 2008).

References

Baker, Kenneth. 2007. "Great politicians rise above ridicule." *British Journalism Review* 28: 19–26.

Baym, Geoffrey. 2005. "*The Daily Show*: Discursive integration and the reinvention of political journalism." *Political Communication* 22: 259–276.

Bennett, Lance W. 2003. "Identity, communication and political action in late modern society." In *Media and the Restyling of Politics: Consumerism, Celebrity and Cynicism*, John Corner and Dick Pels (eds), 137–150. London: Sage.

Berger, Arthur A. 1998. *An Anatomy of Humour*. London: New Brunswick: Transaction Publishers.

Brewer, Paul and Marquardt, Emily. 2007. "Mock news and democracy: Analyzing *The Daily Show*." *Atlantic Journal of Communication* 15: 90–99.

Buijzen, Moniek and Valkenburg, Patti M. 2004. "Developing a typology of humour in audio-visual media." *Media Psychology* 6: 147–167.

Calen, Ioana and Nicoleanu, Anca. 2008. "*Animat Planet* băgat în vacanță forțată de PSD" (*Animat Planet* sent on a 'forced' vacation because by the Social Democrats). *Cotidianul.ro*, October 22. http://www.cotidianul.ro/animat_planet_bagat_in_vacanta_fortata_de_psd-61906.html (accessed January 9, 2009). [in Romanian]

Conners, Joan L. 2005. "Visual representations of the 2004 presidential campaign: Political cartoons and popular culture references." *American Behavioral Scientist* 49: 479–487.

Corner, John. 2003. Mediated persona and political culture. In *Media and the Restyling of Politics: Consumerism, Celebrity and Cynicism*, John Corner and Dick Pels (eds), 67–84. London: Sage.

Cottle, Simon. 1998. "Ulrich Beck, 'risk society' and the media: A catastrophic view?" *European Journal of Communication* 13: 5–32.

Craig, Geoffrey. 2004. *The Media, Politics and Public Life*. Crows Nest: Allen and Unwin Academic.

Dahlgren, Peter. 2003. "Reconfiguring civic culture in the New Media Milieu." In *Media and the Restyling of Politics: Consumerism, Celebrity and Cynicism*, John Corner and Dick Pels (eds), 151–170. London: Sage.

Davidson, Jiton Sharmayne. 2003. "Sometimes funny, but most times deadly serious: Amir Baraka as political satirist." *African American Review* 37: 399–405.

Davies, Christie. 2007. "Humour and protest: Jokes under Communism." *International Review of Social History* 52: 291–305.

Divertis audiența-record. 2006. http://www.libertatea.ro/stire/divertis-audienta-record-165467.html (accessed December 21, 2009). [in Romanian]

Edwards, Janis L. 2001. "Running in the shadows in Campaign 2000: Candidate metaphors in editorial cartoons." *American Behavioral Scientist* 44: 2140–2151.

El Refaie, Elizabeth. 2009. "Metaphor in political cartoons: Exploring audience responses." In *Multimodal Metaphor* [Applications of Cognitive Linguistics 11], Charles Forceville and Eduardo Urios-Aparisi (eds), 173–196. Berlin/New York: Mouton de Gruyter.

Fiske, John. 1987. *Television Culture.* London/New York: Routledge.

Forceville, Charles. 2002. "Further thoughts on delimitating pictorial metaphor." *Theoria et Historia Scientiarum* 6: 213–227.

Forceville, Charles. 2009. "Non-verbal and multimodal metaphor in a cognitivist framework: Agendas for research." In *Multimodal Metaphor* [Applications of Cognitive Linguistics 11], Charles Forceville and Eduardo Urios-Aparisi (eds), 19–42. Berlin/New York: Mouton de Gruyter.

Gaines, Elliot. 2007. "The narrative semiotics of *The Daily Show.*" *Semiotica* 166: 81–96.

Ginman, Mariam and von Ungern-Sternberg, Sara. 2003. "Cartoons as information." *Journal of Information Science* 29: 69–77.

Gray, Jonathan, Jones, Jeffrey P. and Thompson, Ethan (eds). 2009. *Satire TV: Politics and Comedy in the Post-Network Era.* New York/London: New York University Press.

Greenberg, Josh. 2002. "Framing and temporality in political cartoons: A critical analysis of visual news discourse." *The Canadian Review of Sociology and Anthropology* 39: 181–198.

Hartley, John. 1999. *Uses of Television.* London/New York: Routledge.

Hartley, John. 2007. "Reality" and the plebiscite. In Kristina Riegert (ed.), *Politicotainment: Television's Take on the Real* [Popular Culture and Everyday Life 13], 21–58. New York: Peter Lang.

Holland, Patricia. 2000. *The Television Handbook* (2nd edition) [Media Practice]. London: Routledge.

Jones, Jeffrey P. 2010. *Entertaining Politics. Satiric Television and Political Engagement* (2nd edition) [Communication, Media and Politics]. New York/Toronto/Plymouth: Rowan and Littlefield.

Krikmann, Arvo and Laineste, Liisi. 2009. *Permitted Laughter. Socialist, Post-Socialist and Never-Socialist Humour.* Tartu: ELM Scholarly Press.

Kuipers, Giselinde. 2008. "The sociology of humour." In *The Primer of Humour Research* [Humour Research 8], Victor Raskin (ed.), 361–398. Berlin/New York: Mouton de Gruyter.

Lazăr, Ovidiu. 2008. "Satira politică televizuală ca divertisment. Percepția tinerilor asupra emisiunii *Animat Planet Show*" (Television political satire as a form of entertainment. The young perception of the *Animat Planet Show*). Unpublished Graduation Paper, National School of Political and Administrative Studies, Bucharest, Romania. [in Romanian]

Lockyer, Sharon. 2006. "A TWO-PROLONGED ATTACK? Exploring *Private Eye*'s satirical humour and investigating reporting." *Journalism Studies* 7: 765–781.

Maggio, Joe. 2007. "Comics and cartoons: A democratic art-form." *PS: Political Science and Politics* 40: 237–239.

Müller, Beate. 1995. *Parody: Dimensions and Perspectives*. Amsterdam: Rodopi.

Nilsen, Alleen P. and Nilsen, Don L. F. 2000. *Encyclopedia of 20th-Century American Humour*. Phoenix: Oryx Press.

Pădurarü, Adriana. 2008. "Romania animată" (Animated Romania). *Jurnalul National*, September 31. [in Romanian]

Paletz, David L. 1990. "Political humour and authority." *International Political Science Review* 11: 483–493.

Popa, Diana Elena 2002. "The absence of reference in Romanian joke translation." *Antares* V: 13.

Popa, Diana Elena 2003. "The language of humour and the social context: English vs. Romanian." *Antares* VI: 53–60.

Quintero, Ruben. 2007. *A Companion to Satire: Ancient to Modern* [Blackwell Companions to Literature and Culture 46]. Oxford: Blackwell.

Rădulescu, George. 2008. "Toni Grecu: 'Politicienii mi-au luat pâinea'" (Toni Grecu: "The politicians took away my job"). *Adevarul*, October 10. http://www.adevarul.ro/articole/industria-de-divertisment-e-confiscata-de-politicieni.html (accessed January 20, 2009). [in Romanian]

Riegert, Kristina (ed.). 2007. *Politicotainment: Television's Take on the Real* [Popular Culture and Everyday Life 13]. New York: Peter Lang.

Rose, Alexander. 2001. "When politics is a laughing matter." *Policy Review* 110: 59–71.

Rose, Margaret A. 1983. *Parody: Ancient, Modern, and Post-Modern* [Literature, Culture, Theory]. Cambridge: Cambridge University Press.

Rose, Margaret A. 1991. "Post modern pastiche." *British Journal of Aesthetics* 31: 26–38.

Speier, Hans. 1998. "Wit and politics: An essay on laughter and power." *American Journal of Sociology* 103: 1352–1401.

Street, John. 1997. *Politics and Popular Culture*. Philadelphia: Temple University Press.

Street, John. 2001. *Mass Media, Politics and Democracy*. Basingstoke: Palgrave.

Strukov, Vlad. 2007. "Video anekdot: Auteurs and voyeurs of Russian flash animation." *Animation: An Interdisciplinary Journal* 2: 129–151.

Teng, Norman Y. 2009. "Image alignment in multimodal metaphor." In *Multimodal Metaphor* [Applications of Cognitive Linguistics 11], Charles Forceville and Eduardo Urios-Aparisi (eds), 197–212. Berlin/New York: Mouton de Gruyter.

Terdiman, Richard. 1985. *Discourse/Counter-Discourse: The Theory and Practice of Symbolic Resistance in Nineteenth-Century France*. Ithaca/London: Cornell University Press.

Tsakona, Villy. 2009. "Language and image interaction in cartoons: Towards a multimodal theory of humour". *Journal of Pragmatics* 41: 1171–1188.

Tsakona, Villy. 2011. "Humour, religion and politics in Greek cartoons: Symbiosis or conflict?" In *Humour and Religion. Challenges and Ambiguities*, Hans Geybels and Walter Van Herck (eds), 248–267. London/New York: Continuum.

van Zoonen, Liesbet. 2005. *Entertaining the Citizen: When Politics and Popular Culture Converge* [Critical Media Studies]. Lanham: Rowman and Littlefield.

Wagg, Stephen and Strinati, Dominic (eds). 1992. *Come on Down? Popular Media Culture in Post-War Britain*. London: Routledge.

Warner, Jamie. 2007. "Political culture jamming: The dissident humour of *The Daily Show with Jon Stewart*". *Popular Communication* 5: 17–36.

Appendix I

List of proper names of the Romanian political figures and parties appearing in the examples analysed

Băsescu, Traian – politician, currently the President of Romania. Until 2004, he was the President of the Democratic Party. From 2000 to 2004, he was the Mayor of Bucharest. In 2004, he ran in and won in the presidential elections for the Justice and Truth Alliance between the National Liberal Party and the Democratic Party.

Democratic Party – a center-right party of Romania. In 2008, it merged with the Liberal Democratic Party to form the Democratic Liberal Party. From 2004 to 2007, this party was the smallest party of the governing Justice and Truth Alliance. Although he had formally suspended his leadership of the party when elected President in 2004, T. Băsescu is largely associated with the Democratic Party. The current leader of the party is M. Geoană, who was elected in April 2005. I. Iliescu is a former President of this party.

Flutur, Gheorghe – politician, former Minister of Agriculture, Forests, and Rural Development under the Tariceanu government, from 2004 to 2006. In 2002, he was Vice President of the Liberal National Party. In 2007, when a faction in the National Liberal Party formed the Liberal Democratic Party, he became the new party's Vice President.

Geoană, Mircea – politician, currently President of the Romanian Senate. From 2000 to 2004, he was Minister of Foreign Affairs, as part of Adrian Năstase's Social Democratic government. In 2005, he was elected President of the Social Democratic Party. His victory represented a surprise defeat for the former President and founder of the Social Democrats, I. Iliescu. M. Geoană's win was attributed by the media to last-minute backroom dealing by party members opposed to I. Iliescu, as well as to public gaffes made by I. Iliescu at the party congress, including the use of old Communist appellatives in a reference to party colleagues.

Hrebenciuc, Victor – businessman and influential politician, member of the Social Democratic Party.

Iliescu, Ion – politician who joined the Communist Party in 1953. He became a member of the Central Committee in 1965, serving in various positions until Nicolae Ceauşescu was overthrown in 1989. From 1990 to 1996 and from 2000 to 2004, he was the President of Romania. He was often accused by political opponents and journalists of retaining Communist convictions and allegiances as well as of tolerating party corruption.

National Liberal Party – a liberal party in Romania. Until 2007, it was the largest member of the governing Justice and Truth Alliance, which enjoyed a parliamentary majority due to an alliance between the Liberal Party, the Democratic Party, and the Democratic Union of Hungarians in Romania. In April 2007, the Prime Minister at the time, C. P. Tăriceanu, formed a minority government that included only the Democratic Union of Hungarians. In the 2008 legislative elections, it entered the opposition.

National Salvation Front – the governing body of Romania during the first few weeks after the Romanian Revolution of 1989; subsequently, it turned into a political party. It is the common root of the Social Democratic Party and the Democratic Party. In 1992, I. Iliescu and other members left the National Salvation Front and created the Democratic National Salvation Front, which eventually developed into today's Social Democratic Party.

Social Democratic Party – loosely classified as a center-left party, although the right-left division in Romania is quite blurred. After the 2008 Romanian legislative elections, the party entered the coalition together with the Democratic Liberal Party and formed a government led by Emil Boc, the President of the Democratic Liberal Party. From 2005 to 2008, the Social Democratic Party was an opposition party, as it lost in the 2004 legislative elections to the now non-existent Justice and Truth Alliance comprised of the National Liberal Party and the Democratic Party.

Tăriceanu, Călin Popescu – the Prime Minister of Romania from 2004 to 2008. Since 2004, he has been the President of the National Liberal Party and the Vice President of the European Liberal Democratic and Reform Party. Although T. Băsescu appointed him Prime Minister, their political relationship eroded, partly because of E. Udrea publicly accused C. P. Tăriceanu of interfering with justice in the case of Dinu Patriciu, an influential Romanian businessman.

Udrea, Elena – a politician and former member of the National Liberal Party, from which she resigned, and a current a member of the Liberal Democratic Party. In 2008, she was appointed Minister of Tourism under the Boc government. E. Udrea was also Counselor to President T. Băsescu, a function from which she resigned in 2005. E. Udrea has been accused by the media of being emotionally involved with President T. Băsescu.

Videanu, Adriean – politician, former Vice President of the Executive Office of the Democratic Party, and now leader of the Liberal Democratic Party. In 2008, he became the Minister of Economy under the Boc government. From 2005 to 2008, he was the Mayor of Bucharest.

Appendix II

Extract taken from the episode on December 2nd, 2007 (*Animat Planet Show* 2007b). The English translation appears in Example (3) of this chapter.

O voce din pubic strigă:
– Gala Animat Planet – Premiile de Cacao. Animat Planet premiază cele mai de desen animat alegeri din Romania sub genericul *Ăştia-s oamneii, cu ăştia votăm!* ...
Premiul apare sub forma unui morcov de aur.
Iliescu şi Hrebenciuc intră în scenă. Iliescu este îmbrăcat în roşu iar Hrebenciuc în roz.
Iliescu spune:
– Am obţinut cel mai slab rezultat de când este PSD-ul. Îmi vine să plâng. Hrebe, ce facem să salvăm partidul? Iliescu îl înghionteşte pe Hrebenciuc iar Hrebenciuc cască şi răspunde :
– Dacă reuşec să-l căstoresc pe baiatul meu cu fata lui Băsescu, treaba e rezolvată. Facem nunta şi coaliţie cu PD-ul. Refacem FSN-ul, şefu'!
– Dacă iese, eu îi cunun pe copii. Vreau să le fiu naş!
– Si cine o sa fie şeful noii coaliţii, şefu'? întrabă Hrebenciuc.
Deodată Geoană apare călare pe un cal verde înaripat şi spune :
– Eu, normal! Eu sunt Preşedintele PSD-ului! Sunt pe cai mari! Mimează zborul cu mâinile.
Iliescu îi răspunde:

– Eşti pe cai verzi, Mircea! Na! si loveşte calul care nechează şi dispare. Săracu', visează numai cai verzi!

Se anunţă premiile:

– Locul trei şi medalia de bronz – PNL – pentru că se menţine în cursă deşi ia bobârnacele guvernării!

Publicul strigă: "PSD-ul n-a murit!" […]

Tăriceanu intră în scena pe motocicletă, imbrăcat elegant şi purtând un joben pe cap.

– Noi cu 13% suntem la guvernare iar PD-ul cu 30 % stă pe bară. E bine! Doar PDL-ul m-a enervate rău că a furat din voturile noastre!

Flutur apare suspendat, cu urechile ca nişte aripi de fluture şi zburînd.

– Da' ce, voiai sa stăm ca proştii?! Tu ne-ai facut, fraiere! Îţi mulţumim! Începe să râdă batjocoritor.

Publicul apludă.

O voce anunţă:

– Următorul premiat este PSD-ul, care trebuie să se mulţumească doar cu medalia de argint.

Geoană intră călare pe calul verde înaripat:

– Atenţie! Vreau să vă spun un secret! Ne vom uni cu PD-ul şi voi fi Preşedintele Partidului Democrat Social Democrat! Ridică mâinile în sus a victorie. Hrebe aranjează nunta!

Iliescu îi spune lui Hrebenciuc:

– Auzi ce spune, neghiobul?! Vinde secretele din casă! Viorele, trebuie să facem un Congres extraordinar! Ăsta distruge stânga românească!

– Eu sunt motorul partidului! Iha! Di, mârţoaga! Le-arăt eu ce dresură fac eu în PSD cu toata lumea! Dii! Dii! strigă Geoană.

– Eeehee! Să-i spui marţoagă lu' cine vrei! Îl dă jos din şa pe Geoană, se supără calul. Gata! Campania s-a terminat! Caii verzi merg la odihnă până la viitoarele alegeri! Calul nechează şi-şi ia zborul de pe scenă.

[…]

Băsescu intră în scenă şi umflă cu pompa sigla portocalie a PD-ului.

O voce anunţă:

– Premiul întâi este acordat Partidului Democrat! Cel mai tare partid al momentului! Sigla se sparge.

Videanu apare din culise cu o cască de şantier şi cu o lopată în mână.

– Mă scuzaţi că umblu aşa însă am început săpăturile la tunelul care va debloca total traficul din Bucureşti!

Din public strigă cineva:

– Unde sapi dom' Primar?

– Sub Guvernul Tăriceanu, unde să sap?! Acolo e blocajul! Multumesc pentru medalie, am caştigat pe merit! Suntem cei mai buni!

– Cel mai bun e Băse, nea Videanu! strigă cineva din public. Fără locomotiva Băse, nu existaţi!

– Este o falsă impresie! Domnul Preşedinte nu e locomotiva partidului! Spune Videanu.

Din public strigă cineva:

– Aşa-i! El e tot trenul!

Pe scena apare o locomotivă care-l calcă pe Videanu. Băsescu este în locomotivă şi apare imbrăcat ca un şef de tren.

– Poftiți în vagoane! Trenul cursă de persoane Cotroceni - Palatul Parlamentului - Piața Victoriei pleacă din stație acuma! Celelalte partide sunt rugate să ne aștepte pe linie! Râde. Ce-mi place să fiu locomotivă! Îi calc pe toți! Râde batjocoritor și face ca trenul.

[…]

Elena Udrea este și ea în tren.

– Hmmm, Traian! Îmi place cand ești sub presiune! Hai, bagă cărbune! Hmmm!

Ține-te bine, Elena! strigă Băsescu.

Trenul pleacă.

CHAPTER 7

Being Berlusconi

Sabina Guzzanti's impersonation of the Italian Prime Minister between stage and screen

Clare Watters
University of Birmingham, United Kingdom

The present study explores the function of satirical impersonation in contemporary Italian society through an examination of the work of satirist Sabina Guzzanti and her impersonation of the current Italian Prime Minister Silvio Berlusconi. The movement of Guzzanti's work away from television after the removal of the satirical show *RaiOt* from the airwaves allows for an assessment of political impersonation as a humour strategy on both stage and screen. The analysis reveals the role which impersonation has to play in redefining the image of Berlusconi, the restrictions which are placed on television satire in the Berlusconi era, and the development and politicisation of humour which stage appearances have encouraged in Guzzanti's work.

> There is no-one on the world stage who can compete with me.
> Silvio Berlusconi (quoted in Fox 2002)

1. Introduction

In contemporary Italy, where Silvio Berlusconi's control over the media has allowed him to champion his media image and restrict the visibility of political debate and satirical intervention on state television, the work of certain satirists has undergone a visible transformation and radicalisation. The sense of political urgency shown by Italian comedians makes Italian satire a privileged example in understanding the function of satire in contemporary democratic societies.

During the Berlusconi era, comedians have been a recurrent target for censorship (Gomez and Travaglio 2004; Abruzzese 2005; Boria 2009). For example, popular humorists Daniele Luttazzi, Sabina Guzzanti, Paolo Rossi, Dario Fo, and

Franca Rame all saw obstacles put in the way of their television appearances during Berlusconi's second government between 2001 and 2005, by those who, like the Prime Minister's company *Mediaset*, claim that the task of satire should be merely to

> smitizzare e umanizzare i personaggi famosi […] favorendo un clima di tolleranza che attenuerebbe le tensioni sociali.   (Guzzanti 2005)
>
> deglamourise and humanise famous people […] offering a climate of tolerance which relieves social tension.[1]

Thus, they take a narrowly Freudian or relief perspective (Freud 1905/1991) on the role of humour, failing to acknowledge that satire could be able to have any other role to play in a democratic society. Censorship has greatly impacted on the prominence of these figures in the public eye and has been widely decried by public intellectuals. On the other hand, it has led to a renewed focus by these humorists on theatre, political activism, and the internet, which has in turn brought about changes and innovations in their use of humour.

This paper focuses on one of the many performance strategies employed by the comedian Sabina Guzzanti in opposition to Berlusconi since his arrival on the Italian political scene as a candidate, soon to be victorious, in the 1994 parliamentary elections. Guzzanti's impersonation of the current Italian Prime Minister has made her a household name, as well as bringing her fame in the international context through her character's television appearances with the British impersonator Rory Bremner in the guise of Tony Blair (see Figure 7).

Silvio, as he will be called here to distinguish the character from Berlusconi himself, has appeared regularly on satirical and cabaret programmes from the time of Berlusconi's first candidature at a national election in 1994, until the removal of Guzzanti's television programme *RaiOt* from the airwaves in 2003, which left her a fugitive from the small screen until her brief return from the end of 2008 to early 2009.

Through a discussion of Guzzanti's transition and the transformation of Silvio between television and stage performance, this chapter will outline how her humour and use of impersonation has evolved in terms of technique and political content. These developments are due in no small part to the process of television censorship of which Guzzanti has been the target. While Sabina Guzzanti's case is part of a much wider phenomenon during the Berlusconi era of "a flood of censorship of a rather crude kind" (Abruzzese 2005: 182), it offers, as Boria (2009: 100) rightly suggests, the clearest example of how a satirist can overcome television

---

1.   All translations are by the author unless otherwise stated.

Figure 7. Silvio and Tony Blair in *Viva Zapatero!* (Guzzanti 2005)

censorship and extend their comic output. Furthermore, it demonstrates how such obstacles can propel satirists towards a stronger and more forceful means of critique, as opposed to the self-censorship which is unfortunately so often practised by television comedians, depriving their work of any political significance (Freedman 2009; Jones 2009: 52). As this chapter expounds, Guzzanti's removal from television has not had the restraining influence which censors may have sought, but has compelled her instead to further test the boundaries between the humorous and the political.

The focus here will be an examination of Guzzanti's longstanding impersonation in which she presents a dynamic, ever-transforming counter-image to the Premier, in order to repeatedly expose his negative traits and to challenge his authority. In so doing, Guzzanti's work is consistent with Schechter's (1994: 4) definition of satiric impersonation, where impersonation is regarded "not only as the art through which one living person appears to be another; it is also an act that reveals the person imitated to be a fraud or 'gross impostor'". In uncovering the impostor for social or political purposes, the work of the impersonator, as Schechter (1994: 4) argues, "begins to 'pass out of the arts and into action'" and thus from humour for amusement's sake alone to humour as a political tool. While satire always risks falling back into providing mere entertainment, it is precisely this uneasy balance between humour and political action that effective satire embodies. It is Guzzanti's successful maintenance, and later radicalisation, of this tension that will be elucidated below.

The chapter will first examine Berlusconi's own media image (Section 2), before focusing more concretely in Section 3 on early images of Berlusconi in

Guzzanti's work through her impersonation character, Silvio, and the evolution of this figure. In Sections 4 and 5, I analyse Silvio's role in Guzzanti's censored television show *RaiOt* (2003) and the impact of this censorship on the increased politicisation and radicalisation of her impersonation and her satire more generally. The main points of the study are recapitulated in Section 6.

2.   Being Berlusconi: The image of a leader

The longevity of the impersonation of Silvio and its place in Guzzanti's career is due in no small part to Berlusconi's own success in the political sphere. Impersonations are based on recognition, hence audience identification with the character is a key factor in determining not only its popularity but the potential to create meaningful critique (see also Mascha this volume). Indeed, in his discussion of jokes, Raskin (1985:223) has argued that the denigration of a political figure constitutes "the most popular and universal type of political humour".

Having led the largest political parties in Italy into government through centre-right coalitions on four occasions, Berlusconi has become a prominent figure in international politics over the last fifteen years. However, his influence goes further than the political, given his status as a media magnate, a position which he has retained during his time in power (Albertazzi and Rothenburg 2009:1–2), allowing him to combine, as stated in the documentary *Citizen Berlusconi* (Cairola and Gray 2003), "the political power of President Bush, the media influence of Rupert Murdoch and the wealth and ambition of Ross Perot and Steve Forbes".

Berlusconi's image as a politician has been created through the mass media, with television playing a crucial role in political campaigning. Gundle (1997:61) goes as far as claiming that Berlusconi's first political party *Forza Italia* was constructed directly by his broadcasting company. Gundle (1997) and Ginsborg (2005) both describe Berlusconi in terms of his "charismatic" media image, which Ginsborg (2005:110) sees as being "forged, in the sense of being constructed within the confines, practices and symbols of modern communication and construction; carefully *manufactured*" (my emphasis).

Italy is not alone in the reliance of its political leaders on media image; the trend has developed in Western democracies over the last fifty years, since John F. Kennedy arguably became "the first candidate to get elected (in 1960) on the strength of his media presence" (Bruzzi 2000:128). Nor is it the first time in Italian history that a political figure has exerted his power over the media; Benito Mussolini was a prime example (see Mascha this volume). Nonetheless, Silvio Berlusconi's case is unique within the current democratic sphere, given his control, both direct and indirect, over a substantial part of the Italian visual and print media.

Berlusconi's own use of humour is a key element in the construction of this image and has led, along with the emphasis placed on his status as a self-made businessman, to his reception by certain centre-right voters as a "boy-next-door" figure.[2] His playful image has been less well-received abroad, particularly with regard to his many gaffes, which have led to him being targeted by comedians around the globe (Pickering and Lockyer 2005: 1). Nonetheless, at home, the danger remains that his strong influence over the information media may result in his manufactured image being passively accepted as reality. While the "real" in politics can often be difficult to identify, television satire and satirical impersonation in particular can have an important role in democratic countries in discerning the aspects of a politician's image which have been manufactured, and ridiculing them. According to Billig (2005: 190), this ridicule "far from being a detachable negative, lies at the heart of humor". Such ridicule and humour is made possible by the ability of the impersonator to expose the incongruities between the media image and the hidden reality of the political figure, many of which will be humorous and further exaggerated for comedic effect. As Schechter (1994: 153) states, "if our society has lost its sense of reality and accepted images or simulacra as reality, satirists and actors can reverse the process on occasion".

Although the complete reversal of the process of media image creation may not be possible, the exploration of Sabina Guzzanti's impression of Berlusconi that follows will demonstrate satiric impersonation's specific cultural role as a form of professional humour, which determines and criticises the elements which make up his image, including physical appearance, voice, use of language, humour, and textual content of speeches. Through such critique, Guzzanti invites the public to "reconsider the theatrical masks of media-dependent power" (Schechter 1994: 153) and "analyze and interrogate power and the realm of politics rather than remain simple subjects of it" (Gray et al. 2009: 17).

---

2. For further discussion of humour used by politicians, see Archakis and Tsakona (this volume), Dynel (this volume), Georgalidou (this volume), Mueller (this volume), and references therein. Berlusconi's intended and unintended humour has been reproduced in a *Berlusconario* dictionary (Belfiori and Santelli 2010) and has also been analysed by scholars (Billig 2005; Bolasco et al. 2006).

3.   Silvio: Guzzanti's interpretation of Berlusconi

3.1   The beginnings of an impersonation

In early manifestations of Silvio, physical elements are simplified and closely mimicked to enable instant recognition. On her first appearance as Silvio on the television programme *Tunnel* (1994), shortly before Berlusconi's victory at the 1994 General Elections, Guzzanti copies the hair (or lack thereof), incessant smile, and pristine suit of the future Premier in order to create a careful physical resemblance to Berlusconi, down to his *Forza Italia* rosette. The same can also be said of Silvio's piercing Milanese accent and peculiar gestures. Thus, Silvio's image is rooted firmly in caricature. The effect of this exaggerated persona is made more humorous by the incongruity of Guzzanti's transvestism, a young, funny woman dressed as an old male politician: the ultimate mismatch in impersonation (see Figure 8).

In comparison to the serious themes which Guzzanti broaches through her mimicry, at first glance, Silvio seems little more than an instance of the spiteful name-calling which describes Berlusconi as follows:

> L'Unto, il Pelato, il Nano, l'Orecchione, il Liftato, Quello-coi-tacchi-a-spillo, Dop-piopettato, l'Amico-degli-amici, il Puffo, il Padrone, il Mister, l'Improbabile, il Buffone, il Cantante-di-crociera, il Costruttore-senza-portafoglio, il Massone, Impunità [...]. (Guzzanti 2005b: 11)

> The Greasy One, the Bald One, the Dwarf, Big Ears, the One with the Face Lift, the One with the High Heels, the Double-Breasted Jacket, the Friend-of-a-Friend, the Smurf, the Godfather, the Boss, the Improbable, the Buffoon, the Cruiseship Singer, the Constructor with No Wallet, the Mason, Impunity [...].

Figure 8. Silvio in his dressing room (*Tunnel* 1994)

Indeed, Berlusconi has been portrayed in jokes, cartoons, and satirical texts as adhering to all of these types. Because of this common stereotyping, scholars may look no further than such visual caricatures when assessing the contribution that impersonations can make as a part of cultural opposition to politicians. Indeed, many academics consider them to, by definition, skim the surface of the private individual, not addressing the more pressing issues of policies put forward by parties and the governmental system as a whole; an oversight arguably made by Jones (2009: 38) in his discussion of American satire TV.

Impersonation often chooses to toothlessly address only the visual, particularly American presidential impersonations, which often consist of a more conservative form of humour. This has led to politicians being invited on comedy shows and comedians participating in White House dinners (Anonymous 2006; Moore 2008). However, while many impersonations are not necessarily created with a view to criticising the political system in its entirety, this does not justify the frequent denunciation of mimetic impersonations typified by Jones' claim (2009: 39) that they constitute "the lowest common denominator of political humour, with little to offend or provoke".

In a country like contemporary Italy, where campaign publicity in 2001 came in the form of a glossy brochure on Berlusconi's life entitled *An Italian Story* (Berlusconi 2001), the caricatures of any impressionist acquire a new significance. Consequently, through her television imitation, Guzzanti offers the Italian public the most readily available counter-image of Berlusconi. Through holding this human mirror up to his image, Guzzanti reflects back a distorted version of the Premier at odds with the "real" mediated vision penetrating it through a process of countermimesis. Guzzanti's focus on the physical, although perhaps at times overemphasised, is nonetheless central to her attack on Berlusconi and to its humour content. A further analysis of Silvio, with specific reference to his origins, his discourse, and the evolution which takes place in Guzzanti's performance as time goes on, will demonstrate that Guzzanti's work is best understood as a calculated distortion of Berlusconi's media image.

Firstly, satirical impersonation requires far more than a simple application of make-up and the perfecting of a politician's accent. Attention to these details alone is described by the Nobel-prizewinning playwright and satirist Dario Fo, when criticising the work performed by artists on the Italian satirical television programme *Biberon*, as resulting not in *satire* but what Fo calls *sfottò*, merely making fun or teasing:

> L'ironia fatta sui tic, sulla caricature dei connotati più o meno grotteschi dei politici presi di mira dei loro eventuali diffetti fisici, della loro pronuncia, dei loro vezzi, del loro modo di vestire, del modo di camminare, le frase tipiche che vanno ripetendo.   (Fo 1990: 1)

Irony that plays on tics, caricatures of more or less grotesque characteristics of politicians in their sights, their physical defects, their pronunciation, their vices, their way of dressing, their way of walking, typical phrases they go around repeating.

Fo highlights the aspects of impersonation which are most associated with laughter, but denounces "humour for humour's sake" in satirical impersonation. He has also, it should be noted, shown public support for Guzzanti's work, including an appearance in her film on the censorship of cultural figures in Italy, *Viva Zapatero!* (Guzzanti 2005), which hints at a possible recognition on his part that Guzzanti's work exceeds the purely humorous content of *sfottò*, as satire which contains a political message. Indeed, Guzzanti's characterisation of Berlusconi goes beyond the physical (is more than skin deep) and is well-researched and continually updated, to reflect new developments in the media narrative surrounding Berlusconi. Through this process, Silvio takes on a life of his own, evolving beyond a simple, humorous mirror image into a succession of politically charged counter-images, which serve to disrupt and displace the dominance of the image promulgated by the mainstream Italian media. Thus, contrary to its dismissal by some scholars, impersonation is, as I will demonstrate below, arguably uniquely suited to the end of political critique in an era where the image is such a powerful political tool.

Many of Silvio's characteristics remain constant over time. These include the physical attributes which have already been considered, as well as his general behaviour, but also textual elements of speeches made by Berlusconi, and the way he uses language to mould his discourse to suit a populist audience: the repetition of typical set phrases, the addressing of his audience as *italiani* "[my fellow] Italians", the constant denigration of his opponents as Communists (Bolasco et al. 2006). These recurring qualities prompt Fano (2003: v) to equate Guzzanti's impersonations of Berlusconi to a stock character from the 16th century Italian comic theatre *Commedia dell'Arte*, with traits that place Silvio somewhere between the old, lecherous, and money-grabbing Pantalone, and Brighella, a Milanese rogue who has risen from the lower echelons and is ruthless towards anyone who stands in his way. Fano (2003) goes on to claim that because of this constancy, Guzzanti's impersonation has a pacifying effect on its spectators, its humour doing little to attack existing ideologies, as "[a] poco a poco si abbandonano a quelle caratterizzazioni dimenticando anche la funzione sociale e politica" ("[l]ittle by little they abandon themselves to those characterisations, forgetting their social and political function"; Fano 2003: vi).

While it is possible to say that Silvio becomes such a figure in his own right, he is best understood not as a jovial caricature of a social type, but as way of exposing the mediated Berlusconi as an impostor. Unlike Pantalone, Silvio cannot be seen as a stock character who could be related to any number of public figures, nor can the jokes made against him be applied to another leader,[3] but rather are created to attack a politician who himself is as unique as he is powerful, even if he may seemingly aim to appear an "everyman". Not only is the extent to which Silvio can be detached from the media mask of Berlusconi debatable, but, as the following section on his evolution testifies, at no point does Guzzanti allow Silvio to become mere entertainment devoid of a political statement. Even at its most absurd and creative, through the arguments discussed and its exaggerated mimesis, the impersonation reminds the audience that Berlusconi is Guzzanti's "impostor" under attack.

3.2   Moving up the ranks of characterisation

In sketches shown before Berlusconi's second government, which appeared regularly on late night satirical programmes, Silvio demonstrates a desire to present a positive image to his public. First, he is shown in his dressing room, dressing up while discussing how changing his image will help him to win in the opinion polls (*Tunnel* 1994), through which the impersonator demonstrates the constructed and temporary nature of politics as Silvio makes constant costume changes to suit his public's every whim. Later, during his 2001 candidature, as Berlusconi's own image is plastered on billboards, so too is that of Silvio, through whom Guzzanti attacks the policies and slogans of *Forza Italia* in farcical sketches in front of a relevant backdrop (*L'Ottavo Nano* 2001; see Figure 9).

Figure 9. Silvio campaigning as *Presidente operaio* (*L'Ottavo Nano* 2001)

---

3.   Raskin (1985) argues that political jokes can often be transposed and travel to attack multiple political figures.

Superimposed on a typical campaign poster background, Silvio in his billboard manifestation demonstrates both the omnipresence of the Berlusconi image in the run-up to the elections and the Premier's inability to fulfil his election promises of being either a *Presidente operaio* "a working-class Prime Minister" or offering *città più sicure* "safer cities". Instead, as he talks of his presumed working-class origins, workmen throw food at him; and, after assaulting a passing voter with a brick, he attempts to blame the incident on the immigrants who the centre-right had claimed constitute a threat to Italy's security. Thus, while using physical humour through the brick and the food thrown to provoke laughter, Guzzanti uses the perceived incongruity between the "working-class Premier" and his working class citizens to create both a humorous juxtaposition and to emphasise that Berlusconi might not be as adulated as his press office make out. More generally, through Silvio's comic sketch, Guzzanti highlights the false claims and promises that may be made during election campaigns, and the obsessive attention to image that has become central to success in contemporary Italian politics.

From the apparently humble beginnings of Berlusconi's first and second candidatures, where image meant votes, Silvio appears during his second and third terms in office against increasingly elaborate backdrops of chambers of almost regal grandeur. The power which, as Guzzanti claims, Berlusconi has amassed over the country is thus reflected physically in the props and backgrounds surrounding Silvio, but also in the situations targeted as humorous. The culmination of this reflection can be found in his final appearance on screen before the removal of Guzzanti's television programme from the airwaves, in which Silvio speaks from a parliamentary office filled with antique goods including a jewel-filled treasure chest and the Mona Lisa. In parallel with this change to his surroundings, Silvio's desire for grandeur is realised to an ever greater extent, as the control Guzzanti perceives Berlusconi to hold over Italy increases.

The Prime Minister's perceived dominance is physically manifested through Silvio's acquisition of increasingly influential roles. On his return to power in 2001, Silvio is depicted as a "not-so-great" dictator on the *Inaugurazione* (2001) of the seventh national TV channel *La7*. There, he is represented playing with a globe in a manner not dissimilar to that of Hynkel in Charlie Chaplin's masterpiece *The Great Dictator* (Chaplin 1940). Guzzanti places the *Presidente del Consiglio* momentarily on a par with Hynkel, Chaplin's Hitler parody, in order to demonstrate the amount of power he has gathered, despite his absurdity, thereby pinpointing his apparent aspirations to authoritarian power (see Figure 10).

Drawing parallels between democratic leaders and dictators to undermine any excess of power is a common form of humour. Indeed, Guzzanti is not the only artist to compare Berlusconi with a well-known dictator. On his internationally renowned weblog, fellow comedian Beppe Grillo has compared Berlusconi

Figure 10. Silvio's authoritarian desires in *Viva Zapatero!* (Guzzanti 2005)

to Mussolini, a comparison also drawn by the Sicilian writer Vincenzo Consolo (Vaccari 2009:140; O'Connell 2009:154). In Guzzanti's version, in contrast to Hynkel's graceful display of gymnastic control, Silvio clumsily attempts to mount the globe, failing repeatedly and eventually perching awkwardly to discuss his position as Prime Minister and the protests which took place during the G8 summit in Genoa. In this uncomfortable position, Silvio is once again depicted as an impostor in the political sphere, proving not only to be incongruous as a down-to-earth, democratic politician, but also failing as a dictator.

Furthermore, on Silvio's return to television, Guzzanti makes a more explicit reference to authoritarianism by superimposing Silvio giving a speech to a cheering crowd on the famous balcony of *Piazza Venezia* in Rome, which served as the *Duce*'s podium to address the Italian public (*Annozero* 2009). Although eight years have passed, these aspects of Guzzanti's humour and political criticism, as well as the political situation she is addressing, remain unchanged.

The elaboration of the figure of Silvio demonstrates that, far from being what Guzzanti calls *armi di distrazione di massa* "arms of mass distraction" (Guzzanti 2005a:15) provided by much infotainment on Italian television, the character offers a critical insight into the world of Berlusconi. Such a commentary holds the image central to its counterattack, but, using the humorous aspects of his character to expound a political message, goes beyond the surface or *sfottò*. The transformation is enabled through the placing of Silvio against different backgrounds and comparing his character physically with those of dictators both real and fictional, in order to denounce Berlusconi's increasing control over contemporary Italy and his alleged aspirations for further power.

4.   Causing a *RaiOt*: The removal of Guzzanti from the airwaves

Silvio's last stand on television before Guzzanti's removal from the airwaves at the end of 2003 appeared on her own satirical show.[4] *RaiOt*, the name being a play on the English *riot* combined with the state broadcaster's name, RAI, was, from the very beginning, set to cause a stir.

In the first episode of *RaiOt* (2003), the only one to be aired, Berlusconi makes two short appearances in the setting of a lavishly furnished office (Gomez and Travaglio 2004: 165). The first notably takes the form of a mock emergency broadcast to all channels:

> Italiani, purtroppo viaggiando e confrontandomi con tanti altri grandi del mondo ho appreso che in Italia l'informazione è nelle mani di una sola persona. Ma voglio rassicurarvi: la stiamo cercando e la troveremo.   (*RaiOt* 2003)

> [My fellow] Italians, unfortunately, while on my travels and meeting many other great men of the world, I have learnt that in Italy the information media lie entirely in the hands of one man. But I want to reassure you, we are searching and we will find him.

Throughout the 50 minute programme, Guzzanti and her collaborators investigate the control that Berlusconi has over the media and the effect which his use of censorship has had on performers and presenters, while also denouncing the key figures that have allowed this to occur, a prime example being Lucia Annunziata, the RAI President at the time. Impersonations, which had been Guzzanti's mainstay on television, are interwoven with a satirical monologue which many critics within the press were to denounce as entirely lacking in humour (Gomez and Travaglio 2004: 174). However, as scholars have convincingly argued, satire does not always have to be funny (Keighron 1998: 128; Gray et al. 2009). Nonetheless, this insight runs contrary to expectations of television producers, for whom the emphasis is placed squarely on entertainment.

As Guzzanti's first time at the helm of a television show, *RaiOt* represented a unique opportunity to discuss themes which she felt had been either silenced or treated in a politically biased way by the Italian media, with a second episode which was planned to address the war in Iraq (Guzzanti 2005). However, a decision had to be made as to how to approach these subjects, given the constraints that operate on Italian television. Thus, when Guzzanti was first offered the opportunity to do the show, the team agreed on the best way to proceed, as quoted by Gomez and Travaglio (2004: 164):

---

4.   Co-written with Curzio Maltese, Emanuela Imparato, and Paolo Santolini, under the direction of Igor Skofic.

Ne ha parlato a lungo con i suoi collaboratori: "Che facciamo, ci autocensuriamo per passare indenni alla censura, oppure ce ne freghiamo, diciamo quello che pensiamo, quello che diremmo in teatro, in piazza, nella tv di un paese libero?"

She spoke at length with her collaborators about it: "What shall we do - self-censor in order to be left unscathed by the censors, or not give a damn, say what we think, what we say on stage, in the piazza, on TV in a free country?"

The answer for this politically motivated team was clear; every effort must be made to remain true to the political aims of the piece, as to self-censor would constitute a lapse into *sfottò* and humour without a message.

As expected, the censors did not leave the show "unscathed". In fact, the state broadcaster was wary of letting the highly-charged satirical content of *RaiOt* on air, and at first threatened to postpone its broadcast (see Figure 11). However, after due consideration, and the threat on Guzzanti's part to call a press conference, the first episode was aired on 16th November 2003.

Constraints placed on the content of television satire, as faced by *RaiOt*, are by no means exclusive to Italy, but are evident in other European nations in diverse forms (see Freedman 2009; Popa this volume). In Britain, the fear of political backlash is one of the many factors which result in political comedy programmes being few and far between in the larger scheme of humour entertainment. As Bignell notes, there is a fear of provoking "confrontation with the government" (cited in Keighron 1998: 129). Jon Plowman, then BBC Head of Entertainment,

Figure 11. Guzzanti defends herself against *RaiOt*'s censorship in *Viva Zapatero!* (Guzzanti 2005)

reiterates this position when discussing the reasons for impersonator Rory Bremner's move from the public broadcaster to the private station, Channel 4: "balancing politics and comedy, in the way that Bremner attempts, is not worth the risk" (cited in Keighron 1998: 129). For a public broadcaster, be they RAI or the BBC, satire is invariably problematic. In the USA, the unpredictability of satire pushes broadcasters towards safer brands of humour, such as sitcoms, whose very form makes direct attacks on specific politicians or policies unlikely (Mulkay 1988: 185; Gray et al. 2009: 14). The view of what constitutes acceptable political humour for television audiences therefore varies from channel to channel, from country to country, as do the means by which undesired humour is contained.

The case of *RaiOt* did not stop at the more conventional use of political pressure, but was followed by a multi-million euro lawsuit from the Berlusconi-owned company *Mediaset* against RAI and Guzzanti. Surprisingly, the sketch which was the target of the lawsuit was not one featuring Silvio, nor was it the pieces of the monologue which had been badly received by the press. Instead, it was a sketch analysing the controversial Gasparri law on television through an interview with Neri Marcoré in the guise of the then Minister of Communications, Maurizio Gasparri (Boria 2009: 103; Gomez and Travaglio 2004: 179).

The Gasparri law became an infamous addition to the policies of the Berlusconi era, as it imposed changes to the limits of media ownership in Italy – a matter in which many critics consider Berlusconi to have conflicting interests. The sketch depicted Gasparri asking the foreign interviewer to make a list of the main points of the bill, as he had not read it, thereby implying both Gasparri's ineptitude as a Minister of Communications and indicating the subordination of the Italian press to the government. Collaboration of this kind between the media and politicians is echoed in Silvio's press conference with Rory Bremner's Tony Blair during the film *Viva Zapatero!* (Guzzanti 2005), in which Silvio chastises Tony for answering the questions of a press whom he has not paid off. By placing both Silvio and the Gasparri impersonation in an international context, Guzzanti highlights the humour which Berlusconi and his politics elicit abroad and taps into widespread criticism of him in the international press, a position which would also be taken by an Italian protest public.

Directly after the television show was cancelled, a one-off performance protest at the Auditorium in Rome, *Varietà di Protesta* ("Variety of Protest"), showed the support of fans and fellow artists for Guzzanti's cause. The performance attracted an audience of around 15,000 people, the majority of whom were unable to enter the venue and watched from outside on a big screen. The performance focused on the issues of freedom of speech and the censorship that many of the artists present had faced. Moreover, the removal of *RaiOt* from television provoked more than a one-off coming together of cultural figures in support of satire and freedom of speech on television. As Boria (2009: 100) rightly observes, "the censorship and legal action sparked a creative process and a mobilization" in Guzzanti. Sidelined from television, Guzzanti would continue her satirical attack on the political elite through other media, including film, books, and the internet, but most notably through the continuation and radicalisation of her stage performance. The censorship of *RaiOt* can also be seen as a key motivating factor in Guzzanti's increasingly politicised style on stage, where no holds would be barred.

5.   *Reperto RaiOt* and beyond

Directly after the cancellation of the television show and the one-off performance protest *Varietà di Protesta*, Guzzanti took the programme *RaiOt* to the stage. Guzzanti's one-woman show *Reperto RaiOt* ("The RaiOt Exhibition", Guzzanti 2004) evolved into something much more than a live incarnation of the axed television show.[5] Through an analysis of Guzzanti's impersonation in this context, I will demonstrate how live impersonation can

> free the public from the thrall of simulated identities by quotation, by removing identities from their usual context, and by bringing public officials or their doubles out from behind television screens onto stages and into other arenas where speakers stand accountable for their acts in front of a live, spontaneously responsive audience that hears more than sound bites   (Schechter 1994: 153)

Silvio's appearance on stage takes place outside Berlusconi's mediated world of television and beyond the limitations which it has placed on Guzzanti's satirical creation.

Although *Reperto RaiOt* begins as though merely mimicking the farcical sketches of the television programmes through which she first made her name, after only half an hour Guzzanti disappears off stage for a short, tense interlude, returning to inform the audience that the show is over to discuss important matters. While the performance will actually continue, the interlude denies the audience members any expectation that the show will seek only to recreate the hilarity of past television sketches, as is often the case with comedy shows which make the move from screen to stage. Instead, a politically-charged comic monologue

---

5.   The title plays on the idea of Guzzanti's censorship as an historical artefact, a museum piece documenting this aspect of the Berlusconi era. Throughout the show, Guzzanti makes reference to a new *Museo della Resistenza* "Museum of the Resistance", where all forms of Berlusconian society and the cultural resistance to it are displayed.

Figure 12. Guzzanti as Silvio in *Reperto RaiOt* (Guzzanti 2004)

ensues with interjections from characters through impersonation and musical sketches.

In this second section of *Reperto RaiOt*, Silvio makes an inevitable appearance. In a similar physical form to his appearance in an earlier stage performance, *Giuro di Dire la Varietà* ("I Promise to Tell the Variety", Guzzanti 2002),[6] *Guzzanti* uses only a makeshift suit-apron and a pull-on rubber mask in order to adapt physically to the role the impersonator, at far remove from the pristine make-up and costume of Silvio's screen incarnation (see Figure 12). The simplistic make-up does not detract from the impersonation; indeed, if anything, it highlights its distance from the form of mimicry defined above as *sfottò*, in eschewing accurate physical resemblance. No longer working within the constraints of the small screen, the character is able to take on a life of his own. The scripted monologue of Silvio is developed at far greater length on stage, with freer speech and room for improvisation through which it is transformed into a scathing political critique.

Guzzanti continually berates Berlusconi's apparent conflict of interests with regard to his media empire and the ways in which he is perceived to have abused his power as a leader, by viewing himself as above his electorate. She also denounces his alleged mafia connections. Silvio discusses the elections, claiming that

---

6. Guzzanti here plays on the courtroom oath "I promise to tell the truth…", exchanging the Italian word *verità* "truth" with *varietà* "variety", normally associated with cabaret "variety" shows.

le elezioni io le ho vinte, gli italiani le hanno perse [...]. Lo sapete, questo i gior-
nali comunisti non l'hanno detto, «l'Unità» non l'ha scritto: io sono stato, su 56
milioni di persone, l'unico che ha vinto le elezioni.   (Guzzanti 2005b: 64)

I won the elections and the Italian people lost [...]. You know, the Communist
newspapers haven't told you this, *L'Unità*[7] didn't write about it, but out of 56 million people, I was the only one who won the elections.

Guzzanti claims to have placed a decoder in the head of Silvio, and halfway
through his speech on tax cuts, his speech morphs into that of a character which
she sees as hiding behind his media mask: a mafia boss. The characterisation is
formed through a thick Sicilian accent and a liberal use of strong language. Such
discourse would have been unwelcome on television, both for its political message, that Berlusconi is comparable to Italy's most worrying form of criminal, and
for one of the means through which it elicits laughter, through frequent recourse
to coarse language. The figure of the mafia boss constitutes an equally sinister
breed of leader to the dictator and another guise of Italian power reflected back at
Berlusconi, playing on the parallels between them, as well as Berlusconi's alleged
association with the mafia during his assent to power (Travaglio and Veltri 2001;
Anonymous 2003).

Moving away from television, Silvio thus fulfils the aims of stage impersonation, "removing identities from their usual context", namely those of Silvio and
the mafia boss, and making them "stand accountable for their acts in front of a
live, spontaneously responsive audience" (Schechter 1994: 153). In transferring
Silvio from his television base, as she does in *Reperto RaiOt*, Guzzanti has further
removed his image from its mimetic origins, and forces both Berlusconi and the
live audience to confront the implications of his alleged mafia connections.

Within the space of her most recent stage tour, *Vilipendio* (Guzzanti 2009),
the performative freedom of live performance in humour creation can be seen
to an even greater extent. Guzzanti's text changes day-in day-out, mimicking the
style of satirical playwright Dario Fo who believes his work to be "throwaway theatre [*un teatro da bruciare*], a theatre which won't go down in bourgeois history,
but which is useful, like a newspaper article, a debate or a political action" (Fo,
cited in Mitchell 1986: 85). Guzzanti plays constantly with the text of *Vilipendio*,
meaning that between the beginning of the tour in October 2008 and the last
show in November 2009, almost half of the text had been rescripted. Guzzanti's
decision to constantly change the jokes and political discussions of her monologue demonstrate that she too is engaged in current affairs and that much of her
"entertainment" is context dependent. Humour cannot stand alone, but requires

---

7.   A popular Italian left-wing national daily.

acknowledgement of the political situation and current events on the part of the audience (Tsakona and Popa this volume).

As a key political figure and source of humour, once again, Silvio is present, despite Guzzanti's apparent fears, as suggested in a post on her blog (Guzzanti 2009a), that little more could be achieved with the character, as he had already appeared in so many forms. In *Vilipendio* (Guzzanti 2009d), he stars in a recorded introduction, which welcomes the audience to their seats. Silvio is dressed as a Roman emperor, the culmination of his delusions of authoritarian power, a parallel also drawn by other cultural figures (see Fo 2002 and Virzì 2006).

The character may in fact here be seen as a regression to amusing television entertainment of absurdist qualities. Indeed, watching him bounce around the screen on a bed reputedly bought for him by Vladimir Putin, this is certainly how he first appears (see the video at Guzzanti 2009a). However, he still has suggestive comments to make on the Berlusconi phenomenon. Silvio invites the ladies of the audience to enter the screen with him, offering them in return:

> La prima volta un bracciale, la seconda volta orecchini, la terza volta, se sono veramente carine con me, una collana: la parure completa. Non posso promettere a tutti quanti un ministero ma un piatto di minestra, quello sicuramente sì.
> (Guzzanti 2009)

> The first time a bracelet, the second time earrings, the third time, if they're really nice to me, a necklace: the complete set. I can't offer everyone a ministry, but a bowl of minestrone, I certainly can.

Written in October 2008, the sketch, in fact, foreshadows the scandals of Berlusconi's apparently dubious criteria in choosing female candidates for the European elections and his alleged association with minors and prostitutes which would dominate international coverage from 2009 onwards (Hooper 2009; Donadio 2011).

The only constant in an ever-changing production, Silvio here takes on a new function within the work of Guzzanti. In this context, the lively impersonation becomes an entertaining means of easing the audience into a two and a half hour barrage of biting satire, in which Guzzanti constantly denounces Berlusconi's perceived abuses of power, the corruption of the centre-right and the inability of the centre-left to create a united opposition. The show peaks in a deluge of images and sound, in which Italian parliament burns like Sodom and Gomorrah (see Figure 13).

As biting as it is topical, *Vilipendio* is strong evidence that Guzzanti's satire, despite its constant recourse to media images, sounds and effects, has completely outgrown its television base, using the humour of her impersonation gain audience approval before focusing on her political monologue.

Figure 13. Guzzanti denounces parliament in front of a flame-filled screen in *Vilipendio*
(Guzzanti 2009d)

It is therefore surprising that at this point of Guzzanti's career Silvio should make his return to television. In late 2008 to early 2009, Guzzanti made several guest appearances on the current affairs show *Annozero* (2008, 2009), where Silvio appears initially in a physical form similar to that shown in *Vilipendio*. Through pre-recorded faux video link-ups, Silvio reflects on weekly discussions on the topical programme, which addresses a different political or social theme every episode.

The space afforded to her impersonations on *Annozero* (2008, 2009) is considerably longer than Silvio's earlier television appearances, averaging around ten minutes in duration, thereby providing greater scope for political comment. However, in personal communication with her in April 2009, she complained about the threats of censorship to the show, pressures on her work to conform to the format of the programme, and concerns that she did not always identify with the opinions put forward. The day before the interview, she had made her last live appearance as Silvio on Italian television to date. Since then, Silvio has appeared only in his recorded form on the *Vilipendio* tour, at the launch of the "independent" newspaper *Il Fatto Quotidiano* hosted by Marco Travaglio, an investigative journalist and expert on Berlusconi's corruption trials, and both live, as a film clip on *Annozero*, and displayed online in adverts to bring public attention to the situation in the earthquake-hit town of L'Aquila (Guzzanti 2009b; Guzzanti 2009c). In the selection of these recent appearances, Guzzanti clearly demonstrates her heightened political agenda, using Silvio to publicly support campaigns which are either at odds with Berlusconi's control of the media or attempting to improve Italy without government involvement.

Furthermore, Guzzanti's brief return to TV as a guest on *Annozero* (2008, 2009) demonstrates that both the character of Silvio and the satire of his creator have evolved. Although appearing on a current affairs programme allowed for more transgression than the satirical comedy sketch shows and variety shows of her past, Guzzanti's return to television was short-lived, as her politicised satire has surpassed the limits within which it was first brought into being. It has, in other words, outgrown the strict confines of television appearances, making her return to the small screen an uneasy one. She is confronted with a harsh choice: conform to the demands of the televisual format, inevitably sacrificing a degree of control to censors, presenters, and television executives, but win far greater exposure; or operate within the more permissive confines of theatre and reach only a fraction of that audience. In choosing to make no further television appearances, it would seem that Guzzanti has opted for the latter, but she has also increased her political humour output to film, a weblog, and speeches at demonstrations.

6. Conclusions

By comically distorting the accepted image of a politician, impersonators can begin to displace the power that such images hold over media-centred democratic societies. By manipulating the image of politicians through humour, impersonators are able to show the moral flaws that lurk behind their masks, as well as demonstrating the negative impact that media-constructed images have on the political process in general.

For Sabina Guzzanti, this image-based politics constitutes an erosion of democracy itself, with parliament resembling Sodom and Gomorrah (Guzzanti 2009d). By deconstructing these images through impersonations, she and other satirists form an important part of the cultural resistance to the political domination of the constructed image in the Berlusconi era. Be it on screen or stage, throughout his career in politics, Berlusconi has been shadowed by Guzzanti's Silvio, who has constantly drawn attention to the incongruities of the Prime Minister's media mask, and confronted the Italian public with a succession of counter-images of which both they and Berlusconi are forced to take account. They do so through performances which are steeped in humour, but which avoid making fun through *sfottò*, focusing equally attentively on the political message they wish to make.

In the opening sketch of the stage show *Giuro di Dire la Verità* (2002), Silvio encounters Death who, instead of sending him to Hell, declares that Silvio is to spend eternity face to face with himself, a punishment which is more than his sanity can endure. Guzzanti has condemned Berlusconi to a similar sentence since the beginning of his political career, reflecting back distorted and humorous versions of his actions and his mediated mask which mock him at every turn, competing with him in the public eye, where his political opposition have failed.

Although necessitated by the censorship of her television show *RaiOt*, Guzzanti's move away from television has led to the political aspects of her humour, along with the character of Silvio, developing further than was possible on the small screen. Ultimately the removal of television from her repertoire has allowed her to play not only with the accepted images of the political elite, but also with the perception of the work of comedians in Italy and their role within Italian society. Although television provided her with a larger audience than theatre, due to both the publicity that censorship afforded her and her talents for impersonation, she has retained a high profile. Having been forced away from televison, Guzzanti has exploited the opportunity to intensify the political aspects of her humour, developing her most well-known impersonation, Silvio, into a kaleidoscopic diffraction of his real-life equivalent's media image. Furthermore, the overall style of her comedy has evolved into a more rigorously political form, so much so that both style and content of her humour have moved beyond the bounds of what Italian television can allow.

Multimedia sources

Cairola, Andrea and Gray, Susan. 2003. *Citizen Berlusconi*. Italy and USA.

Chaplin, Charles. 1940. *The Great Dictator*. USA.

Fo, Dario. 2002. *Ubu Roi, Ubu Bas e Altre Storie*. Italy.

Guzzanti, Sabina. 2002. *Giuro di Dire la Varietà*. Italy.

Guzzanti, Sabina. 2004. *Reperto RaiOt*. Italy.

Guzzanti, Sabina. 2005. *Viva Zapatero!* Italy.

Guzzanti, Sabina. 2009. *Vilipendio*. Italy.

Virzì, Paolo. 2006. *N (io e Napoleone)*. Italy/Spain/France.

Television

Annozero. 2008. *RAI 2*, October 30 (accessed at *RAI Medioteca*, July 5, 2009; also available at: www.annozero.rai.it).

Annozero. 2009. *RAI 2*, March 26 (accessed at *RAI Medioteca*, July 5, 2009; also available at: www.annozero.rai.it).

Inaugurazione. 2001. *La7*. Clips re-released in edited video: *Una Ragazza Terra e Sapone*, Sabina Guzzanti and Nicola Fano (eds), 2003. Italy: Einaudi. www.youtube.com/watch?v= YGNcA3ISw1c&feature=related (accessed March 11, 2011).

L'Ottavo Nano. 2001. *RAI 2*. Clips re-released in edited video: *Una Ragazza Terra e Sapone*, Sabina Guzzanti and Nicola Fano (eds), 2003. Italy: Einaudi. http://www.youtube.com/ watch?v=Drqv6K01Q6g,   http://www.youtube.com/watch?v=2nLDlNYqkuY&feature= related (accessed March 11, 2011).

RaiOt: Armi di Distrazione di Massa. 2003. *RAI 3*, November 16. http://www.youtube.com/ watch?v=OKGArgcSQFA (accessed January 11, 2011).

Tunnel. 1994. *RAI 3*, February 13 (accessed at *RAI Medioteca*, July 5, 2009).

References

Abruzzese, Alberto. 2005. "Censorship in the time of Berlusconi." In *Culture, Censorship and the State in Twentieth-Century Italy* [Legenda Main Series], Guido Bonsaver and Robert S. C. Gordon (eds), 179–191. London: MHRA/Maney.

Albertazzi, Daniele and Rothenburg, Nina. 2009. "Introduction. This tide is not for turning." In *Resisting the Tide: Cultures of Opposition under Berlusconi (2001–2006)*, Daniele Albertazzi, Clodagh Brook, Charlotte Ross and Nina Rothenburg (eds), 1–16. London: Continuum.

Anonymous. 2003. Berlusconi accused of mafia links. *BBC Online*, January 8. http://news.bbc.co.uk/1/hi/world/europe/2638609.stm (accessed November 15, 2009).

Anonymous. 2006. "Double-you" Bush delights media. *BBC Online*, April 30. http://news.bbc.co.uk/1/hi/world/americas/4959380.stm (accessed November 18, 2009).

Belfiori, Giovanni and Santelli, Giorgio. 2010. *Berlusconario: Tutte le Gaffe del Presidente.* Milan: Melampo Editore.

Berlusconi, Silvio. 2001. *Una Storia Italiana.* New York: Gotham.

Billig, Michael. 2005. *Laughter and Ridicule. Towards a Social Critique of Humour* [Theory, Culture and Society]. London: Sage.

Bolasco, Sergio, Giuliano, Luca and Galli de' Paratesi, Nora. 2006. *Parole in Libertà. Un' Analisi Statistica e Linguistica dei Discorsi di Berlusconi* [Contemporanea]. Rome: Manifestolibri.

Boria, Monica. 2009. "Silenced humour on RAI TV: Daniele Luttazzi, Sabina Guzzanti & Co." In *Resisting the Tide: Cultures of Opposition under Berlusconi (2001–2006)*, Daniele Albertazzi, Clodagh Brook, Charlotte Ross and Nina Rothenburg (eds), 97–109. London: Continuum.

Bruzzi, Stella. 2000. *New Documentary: A Critical Introduction.* London: Routledge.

Donadio, Rachel. 2011. "Surreal: A Soap Opera Starring Berlusconi". *New York Times*, January 22. http://www.nytimes.com/2011/01/23/weekinreview/23donadio.html (accessed January 22, 2011).

Fano, Nicola. 2003. "Arlecchini, Pantaloni e Berlusconi." In *Il Diario di Sabna Guzz*, Sabina Guzzanti, iii–x. Turin: Einaudi.

Fo, Dario. 1990. *Dialogo Provocatorio sul Comico, il Tragico, la Follia e la Ragione, con Luigi Allegi.* Rome: Laterza.

Fox, James. 2002. First among billionaires. *Guardian*, September 28. http://www.guardian.co.uk/world/2002/sep/28/italy.weekend7 (accessed November 15, 2009).

Freedman, Leonard. 2009. *The Offensive Art: Political Satire and its Censorship around the World from Beerbohm to Borat.* London: Praeger.

Freud, Sigmund. 1905/1991. *Jokes and their Relations to the Unconscious.* Transl. James Strachey [The Penguin Freud Library 6]. London: Penguin.

Ginsborg, Paul. 2005. *Silvio Berlusconi: Television, Power and Patrimony.* London: Verso.

Gomez, Peter and Travaglio, Marco. 2004. *Regime.* Milan: BUR.

Gray, Jonathan, Jones, Jeffrey P. and Thompson, Ethan. (eds). 2009. *Satire TV. Politics and Comedy in the Post-Network Era.* New York: New York University Press.

Gundle, Stephen. 1997. "Television in Italy." In *Television in Europe* [Intellect. European Studies Series], James A. Coleman and Brigitte Rollet (eds), 61–76. Bristol: Intellect Books.

Guzzanti, Sabina. 2005a. *Viva Zapatero!* Milan: BUR.

Guzzanti, Sabina. 2005b. *Reperto RaiOt.* Milan: BUR.

Guzzanti, Sabina. 2009a. Comment on and video of Berlusconi impersonation, *Sabinaguzzanti. it*, July 1. http://www.sabinaguzzanti.it/?s=berlusconi+gay (accessed November 1, 2009).

Guzzanti, Sabina. 2009b. Post on "Attenzione all'ecovillaggio umano a L'Aquila." *Sabinaguzzanti.it*, November 19. http://www.sabinaguzzanti.it/2009/11/19/attenzione-a-lecovillaggio (accessed November 19, 2009).

Guzzanti, Sabina. 2009c. Post on "Raccolte fondi per Pescomaggiore." *Sabinaguzzanti.it*, November 27. http://www.sabinaguzzanti.it/2009/11/27/raccolta-fondi-per-pescomaggiore (accessed November 27, 2009).

Guzzanti, Sabina. 2009d. *Vilipendio.* Milan: BUR.

Hooper, John. 2009. "Being Silvio Berlusconi." *Guardian*, October 31. http://www.guardian. co.uk/world/2009/oct/31/silvio-berlusconi-profile (accessed March 11, 2011).

Jones, Jeffrey P. 2009. "With all due respect: Satirizing presidents from *Saturday Night Live* to *Lil' Bush*." In *Satire TV. Politics and Comedy in the Post-Network Era*, Jonathan Gray, Jeffrey P. Jones and Ethan Thompson (eds), 37–63. New York: New York University Press.

Keighron, Peter. 1998. "The politics of ridicule: Satire and television." In *Dissident Voices: The Politics of Television and Cultural Change*, Mike Wayne (ed.), 127–144. London: Pluto Press.

Mitchell, Tony. 1986. *Dario Fo: People's Court Jester.* London: Methuen.

Moore, Matthew. 2008. "Sarah Palin's appearance with Tina Fey boosts *Saturday Night Live*." *Telegraph.co.uk*, October 20. www.telegraph.co.uk/news/worldnews/northamerica/usa/ sarah-palin/3228386/Sarah-Palins-appearance-with-tina-fey-boosts-saturday-night-live. html (accessed November 18, 2009).

Mulkay, Michael. 1988. *On Humour. Its Nature and Place in Modern Society.* Oxford: Blackwell.

O'Connell, Daragh. 2009. "Mascelloni, masks and mascara: Writing, language and power in Vincenzo Consolo." In *Resisting the Tide: Cultures of Opposition under Berlusconi (2001– 2006)*, Daniele Albertazzi, Clodagh Brook, Charlotte Ross and Nina Rothenburg (eds), 148–160. London: Continuum.

Pickering, Michael and Lockyer, Sharon. 2005. "Introduction: The Ethics and Aesthetics of Humour and Comedy." In *Beyond a Joke. The Limits of Humour*, Sharon Lockyer and Michael Pickering (eds), 1–24. Basingstoke: Palgrave Macmillan.

Raskin, Victor. 1985. *Semantic Mechanisms of Humour* [Studies in Linguistics and Philosophy 24]. Dordrecht: D. Reidel.

Schechter, Joel. 1994. *Satiric Impersonations: From Aristophanes to the Guerrilla Girls.* Carbondale/Edwardsville: Southern Illinois University Press.

Travaglio, Marco and Veltri, Elio. 2001. *L'Odore dei Soldi. Origini e Misteri delle Fortune di Silvio Berlusconi* [Primo Piano]. Rome: Editori Riuniti.

Vaccari, Cristian. 2009. "Web challenges to Berlusconi: An analysis of oppositional sites." In *Resisting the Tide: Cultures of Opposition under Berlusconi (2001–06)*, Daniele Albertazzi, Clodagh Brook, Charlotte Ross and Nina Rothenburg (eds), 135–147. London: Continuum.

CHAPTER 8

Mocking Fascism

Popular culture and political satire as counter-hegemony

Efharis Mascha

Hellenic Open University, Greece

Political satire can be considered a significant part of popular culture, but has been systematically neglected by theorists of popular culture. This study discusses how popular culture and political satire reflect their counter-hegemonic project against the Fascist hegemony of Mussolini. All the necessary elements are put into practice in order to eliminate the Fascist power, overthrow the regime, and, most importantly, resist the Fascist standardisation of late modernity. The paper will start with an account of the role of popular culture and its relation to hegemony. Examples and illustrations will facilitate our understanding of political satire as a significant contributor to resistance, change, and the formation of political consciousness.

> The people (oh!), the public (oh!). The political adventurists ask with the scowl of those who know what's what, "The people! But what is this people? Who knows them? Who has ever defined them?"
>
> (Gramsci 1985: 273)

> Popular culture was not identified by the people but by others.
>
> (Williams 1983: 237)

1. Introduction

"Oh, the people! [...] But what is this people?" asks Gramsci, trying to define the political identity of the "people" and their role in the realm of popular culture. "The people" and what constitutes popular culture is not a homogeneous whole, "a homogeneous cultural collectivity" in Brandist's (1996: 235) words. Furthermore, in contrast to the official culture, popular culture is characterised by a fragmentary, "unorganic" nature (Brandist 1996: 235). This fragmentary nature of popular culture makes the task of defining it difficult, and the understanding of its purpose and role – in comparison to the official culture – even more so. Similar problems occur while attempting to understand political satire as part of popular culture. What are the elements of the official culture that political satire uses, and how does it integrate them into something that produces laughter? What is the political role of satirical laughter and how is it achieved? These are questions addressed in this paper. Furthermore, my aim is to show how Gramsci's theory of hegemony can facilitate an understanding of popular culture, clarify its "unorganic" nature, and, consequently, provide us with answers regarding the above questions related to political satire during Mussolini's Fascism.

Before entering the discussion of political satire as part of Italian popular culture, I will briefly describe the data under examination (Section 2). Following that, in Section 3, I will discuss the relationship between popular culture and hegemony together with the role of political cartooning as a counter-hegemonic project. This project is supplemented by the role of the cartoonist as organic intellectual (Section 4) and the notion of contradictory consciousness of popular culture (Section 5). Section 6 includes the analysis of the caricatures based on the aforementioned principles, while the final section summarizes the findings of the study.

2.   The data of the study

The data analysed consists of caricatures published in satirical weekly journals, in particular *L'Asino* and *Becco Giallo* of 1919–1925, by Gabriele Galantara and Giuseppe Scallarini, who were the most popular cartoonists of that time (see also Mascha 2008). Both journals were anti-clerical and anti-Fascist due to their leftist background. *L'Asino* ("The Donkey") was the first Socialist satirical weekly journal published by Guido Podrecca and Gabriele Galantara in Rome starting in 1892. From 1921 it was published in Milan under the direction of G. Galantara alone and its weekly circulation was 100,000 copies. It was suppressed by the Fascist regime by 1925. The *Becco Giallo* ("Yellow Beak") was also an anti-Fascist satirical weekly journal published in Rome. Founded by Alberto Giannini in 1924, it was published in Italy until 1926, and resumed its publication in France until 1931. During this period its circulation figures varied between 50,000 and 450,000 copies per week (see Vallini and Candeloro 1970; Del Buono and Tornabuoni 1972; Gianeri and Rauch 1976).

Both journals were exclusively satirical and were popular amongst the workers of the North and the peasants of the South.[1] Official and unofficial censorship targeted both journals and that is why their circulation varied significantly. Official censorship was imposed on the journals starting with the decree of 1923, which was finalised and implemented as a law on the press by the end of 1926. Unofficial censorship targeted the journals and their contributors since 1919, when Fascists were still a movement and Fascist squads tended to exercise their power through acts of violence against the opposition. At that time, Fascism was an ascendant power, a power to become, and not yet an established hegemonic project. At this stage, there seemed to be no signs of a Fascist satire as a counter satirical project to the leftist one. On the contrary, the Fascist answer to the leftist laughter was violence and exile for the cartoonists.

The main actors of this anti-Fascist satirical project, G. Galantara and G. Scallarini, resisted Fascism by putting their lives in danger and suffering in exile. Their contribution has been vastly neglected by the literature so far, hence in the following section I shall discuss the role of hegemony and counter-hegemony based on the work of Antonio Gramsci, which will set the foreground for my analysis and will account for the cartoonist's role as an organic intellectual in this context.

3. Popular culture as counter-hegemony

This section discusses the role of popular culture in relation to hegemony. This will enable us to theorise the ideological-cultural articulation of the Left when Fascism emerged. Bennett's reading of popular culture through the lenses of hegemony is indicative here.

Following Bennett (1980: 26),

> to rethink the concept of popular culture in and through the concept of hegemony is thus to define it as a system of relations – between classes – which constitutes one of the primary sites upon which the ideological struggle for the production of class alliances or the production of consent, active or passive, is conducted.

Bennett's position raises two important issues regarding popular culture. First, he defines popular culture as a "system of relations between classes". Popular culture

---

1. In his autobiography, Amiconi (1977), a Socialist of Abruzzo, mentions that at home they were reading *L'Avanti!* (i.e. the official Socialist newspaper) and *Becco Giallo* with its famous caricatures, which became significantly popular under the directorship of Alberto Giannini (Salvatorelli and Mira 1964: 340).

is not the culture of a specific class, "it is not the culture of the subdued", as Fiske (1989:69) would say, but is a dynamic process of negotiation between the dominant and subaltern cultural forms. Second, the outcome of this dynamic process is the production of ideology. Similarly, Gramsci suggests an understanding of culture and ideology as two spheres that are linked together in a constant process of mutual determination, which in the end will form the basis of different ideological/cultural articulation. Both issues need further elaboration in order to understand why hegemony is a useful analytical tool for the study of popular culture.

Hegemony refers to the realm of civil society and more specifically to the relation between the power bloc and the subaltern classes.[2] Hence, "one or more groups or classes" can become hegemonic if they are ideologically in ascent "over others in civil society" (Bellamy 1987:126). How exactly does this take place? A "dominant group" manages to "incorporate some popular opinions and aspects of the *common sense* of the subordinate groups into a specific hegemonic discourse of its own" (Harris 1992:27; my emphasis). This process of ideological subordination of the subaltern groups to the hegemonic discourse of the dominant group is fundamental to Gramsci's analysis and can be exemplified extensively in the case of the Fascist and nationalist ideologues who "continuously paid homage to the idea of a unified and unifying national culture" (De Grazia 1981:187). The purpose of *Opera Nazionale Dopolavoro* (the Organisation of Dopolavoro; henceforth OND) or *Instituto Nazionale di Cultura Fascista* ("National Fascist Institute of Culture"; henceforth INCF) was to hegemonise the bourgeois culture (i.e. the culture of the elite) as national culture, and to legitimise the regime and its rule.[3] The dominant ideology of Fascism was practised in these institutions and the Fascist elite aimed to transform and homogenise the masses. Common sense had to be transformed to Fascist sense.

In this context, what was the role of popular culture during Fascism? Following De Grazia (1981:189),

> in the regime's definition, "popular" culture simply involved the transmission of an already formulated body of precepts and information, whereas true culture was formed by the elite and purveyed to the masses.

---

2.   Both terms, *power bloc* and *subaltern classes*, were used by Gramsci in replacement of *Fascism* and *proletariat*, in order to evade the prison censors. *Subalternity*, however, has been employed in a series of different and broader meanings (see Buttigieg 1995:55–62).

3.   *Opera Nazionale Dopolavoro* (OND) was a leisure-time organisation created by the Fascists. Both OND and the INCF made an effort to draw on popular culture and offer art education. In fact, they supported popular culture, "combining genuine pre-industrial hangovers with pseudo-popular festivals invented by the regime" (Passerini 1987:116).

This top-down cultural formation of the Italian society legitimised the role of the Fascist intellectuals and the Fascist elite, and sustained the regime in general. The understanding of "popular culture" was limited to folklore and the regime aimed at creating the "New Italian" with a homogenous political identity eliminating – if possible – the political diversity and opposition to the Fascist rule, as well as the cultural diversity due to the regional particularity of traditions and customs. Their aim was to make a homogenous civil society that would reinforce Fascist hegemony and the state.

On the contrary, popular culture for Gramsci and the Left is a meaningful ideological sphere that moulded the consciousness of the subaltern groups and a place for action for the organic intellectual. Gramsci's understanding of popular culture begins with his critique of the Fascist "statolatry" and his eagerness for a "resurgent vibrant civil society" (Gramsci 1971:268). With regards to the role of the state, he suggested a balance among the state, the civil society, and the private sphere, so that the weakest will not be overcome by the strongest (Gramsci 1971:238). Following Adamson (1980:496), "the best hope for such a balance of power lies in a resurgence of civil society". More precisely, civil society in Gramsci's theory is the public space between the state and the private sphere (Gramsci 1971:238) and the "location of all culture or 'ethical' life publicly expressed" (Adamson 1980:480). Following that train of thought, I consider popular culture as part of "all culture" and, consequently, as part of civil society.

However, a legitimate question would be the following: is popular culture a well-organised part of civil society and, specifically in the case of Fascist ascent, was its role a type of folklore due to the contribution of the organisation of the Fascist political institutions, such as OND and LUCE (*L'Unione Cinematografica Educativa*)?

In the case of Fascism, I consider popular culture to be a discourse organised as counter-hegemony. Popular culture is formed as a counter-discourse to the dominant discourse of Fascist political institutions, which were the main producers of Fascist ideology. Political satire is a typical example of this counter-hegemony, since its primary aim is to subvert official discourse. Gramsci's analysis of hegemony provides us with two important mechanisms that significantly contribute to the establishment of a hegemonic project: *a war of position* and *a war of manoeuvre*.[4] Political satire, as a counter-hegemonic project, systematically

---

4. Following Martin (1998:95), the distinction between *war of position* (*guerra di posizione*) and *war of manoeuvre* (*guerra manovrata*) or *war of movement* (*guerra di movimento*) was originally a military one. Whereas a war of manoeuvre denoted the moment in a military operation in which a frontal attack was directed at an enemy's power base, signifying a coercive assault on the major apparatus of power, a war of position indicated a prolonged series of attacks on the outer defences.

operates as a *war of position*, since it smoothly degrades official discourse by revealing the weak aspects of the regime and not by actually confronting the power
base of the regime, as a *war of manoeuvre* would do. Hence, Mussolini was mocked
for his megalomaniac attitude, his theory of omnipresence and omnipotence, his
attempt to revive the Roman Empire, etc.

Mockery exploited the same tools the regime used to establish its hegemony.
It aimed primarily at subversion (see Dynel this volume; Watters this volume; see
also Tsakona and Popa this volume) and two tropes operated in this effect, namely
condensation and *displacement*, as illustrated by Freud (1905/1991). For Freud the
use of condensation and thus the formation of substitutes establish significant
brevity in the humour device. This process is the first common element between
the joke-work and the dream-work, although in dreams the work of condensation
takes place in pictures, which "exactly resemble one thing or one person except
for an addition or alteration derived from another source – modifications" (Freud
1905/1991:61–62). This is exactly the case of condensation in caricatures.

Since all laconic expressions are not necessarily humorous, displacement is
another fundamental technique that Freud observed in dream-work, as "[it] is
responsible for the puzzling appearance of dreams, which prevents our recognising that they are a continuation of our waking life" (Freud 1905/1991:130). This is
achieved by political caricatures, which use displacement to indirectly mock the
politician's faults or criticise political practices that could have been censored in
case of direct representation.

Via condensation and displacement the cartoonist mocks and subverts official discourse. Both mechanisms function as a *war of position* pulling down the
ideological edifice of Mussolini's immortality and powerfulness. In most cases,
they are used to negatively evaluate and undermine this ideology. *War of position*
was widely exploited during Mussolini's ascent to power due to the growing development of official and unofficial censorship, which would not allow for a *war
of manoeuvre* as an act of resistance. Hence, condensation and displacement were
systematically operated by cartoonists as an ultimate way to lull the vigilance of
the censor and produce laughter. Cartoonists had to strike a balance between the
permitted and the censored and to produce laughter at the same time (see also
Mascha 2008).

The question raised by the proposed analysis of the counter-hegemonic project and the ways it was deployed as a *war of position*, is the following: what was the
specific role of the cartoonist in this context?

4. The role of the cartoonist

The cartoonist shaped and expressed public views and demands. He[5] was in position to criticise official discourse and at the same time educate the illiterate. During the ascendance of Fascism, the level of illiteracy was nearly 40% (De Felice 1966). This level of illiteracy attributed to the cartoonist a special educative role: he was the one who would politically educate the people of the subaltern classes, those of the petite-bourgeoisie and the working class, the subdued, those who resisted not only Fascism, but also the Catholic Church. Hence, he becomes the *organic intellectual* pointed out by Gramsci, suggesting that the organic intellectual was the *esprit de corps,* namely autonomous and independent from the dominant group and aiming at educating and organising the avanguard.[6] As Gramsci (1971:12) notes, "the intellectuals are the dominant group's 'deputies' exercising the subaltern functions of social hegemony and political government". So, the cartoonist can be viewed as the coordinator of the subaltern groups, organising what I called a counter-hegemonic project to the Fascist hegemony (see Section 3).

Both G. Galantara and G. Scallarini's biographies explicitly mention that they were at the hearts of the people (De Micheli 1978; Chiesa 1990). Gramsci's instructions in a letter to Palmiro Togliatti[7] further reveal the guidelines of the opposition concerning the target group of the satirical journals:

> I thought that our party [i.e. the Communist party] could revive on its own behalf the old PSI [i.e. the Italian Socialist Party] paper *Il Seme*[8] as a fortnightly or a monthly. It should be done like the old one, with a modernised content, but of the same type. It should cost no more than one soldo,[9] so that it can circulate among the poorest peasants and it should have many simple cartoons, short articles, etc. It should be aimed at popularising the slogan of the workers' and peasants'

---

5. I only refer to cartoonists as male artists, because there have been no records of any female cartoonists in that period in Italy.

6. Gramsci used the term *avanguard* to refer to the Socialist and, later on, to the Communist party that resisted Fascism. In the case of cartoonists, who also belonged to the Left, I consider all the realm of popular culture as the *avanguard.*

7. P. Togliatti was one of the founders of the Communist Party and replaced Gramsci as a representative of the Communist Party in Moscow (see Mack Smith 1997). The letter was sent to P. Togliatti on March 27, 1924.

8. Old Socialist satirical journal which was published between 1901 and 1914 and, due to the Fascist oppression, did not manage to be republished (Gianeri and Rauch 1976).

9. At that time, 20 soldi were equal to 1 lira. Lira used to be the Italian currency until euro was introduced.

government, at reviving the anticlericalism campaign, because I think that four years of reaction must have thrown the masses in the countryside back to super-stitious mysticism, and also at spreading our own general propaganda.

(Gramsci, cited in Germino 1990: 122)

Thus, caricatures and the comic would be offered to peasants at a very low price, so as to achieve good circulation, revive anticlericalism, and intensify Communist propaganda. The same guidelines were followed by G. Galantara and G. Podrecca for *L'Asino*, by A. Giannini for the *Becco Giallo* and by Guglielmo Guasta for *Il Travaso* (Del Buono 1971; Gianeri and Rauch 1976; Neri 1980; Chiesa 1990; Bergamasco 1995).

To sum up, Mussolini's regime attempted to construct a consensus between the different elements of civil society by creating its own means of civil society (e.g. OND, Fascist organisations, Fascist journals). Mussolini aimed at homoge-nising the civil society and at emerging as a triumphant charismatic leader in Italian politics, who sought to revive the Roman myth of Imperial Italy, a su-perpower among the rest of European countries. His influence was significant among the ranks of the petite bourgeoisie and the working class, who suffered the consequences of World War I and needed an ideological-political bench to lean on. At the same time, a counter-hegemony to his hegemonic project took place step by step as *a war of position* signifying a resistance movement in the ranks of the civil society that resisted the homogenisation and standardisation of everyday life. Political satire played a significant role in this counter-hegemonic project, which is worth looking into and, although it did not manage to actually subvert the regime, it contributed to the "negative evaluation", as Hutcheon (1989) would suggest, of the Fascist myth. It also contributed significantly to the education and the self-determination of subaltern groups, who were able to identify themselves as a group opposing Fascism and laughing at the Fascist mythology. This evalu-ation resulted in a significant change in citizens' common sense, which will be discussed in the following section.

5.   Contradictory consciousness and popular culture

In order to see more clearly how counter-hegemony functions, I would like to discuss the difference between popular culture and folklore, the relationship of popular culture with common sense, resistance, and contradictory consciousness. I consider all these elements to be constitutive parts of a counter-hegemonic pro-cess and, most importantly, the targets of cartoonists' satire.

Popular culture is not folk culture, although they may share some common features. Fiske's (1989, 2002) account is useful in this respect. Fiske (1989:170) claims that

> conceiving popular culture as a form of folk culture denies its conflictual elements. It denies, also, its constantly changing surface as the allegiances that constitute the people are constantly formed and reformed across the social grid.

Fiske here raises two very important issues. First of all, the role of the "conflictual elements" embedded both in satire and popular culture denotes their counter-hegemonic character. Popular discourses entail conflict with the power bloc, thus creating a distance between the worlds of the subaltern and the dominant. In political satire, the opposition to the dominant power is characteristic as a form of irony, ridicule, sarcasm, or cynicism against the power elite (see Manteli this volume; Popa this volume; Tsakona and Popa this volume). The element of opposition or conflict is typical in popular culture, but it is not present on its own as pure negativity of the dominant order. Therefore, it is argued (Bennett et al. 1986:19) that

> popular culture consists of those cultural forms and practices – varying in content from one historical period to another – which constitute the terrain on which dominant, subordinate, and oppositional cultural values and ideologies meet and intermingle, in different mixes and permutations, vying with one another in their attempt to secure the spaces within which they can become influential in framing and organising popular experience and consciousness.

Consequently, popular culture is not an autonomous sphere consisting of discourses, practices, and manifestations purely oppositional to the dominant order. It is a discursive field where popular consciousness is shaped by a dialectical process between the dominant and subordinate culture.

My personal understanding of popular culture entails the element of counter-hegemony under *certain* conditions, where popular culture can become a framework of organising "popular experience and consciousness". Popular media, such as the satirical journals examined here, incorporate this organising element and were highly politicised during this specific historical period, thus creating a kind of counter-hegemony to Fascism. This organisation of the "popular experience and consciousness" was synonymous with the educative aspect of political cartooning, as political cartoonists played the role of the popular intellectuals, who would educate the illiterate Italians away from the superstitiousness and religious values. Italian political satire belonged to the Italian popular culture, of which Fascism was constantly denying existence – by considering it as folklore – due to

Fascists' failure to control it or their inability to create a Fascist political satire. As Fiske (1989:69) insightfully points out,

> the signs of the subordinate out of control terrify the forces of order (whether moral, legal or aesthetic) [i.e. official and unofficial Fascist censorship] [...]; they demonstrate how escaping social control, even momentarily, produces a sense of freedom.

Laughing at the dominant order, if nothing else, gives a great sense of freedom to the subordinate.

Freud's (1905/1991) thesis of humour as a relief mechanism comes to the fore at this point.[10] Laughter escapes social control and the order of the power bloc, while also creating a common sense with the ones that can share the same laughter. The subaltern class laughed, for instance, at Mussolini dressed as a ballet dancer (see Figure 16 in Section 6) and at the same time shared this laughter with other people in the private or public sphere, thus raising their political consciousness. Laughter is an element that brings together people who can share the same sense of humour and consequently share a common understanding of the object that is being laughed at. Hence, subaltern groups may have felt excluded from the power bloc, but still, via political humour and other forms of popular culture, they could create a culture of their own, which was resisting the dominant order and was also conscious of this resistance.

Two immediate questions are raised with regards to consciousness: firstly, what type of consciousness characterises Italian subaltern groups and, secondly, what type of resistance can be formed out of this consciousness?

I began my paper by discussing the role of "the people" and denoted the fragmentary character of what might constitute "the people" and, consequently, the "popular culture". The analysis of the popular consciousness of subaltern groups during the ascent of Fascism to power reveals a variety of social groups. Following Gramsci, subaltern groups,

> although differing from one another in other respects [...] are distinguished from the economically, politically, and culturally powerful groups within society

---

10. Freud (1905/1991:145) argues that "[t]he repressive activity of civilisation brings it about that primary possibilities of enjoyment, which have now, however, been repudiated by the censorship in us, are lost to us". Hence, during the process of civilisation, the expressions of human hostility and aggressiveness have been reduced to the level of tendentious humour. In other words, the socially constructed framework of everyday life creates a number of serious repressions which push the individual back to the level of the unconscious and laughter will emerge with the purpose of unblocking them.

and are hence *potentially* capable of being united – of being organised into "the people versus the power bloc" – if their separate struggles are connected

(Gramsci, cited in Bennett et al. 1986: 20; my emphasis)

This *potential* unity in Gramsci's work allows for the development of a counter-hegemony of "the people versus the power bloc" and, at the same time, moves a step forward class determinism. He also sees this *potential* unity away from the class consciousness of each group, but in connection with their "separate struggles".

The crucial point at this stage of struggling is the type of consciousness that the subaltern groups attain regarding their relation with the power bloc and the tools for transforming the conditions of their lives, whether or not they can effectively comprehend their relation of subordination with the power bloc and act upon it. For Gramsci the masses lack a "clear theoretical consciousness" (Gramsci, cited in Femia 1987: 43–44). Hence,

> the active man-in-the-mass has a practical activity, but has no clear theoretical consciousness of this activity. [...] One might almost say that he has two theoretical consciousnesses (*or one contradictory consciousness*): one which is implicit in his activity and which truly unites him with all his fellow-workers in the practical transformation of reality; and one, superficially explicit or verbal, which he has inherited from the past and uncritically accepted.
>
> (Gramsci, cited in Femia 1987: 43; my emphasis)

The concept of *contradictory consciousness* can explain the fragmentary unity of popular culture and the struggle of the latter to become a counter-hegemonic discourse that would be embraced by the subaltern groups who would thus achieve consensus. Political satire plays an important role in the consciousness of subalternity since it denigrates the past which the active-man-in-the-mass has "uncritically accepted". Political satire challenges the norms and order that aim at controlling and homogenising the subordinate groups by constraining their lives in order to maintain the status quo. That is why I consider political satire a part of popular culture which aims at creating "a space in which contradictory values can echo, reverberate and be heard" (Bennett et al. 1986: 19).

The first step towards change can take place in what constitutes the common sense of the people. Fiske also raises the issue of change and reformation, which brings us back to what Gramsci considered common sense, namely a constitutive part of popular culture being in "continuous transformation". For Gramsci (1971: 326),

> common sense is not something rigid and stationary, but is in continuous transformation, becoming enriched with scientific notions and philosophical opinions that have entered into common circulation. Common sense is the folklore of

philosophy and always stands midway between folklore proper and the philosophy science, and economics of the scientists. Common sense creates the folklore of the future, a relatively rigidified phase of popular knowledge in a given time and place.

Political satire challenges common sense attitudes and preconceptions of the world. It reverses the world created by the dominant order. Was Mussolini's government a legitimate one? How did he deal with Fascist violence? What was the pacification pact? Or, who was against normalisation? Via Fascist media and propaganda, the Fascist government was creating a "common sense" of political stability, legitimate government, and a strong ability to deal with the currents of violence spreading in the periphery. Political satire systematically mocked this propaganda by creating a counter-hegemonic discourse and showing the opposite side of the coin, thus reducing the power of the dictator in the eyes of the disempowered people.

Keeping in mind popular culture and political satire as a discourse of counter-hegemony, it remains to discuss the role of *resistance*. In other words, is popular culture and, in the present case, political satire a form of resistance? If it is, what type of resistance is it? Is resistance expressed as discomfort at the individual level and is this discomfort translated into cynicism or irony? Or is resistance promoted to a level of sociopolitical action? Political satire has been already examined in different social contexts and their common denominator was political humour as "peaceful protest" and not as a radical change in the system (Brandes 1977; Pi-Sunyer 1977).

Popular culture can classify change as either radical or popular (Fiske 1989). In the case of radical change, we have the emergence of a revolutionary movement where radical change takes place in social structure. In the case of popular change, we are faced with a progressive, on-going process, which is normally "politicised at the micro-political level *only*" (Fiske 1989: 172; my emphasis). As a result, it can be argued that political satire (i.e. political cartoons such as the *Uncertainties of Consensus* in Figure 14 and *Lazzarina between the Knives* in Figure 16; see Section 6) is a form of resistance, expressed as a counter-hegemony to the dominant order, and constitutes an on-going process which changes the common sense, the preconceptions, and stereotypes of "the people", relieving them from the power of their oppressors. For Gramsci (1998), the *contradictory consciousness* of the masses can be developed through education and through the strong leadership of the organic intellectual, who would be able to give the people and, more specifically, the proletariat a strategic plan for becoming hegemonic. At a micro-political level, the cartoonist functions as a type of "popular intellectual", since he refers to the illiterate masses, who can laugh at his drawings and receive his political message.

I would like to suggest here that laughing at the system of order does not necessarily change the *big structure*, but is attributed to a micro-level change in the realm of common sense and relieves those oppressed by the power bloc. This point will be further illustrated in the next section via the analysis of examples coming from my data.

6. The analysis of caricatures

Before entering into the analysis of specific caricatures, I need to refer to how Mussolini's image created and projected his megalomaniac identity. By the time he became Prime Minister, he was the youngest one in Italian history and he insisted on reproducing the image of the young Duce through "the government's communications to the press, via *Ufficio Stampa* [i.e. the government's press office], and by forbidding journalists from publicizing Mussolini's birthdays" (Falasca-Zamponi 2000: 72–73). Together with his young, healthy, and serious profile, his qualities, superhuman capacities, and daily activities (e.g. daily horse riding, daily walk, daily car ride) were being analysed daily in the press, while the number of his photos outnumbered those of any previous Prime Minister.

Via controlling the press, Mussolini created the myth of the superhuman. He visited Sicily in 1923 whilst Etna was erupting. The moment Mussolini arrived, the lava stopped, and a village that was in danger was saved. So, after the event the newspapers wrote the following: "The river of flowing lava had to stop in the face of the fire, much more ardent, of the Duce's eyes" (Falasca-Zamponi 2000: 71). He also built a legend of immortality, as numerous attempts on his life failed. In April 1926, Violet Gibson shot him and missed, and Mussolini said to the crowd in Milan: "Bullets pass and Mussolini stays" (Falasca-Zamponi 2000: 75). His omnipotence and his immortality were reproduced successfully by the Fascist rhetoric and were being degraded by political satire. The only outcome of all these attempts on Mussolini's life was the enforcement of very strict laws against the opposition and its actual elimination by 1926. Mussolini's image sold well, "whether in postcards or soap bars or as a model of style" (Falasca-Zamponi 2000: 145). He built his personality in a political culture capitalising on the role of the political leader and he succeeded in creating the myth that he had everything under his control. He supposedly worked twenty-four hours a day, leaving the light of his office on even at night in order to show that the regime never rested. Congruent with his superhuman capacities and his immortality, he did not create any institutional means of transference of power. He did not need a successor as "the Duce was eternal" (Falasca-Zamponi 2000: 77).

In Figure 14, Mussolini is portrayed in exactly the opposite way from the official Fascist discourse wishes to present him, thus creating a project of counter-hegemony: he is portrayed with a stupid face, as a helpless fat assistant, and as a poor bureaucrat drowned by paperwork with *Se ne vada!* ("Go away!") written on it.

The Italian cartoonist G. Galantara mocks Mussolini's "belief" that his government is based on consensus by displacing it (in Freud's 1905/1991 sense; see Section 3) with a "Go away!" caption that terrifies Mussolini. *Se ne vada* is the displacement of the Fascist motto *Me ne frego* ("Who gives a damn!"), which accompanied and gave justification to all their violent acts. In 1924, Fascism went through its greatest crisis, the opposition was not yet tamed, violence was spreading throughout the country, and no light of consensus could be seen at the end

Figure 14. *L'Asino* (December 13, 1924), *The Uncertainties of Consensus*

of the tunnel. Mussolini is represented as asking for mercy and with a pitiful, yet ugly face. While the official Fascist propaganda presented Mussolini as worka-holic, omnipresent, and with an incomparable ability to solve problems, political satire degraded Mussolini's authority and his officials, aiming at subverting their power. A comparison of the above political caricature with a photo of Mussolini taken whilst at work leads to a better understanding of the way political satire tried to subvert his power. Figure 15 was carefully composed as a good example of his watchful look (Mack Smith 2001: 148).

In Figure 15, he appears to be calm and serious, definitely not hopeless and drowned by paper work. His watchful look aims to reassure the people that he will solve all the problems that may come his way. This ideological construct of the of-ficial propaganda aimed at reinforcing social security and governmental stability, while the Fascist regime became bureaucratic in its effort to control the economy and the civil society.

In short, political satire functioned as a "value-problematising, de-naturalis-ing form of acknowledging the history of representation" (Hutcheon 1989: 94). It successfully undermined the value system that Fascist hegemony attempted to establish. That is why we could say that, by presenting the opposite picture of the official propaganda, political satire became a successful weapon in the hands of the opposition, as well as a sign of resistance of the "perfect" image the regime attempted to establish. Following Gramsci (1971), I shall call this process of resis-tance *counter-hegemony*.

People resisted Mussolini's "perfect" image as dictator and governor. In Fig-ure 16, the declarations of the government in the parliament are presented as *Lazzarina fra i Coltelli* ("Lazzarina between the Knives"), which constitutes a

Figure 15. Prime Minister Mussolini at his desk in Palazzo Chigi (Mack Smith 1981)

Figure 16. *Becco Giallo* (1924), *Lazzarina between the Knives*

clear example of condensation (in Freud's 1905/1991 sense; see Section 3), since the word *Lazzarina* results from the combination of the word *Lazzarone* "scoundrel"[11] and the ending *-ina* denoting a female noun, thus denigrating Mussolini's political actions.

Fascism in those first years was equivalent to Mussolinianism; hence, Mussolini's declarations were equivalent to the governments' declarations. By characterising Mussolini as a scoundrel dancing like a "pretty" ballet dancer among sharp knives, the cartoonist degrades Mussolini's regime and his ability to deal with their problems. The cartoonist portrays the problems as sharp knives which are difficult to avoid. Femininity is used here to metaphorically symbolise Mussolini's

---

11. *Lazzaroni* or *lazzari* comes from the Spanish *lazaro* "poor" (which in turn derives from the Biblical figure of Lazarus the beggar). From the 16th century onwards this word was applied by the Spanish rulers to the urban mob of Naples (and, by extension, of other cities). In Naples, this sub-proletariat was strongly monarchist and in 1799 they rose in the Sanfedista rising against the bourgeois Jacobin regime of the Parthenopean Republic. It continued to be the bastion of the Bourbons to the end. The term itself is pejorative, stressing the wretched condition of that sub-proletariat and its supposed laziness and dishonesty. Gramsci refers to these *lazzaroni* of the South as "vagabondry", due to whom the legend of the underdeveloped South was theorised by positivists and sustained the conflict between South and North Italy (see Gramsci 1971:71).

weakness and his inability to deal with public affairs, since the role of the woman for the official Fascist discourse is to stay at home, raise children, and be a good wife (see among others De Grazia 1992; Pickering-Iazzi 1993). On the other hand, femininity contradicts Mussolini's expression of masculinity on every public occasion and the prevailing discourse regarding the role of man as the cornerstone of the family, a good soldier, a member of the Fascists serving the nation, and, ultimately, as a politician-artist (male pole) creating wise laws/sculptures for the masses (female pole). The displacement between femininity-masculinity, which is a common method in most political satire even today, makes the caricature funny and reveals once more the paternalistic norms of the Italian society. Such norms are related to the Italian tradition and reflect sentiments of inferiority with regards to woman's role in the public sphere (De Grazia 1992; Pickering-Iazzi 1993; Mascha 2010). In other words, in the traditional margins of this culture, it is the ultimate resource of political satire to portray a public official (even more so, if he is the powerful, omnipotent, etc. Prime Minister) with feminine features.

So, Mussolini is portrayed as a ballet dancer, being stared at by his assistants and dancing among a series of knives named *illegalismo* "illegalism", *syndicalismo* "syndicalism", *polizia* "police", *industria* "industry", *Socialismo* "Socialism", *Capitalismo* "Capitalism", *opposizione* "opposition", *liberta* "liberty", *debito* "deficit", *stato* "state administration", *militarismo* "military". All these are different, yet equivalent areas of political decision that Mussolini should respond to without getting "injured". A Freudian analysis would pinpoint the role of the knives together with their position in the picture, aiming at the dancer. For Freud (1905/1991), this hidden aggressiveness would be the element that the audience could relate to, and thus becomes the medium through which humour becomes successful. In other words, it is the element that lets laughter sound.

The displacement of Mussolini's masculinity to the femininity of a ballet dancer, who may seem happy and "elegant" but who steps among sharp knives, makes the political satire successful and at the same time brings Mussolini's governmental declarations closer to popular culture. He is not the inaccessible dictator of public speeches in Piazza Victoria of Rome; he is an object of derision through the travesty, and his power is undermined in the eyes of the public. The cartoonist mocks Mussolini's incapacity to govern, scorns the "baseness" of the regime, and challenges his power (Passerini 1987). In fact, Lazzarinismo, being at the heart of the Southern popular culture, had a connotation of the subaltern classes counter-posing the discipline, order, and masculinity of Northern Italy propagated by the regime. Nevertheless, this counter-position seemed to make him more "human" and more sympathetic, instead of the cruel omnipotent dictator of his official propaganda (see Figure 17; see also Mascha 2008), thus breaking the face of the cruel dictator who governs the people against their will.

Figure 17. Prime Minister Mussolini addressing the Fascists (Mack Smith 1981)

In this respect, political satire, as part of Italian popular culture, played a significant role in constructing a certain type of consciousness, and once again counter-posed the official propaganda that wanted Mussolini to look as a legend of masculinity, heroism, militarism, and strength (as shown in Figure 17).

In contrast to this image of immortality and omnipresence, the cartoonist via exaggeration makes Mussolini meet his younger image in the caricature called *Incontro* ("Encounter"; see Figure 18), which actually refers to an accidental meeting rather than a fixed appointment. It is one of the most famous caricatures of 1923 (under medium level of censorship) and has been reproduced in a series of anthologies of political caricatures (Gianeri and Rauch 1976; Neri 1980; Chiesa 1990; Bergamasco 1995). It portrays the meeting of the past and the present, a moment of identification, of who is who. It is a moment of reflection on past political practices which leads to the following dialogue:

> – Chi siete?
> – Sono… Benito del '14!
> – Mi meraviglio…che siete ancora libero!
> (Figure 18)
>
> Old Benito (on the left): Who are you?
> Young Benito (on the right): I am… Benito of '14!
> Old Benito: I am amazed… you are still free!

Young Benito's pause (indicated with dots) signifies his surprise, a moment of identification, as if to say "You know who I am!", which is also reflected in his look, the nod of his head, and the movement of his hand. On the other hand, the

Figure 18. *L'Asino* (February 3, 1923), *The Encounter*

pause following the "surprise" in the old Mussolini's answer, together with his eyes and gesture, signify an act of aggression. He is not the red-coated Mussolini, but rather belongs to the blackshirts and is ready to imprison anyone who belongs to the opposite camp. He is surprised by his past and would be happy if he could erase it somehow:

The cartoonist degrades his current political identity by reminding the audience of who he was back in 1914. The caricature entails an act of aggression, especially on the side of the old Mussolini, since he represents the aggression of Fascist squads, and this aggression justifies the Freudian theory (Freud 1905/1991) concerning the release of hidden elements of aggression from the unconscious through the humorous device. Simultaneously, this act of aggression and the process of identification are constitutive parts of the Gramsci's *contradictory consciousness* (see Section 5). The cartoonist mocks Mussolini's political identity and his transformation from the ranks of Socialism to Fascism. His transformation is so rigid that one cannot help but wonder why he has not killed or imprisoned himself for once being a Socialist. The past meets the present and what was once in favour of Socialism is now against it. The official Fascist propaganda during 1923 would not suggest a similar *encounter*, since Fascism was linked with the Imperial Rome and not Socialism.

Hence, political satire brings forth elements of this contradictory consciousness in the process of self-determination and, whilst challenging the official interpretation of history, makes a step towards change.

7.   Conclusions

My theoretical encounter with popular culture focused on the work of Gramsci and revealed that popular culture can – under certain conditions – become a counter-hegemony to the dominant order. I have discussed Gramsci's theory of hegemony as it "constitutes the focal, terminal point of the history of the subaltern classes" (Salamini 1981:126). My discussion of hegemony serves the purpose of clearly understanding the role of popular culture in the context of Fascism. The possibility of a hegemonic leadership as the outcome of an enlarged consensus among the dominant order and the proletariat (i.e. a homogeneous civil society) was expected to develop popular culture. Nevertheless, this consensus, namely the "collective will" that would transcend the particularity of every political identity (whether Left or Right), was *not* an achievement of Fascism: Fascism achieved only a partial consensus. That is why this lack of consensus was at the core of the opposition's political satire.

Gramsci's understanding of hegemony is crucial for the reading of political satire as it throws light on the alternative (i.e. the counter-hegemony) of Mussolini's ascent to power. This counter-hegemony would result from an active consensus and not a coercive system that aimed at controlling the media, silencing the press, and establishing itself through the control of an enlarged state and its functionaries. Mussolini's dream of the new empowered Italy and the new Italian was based on violence and censorship, thus it became the target of political satire. This project can be understood only by means of a hegemonic project based on the ethico-political maturity of the civil society that organically links the level of the superstructures. This ethico-political maturity of the civil society was represented in popular culture, in which political satire was embedded and had an educative role towards the illiterate masses that would otherwise be guided by Catholicism and religiosity, superstitiousness, and myths presenting Mussolini as omnipotent and immortal, a true descendent of the Romans and Emperor of a future Italian Empire (Falasca-Zamponi 2000).

Hence, starting with Gramsci and his account of hegemony, I moved forward to the discussion of popular culture, as it has been examined by more recent theorists of popular culture (e.g. Bennett 1980; Fiske 1989, 2002), who point out the "conflictual" element of popular culture, its role in organising popular consciousness, and, finally, the possibility of change not as a radical change of the structure, but as an on-going process of change at the micro-political level. So, on the one hand, political satire can portray a form of resistance and direct conflict with the dominant system, but, on the other hand, the process of change is more developed at the micro-political level, leaving the bigger structure of the power-system untouched.

In the present case study, the role of political satire functioned within the margins of popular culture without directly affecting the emergence of Fascism and its hegemonic power. Political satire and political cartoonists as popular intellectuals played an important role in politically educating the illiterate masses through laughter. In addition, with their own life experience – being chased, imprisoned, and sometimes even executed by the Fascists – they contributed to the resistance movement. During the Fascist ascent (1919-1925), the resistance movement was not well-organised and the counter-hegemonic project of the cartoonists was step by step censored: popular satirical journals were officially banned (Mascha 2008:71–73). In the realm of popular culture, however, the cartoonists and their caricatures were kept alive in the memory of the people, which was actually a step towards the counter-hegemony of a better organised and more efficient resistance movement during the mid 1930s, when some of the satirical journals emerged again and the regime's power was doomed to collapse.

Acknowledgments

The author would like to thank Villy Tsakona and Diana Popa, as well as the two anonymous reviewers for their extremely insightful comments on an earlier version of this paper.

References

Adamson, Walter L. 1980. *Hegemony and Revolution. A Study of Antonio Gramsci's Political and Cultural Theory*. Berkeley: California Press University.
Bellamy, Richard P. 1987. *Modern Italian Social Theory*. London: Polity Press.
Bennett, Tony. 1980. "Popular culture: A teaching object." *Screen Education* 34: 17–29.

Bennett, Tony, Mercer, Colin and Woollacott, Janet. (eds). 1986. *Popular Culture and Social Relations*. Milton Keynes: Open University Press.

Bergamasco, Franco. 1995. *L'Italia in Caricatura*. Rome: Newton Compton.

Brandes, Stanley H. 1977. "Peaceful protest: Spanish political humour in a time of crisis." *Western Folklore* 36: 331–346.

Brandist, Craig. 1996. "The official and popular in Gramsci and Bakhtin." *Theory, Culture and Society* 13: 59–74.

Buttigieg, Joseph A. 1995. "Gramsci on civil society." *Boundary 2* 22: 1–32.

Chiesa, Adolfo. 1990. *La Satira Politica in Italia*. Rome: Laterza.

De Felice, Renzo. 1966. *Mussolini il Fascista: La Conquista del Potere 1921–1925*. Rome: Einaudi Tascabili.

De Grazia, Victoria. 1981. *The Culture of Consent: Mass Organisation of Leisure in Fascist Italy*. Cambridge: Cambridge University Press.

De Grazia, Victoria. 1992. *How Fascism Ruled Women: Italy 1922–1945*. Berkeley: University of California Press.

De Micheli, Mario. 1978. *Scalarini. Vita e Disegni del Grande Caricaturista Politico*. Milan: Feltrinelli.

Del Buono, Oreste. (ed.). 1971. *Eia, Eia, Eia, Alalà. La Stampa Italiana sotto il Fascismo*. Milan: Feltrinelli.

Del Buono, Oreste and Tornabuoni, Lietta. (eds). 1972. *Il Becco Giallo. Dinamico di Opinione Publica, 1924–1931*. Milan: Feltrinelli.

Falasca-Zamponi, Simonetta. 2000. *Fascist Spectacle. The Aesthetics of Power in Mussolini's Italy* [Studies on the History of Society and Culture 28]. Berkeley/Los Angeles: University of California Press.

Femia, Joseph V. 1987. *Gramsci's Political Thought. Hegemony, Consciousness, and the Revolutionary Process*. Oxford: Clarendon Press, Oxford University Press.

Fiske, John. 1989. *Understanding Popular Culture*. London: Routledge.

Fiske, John. 2002. *Reading the Popular*. London: Routledge.

Freud, Sigmund. 1905/1991. *Jokes and their Relations to the Unconscious*. Transl. James Strachey [The Penguin Freud Library 6]. London: Penguin.

Germino, Dante. 1990. *Antonio Gramsci: Architect of a New Politics* [Political Traditions in Foreign Policy]. Louisiana: Louisiana State University Press.

Gianeri, Enrico and Rauch, Andrea. 1976. *Cento Anni di Satira Politica in Italia (1876–1976)*. Florence: Guaraldi.

Gramsci, Antonio. 1971. *Prison Notebooks*. Ed./transl. Q. Hoare and G. N. Smith. London: Lawrence and Wishart.

Gramsci, Antonio. 1985. *Selection from Cultural Writings*. Ed. D. Forgacs and G. Nowell-Smith. London: Lawrence and Wishart.

Harris, David. 1992. *From Class Struggle to the Politics of Pleasure. The Effects of Gramscianism on Cultural Studies*. London: Routledge.

Hutcheon, Linda.1989. *The Politics of Postmodernism* [New Accents]. London/New York: Routledge.

Mack Smith, Denis. 1981. *Italy and its Monarchy*. New Haven/London: Yale University Press.

Mack Smith, Denis. 1997. *Modern Italy: A Political History*. Ann Arbor: The University of Michigan Press.

Mack Smith, Denis. 2001. *Mussolini*. London: Weidenfeld and Nicolson History.

Martin, James. 1998. *Gramsci's Political Analysis: A Critical Introduction.* Houndmills: McMillan.

Mascha, Efharis. 2008. "Political satire and hegemony: A case of 'passive revolution' during Mussolini's ascendance to power 1915–1925." *Humour: International Journal of Humour Research* 21: 69–98.

Mascha, Efharis. 2010. "Contradictions and the role of the 'floating signifier': Identity and the 'New Woman' in Italian cartoons during Fascism." *Journal of International Women's Studies* 11. http://www.bridgew.edu/SoAS/jiws/May10/FloatingSignifier.pdf (accessed March 20, 2011).

Neri, Guido Davide. 1980. *Galantara: Il Morso dell'Asino.* Milan: Feltrinelli.

Passerini, Luisa. 1987. *Fascism in Popular Memory. The Cultural Experience of the Turin Working Class* [Studies in Modern Capitalism]. Transl. Robert Lumley and Jude Bloomfield. Cambridge: Cambridge University Press.

Pickering-Iazzi, Robin. (ed./transl.). 1993. *Unspeakable Women. Selected Short Stories Written by Italian Women during Fascism.* New York: Feminist Press at the University of New York.

Pi-Sunyer, Oriol. 1977. "Political humour in a dictatorial state: The case of Spain." *Ethnohistory* 24: 179–190.

Salamini, Leonardo. 1981. *The Sociology of Political Praxis. An Introduction to Gramsci's Theory.* London: Routledge and Kegan Paul.

Vallini, Edio and Candeloro, Giorgio. 1970. *L'Asino di Podrecca e Galantara (1892–1925).* Milan: Feltrinelli.

Williams, Raymond. 1983. *Keywords. A Vocabulary of Culture and Society* (revised edition). London: Fontana.

PART III

Public debates and political humour

CHAPTER 9

Politics of taste in a post-Socialist state

A case study

Liisi Laineste

Estonian Literary Museum, Estonia

The link between jokes and social reality is visible in the way jokes adapt to different sociopolitical contexts by dealing with the most salient issues of such contexts. This chapter casts light on another facet of the relationship of jokes and their social context. Ideas *about* jokes are influenced by their social context, being continuously reformulated by social change or political manipulation. This case study analyses the official and unofficial media discourses that address the issues of taste and sense of humour, as emerging from a recent polemics about Estonian ethnic jokes. The different standpoints reflect ideas about the content and functions of the jokelore, characterising jokes either as an essentially racist or as a funny (i.e. harmless) genre.

1. Introduction

Among small communities, joke-telling (and humorous communication, in general) is often motivated by a desire to indicate and create positive effect. At the same time, joking about something means excluding people who do not understand the in-group jokes, or those that the jokes are about (Martin 2007: 116). Based on the conclusions of several studies in personality psychology, Martin (2008: 16–21) suggests that exposure to aggressive jokes can have an influence on the attitude of listeners, albeit a complicated one. Racist jokes may reinforce the joke-teller's negative stereotypes and make them more salient for the listener (see among others Ford 2000; Ford and Ferguson 2004).

However, whenever we want to describe the influence of jokes on society as a whole, or when we are looking for reasons why certain jokes exist in certain societies and why targets vary between regions and through time, the conclusions from studies on personality and interpersonal communication are insufficient or even misleading. There are no adequate methods to evaluate the change of attitudes in a society after exposure to the stimulus, namely the (potentially aggressive and racist) joke text. A careful analysis of historical, political, and cultural arguments is necessary, conducted on a wider scale and via juxtaposing data from different periods and places, namely by methods of cross-cultural comparison (Davies 2008; Kuipers 2008).

The present study explores the relationship between jokes and their social context by addressing their function as politicised texts. Describing certain instances of joking that balance on the thin line between humour and insult will help explain the politics of humour taste: what aspects of jokelore become relevant in public discussions of humour, how well does humour travels between different social groups, and what happens if people's interpretations and ideas about humour are not compatible?

To this end, after a brief overview of some of the relevant literature (Section 2), I will give a short history of the search for ethnic identity in Estonia and its connection with ideas of nationalism and xenophobia (Section 3). In Section 4, based on the two-dimensional model of attitudes towards racism (Vihalemm and Timmi 2007), I will analyse the recent polemics about Estonian ethnic jokes in a public debate. This case study uses material from two types of sources: published newspaper articles representing official discourse through the voices of government officials and journalists, and the unofficial responses to these articles in online forums by Estonian citizens. The four-way categorisation of the material will describe the data in terms of the opinions expressed about ethnic jokes, simultaneously revealing the discussants' thoughts about nationalism and racism. Section 5 discusses well-known similar cases, such as the Danish Mohammad cartoons and the *Borat* film, and draws parallels among them. It will thus be possible (in Section 6) to draw some conclusions about the way jokes interact with society at large, contribute to the negotiation of taste and ethics, and influence the construction of identity and the meaning of censorship in a post-totalitarian society.

2.   Ethnic jokes, ethnic identity, and political correctness

The relationship between society and jokes is played out on different levels, the former influencing the popularity of, and attitudes towards, the latter. The common sense view about the relationship between society and jokes maintains that jokes are a straightforward reflection of society, its prejudices, stereotypes, etc., so that racist jokes mirror the racist attitudes of a group. The existence of racist jokes can therefore be interpreted as evidence of xenophobia: a group of people selecting particular targets and joke types can be assumed to foster racist attitudes. Thus, the claim that jokes reveal racist attitudes often becomes a political statement. Jokes are transformed into a political argument, as they are considered texts of ambiguous moral and ethical quality.

Nevertheless, there are several problems with this line of reasoning. First, the relationship between jokes and society is not straightforward and jokes are better explained by certain social, economic, and other relations between groups; secondly, jokes are ambivalent and offer the joke-teller the opportunity to claim that s/he was "only joking" (see among others Tannen 1992); and last but not least, not everybody who tells racist jokes necessarily has negative attitudes towards joke targets (Attardo and Raskin 1991).

The present analysis offers an example of how politics interferes with ethnic jokes by forcing them to become political, in the sense that they are manipulated to stand for more than they actually do.[1] This is particularly evident under certain social circumstances: under political oppression or social transition, which bring along a number of unexpected cultural encounters, blur social boundaries, and prioritise issues of identity. Rather than being just a reflection of a relationship between a teller and a target, jokes acquire their meaning in relation to a particular society, its specific cultural, economic, and, above all, political contexts.

Ethnic identity is primarily understood and defined as a characteristic of both the individual and society as a whole, which is constantly reconstructed via internal and external processes, including politics (Nagel 1994). Ethnic identity is not a stable entity, but is rather shaped by a constant dialogue between individuals and their social contexts, narrow or broadly described. It can also become stronger at times of perceived threat. Studies of intolerance and racism have drawn their conclusions mainly based on large-scale opinion surveys and national polls (see among others Wallace 2002; Goldman 1997, and references therein). Many of them involve post-Socialist countries, which are often perceived as a threat to the stability of interethnic relations in Europe. Furthermore, interviews and analysis of media texts are common (see among others Žagar 2002). The transition of totalitarian regimes into young democracies has turned Eastern Europe into a hotbed of ethnic tension (Gurin 2004; Hann 2002; Pajnik 2002; Wallace 2002; Spohn and Triandafyllidou 2003). In the context of pre-existing conflicts, the various difficulties resulting from transition may bring about heightened feelings of nationalism (the Estonian example is discussed in greater length in Section 3, following Lokk 2003).

Considered relatively harmless and ambiguous, ethnic jokes have not been addressed in studies concerning group attitudes. On the other hand, ethnic or racist humour has been excluded from public discourse as tasteless in many

---

1. Other types of jokes have also been described in the context of a totalitarian society, for example, the ethno-political joke; see Laineste (2009).

Western European countries (Davies 1996; Kuipers 2006). The need to be politically correct especially in the context of increasing migration and cultural diversity stigmatises such jokes as hostile (Billig 2005). Researchers have described the attitudes displayed in ethnic jokes as negative and stereotype reinforcing rather than moderating and enabling to overcome the tensions present in a society (see among others Lockyer and Pickering 2005). The view that jokes are thermometers (and not thermostats; Davies 1990) maintains that they reveal attitudes that are left undercover (see also Mesropova 2007). It is therefore useful to investigate jokes in the context of ethnic struggle, where a quest for a (new) national identity brings to the surface attempts to censor jokes, and reveals the limits of humour. The contemporary Estonian joke tradition presents a relevant example as ethnic jokes are available without censorship and the negotiations of taste are still underway.

Previous research (Laineste 2008) has shown that Estonians currently tend to make Latvians, Finns, and themselves the targets of their stupidity jokes. In addition, some groups mocked a century ago are now re-emerging in Estonian jokelore: Saare, Hiiu, and Muhu islanders; Setus and Mulks from Southern Estonia. All the "exotic" nations (Turks, blacks, Indians, Latin Americans, but also Frenchmen or Swedes) introduced during the early post-Socialism have disappeared from contemporary Estonian jokelore. Estonians do not even joke about their biggest and most powerful neighbours, the Russians, anymore (Laineste 2008:134–135).

Nevertheless, autumn 2007 saw a heated discussion in the Estonian and Russian media about the ethical dimension of ethnic jokes. The argument revealed two contradicting positions about the relationship of jokes and insult, advocating that jokes are a form of aggressive racism or, on the contrary, that they are harmless fun. Similarly to what happened with the cartoons depicting Mohammad in 2006, no compromise could be found between the two parties. The limits of humour and aggression were being defined by both sides. As revealed in the present study, it seems that the official discourse finds the jokes abusive and not funny, while the unofficial sources stress that jokes belong above all to a funny genre that can at times seem racist, but should not be censored in any case.

3.   The cultural and historical background of the polemics

Heterogeneous groups should, in an ideal state, form an assimilated community based on a common territory, culture, language, religion, etc. Among the four types of acculturation identified by Berry (1980), namely marginalisation, separation, assimilation, and integration, it has been suggested that the Russian minority in Estonia displays all four of the above-mentioned types of acculturation (Tammaru 1997). In reality, because of different education systems and territorial separation, the two communities of local Estonians and Russian immigrants in Estonia have always lived separate lives. The same social distancing has been carried over into post-Socialism: for example, there are few intermarriages or informal relations between Estonians and Russian immigrants, and different social networks, even different media channels are used (Heidmets 1998). As a result, ethnic Russian immigrants in Estonia have posed a problem for post-Socialist Estonia, as internal homogeneity has often been considered by the Estonian majority to be the starting point of a fully functioning society.

Certain socio-psychological factors inherited from the recent past hindered the process of acculturation of the Russian minority in the 1990s (Lokk 2003): (1) the existential fears about the strength of the nation connected with the immediate presence of a large and "alien" community (Pettai 2000); (2) the cultural and language barrier (Laitin 1998); (3) the historical memory of the recent occupation with moral responsibility being assigned to the younger generation of Russians in Estonia; and (4) the suspicions towards the political identity and loyalty of the Russian minority.

Such "fears" lasted until the middle of the 1990s, when it became clear that only a small percentage of ethnic Russians would emigrate from Estonia to Russia, that is, approximately 1/5 of the Russian population in Estonia (Kirch 1999). Integration then became an issue which had to be dealt with. This change of mentality was also brought about by a more general shift of interest, from an existentialist collective focus (directed towards the nation and state) to an individualistic and pragmatic focus (on economy and living standards), which in turn led to a revision of attitudes towards interethnic relations. The identity issues had to be addressed in one way or another, be it due to European regulations or in the name of local social equilibrium. At times, the Estonian response to European regulations about handling minorities has been quite ambiguous. As a consequence, in September 2007, Rene van der Linden, the President of the Parliamentary Assembly of the Council of Europe, criticised the status of ethnic minorities in Estonia. His public statement was followed by a vigorous discussion about the rights of ethnic Russians (see among others Stadnikov 2007). Many Estonians felt that (misinformed) European Union officials should not have a say in issues of Estonian internal politics.

During the last decade, Estonian politics have turned more and more to displaying and stressing the difference in identity between Estonian and ethnic Russians, thus deliberately constructing the *us versus them* cleavage. As a result,

Estonian's perceived uniqueness and constructed difference from ethnic Russians in Estonia is employed to legitimise the xenophobic and nationalist attitudes of Estonians. Politicians and the media manipulate the nationalist feelings and identities of both Estonians and Russians immigrants, thus influencing the reactions of the wider public. At times such reactions become quite unpredictable, as happened in the case of relocating the Bronze Soldier monument. The Bronze Soldier has significant symbolic value to Estonia's community of post-World War II immigrants (mostly ethnic Russians), symbolising not only Soviet victory over Nazi Germany in the Great Patriotic War, but also advocating for their rights in Estonia. At the same time, Estonians consider the Bronze Soldier to be a symbol of Soviet occupation and repression. The statue was removed under great secrecy and considerable haste a few days before May 9th, 2007, a day of primary significance to Russian World War II veterans. The primarily politically motivated relocation escalated into two nights of looting and riots in Tallinn (which left one dead, 153 injured, and over 800 arrested), and also resulted in the siege and week-long occupation of the Estonian embassy in Moscow. Coincidently, miniature Estonian car flags entered the market and were displayed with great pride all over the country, sometimes also evoking aggressive responses from local Russians. The period was characterised by an overall rise in nationalist feelings on both sides.

The tense atmosphere during this period was also expressed indirectly, namely in informal communication and jokes. Laughter after the riots, following the relocation of the Bronze Soldier monument, certainly escalated, while jokes in Russian which targeted Estonians appeared on the internet (Kall 2007; this tendency was, however, visible before spring 2007; see among others Krikmann 2006). At the same time, Estonians tend to laugh more and more with/at themselves. Even the Soviet three-nation stupidity jokes, traditionally featuring the Estonian, the German, and the Russian, and circulating among Estonian schoolchildren, have by now switched the nationalities which appear in the first and last positions: instead of the Russian, it is now the Estonian who is defeated (Tuisk 2009).

Political decisions and attitudes concerning immigrants in Estonia have been much-manipulated facets of Estonian national revival and also typical of a nation-state where ethnic conflicts are prone to arise. Describing the array of opinions and attitudes towards racism, a research group of the Ministry of Justice, in their report on xenophobia in the Estonian press (Vihalemm and Timmi 2007), presented a two-dimensional model of possible attitudes towards racism (see Figure 19).[2]

---

2. The labels for the four categories are borrowed from Vihalemm and Timmi (2007), and will be used throughout the article. At times, for the sake of brevity, four abbreviations will alternatively be used:

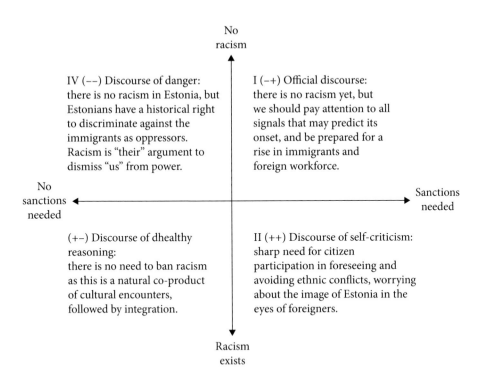

Figure 19. Two-dimensional model of attitudes towards racism

The model is based on the analysis of articles in the Estonian print media from 2000 to 2007. The four types describe the majority of displayed attitudes towards immigrants. The study presented two main findings that are relevant to the present analysis: the amount of articles dealing with racism has increased during the last few years, and the focus of discussion has shifted from racism being a foreign problem to it being a highly relevant issue. Another development concerns the diminishing importance of the *discourse of healthy reasoning*, which has gradually been replaced by the *discourse of danger* in some of the more recent racial polemics. This development is indicative of Estonians' tendency to justify their politically incorrect behaviour by referring to (often distorted) historical arguments.

---

discourse of danger: no racism and no sanctions needed (−−)
discourse of self-criticism: racism exists and sanctions are needed (++)
official discourse: no rasicm, but sanctions are needed (−+)
discourse of healthy reasoning: racism exists, but sanctions are not needed (+−)

All Estonian texts were translated into English by the author.

4. The case study

4.1   Official responses: Newspaper articles and other media

In autumn 2007, a complaint was filed, pointing out that Estonian schoolbooks recommend racist joke collections as advisory supplementary reading material in primary schools. The parent who complained protested that, in 2001, the Estonian Ministry of Education had accepted the joke collections *Banaanil on Nohu: Valik Koolinalju ja Muud* ("Banana Has a Cold"; Kalmre 1996), *Neeger Päevitab: Maailma Rahvad Eesti Laste Naljades* ("Black Man Sunbathing: Nations in Estonian Children's Jokes"; Tuisk 1996), and *Elevant Külmkapis: Kimbuke Keerdküsimusi Koolilaste Suust* ("Elephant in the Cupboard: Some Riddles from Estonian Schoolchildren"; Voolaid 1998) as recommended extra reading-material for the seventh grade, despite of the fact that these books included racist jokes. The joke collections were compiled on the basis of a nationwide child lore collection that took place in 1992. In other words, these were jokes told by children in the beginning of 1990s. Jokes like the following were included in these collections:

(1)   Miks kannavad venelased õlgkübarat?
       Sest sõnnik kaetakse ikka õlgedega kinni.

       Why do Russians wear straw hats?
       Because you always must put hay on manure.

(2)   Kes on kõige levinum loom Eestis?
       Venelane.

       What is the most common animal in Estonia?
       Russians.

(3)   Mis vahe on neegril ja sibulal?
       Sibulat lõikudes tuleb vesi silma.

       What is the difference between a black man and an onion?
       When you cut an onion you cry.

The complaint was left unanswered for two weeks, hence the parent decided to publicise the problem by bringing it to the attention of the Russian-speaking audience first.

In October 2007, a Russian newspaper in Estonia, *MK Estonija*, published an article about the inappropriateness of encouraging schoolchildren of vulnerable age to harbour racist attitudes. The parent particularly stressed the fact that there were no political manipulations behind the upsurge of the issue: "Я не хочу влезать в политические дрязги, я смотрю со своей колокольни – с позиции педагога и отца, – отметил учитель" ("I do not want to get into political squabbles; I look at it from the position of a teacher and father"; Gusev 2007). The question of ethics is further developed in all the consequent media texts, claiming that "Учебники учат эстонских детей смеяться над русскими" ("School textbooks teach Estonian children to laugh at Russians"; Gusev 2007). Russian television interviewed ethnic Russians in Estonia, who were upset by the idea that Estonian schoolchildren (and Russian ones attending Estonian schools) should study deprecating jokes about the Russians as a part of the education programme.

As a reaction to this, several articles were published. The present study analyses the content of 8 articles and 407 comments written to these articles from various daily news portals (*Delfi* 2007; *Eesti Ekspress* 2007; *Eesti Päevaleht* 2007; *Õhtuleht* 2007; *Postimees* 2007; *Reporter* 2007), which are among the largest and most influential Estonian online news sites. First, I will offer a brief summary of the viewpoints cited in the newspapers, which involve opinions expressed by politicians and journalists – the latter can be seen as somewhere between the official and unofficial opinions. Then, I will turn to the description of the unofficial forum content. In both cases, the quantitative analysis programme QDA Miner was used to tag texts according to the opinions expressed. The articles appeared in the following chronological order (see Table 4).

The titles of the 8 articles (A–H) illustrate the arguments put forward by each of them. The first two articles (A–B: *Lapsevanema arvates soovitab õpik lugeda rassistlikke naljakogumikke* "Parent believes that the recommended reading material of school textbooks is racist" and *Õpiku autor eitab rassistlike naljade soovitamist* "Author of the textbook denies recommending racist jokes") are quite neutral, representing the two different standpoints: the parent who accuses the government of accepting racist reading material (although the phrase "*Parent* believes" hints at the fact that others do not necessarily agree with the parent) versus the view that, according to the opinion of the author, her textbook is not designed to promote racist jokes, and she was not aware of the fact that the joke books were even included in the recommended extra reading material. At first, public discourse joins the accusers and suggests the idea that using such jokes in textbooks is a mistake. The first article describes the futile attempts of the parent and teacher to contact the Ministry of Education: "Lapsevanem pöördus haridusministeeriumi poole poolteist nädalat tagasi […]. Minister ei ole veel vastanud" ("The parent turned to Ministry of Education a week and a half ago […]. The Minister has still not answered"; in article A). The whole text is written from the viewpoint of the complaining parent. The contrasting point of view is only represented indirectly, namely via stating that the news portal got an answer from a specialist: "[…]

Table 4. Articles/news texts included in the case study

No	Source	Title	Date
A	*Postimees*	Lapsevanema arvates soovitab õpik lugeda rassistlikke naljakogumikke "Parent believes that the recommended reading material of school textbooks is racist"	Oct. 17
B	*Postimees*	Õpiku autor eitab rassistlike naljade soovitamist "Author of the textbook denies recommending racist jokes"	Oct. 17
C	*Eesti Ekspress*	Kuidas hoida neegrid oma aiast eemal "How to keep a nigger off your yard"	Oct. 25
D	*Reporter*	Venemaa kasutab eestlaste mustamiseks Eesti koolilaste anekdoote "Russia uses Estonian jokes to denigrate Estonians"	Oct. 25
E	*Postimees*	Lukas vabandas rassistlike naljakogumike pärast "[Tõnis] Lukas [i.e. the Minister of Education] apologised for racist joke collections"	Oct. 31
F	*Delfi*	Tõnis Lukas vabandas rassistlike naljakogumike pärast "Tõnis Lukas apologised for racist jokes"	Oct. 31
G	*Eesti Päevaleht*	Muuseum võitleb rassismi levitamise süüdistustega "Museum fights with accusations of racism"	Nov. 1
H	*Õhtuleht*	Neegrinaljad peidetakse tavakasutaja eest? "Ethnic jokes will be hidden from Internet users?"	Nov. 1

kodune ülesanne puudutab vaid raamatut *Banaanil on Nohu*, selgitab oma vastuses ametnik" ("[…] the government official explains that the task only concerns the joke collection titled *Banana Has a Cold*"), thus creating an allusion to the fact that the "government official" is being very formal in her answer or even delegating the blame, as well as accusing the teacher of adding extra reading material. The author is portrayed as quite irrational:

> (4)   Nahkuri sõnul pole ta seda kogumikku päris rida-realt läbi lugenud, vaid sirvinud. […] Tema sõnul jääb talle küll veidi arusaamatuks, miks ei võiks lapsed neid nalju lugeda, kui need on laste endi poolt rahvaluulearhiivile saadetud, teadlaste poolt välja valitud ja töödeldud ning avaldatud.   (article B)

> The author of the textbook Anne Nahkur admitted yesterday to *Postimees.ee* that she has only flicked through and not read the joke collection. […] She says that it is unclear to her why it should be forbidden to read the jokes that were sent in by schoolchildren and edited by researchers.

The following texts are more critical, as the "unpleasant and shameful story" (as it was labelled by a conservative alternative news site; see *Infopartisan* 2007) catches the attention of critically-minded group of young people contributing to a communal blog site. Article (C), provokingly and sarcastically titled *Kuidas hoida neegrid oma aiast eemal* ("How to keep a nigger off your yard"), borrowing the question from a conundrum available on a public search engine of Estonian riddles, reinforces the critical stance. A change is brought about by the intensive public debate concerning the reasons why such claims should be raised about some old jokes. Debate participants speculate about the motives of the Russian media, and the self-defensive mode emerges in titles as *Venemaa kasutab eestlaste mustamiseks Eesti koolilaste anekdoote* ("Russia uses Estonian jokes to denigrate Estonians"; in article D). Finally, after the Minister of Education has officially apologised for the inappropriate reading material, the titles fight against the accusations and try to draw the line between an insult and a joke. The hasty and, to many, obsequious decisions made by government officials not only upset the wider public, but also motivate journalists to post quite ambivalent articles that fluctuate between the politically correct and incorrect. Their primary aim is to stress the desire to censor folklore databases and potentially harmful jokes in general, but, willingly or unwillingly, they provoke a heated debate about the thin line between humour and insult.

In the course of discussion, after official discourse enters and takes over the role of the scapegoat, journalists move to the side of the unofficial discourse. They foster the nationalist feelings of internet commentators by using titles such as *Lukas vabandas rassistlike naljakogumike pärast* ("Lukas apologised for racist joke collections"; in article E) or *Neegrinaljad peidetakse tavakasutaja eest?* ("Ethnic jokes will be hidden from internet users?"; in article H). On October 25, 2007, the Minister of Education is still cautious and refrains from taking an explicit standpoint in the matter: "Lukas tunnistas ajalehele, et ta on mainitud anekdoodikogumikest ajakirjandusest lugenud, kuid ise neid sirvinud ei ole" ("Minister Lukas confessed that he has read about the joke collections only from the media and has not flicked through the books himself"; in article F). We see the opposition of the two opinions: that of the official discourse attempting to be politically correct, and the more provoking popular ideas about the ethical side of these jokes embedded in the same text. The title of article (D) (*Venemaa kasutab eestlaste mustamiseks Eesti koolilaste anekdoote* "Russia uses Estonian jokes to denigrate Estonians") clearly puts Estonians in the victimised position, stating that the Russians use Estonian jokes to make a statement against Estonian people and hinting at the fact that Estonian politicians are pairing up with Russians against Estonia's interests.

The message of the Minister of Education is also ambiguous,[3] but the fact that he apologises is used by journalists to provoke a counter-reaction from readers.

Adding fuel to the fire, the choice of the webmaster to publish the articles on the database.[4] In article F, it is stated that

(5) [k]a ajakirjanik Krister Kivi juhtis viimases Eesti Ekspressis tähelepanu sei-
     gale, et riiklikult finantseeritavas kirjandusmuuseumi serveris www.folklore.
     ee avaldatakse eriti rassistlikke anekdoote. Viimaste nädalate sündmuste
     mõjul peeti kirjandusmuuseumis teisipäeval koosolek, kus leiti, et üheks
     lahenduseks võib olla serveris leiduvate, üliõpilastele ja teadlastele uurimis-
     tööde tegemise lihtsustamiseks avatud andmebaaside sulgemine registreeri-
     mata ning kasutajatunnuseta isikutele.

     [t]he journalist Krister Kivi drew attention to the fact that a state-financed
     public folklore server is publishing extremely racist jokes. On Tuesday, the
     Estonian Literary Museum held a meeting and decided that it may be neces-
     sary to make the database intended for humour research available only to
     registered users.

Media discourse can be very powerful and influential, especially as it tends to dramatise events and is keen on engaging its audience. The more provoking the subject and the way it is conveyed, the more audience feedback there appears to be. The media decontextualises events so that they can be recast within the frame of a broader ideology (see also Smith and Saltzman 1995). Reframing often means that some more sensitive sides of an issue are brought forward, so as to trigger angry and confrontational responses from the audience. In the present case, the media focused on (both historical and present-day) interethnic relations in Esto-nia, taking the current polemics as an example of a long-lasting and inequitable struggle.

In light of the two-dimensional model introduced earlier (see Figure 19, in Section 3), the newspaper articles primarily support the claim that there is a need for citizens to understand and anticipate the dangers of racism, thus represent-ing the *discourse of self-criticism*. Especially at the beginning of the polemics, the journalists display opinions such as the following:

---

3. In the same article, he says: "Kas me hakkame "Pipi Pikksukka" selle pärast ümber kirju-tama, et seal on Pipi isa neegripealik?" ("Should we also ban *Pippi Longstocking* because her father was Negro King?"). It should be noted here that Negro King was renamed in the English translation of *Pippi Longstocking* into South Sea King.

4. The database of Estonian contemporary jokes (*Eesti Kaasaegsed Anekdoodid* 2004) con-sists of approximately 50,000 joke texts from 1950s to date. For more information, see Laineste (2005, 2006).

(6) [...] ministeeriumi poolt kinnitatud õpik soovitab 12- kuni 13-aastastele lastele raamatuid, mis sisaldavad rassistlike nalju stiilis – mis vahe on neegril ja batuudil? Batuudil hüpates on vaja kingad jalast võtta. (article A)

[...] a school textbook approved by the Minister of Education recommends 12- and 13-year-olds read racist jokes such as: What is the difference between a black man and a trampoline? – When you jump on a trampoline, you have to take your shoes off first.

But even the official media is not so willing to take a unanimous standpoint about the nature of these jokes. For example, trying to define the distinction between good and bad humour, the Minister of Education Tõnis Lukas states that "[...] kui suur osa inimestest näeb siin probleemi, siis järelikult on probleem olemas" ("[...] if the majority sees a problem here, then it means the problem must exist"; in article E). This makes room for the *official discourse* to enter the discussion. It also transfers the responsibility of labelling jokes to the people, as Lukas indicates that he, nevertheless, believes the jokes are just jokes:

(7) Lukase sõnul otsib Vene propaganda kohti, kus saaks näidata Eestile näpuga. [...] Lukase sõnul ei hakata aastate jooksul laste poolt koostatud anekdoodi-kogumikke selle kampaania pärast tuleriidal põletama. (article F)

Lukas says that Russian propaganda is just searching for instances where it can blame Estonia. [...] Lukas says that the joke books will not be burned on the stake because of the Russian media's campaign.

Moreover, there is evidence of the *discourse of danger*. One of the articles asked for an expert to comment on the polemics and her response was the following:

(8) [...] Nali ja folkloor pole tegelikkuse peegel. Näiteks naljad neegritest on rahvusvahelised ning nende sagedase esinemise põhjuseks pole eestlaste seas leviv rassism. (article H)

[...] Jokes, in the same way as folklore in general, is not a true mirror of society. Jokes about blacks are international and the reason for their frequent occurrence is not Estonians' racism.

This statement asserts that there is no racism in the jokes and even if there was, the jokes should not be sanctioned. At the same time, it implies that there is a constant threat that jokes will be taken as evidence of Estonians' xenophobic feelings. Such accusations do not take into account the history of oppression that is used to justify racist jokes and other expressions of xenophobia in Estonia.

4.2   Unofficial responses: Internet discussion boards

Forum responses reacting to the apologies by the Minister of Education were sharp and discontented. The unofficial discourse was partly fuelled by the provocative journalists playing on Estonians' nationalist feelings. In this section, examples from the four modes of reasoning about racism are presented. The quantitative analysis of the data reveals that the most numerous comments fall into the category of *discourse of danger*, which stresses Estonians' historical right to demand full assimilation from those who are not Estonian but wish to live in Estonia. The following Examples (9)–(12) give an overview of the informal opinions expressed in the discussion boards:

(9)   *Official discourse*

    a.   Me peaksime tegema selge vahe, mis on huumor ja mis mitte, siis ei ole kellegi põhjust kaevata.

        We should clearly define when we are dealing with humour and when not, then nobody will have any reason to complain.

(10)   *Discourse of danger*

    a.   Põhjendamatu foobia. Kui eestlaste kohta nalja tegakse siis naerab ka eestlane kaasa. Milles probleem? Inimesed hakkavad vist manduma (amerikaniseeruma), et huumorit huumoriga võtta enam ei suuda.

        Their phobias are unreasonable. People are beginning to degenerate [read: Americanise] and cannot take humour with a sense of humour.

    b.   Pole need ju midagi muud kui lihtsad naljakesed. Inimesed, kes siit rassismi välja loevad, on ise rassistid. Normaalne inimene, olgu siis eestlane või venelane saab naljast aru ja naerab.

        These texts are nothing more than simple jokes. Everyone who sees them as racist, is him/herself a racist. A normal Estonian or Russian will understand and just laugh along with the others.

    c.   Olen igasuguse rassismi vastu ja samamoodi ka liba anti-rassismi vastu, nagu vingumine anektootide teemal. Anektoot võib olla naljakas, ükskõik kas naerdakse eestlase, venelase, parntslase või kelleiganes üle.

        I cannot see anything bad in these jokes. I am against racism and against quasi anti-racism.[5] A joke can be funny, no matter if it targets Russians, Estonians, French, or whomever.

---

5.   *Quasi anti-racism* here involves complaints against the racism in jokes.

d. Ma vabandan petka ja tshapai ees, samuti kõikide tshuktshide, venelaste-
sakslaste-ameeriklaste, rebase, karu ja jänese, neegrite ja juutide… ja üldse
kõigi ees kellest anekdoote olen rääkinud või nende üle naernud…

I would like to apologise to Petka and Chapaev, all Chukchis, Russians,
Germans, Americans… the fox, the bear, and the rabbit, the blacks, Jews
and everyone I've ever told jokes about…

(11) *Discourse of healthy reasoning*

a. Nemad ei ole mustlased ega juudid […]. Kohtusin nendega Leningradis
õppides: nende häbitunne erineb meie omast, kõik teised käitumisviisid
on erinevad. Meil on kergem aru saada vene pätist,kui neist. Kui ei usu
siis küsi pranslaselt või hollandlaselt […]. Parem karta, kui kahetseda!

We are not talking about Gypsies or Jews […]. I met them [i.e. people of
African origin] while studying in Leningrad [i.e. St. Petersburg]: they are
never ashamed of anything, they are different in their behaviour [from
us]. It's easier for us to understand a Russian lowlife than them. If you
don't believe me, ask any Dutch or Frenchman […]. Better to be safe than
sorry.

b. Venelased katsugu ikka omal maal hakkama saada, aga millegipärast
oleme seal populaarsed, viisa mittesaamise puhul nälgitakse ja naljade
puhul kuulutatakse või sõda.

Russians should try to get by on their own. For some reason, we are
popular there. They go on a hunger strike when they don't get a visa, and
some jokes make them launch a holy war.

c. Lukas üritab olla, jah, "poliitiliselt-hüper-korrektne". Täiesti tarbetu, isegi
budda naeraks selle nirvaanaküünituse ees kolm lõuatäit ja ütleks siis
Lukasele, "lase rahus olla. kuigi deemonite vägi on lõputu, väsivad nad
alati enne sind ja püüavad su kaasa tõmmata".

Lukas [i.e. the Minister of Education] is trying to be politically "hyper-
super-correct". This is completely pointless. Even Buddha would laugh at
this endeavour and tell him "the power of evil is endless, but the demons
will always tire before you".

d. See, et tibla on loll, ei ole anekdoot. See on TÕDE ise.

The claim that Russkies [i.e. Russians] are stupid, is not a joke. It is the
TRUTH.

e. Naabrid ja ka muud on alati üksteist aasinud ja töganud. Pealgi ei keela
keegi neegritel valgete kohta nalju teha või siin avaldada. Kõige lihtsam
on keelata.

Neighbours have always mocked and teased one another. Nobody denies them the right to make jokes about us. It's always very easy to ban things.

(12)   *Discourse of self-criticism*

    a.   Pärast hakkame kurtma: miks lapsed nii vägivaldsed on? Kas õpetajad ei tea, et bumerang tuleb tagasi?

        We start to complain later: why do our children become so violent [read: xenophobic]? These teachers should know that the boomerang will return.

    b.   korralikkus riigis (kas USAs ehk Kanadas) oleksid koolist visatud ning isegi kriminaal recordi saanud… aga EeSStis see on ju normaalne… kui mitte eeSStlastest jutt…

        In a decent country (in USA and maybe in Canada) such teachers would have been expelled from schools or even be sued, but in eSStonia[6] this is perfectly normal, when we are talking about attitudes towards non-eSStonians.

    c.   Masendav koht see Eesti! Rassistlik, fashistlik, seksistlik, homo- ja kseno-foobne. Ainult valge mees saab Eestis rahulikult elada – kõik ülejäänud, kes sellesse kategooriasse ei mahu (naised, homod, mustanahalised, muulased) mürgitatakse vihkamise kibeda sapiga.

        Estonia, a depressing place. Racist, Fascist, sexist, homophobic and xenophobic, only white men can live here peacefully, while the lives of all the rest who do belong not to this category (women, gay, blacks, and immigrants) will be poisoned with the bitterness of hatred.

The examples above show that all four discourses are present in the unofficial sources, with some more salient than others (see Figure 20). Every group displays multiple standpoints which do not merge into one in the course of discussion, but rather tend to result in attitude polarisation (Mackie and Cooper 1984). This makes generalisations quite risky: the majority of commentators in internet forums choose the (quite openly racist) *discourse of danger*, while at the same time the other extreme, namely the *discourse of self-criticism*, is also present. If we break the comment categorisation down to see a temporal development by looking at how the frequency of the four categories of comments changes in the course of the 16 days, during which the polemics was a hot topic in (online)

---

6. The terms *eSStonia* and *eSStonians* constitute a popular ethnonym in the internet and are used to stress the (assumed) nationalist attitudes of Estonians. The *SS* in the ethnonym alludes to the voluntary armed forces (*Schutzstaffel*) of the Nazis.

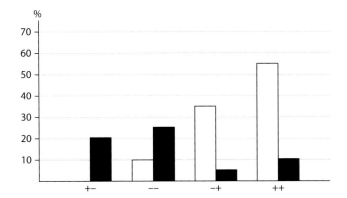

* +– (discourse of healthy reasoning): no need to sanction ethnocentrism as a nation needs to maintain its ability of self-regulation; –– (discourse of danger): anti-racist arguments do not consider the historical background in Estonia, victimisation of the nation to justify xenophobia; –+ (official discourse): integration, preparations for receiving immigrants; ++ (discourse of self-criticism): recognising a threat to Estonian international image and the need to actively involve citizens in understanding the need for tolerance

Figure 20. Percentage of the four types of attitudes towards racism (%) in the articles (white columns) and their subsequent comments (black columns)

journalism, the growing tendency of the *discourse of danger* (––) and the falling one of the *discourse of self-criticism* (++) does not straightforwardly support the idea of polarisation, but this seems to correlate with the switch of focus and blame in the news texts throughout the polemics.

We can also compare the voices present in the newspaper articles to the opinions articulated in the forums (Figure 20), with the share of commentaries from the four different discourses (x-axes).

Figure 20 shows that the voices of the official and unofficial media are incompatible. The news texts, especially in the beginning of the polemics, displayed a concern for the image of Estonians in the foreign media, and portrayed the people responsible for accepting racist jokes onto the school curriculum as irresponsible, irrational, and quite confused (see examples from article A and B, in Section 4.1). The official voice reacted mostly in the vein of *discourse of self-criticism* (i.e. "we need sanctions for this kind of racism"), while forum entries represented the *discourse of danger* (i.e. "these are just jokes, no sanctions are needed"). This points to a serious disparity in views about racism in general and jokes in particular. Such diverse discourses are hardly compatible, especially because the racist ideas represented by the forum discussants are, at times, reinforced by those of politicians as the latter manipulate nationalist ideas.

The insertion of jokes into online comments reveals that people want to make a statement by posting a racist joke during the discussion of racism, thus highlighting the non serious aspect of joke-telling. Several anonymous commentators chose to take part in the discussion of the online articles by posting jokes not only about Russians or blacks, but also about European regulations about racism. The following example was posted as a comment to article (F):

(13)   Mitut europolitrukki on vaja, et lampi lakke keerata ? – Arv ei oma tähtsust, sest puudub eurodirektiiv.

How many European Union politruks [i.e. political commissars] are needed to screw in a light-bulb? – The number is not important, if the directive is missing.

The latter joke is triggered by the link between censoring jokes and the regulations on racism, supposedly advocated by the European Union.

It seems that the unofficial discourse of nation-building is more radical and exaggerated than the politically correct opinion fostered by the print media. It originates in a public discourse that enjoys playing with potential fears, extreme opinions, and feelings of nationalism. In addition, exposing covert feelings of aggressiveness is typical of online communication, as users experience more freedom to joke, tease, and provoke others during the discussion of sensitive issues. It also means that the need for free press and freedom of speech seems to be increased in Estonia, and advocates of censorship will be met with aggressive responses. The long period of silence enforced by the totalitarian regime has brought about a strong reaction since the late 1980s, that is, after the ideas of *glasnost* (i.e. bringing the truth before the public) were introduced. Freedom of speech currently bears a clear ideological significance closely tied to Estonia's recent past.

5.   The public negotiation of "good" and "bad" humour

The present case study exhibits some parallels with other cases involving media manipulated humour and international negotiations of "good" and "bad" taste in humour, hence a comparative approach could be revealing. In other words, it is fruitful to juxtapose similar events that display public demonization of humour, such as the case of the Danish cartoon controversy (for references, see Tsakona and Popa this volume), where humour caused offence and mobilisation against the "humorous aggressor". Throwing the Mohammad cartoons into an international arena widened the audience of the debate, and even led some people to conceptualise it as a "clash of civilisations" (Harding 2006; see also Lewis 2008a).

Issues of free speech and censorship also accompanied the screening of Baron Cohen's film *Borat: Cultural Learnings of America to Make Benefit Glorious Nation of Kazakhstan* (2007; see among others Lewis 008b).

In all cases, the size of the two opposing sides was incompatible: a Danish newspaper versus Islam; a film director with his team versus the Kazakhs, the Jews, and U.S. Americans; Russian immigrants versus the Estonian majority. Humour was subsequently taken out of context, a process much aided by the involvement of the (international or local) media. The initially humorous texts were framed as indicative of the (alleged) blasphemous and/or aggressive intention of joke-tellers. In fact, the targeted groups were the ones who tried to publicise the discussion in the media. Being indignant at the unjustified attack, they sought for justification and demanded public apologies. But the context of exhibiting their hurt feelings in combination with the (highly projected) humorous dimension of the jokes was inappropriate and caused an amplification of the conflict.

The targets were, as a result, perceived as even more different from the joke-tellers. They were the ones with a different culture, different values concerning individual freedom, and, what is even worse, a different sense of humour - or, alternatively, no sense of humour at all. Another common issue that was brought up in all these polemics is the negotiation of issues regarding censorship and freedom of speech as part of the political identity of the insulted party. The offended groups are allegedly depicted as non-democratic and, at the same time, major global forces: Russia as the former "1/6 of the world" and Islam as the "rising world religion", also a majority religion in Kazakhstan. Both Russia and Islam are known for using harsh measures to limit freedom of speech and discriminate its citizens for gender or nationality in their own country (e.g. the governmental control of the mass media in Russia, the deprivation of women's civil rights in Islam, Kazakhstan and Russia as the home countries of many Western European prostitutes). Such "out-groups" can be regarded as a threat to the Western way of living and thinking.

On the other hand, the party that (allegedly) suffered from the attack actually benefited from the heightened sense of group solidarity. A public and well-orchestrated crusade against an enemy is a strong group adhesive. Even the government of Kazakhstan, who appeared to be emotionally hurt and as though the losers in somebody else's game, would probably have not braced up and mobilised themselves with such international reverberation if it were not for the humorous "offence" they "suffered". The government of Kazakhstan even published a four-page advertising section in *The New York Times* (see among others Fletcher 2006), in an effort to create a positive image of the current quality of life in the country. Although the scope of these cases is quite different (mostly national in Estonia and Russia, highly international in the Danish cartoons and *Borat*), there seem to be similarities connecting them: humour was used as an emotionally effective argument to wind up aggressive acts and attitudes.

In all cases, there is a clear cultural clash between the joke-tellers and their targets which frames the conflict. And even if joke-tellers are geographically situated at the margins between the joke target and the rest of the world (as is the case of Estonia and Russia), they live in a country that has a good insight into the background of the joke targets, but also of those who laugh at the targets.

6.   Discussion

Although the polemics about Estonian ethnic jokes started out from a political-ly correct stance, the will to prompt more radical responses from the audience gradually evolved, as the analysis of the headlines reveals. The official and unof-ficial sources expressed their ideas about humour and jokes, with the first stating that the censorship was in order. The responses posted in the unofficial sources, namely the forums, confronted the official statements: the commentators began to fight for their right to joke (for reaction against censorship, see also Watters this volume), going as far as adding more "racist" jokes into their comments. The most frequent of the different discourses in the unofficial internet commentaries appear to be the *discourse of danger*, which emphasised the need to strengthen Estonian national integrity through forced assimilation. This shows that the unof-ficial discourse of nation-building is strong, radical, and often manipulated by the media and journalists (since the reactions of the audience also depend on the way the news text is formulated, e.g. its title).

The public discussion increased the public interest in the jokes in general and resulted in the re-emergence of long-forgotten racist jokes which also appeared on online discussion boards. On the official level, the manipulative attack on jokes highlighting the racism of Estonians was successful, even though it did not have any impact beyond the Estonian and Russian media. On the unofficial level, it produced an increased interest in jokes and fostered nationalist feelings.

Lockyer and Pickering (2008) have pointed out that we should ask why hu-mour is sometimes found to be offensive, what social functions offensive humour has, and how we can negotiate the ethical limits of humour in order to define the boundary between the comic and the malevolent. In the present case, we did not look at the offensiveness of the texts as such, but at how the cultural, historical, and political background led (at least part of) a nation to fight for their right to joke about others freely. And it should be noted here that the idea of jokes as a weapon of political propaganda against "dangerous" ideologies, such as racism, has not yet attracted scholarly attention.[7]

Furthermore, when examining the function of humour, its framing and the reactions to it seem to be most revealing. Making fun of a group of people can be a form of exploitation and dominance: joke targets are so funny that they cannot be considered equal partners (e.g. the Chukchis). But also the negative stereotyping of humour can be seen as a weapon in power struggle. It is not only about telling that something is not funny; it is equally important to use the "un-funny" (cf. *un-laughter* in Billig 2005: 175–199) to show the wider audience that a nation's sense of humour constitutes a clear manifestation of its aggressive and xenophobic ways. At the same time, by choosing not to laugh at the jokes, the border between "us" and "them" is drawn. By laughing at others, the out-group is excluded and may feel that this is an indication of the joke-tellers' hostility, thus they will in turn feel hostile towards the excluder, the joke-teller (see also Archakis and Tsakona this volume; Mueller this volume). Looking more closely at instances where humour is not unanimously accepted brings us closer to definitions of humour by its users, as well as to the cultural and political presuppositions of such definitions.

It could also be suggested that the present case study brings to the surface the negotiation on the politics of humour taste. The questions of taste are not only settled in intergroup (e.g. interethnic) conflicts, but also in negotiations within a group as well. The nation consists of different people, all with their own ideas of morality and ethics. Unofficial censorship arises from the generally accepted norms of what is moral and what can be labelled offence or blasphemy, thus unveiling people's orientation towards what is allowed and what will most probably elicit a negative response. The role of journalism (Oring 1995) and online media, such as news portals or communication boards, is significant in establishing the boundary between "good" and "bad" taste. The media takes issues to public display and, by giving voice to one opinion over the other, it implicitly frames and (more or less) controls the negotiations concerning humour and taste. The present case clearly showed that there are three forces trying to make a point about appropriate behaviour: the government, the people, and the press itself – the press reflecting the government, the people, or both. The change of moods in the Estonian audience response was brought about by the way the incident was reported in the press. As long as the official discourse took no standpoint, the audience kept its nationalist impulses under control; but after the Minister of Education apologised for the jokes, an unexpectedly strong reaction was triggered that revealed

---

7.   Billig (2001, 2005) has researched the propaganda of radical racists, but not the use of humour as an argument in the crusade *against* racism.

some of the most aggressive views about ethnic Russians in Estonia, present and even future immigrants.

This incident did not raise a question of taste in the narrow sense: the actual limits were negotiable and not remarkably controversial. Estonians and Russians are already well aware of these jocular perceptions of each other, hence the incident under scrutiny did not pose a "new" problem for either group to deal with it. It was more about setting (temporary) new criteria of taste and creating polarisation between the two incompatible positions. Moreover, it emphasised how a group can be manipulated to take a side, thus becoming part of a polemic that is indicative of the ongoing struggle between the two groups. Politics and the media both set new frames for discussing and perceiving jokes. Bad taste thus became a political argument, together with its allusions to morality, assimilation/integration, cooperation, democracy, and other building blocks for a sustainable society.

Acknowledgements

This research was supported by the *Estonian Science Foundation*, ETF8149.

References

Attardo, Salvatore and Raskin, Victor. 1991. "Script theory revis(it)ed: Joke similarity and joke representation model." *Humour: International Journal of Humour Research* 4: 293–347.

Baron Cohen, Sacha. 2007. *Borat: Cultural Learnings of America to Make Benefit Glorious Nation of Kazakhstan*. USA.

Berry, John W. 1980. "Social and cultural change." In *Handbook of Cross-Cultural Psychology: Social Psychology*, vol. 5, Harry C. Triandis and Richard W. Brislin (eds), 211–279. Boston: Allyn and Bacon.

Billig, Michael. 2001. "Humour and hatred: The racist jokes of the Ku Klux Klan." *Discourse and Society* 12: 267–289.

Billig, Michael. 2005. "Comic racism and violence." In *Beyond a Joke. The Limits of Humour*, Sharon Lockyer and Michael Pickering (eds), 25–44. Basingstoke: Palgrave MacMillan.

Davies, Christie. 1990. *Ethnic Jokes around the World. A Comparative Analysis*. Bloomington: Indiana University Press.

Davies, Christie 1996. "Puritanical and politically correct. A critical historical account of changes in the censorship of comedy by the BBC." In *The Social Faces of Humour: Practices and Issues* [Popular Culture Studies 11], George Paton, Chris Powell and Steve Wagg (eds), 29–61. Aldershot: Arena.

Davies, Christie 2008. "The Danish cartoons, the Muslims and the new battle of Jutland." In "The Muhammad cartoons and Humour Research: A collection of essays," Paul Lewis (ed.), 2–7. *Humour: International Journal of Humour Research* 21: 1–46.

Delfi. 2007. www.delfi.ee (accessed February 9, 2011). [in Estonian]

Eesti Ekspress. 2007. www.ekspress.ee (accessed February 9, 2011). [in Estonian]

Eesti Kaasaegsed Anekdoodid. 2004. http://www.folklore.ee/~liisi/o2 (accessed March 12, 2011).

Eesti Päevaleht. 2007. www.epl.ee (accessed February 9, 2011). [in Estonian]

Fletcher, Phyllis. 2006. "Kasakhstan Embassy responds to Borat." *NPR*, October 16. http://www. npr.org/templates/story/story.php?storyId=6276973 (accessed February 16, 2011).

Ford, Thomas E. 2000. "Effects of sexist humour on tolerance of sexist events." *Personality and Social Psychology Bulletin* 26: 1094–1107.

Ford, Thomas E. and Ferguson, Mark A. 2004. "Some sociology of humour: The joke." *International Social Science Review* 63: 431–446.

Goldman, Minton F. 1997. *Revolution and Change in Central and Eastern Europe: Political, Economic, and Social Challenges*. Armonk: M.E. Sharpe.

Gurin, Carl 2004. "Russian media mulls growing ethnic intolerance." *Eurasia Daily Monitor* 1. http://www.jamestown.org/single/?no_cache=1&tx_ttnews[tt_news]=27054 (accessed February 11, 2011).

Gusev, Aleksei. 2007. ""Учебники учат эстонских детей смеяться над русскими" (Textbooks teach Estonian children to laugh at Russians). *Utro*, October 18. http://www.utro. ru/articles/2007/10/18/688371.shtml (accessed February 17, 2007). [in Russian]

Hann, Chris M. (ed.). 2002. *Postsocialism: Ideals, Ideologies, and Practices in Eurasia*. London/ New York: Routledge.

Harding, Gareth. 2006. "Analysis: A cartoon spat a culture clash?" *The Washington Times*, February 15. http://www.lebanonwire.com/0602MN/06021601UP.asp (accessed February 11, 2011).

Heidmets, Mati. 1998. "The Russian minority: Dilemmas for Estonia." *Trames* 2: 266–269.

Infopartisan. 2007. http://infopartisan.blogspot.com (accessed March 12, 2011). [in Estonian]

Kall, Toomas. 2007. "Kui venelane ajab naeru peale" (If the Russian makes us laugh). *Eesti Ekspress*, October 10. [in Estonian]

Kalmre, Eda (ed). 1996. *Banaanil on Nohu: Valik Koolinalju ja Muud* (Banana Has a Cold). Tallinn: Koolibri. [in Estonian]

Kirch, Aksel. 1999. "Eesti etniline koosseis" (Ethnic groups in Estonia). In *Eesti rahvaste raamat. Rahvusvähemused, -rühmad ja -killud* (Book of Nations Living in Estonia), Jüri Viikberg (ed.), 68–70. Tallinn: Eesti Entsüklopeediakirjastus. [in Estonian]

Kuipers, Giselinde. 2006. *Good Humour, Bad Taste: A Sociology of the Joke* [Humour Research 7]. Berlin/New York: Mouton de Gruyter.

Kuipers, Giselinde. 2008. "The Muhammad cartoon controversy and the globalisation of humour". In *The Muhammad cartoons and Humour Research: A collection of essays*, Paul Lewis (ed.), 7–11. *Humour: International Journal of Humour Research* 21: 1–46.

Laineste, Liisi. 2005. "Targets in Estonian ethnic jokes within the theory of ethnic humour (Ch. Davies)." *Folklore. Electronic Journal of Folklore* 29: 7–24.

Laineste, Liisi. 2006. "Eesti anekdootide digitaalne andmebaas" (Digital database of Estonian contemporary jokes). In *Võim ja Kultuur* (Power and Culture), vol. 2, Mare Kõiva (ed,), 103–125. Tartu: Eesti Kirjandusmuuseum. [in Estonian]

Laineste, Liisi 2008. "The politics of joking: Ethnic jokes and their targets in Estonia (1880s–2007)." *Folklore: Electronic Journal of Folklore* 40: 110–132.

Laineste, Liisi 2009. "Political jokes in post-Socialist Estonia". In *Permitted Laughter: Socialist, Post-Socialist and Never-Socialist Humour*, Arvo Krikmann and Liisi Laineste (eds), 39–68. Tartu: ELM Scholarly Press.

Laitin, David D. 1998. "Nationalism and language: A post-Soviet perspective." In *The State of the Nation: Ernest Gellner and the Theory of Nationalism*, John A. Hall (ed.), 144–155. Cambridge: Cambridge University Press.

Lewis, Paul (ed.). 2008a. "The Muhammad cartoons and Humour Research: A collection of essays." *Humour: International Journal of Humour Research* 21: 1–46.

Lewis, Paul. 2008b. "(Mis)reading Borat: The risks of irony in the digital age." *Electronic Journal of Communication* 18. http://www.cios.org/www/ejc/EJCPUBLIC/018/2/018410.html (accessed March 12, 2011).

Lockyer, Sharon and Pickering, Michael. (eds). 2005. *Beyond a Joke. The Limits of Humour*. Basingstoke: Palgrave MacMillan.

Lockyer, Sharon and Pickering, Michael. 2008. "You must be joking: The sociological critique of humour and comic media." *Sociology Compass* 3: 808–820.

Lokk, Reigo. 2003. "The Russian minority in post-Communist Estonia. A comparison with Czech-Sudeten. German relations between the Wars." In *Tolerance and Intolerance in Historical Perspective*, Csaba Lévai and Vasile Vese (eds), 217–239. Pisa: University of Pisa. www.stm.unipi.it/Clioh/tabs/libri/9/15-Lokk_217-240.pdf (accessed December 21, 2009).

Mackie, Diane and Cooper, Joel. 1984. "Attitude polarisation: Effects of group membership." *Journal of Personality and Social Psychology* 46: 575–585.

Martin, Rod A. 2007. *The Psychology of Humour. An Integrative Approach*. Burlington: Elsevier.

Martin, Rod A. 2008. "Thoughts on the Muhammad cartoon fiasco." In "The Muhammad cartoons and Humour Research: A collection of essays", Paul Lewis (ed.), 16–21. *Humour: International Journal of Humour Research* 21: 1–46.

Mesropova, Olga. 2007. "Pop culture, Russian style." *News of the College of Liberal Arts and Sciences*. http://www.las.iastate.edu/newnews/mesropova0219.shtml (accessed December 21, 2009).

Nagel, Joane. 1994. "Constructing ethnicity: Creating and recreating ethnic identity and culture." *Social Problems* 41: 152–176.

Õhtuleht. 2007. www.sloleht.ee (accessed February 9, 2011). [in Estonian]

Oring, Elliott. 1995. "Arbiters of taste: An afterword." *Journal of Folklore Research* 32: 165–175.

Pajnik, Mojca (ed.). 2002. *Xenophobia and Post-Socialism*. Ljubljana: Peace Institute. http://www2.mirovni-institut.si/eng_html/publications/pdf/MI_politike_symposion_xenophobia.pdf (accessed December 21, 2009).

Pettai, Iris. 2000. "Eestlaste ja mitte-eestlaste integratsiooniparadigma" (Integration paradigm of Estonians and non-Estonians). In *Integratsioonimaastik – ükskõiksusest koosmeeleni* (Integration Landscape. From Indifference to Unity), Agu Laius, Ivi Proos and Iris Pettai (eds), 95. Tallinn: Jaan Tõnissoni Instituut. [in Estonian]

Postimees. 2007. www.postimees.ee (accessed February 10, 2011). [in Estonian]

Reporter. 2007. www.reporter.ee (accessed February 10, 2011). [in Estonian]

Smith, Moira and Saltzman, Rachelle H. 1995. "Introduction to tastelessness." *Journal of Folklore Research* 32: 85–99.

Spohn, Willifried and Triandafyllidou, Anna. 2003. *Changes in Boundary Constructions between Western and Eastern Europe* [Routledge Advances in Sociology 5]. London/New York: Routledge.

Stadnikov, Sergei. 2007. "Võitlus van den Lindeni pärast" (Fight for van den Linden). *Eesti Ekspress*, October 22. [in Estonian]

Tammaru, Tiit. 1997. "Venelaste kohanemise regionaalsed erisused ja kohanemist mõjutavad tegurid" (Regional specificity and factors influencing Russian acculturation). *Akadeemia* 11: 2283–2301. [in Estonian]

Tannen, Deborah. 1992. *That's Not What I Meant! How Conversational Style Makes or Breaks Your Relations with Others*. London: Virago.

Tuisk, Astrid. (ed). 1996. *Neeger Päevitab: Maailma Rahvad Eesti Laste Naljades* (Black Man Sunbathing: Nations in Estonian Children's Jokes). Tallinn: Koolibri. [in Estonian]

Tuisk, Astrid. 2009. "Kolme rahva anekdoodid lastepärimuses: viisteist aastat hiljem" (Three nation jokes in child lore: 15 years later). In *Tulnukad ja internetilapsed. Uurimusi laste- ja noortepärimusest* (UFOs and Internet Children) [Tänapäeva folklorist VIII (Contemporary Folklore 8)], Eda Kalmre (ed.), 161–184. Tartu: EKM Teaduskirjastus. [in Estonian]

Wallace, Claire. 2002. "Opening and closing borders: Migration and mobility in East-Central Europe." *Journal of Ethnic and Migration Studies* 28: 603–625.

Vihalemm, Triin and Timmi, Mailis. 2007. "*Rassism eesti trükimeedias*" (Racism in the Estonian press). Ministry of Justice, Press Conference on the research project "Rassism ja ksenofoobia Eestis" (Racism and Xenophobia in Estonia). October 15. [in Estonian]

Voolaid, Piret (ed). 1998. *Elevant Külmkapis: Kimbuke Keerdküsimusi Koolilaste Suust* (Elephant in the Cupboard: Some Riddles from Estonian Schoolchildren). Tallinn: Koolibri. [in Estonian]

Žagar, Igor. 2002. "Xenophobia and Slovenian media: How the image of the Other is constructed (and what it looks like)". In *Xenophobia and Post-Socialism*, Mojca Pajnik (ed.), 37–45. Ljubljana: Peace Institute. http://www2.mirovni-institut.si/eng_html/publications/pdf/MI_politike_symposion_xenophobia.pdf (accessed December 21, 2009).

CHAPTER 10

Humour and… Stalin in a National Theatre of Greece postmodern production

Stalin: *A Discussion about Greek Theatre*

Vicky Manteli

Hellenic Open University and University of the Peloponnese, Greece

This study focuses on the function of humour in a postmodern performance which explored Stalinism as a paradigm of power politics and suggested that Stalinism is comparable to Modern Greek theatre. The performance suggests that non-conformist art can be denied acceptance and/or success and that both Stalinism and Modern Greek theatre are powerful enough to curb non-conformist artists. This analogy creates a special form of political humour which targets both Stalinism and the Greek theatre, and reveals the Stalinist practices followed in the latter. The study applies a semiotic approach to the analysis of performance and argues that humour, irony, and parody in the production are activated through the complex interaction of verbal, visual, musical, paralinguistic, and intersemiotic signs and codes.

1. Introduction

This study focuses on the function of humour in a postmodern performance of the National Theatre of Greece, which explored Stalinism as a paradigm of power politics and suggested that Stalinism is comparable to Modern Greek theatre. The main idea of the performance is that Stalinism (including the political discourse produced therein) exhibits striking analogies with the discourse produced in/about the Modern Greek theatre by its own people. In the framework of this analogy, images and discourses pertinent to Stalinism are combined and juxtaposed with those of the Modern Greek theatre, in order to criticize both (but mostly the latter one). The perceived analogy throughout the performance is that modernist movements, groups, and people are (or have been) repressed in the history of Stalin's rule and the history of Modern Greek theatre. In addition, the performance hints that non-conformist art can be denied acceptance and/or success and that both systems (i.e. Stalinism and Modern Greek theatre) are powerful enough to curb non-conformist artists. This analogy creates a special form of political humour which targets both Stalinism and the Greek theatre, and reveals the Stalinist practices followed in the latter.

My study applies a semiotic approach to the analysis of performance and suggests a revised look to a linguistic theory, namely the *General Theory of Verbal Humour* (Attardo 2001; henceforth GTVH), to accommodate for the analysis of a multimodal text (i.e. performance text). It argues that humour, irony, and parody in the production *Stalin: A Discussion about Greek Theatre* are activated not only verbally but also through the complex interaction of visual, musical, paralinguistic and intersemiotic signs and codes which may be seen as an extension to Attardo's (2001) theoretical framework of *hyperdetermined humour*. With particular reference to postmodern Greek parodic drama, this study suggests that its discussion should also consider intertextual relationships with oral genres and media discourses. I intend to support the claim that an approach of humour theory extended to be applicable to performance analysis enhances theatre studies, while the multimodality of theatre texts contributes to a fruitful extension of humour theory in order to cover intersemiotic humour.

In 2007–2008 the National Theatre of Greece produced *Stalin: A Discussion about Greek Theatre*. The production can be viewed as an example of Greek postmodern theatre, written, directed, and performed by Michael Marmarinos and Akilas Karazisis, both established as directors and actors outside the National Theatre and acknowledged as respected representatives of the independent Greek theatre scene. Particularly, Marmarinos' recent work with his group *Theseum Ensemble* focuses on re-writing and re-viewing classical dramatic texts, creating thus a new dramatic form based on improvisation and rehearsal reading, interviews, and political commentary. On the performance level, Marmarinos is keen on merging various artistic forms on stage, as well as assigning roles not only to professional actors but also to singers, dancers, audience members, and volunteers (cf. Manteli 2008b: 146).

The production *Stalin: A Discussion about Greek Theatre* competed with sixteen international productions in the 7th Festival *Echt! Politik im Freien Theater* in Cologne, Germany (November 2008) and was awarded first prize. In their decision the jury pointed out the artists' contribution to Greek state theatre as well as the political and theatrical value of the production as "a vision of cooperation and overcoming barriers – whether social, aesthetic, or traditional" (*Kölner Theatre Festival* 2008).

After setting the scene, giving the background of the production and clarifying the objectives of this study and the organisation of this work, in the following section (Section 2), I suggest that humour, irony, and parody are exploited in the production via utterances plus visual and acoustic signs. This complex interaction of different active sources of humour on the performance level may be seen as an extension to Attardo's (2001) theoretical framework of *hyperdetermined humour*. I also propose a revised look at Attardo's (2001) notion of strand to fit the specifics of my data analysis. To give the reader a clear view of the humour and the political discourse in the production, I overview some of its postmodern qualities specifically related to humour and political discourse (Section 3). In Section 4, I first discuss parody related to performance (i.e. parody activated through theatrical signs), as well as the humour (repertoire) of postmodern Greek drama, and then I hint to the genres and text types that the genre appears to draw upon. In Section 5, I discuss hyperdetermined humour in the production in view of parody with reference to toasts performed by the actors (5.1) and to a metatheatrical episode focusing on intertextual and intersemiotic parody (5.2). In Section 6, I discuss hyperdetermination in view of irony with reference to an allegorical episode in which Soviet politics is compared to Modern Greek theatre. It goes without saying that these phenomena (i.e. hyperdetermined instances of parody and irony) are scattered throughout the production and that the episodes analysed are only singled out as typical examples. In fact, hyperdetermination is so often exhibited in the production that it can be considered to form a particularly dense strand in the text. Concluding remarks, implications for further research, and an evaluative approach of the research tools implemented in this study are presented in Section 7.

Overall, *Stalin: A Discussion about Greek Theatre* is shown as an example of Greek postmodern drama and theatre, which heavily draws on political discourse to address dominant ideologies and mythologies of both Left politics and the Modern Greek theatre. Through a variety of humorous mechanisms (humour, parody, irony) expressed verbally, visually, and acoustically, the production compares the Greek theatre system to Stalinism and criticises both systems for their capacity to construct an incongruous reality (cf. Tsakona and Popa this volume). Consequently, while manufacturing the 'real' is discussed notably as a possibility within politics (cf. Watters this volume), my discussion of toasts and the "Siberia episode" (in Section 5) shows that manufactured images and constructed realities are also possible within the world of theatre and its people.

2. Key concepts concerning humour discussion in the production

Humour, irony, and parody can be realised both on the performance level and dramatic discourse. In my study I intend to show that in *Stalin: A Discussion about Greek Theatre*, incongruity is realised through the use of different media, aesthetic forms, and theatrical codes (i.e. text, kinesics, proxemics, actors' appearance and paralinguistic features, painting, video), whose interaction may be said to form *strands*. At this point I should make clear that my use of the term *strand* departs from Attardo's definition (2001:83–84) as a sequence of humorous lines (i.e. punch lines and jab lines; see Attardo 2001; Archakis and Tsakona this volume) formally or thematically linked, possibly established textually or intertextually. Rather than seeing to their role as tools for text segmentation and for structural/formal analysis, I acknowledge the importance of strands as tools for exploring the (humorous) coherence of multimodal texts, such as the theatre performance I study here (cf. Antonopoulou 2003:21 and Chlopicki 2003:157). For the purposes of my discussion then, I apply to strand the notion of co-occurrence of various (textual, performative, intersemiotic) incongruous signs (rather than jab lines or punch lines) whose active participation enhances the performance's coherence, thus facilitating audience reception. I would like to propose that this interaction of different active sources of humour on the performance level may be seen as an extension to Attardo's theoretical framework of *hyperdetermined humour* (Attardo 2001:100–101, 109–110, 122–125). This suggestion may be particularly useful when discussing the humour of more complex (i.e. multimodal) texts, such as performance texts. Attardo (2001:100–101) realises *hyperdetermined humour* as "the presence of more than one active source of humour at the same time, or as the simultaneous activity of a given source of humour in different contexts" and distinguishes between *textual hyperdetermination* (former case) and *punctual hyperdetermination* (latter case). In my discussion of the *Stalin: A Discussion about Greek Theatre* performance text, I intend to show that humour in the dramatic text and performance is simultaneously activated through different codes, including more specifically irony, satire, parody and farce in a certain number of episodes/sequences.

Therefore, the notions of *strand* and *hyperdetermination* are adopted by the GTVH – a theory restricted to verbal humour – and extended to cover the humour of multimodal texts, such as theatrical performances. I consider this approach relevant both to humour theory and theatre studies as it introduces a linguistic methodology and extends it to discuss a performance text.

3.   Humour and political discourse in *Stalin: A Discussion about Greek Theatre*

Postmodern theatre frees itself from the text and the long established dramatic forms and style as well as "grand narratives", which may be said to represent dominant class interests rather than everyone's interests (Allain and Harvie 2006:191).

As a cultural practice of postmodernism, postmodern theatre constructs its multiple meanings around contexts, audiences, and makers. Since one of its main concerns is the representation of meaning, postmodern theatre heavily draws on meta-language (both on text and performance level) and often becomes self-conscious or self-referential. In contrast to naturalist theatre, it questions the value of the image as truthful and real, and concludes that everything is simulation. It also proposes a different approach to acting/performing and emphasises the process rather than the product of theatre performances.

Furthermore, the political character of postmodern performance and its alleged radicalism have been in the centre of much recent debate (Allain and Harvie 2006: 192–193). Thematically, postmodern theatre places emphasis on human relationships with nature, society, culture, and politics. Among its representational practices one should consider the following: the presence of modern technology versus the absence of professional actors on stage, the participation of spectators and/or other artists live on stage, and audience interaction.

Here I present the postmodern aspect of *Stalin: A Discussion about Greek Theatre* with specific reference to characteristic examples related to humour and political discourse. This discussion aims at showing how political discourse is introduced and functions in the production. It also aims at foregrounding the incongruity and absurdity of the production affected by the breaking of dramatic illusion and formal relations between actors and audience, the world of stage and real life.

To start with, there are no dramatic characters or heroes according to traditional theatre conventions. Instead, the audience is presented with an incongruous combination of the following *dramatis personae* defined as "concepts or scenes of history": two Representatives of the Soviet regime, Verico (a Bolshevik princess), Mary (Jesus' mother), a Visitor, a Stuntman (i.e. a dummy), and an undergraduate of Theatre Studies. The Stuntman is present on stage (sits on a sofa) and at certain moments of the dramatic action takes up the role of Mary in order to perform some difficult tasks (e.g. when Mary is supposed to be beaten, or when hung on a bar she is supposed to spit phrases in an ashtray). The dummy also becomes the dancing partner of a Representative when he performs the Kozak dance in the drama episode "Considerations about reality".[1]

---

1. For a full description of the qualifying features of the characters and their role, see the information provided in the published text (Karazisis and Marmarinos 2008) and the theatre bill of the production (*Μικρή Εγκυκλοπαίδεια. Στάλιν: Μια Συζήτηση για το Ελληνικό Θέατρο* 2007–2008). See also Marmarinos and Karazisis' press interviews to Marinou (2008) and Kleftogianni (2008).

Secondly, additional conventions are broken: before the performance starts, the audience can see the actors on stage whispering to each other, engaging in lively conversations, or walking. The stage, designed as a spacious set as big as the auditorium and almost level with the first auditorium rows and covered with the same fitted carpet, gives the impression of a single spatial unit. Just before the dramatic action begins, an usherette removes a member of the audience from their seat and leads them backstage. A couple of minutes later, a shot is heard off-stage.[2] In another episode, a member of the audience addressed as "A Visitor" steps on the stage, engages in dialogue with the actors about Left politics, and narrates his family story dating back to the Greek civil war.

Finally, multimodality is further exploited through the screening of the film *Earth* by Alexander Dovzhenko (1930) at various points of the performance. Besides the symbolism and realism of A. Dovzhenko's film images, the audience is also exposed to made-up shots of texts either referring to the art of cinema (e.g. the generic) or presenting puzzling political discourse. For example:[3]

(1)   Πολιτική ξεπολιτική
      Συγνώμη για τη βρισιά
      Έμενε πάντα κάτι να σπρώχνει την περιπέτεια,
      Αυτήν που έμεινε στη μέση το '89.
      Αυτή που δεν ολοκληρώθηκε.   (Karazisis and Marmarinos 2008:47)

Politics Unpolitics
Pardon my French
Something has always remained to push the adventure,
The one that was not completed in '89.
The one that was not concluded.

Towards the end of the performance a home-made video is also screened featuring private family moments of the two Representatives.

From the above examples it becomes clear that public discourses (e.g. about art and politics) are often mixed with private discourses (informal talk among friends or in family settings) inducing an incongruous (or even absurd) effect on the performance level. The verbal text itself (what is called the *dramatic text* in theatre studies) is also puzzling. It is a hybrid of genres in which private and public discourses merge, in some cases also in different languages (Greek,

---

2.   Matziri (2008) reports this extra-theatrical event as a personal account of her own "execution" as a "guilty" critic who was intentionally picked up among the audience of the specific performance night.

3.   All texts discussed in this study have been translated from Greek into English by the author. Original punctuation and layout of the texts have been preserved and transcribed.

Russian, and Georgian), such as political lectures, politically-oriented asides, conversational talk, personal accounts and narratives, citations from reference books on Communism and Revolution, anecdotes about Stalin's private life and era, self-referential metatheatrical discourse, intertextual allusions to media discourse, popular songs.

4. Theatrical parody: Props, actors' codes, intersemiotic parody

This section discusses parody on the performance level. Consequently, a detailed account of theatrical signs is provided to explain the narrative (drama and performance) and its semiotically-expressed parody. Through a concise presentation of parody which is either related to scenography and acting, or activated intersemiotically, the humour of the production can be appreciated and the comic mechanisms are accounted for. In this section, I will illustrate my argument that in *Stalin: A Discussion about Greek Theatre* any humorous, parodic, or ironic effect is mainly realised through the interaction of various media or aesthetic forms (e.g. painting and cinema), theatrical codes (e.g. paralinguistic signs), genres and discourses (e.g. parodic imitation of the overall organisation and jargon of a public political demonstration).

First, the set includes some incongruous props (i.e. unrelated to the narrative) like a dummy pig which stands at the back of the stage. However, other props are symbolic representations of the narrative of the drama and, therefore, enhance dramatic coherence. For example, Stalin's portrait is being hung on the wall and at some point is removed to be shown to the audience; the two Representatives can be seen as representations of Lenin and Stalin respectively thanks to their costumes and, towards the end of the performance, their masks;[4] standing on a podium in a pose that reminds us of public men delivering political speeches, an actress reads clumsily out of a reference book.[5]

---

4. I consider it is not without significance that, when the production was running, the artists very often chose to pose dressed up as Lenin and Stalin for photographs in the context of interviews.

5. Significantly enough, the entry *podium* with an explanatory picture of Vladimir Ilyich Lenin next to it, is included in the theatre bill of the production, ironically entitled as *Μικρή Εγκυκλοπαίδεια. Στάλιν: Μια Συζήτηση για το Ελληνικό Θέατρο* (Concise Encyclopedia: Stalin. A Discussion about Greek Theatre 2007–2008). The theatre bill imitates the layout and organisation of a reference book and includes the most unlikely information for its genre (i.e. theatre bill).

Secondly, parody can also be detected in the acting codes, particularly para-linguistic and idiolectal codes, and may refer to comic gestures and farcical movements of the performers. A case in point is when actors sit around a table and interrupt abruptly their speech to perform gestures and movements in which the actor's body reminds one of an artificial body or mechanism. Another example is when the male protagonists stop walking on stage and start banging their heads, a kinesic code which imitates automatic machines.[6]

Third, intersemiotic parody is another humorous mechanism employed on the performance level. A case in point is Marmarinos and Karazisis' lying posture on the sofa of the set (see Figure 21). While "Film 3" and "Film 4" are being screened and no action takes place on stage, the two actors retreat from dramatic action and actually become a spatial sign of the performance through a specific configuration of their bodies which imitates J. H. W. Tischbein's art work *Zwei Männer auf einem Sofa* ("Two Men on a Sofa"; see Figure 22). Further on, the two actors resume their roles as Representatives, without changing their posture and adopting an articulation and intonation which recalls recitation, they give a lecture on the duties of the Soviet CK, namely the notorious Soviet state security agency which was important to the survival of the Stalinist regime.

I will now attempt to view the above mentioned signs of parody in *Stalin: A Discussion about Greek Theatre* in the context of a discussion about Modern Greek dramatic and theatrical parody.[7] More specifically, I will attempt to make some comparative remarks following Diamantakou-Agathou's discussion (2007:452–505) on the topic. To start with, I should mention that, unlike most Modern Greek dramas involving parody, the dramatic text of the production does not bear any intertextual relation to Greek myths, ancient Greek or Roman history.[8] By contrast,

---

6. The discussion of automatic gestures and movements should be seen in view of Bergson's (1901/1997) seminal study on laughter and the mechanics of the comic. For a brief explanation of the perception of a mechanism reproduced in human action as comic, see the entry *comic* (Pavis 1998:66).

7. See Diamantakou-Agathou (2007:452–465) for her proposed definition and demarcation of parody in Modern Greek drama, a thematically related classification of parodic Modern Greek dramatic writing (2007:465–487), and a list of "parameters of parody" (2007:488–505). It is important to consider the time span of Modern Greek drama that Diamantakou-Agathou deems valid for such a discussion: "[…] the age of Modern Greek parody of drama tends also to coincide with the age of Modern Greek overall" (Diamantakou-Agathou 2007:458). This literally means that her corpus consists of parodic dramatic texts which might date back to 18th century up to the first decade of 2000.

8. See, for example, the discussion by Chasapi-Christodoulou (2002) on the ways Greek myths have been used in Modern Greek theatre since the era of Cretan theatre (16th and 17th centuries). See also Chatzipantazis (2004) for the dramaturgical influence not only of Aristophanes'

Figure 21. Reprint of photograph from a newspaper interview of Michael Marmarinos and Akilas Karazisis (Marinou 2008)

the text critically approaches Greek post-war politics and myths (either political or theatrical) and Soviet history. Secondly, the text does not use any intertexts from Greek tragedy, another thematically related class from which Modern Greek parodic drama systematically borrows (Diamantakou-Agathou 2007:471). Nor does it allude to any dramatic texts from either contemporary Greek or European literary history which is a case in point for most Modern Greek parodic drama.[9] In fact, the text parodically imitates oral genres as well as metatheatrical, media,

comedy but also European comedy (particularly Molière, Goldoni, and Labiche) on 19th century Modern Greek comedy.

9. For a suggestive Greek bibliography on this discussion, see Diamantakou-Agathou (2007:453–487) and references therein.

J.H.W. Tischbein (1751-1829)

Zwei Männer auf einem Sofa, um 1786/1787

Due uomini su un sofà, 1786/1787 ca.

Casa di Goethe, Roma.

Figure 22. Reprint of photograph of original painting by J. H. W. Tischbein *Zwei Männer auf einem Sofa* (see *Casa di Goethe* 2010; also Μικρή Εγκυκλοπαίδεια. Στάλιν: Μια Συζήτηση για το Ελληνικό Θέατρο 2007–2008: 41)

and political discourses (see Section 5). Consequently, what I will argue is that a discussion of parody of Modern Greek drama should be extended as to include besides theatrical, cinematic and/or literary text types, additional parameters, too, such as intertextual relationships with oral genres and media discourses. From the point of view of this volume, it is interesting that the function of such oral and media intertexts in postmodern drama are often humorous and parodic.[10]

---

10. Cf. Manteli (2010) for a discussion of humour in children's discourse (i.e. nursery rhymes) and songs' parody in *Zorbas: The True Story*, which was also produced by the National Theatre

5.   Parody and hyperdetermination

In this section, I will discuss in detail how oral and media intertexts are used in the National Theatre of Greece performance to create humour. In this context I will argue that hyperdetermination including parody is so often that it forms strands. The political discourse of the discussed episode (see Section 5.1) loaded with allusions to Stalin, totalitarian regimes, and politics in general are mixed with references to the politics of the theatre of the Stalinist era and of Modern Greece, in order to criticize both. This blend of discourses creates a special form of political humour which targets both and reveals any restrictive practices followed in the Modern Greek theatre. Through this blend of discourses the art of theatre and the values of youth, urbanism, revolution, and language are addressed, too.

In Section 5.2, emphasis is given on another type of discourse, often used in modern and postmodern drama, namely self-referential metatheatrical discourse. The discourse in this production is mostly satirical and ironic targeting the people and the audience(s) of the Greek theatre. The basic allusions are that the former (specifically, actors and directors) are crackpots, biased, and retrogressive in their critical approach (specifically, theatre reviewers and critics), and victims of the mass media promotion system(s) (including all the people of the theatre and probably the audience, as well). Another allusion is that the audience(s) consists of unsophisticated or perplexed victims of a postmodern trend which has taken over the Greek theatre. Consequently, the analogy with Stalinism is that there is a manufactured reality in today's Greek theatre which constrains its people's liberties. Significantly enough, this episode is named "Considerations about reality" and, as will be discussed, it is backed up with a series of "virtual reality" executions on the performance level, a parodic allusion to Stalin's executions.

5.1   Cheers to… Stalin: Toasts

The first point concerns the toasts performed by the actors in four different dramatic sequences of the performance. I will only focus on performance toasts which parodically imitate the oral genre of toasting and satirise the absurdity of its content, for example, honouring the dead and parents (see Examples (2), (3), and (6)). The toasts (see Examples (2)–(6)) heavily reside in nonsense humour which is thematically linked to politics or acting. They are proposed by the leading

---

of Greece in 2009. There, I also explore the oral genres and media discourses humour in Greek post-dramatic theatre draws upon.

male actors, particularly one of them who by some theatre conventions (i.e. mask, costume, hairstyle, and beard) appears as a sign of Lenin.

In discussing the parody of the performance toasts, I will use Kotthoff's (1995) discussion of the oral genre of Georgian toasting and compare it with Greek toasting with which it seems to share a number of generic features. Georgian toasting as a genre

> depends on stable textual and contextual factors: alcoholic drinks have to be served; the toast has to be addressed to the whole group; the text should include a good wish; at least one central formula must be expressed, and at least one person has to drink following its presentation.   (Kotthoff 1995:357)

Textually, toasts in the performance imitate the internal organisation of the oral genre with the following highly marked features in Georgian tradition as noted by Kotthoff (1995:354): repetition, formulaic speech, parallelisms, extravagant wording, and other factors of verbal art like improvisation. A Greek audience is expected to recognize these features in their own tradition, too.

I will here present my examples, namely the Greek and translated texts of toasts (Karazisis and Marmarinos 2008):

(2)   Ψηλά τα ποτήρια
      Στη βάρκα
      [...]
      Ψηλά τα ποτήρια
      Στον πατέρα του γιου του. Και στο γιο του πατέρα.
      Την ίδια περίπου εποχή που άλλοι προστάτευαν
      μπαλαρίνες. Όπως έκαναν και θα κάνουν πάντοτε
      οι εκατομμυριούχοι.

      Ψηλά τα ποτήρια
      Στη βάρκα
      Με την αθάνατη Seagull στη ράχη
      Μόνο τρεις ίπποι   (Karazisis and Marmarinos 2008:21)

      Cheers
      To the boat
      [...]
      Cheers
      To the father of his son. And to the father's son.
      At about the same time when others used to protect
      ballet dancers. As the millionaires have been doing
      and will always be doing.

Cheers
To the boat
With the immortal Seagull[11] on the back
Just a three-horsepower engine

(3) Ψηλά τα ποτήρια
Στην πολιτική
που προϋπάρχει της βάρκας.
Που προϋπάρχει της Seagull.
Ό,τι είναι πριν
Στην πολιτική που προϋπάρχει του είναι.

(Karazisis and Marmarinos 2008: 22)

Cheers
To politics
which precedes the boat.
Which precedes Seagull.
Whatever is before
[Cheers] To politics which precedes being.

(4) Ψηλά τα ποτήρια
Στο παίξιμο που δεν υπάρχει
Στο έργο που παίζει μόνο του   (Karazisis and Marmarinos 2008: 29)

Let's raise our glasses
To acting which does not exist
To the play which is on by itself

(5) Ψηλά τα ποτήρια
Στη Δικτατορία του προλεταριάτου
Στην πολιτική που προϋπάρχει του είναι

(Karazisis and Marmarinos 2008: 42)

Cheers
To the Dictatorship of the proletariat
[Cheers] To politics which precedes being

(6) Ψηλά τα ποτήρια
Στο αποσπασματικό
Στο θραυσματικό που ερεθίζει τη φαντασία
Στο θραυσματικό που είναι από μόνο του μια αντίσταση
στην ύπουλη λογοκρισία που μεταμφιέζεται

---

11. The British *Seagull*, an outboard engine, has been considered the best outboard motor of the world.

Στην πιο καινούρια ιδέα που εμφανίστηκε ποτέ
στο δικαίωμα στην αποσπασματική ευτυχία

Τραγούδα Μάνα του Χριστού Τραγούδα

Στη νεότητα Που δεν κατρακυλάει στα άπειρα
πρόσωπα της παραίτησης
Σε μια πόλη που δεν είναι φτιαγμένη μόνο για τη
δυστυχισμένη ευτυχία των μικροαστών
Στη μνήμη Επειδή δεν μπορεί να υπάρξει ποτέ
επανάσταση χωρίς μνήμη
Και στη γλώσσα Γιατί η γλώσσα και η μνήμη
διαλύονται μαζί, χέρι χέρι
Στον πατέρα μου Στον πατέρα σου
Όχι στους δικούς σας, ζουν ακόμα   (Karazisis and Marmarinos 2008: 56)

Cheers
To the fragmentary
To the broken which kindles imagination
To the broken which is a resistance by itself
to sly censorship which disguises itself
To the newest idea which has ever occurred
to the right to fragmentary happiness

Sing Jesus' Mother Sing

To youth Who does not tumble into the infinite
faces of resignation
To a city which is not made only for the
unhappy happiness of the petit bourgeois
To memory Because no revolution can ever occur
without memory
And to language Because language and memory
melt together, hand in hand
To my father To your father
Not to yours, they're still alive

The following are some observations to illustrate the analogy between the overall organisation and jargon of the genre of toasting and the toasts of the dramatic text:

a. *Repetition* of words/phrases (e.g. *βάρκα* "boat" in Examples (2)–(3); *πολιτική*
    "politics" in Examples (3) and (5); *Seagull* in Example (3); *το θραυσματικό*
    "the broken" in Example 6).
b. *Formulaic speech* exemplified through the opening phrase *Ψηλά τα ποτήρια*
    "Cheers to…" (in Examples (2)–(6)).

c. Imaginative parallelism between the protectors of ballet dancers and the millionaires (*Την ίδια περίπου εποχή... οι εκατομμυριούχοι* "At about the same time... always be doing" in Example (2)).

d. *Paradox* or else *extravagant wording* (e.g. *στο έργο που παίζει μόνο του* "to the play which is on by itself" in Example (4); *στην πολιτική που προϋπάρχει του είναι* "to politics which precedes being" in Example (5); *δυστυχισμένη ευτυχία* "*unhappy happiness*" in Example (6)).

Pragmatically, the dramatic situation in which toasts are pronounced imitates real life situations, that is, they are proposed during the sharing of food and drink around a table among male speakers. Alcoholic drinks and particularly Georgian red wine represents an extra-linguistic sign, a prop within the system of the performance. Moreover, the formula *Λίγο καλό γεωργιανό κρασί* ("A little good Georgian wine"; Karazisis and Marmarinos 2008: 15) is often inserted at the opening of a toast proposed by one or both leading male actors either as they walk arm in arm towards or sit at the long wooden table of the set. The particular stage prop, namely the table filled with wine glasses, a teapot, a lamp, and a fruit bowl, provides useful dramatic information about the spatio-temporal conventions of the performance narrative. In addition, the qualification *Georgian* "γεωργιανό (neutr.)" may be taken as an intertextual allusion to Joseph Stalin's country of origin and thus highlights both the dramatic and the political context of the performance.

   Parody is realised here through nonsense humour linked to thematic non-sequiturs associated with paradoxical toasts, absurd phrasing, and pragmatic incongruity. It is also linked to a 'theatrical' speech delivery produced by the actors while performing the toasts (particularly Example (2)), as attested in the performance's DVD (Karazisis and Marmarinos n.d.). This illustrates my hypothesis that humorous mechanisms in the performance are activated because of the co-occurrence of opposed codes (both linguistic and the paralinguistic ones) and incongruous textual and performative signs. Such co-occurrences are, arguably, parallel to the formation of strands, not strictly in terms of jab lines or punch lines, as in the GTVH, but rather in terms of combined activation of textual, intertextual, and performative signs. Parodically exploited incongruity is therefore present both on the linguistic and the performance level. As instances of linguistic paradox consider, for instance, *Ψηλά τα ποτήρια/ Στον πατέρα του γιου του. Και στο γιο του πατέρα* ("Cheers/ To the father of his son. And to the father's son" in Example (2)). Parody exploited on the performance level is exemplified in speech delivery while proposing a toast with the Representatives seated or walking arm-in-arm.

5.2   "Considerations about reality": Parody and the political images of metatheatrical discourse

The episode "Considerations about reality" can be viewed as the most suggestive example of self-referential metatheatrical discourse in the production. The text is a composition of various extracts and allusive phrases from oral and written critical discourses and genres, such as interviews, theatre reviews, popular magazine articles, newspaper headlines, and magazine titles, gossip magazine columns, and lists of names of contemporary Greek theatre directors and critics. Consequently, this illustrates one of the basic arguments proposed in my work, namely that postmodern Greek parodic drama should particularly consider intertextual relationships with oral genres and media discourses (see also Section 4).

The function of the above mentioned intertexts is mostly satirical and ironic targeting actors, directors, and the audience. The production's self-referential discourse is an extended example of how postmodern Greek drama can address humorously the people of the Greek theatre and Greek theatre-goers.

First of all, directors and actors become the target of a biting satire due to their overweening conceit and extraneous propositions regarding their professional choices and artistic style. In the following Example (7), a director talks about his criteria for reviving an ancient Greek comedy by Aristophanes:

(7)   Ο Αριστοφάνης ήταν δική μου επιλογή γιατί σαν άνθρωπος έχω πολύ χιού-
       μορ. Ο γιός μου μάλιστα μου λέει συνέχεια: μπαμπά σκέφτεσαι σαν 17χρονος.
       ΜΠΑΜ   (Karazisis and Marmarinos 2008: 50)

       Aristophanes was my choice because as a person I've got a great sense of
       humour. To be honest, my son keeps telling me: "Dad, you think like a 17-year
       old". BANG

Parody here involves the irrelevant and exaggerated information provided by the targeted director in an interview. Directors and actors are also satirized because of their talking nonsense:

(8)   Πιστεύω στη δύναμη των σπόρων και των βλαστών, στο πρωτογενές ένστικτο
       των ζώων, στον τρόπο που τα αποδημητικά πουλιά βρίσκουν το δρόμο τους,
       στις ερωτικές συνευρέσεις των μεγάλων θηλαστικών. Όλα αυτά μέσα από τη
       μελέτη και την τελετουργία με κάνουν να πιστεύω στο θέατρο ΜΠΑΜ
                                             (Karazisis and Marmarinos 2008: 50–51)

       I believe in the power of seeds and buds, the instinct of animals, the way that
       migrating birds find their way, sexual intercourse among mammals. All these
       through the study and the ritual make me believe in theatre BANG

Greek critics become the butt of criticism for their outdated views (e.g. views about the revival and modern productions of classical Greek tragedy in Epidaurus Festival) as in the following ironic reference:

(9) Αλλά στην Επίδαυρο οι Τούρκοι τη δουλειά είχαν;
                                   (Karazisis and Marmarinos 2008:51)

   What were the Turks doing in Epidaurus Festival, after all?

The intertext is an ironic allusion to a newspaper review by Christidis (2006), an established theatre critic of the older generation, who used a torrent of abuse to review a production of Aeschylus *Persians* by Theo Terzopoulos, among the fewest Greek directors with an international career, with a cast of Greek and Turk actors at the 2006 Epidaurus Summer Festival. The implied irony is that exaggerated patriotic feelings may infuse Greek theatre critics' writing when it comes to reviewing avant-garde performances of classical Greek drama staged at the ancient theatre of Epidaurus. The overall assumption is that Greek theatre criticism irrevocably suffers from outdated established perceptions and cannot really appreciate a modernist or a postmodernist outlook. Moreover, Greek critics are also criticized for their inefficiency to appropriately review theatre performances.

   The promotion system of stars is also mocked for its special attention to private details rather than to the art and the talent of theatre people:

(10) Επιτέλους εγεννήθη υπέροχο θεατρικό ζευγάρι. Και στη ζωή μαθαίνω, αλλά
     και στη σκηνή.   (Karazisis and Marmarinos 2008:52)

   At last! A new theatrical couple is born! Both on stage and in life.

This example is a parodic allusion to a phrase used in a media text by Kraounakis (2007), who addressed humorously the idea of the media's preoccupation with theatre people's private lives and the occasional excitement on drawing analogies with the commotion felt by both critics and audiences in the 1960s and 1970s about the private life of a most popular and successful theatre couple of the older generation, namely Dimitris Horn and Elli Lambeti.

   The audience's reception of postmodern theatre is humorously presented as informal talk between theatre-goers:

(11) Και μη με ρωτάς για υπόθεση. Ακούμε ένα ακορντεόν και μια κουλή σφουγ-
     γαρίζει μια αυλή. Δεν πάει ο Μπέλα Ταρ να θεωρείται ποιητής του σινεμά;
     Μακριά απ' τον κώλο μου κι ας κάνει ό,τι θέλει ΜΠΑΜ
                                   (Karazisis and Marmarinos 2008:51)

And don't ask me about the plot. We just listened to an accordion playing while a dotty female was mopping a yard. Who cares if Bela Tarr[12] is considered a poet of the cinema. So long as he keeps away from my ass let him do whatever he pleases BANG

In this extract, probably an oral intertext from an overheard discussion among Greek spectators, the target is the Greek audience and the implied irony is that Greek audience is fond of watching what might be considered avant-garde and/or postmodern theatre without really enjoying or understanding it.

Furthermore, actors' incongruous reflections on theatre are included in humorous asides:

(12) Εμ, γι' αυτό μ' αρέσει το θέατρο Γιατί; Γιατί μπορείς να σκοτώνεις όποιον θέλεις όποτε θέλεις [...] Και γιατί άλλο; Γιατί μπορείς να γερνάς όποτε θέλεις και όπως θέλεις Εμ, γι' αυτό ξενυχτάμε, γι' αυτό πίνουμε, γι' αυτό βλέπουμε ταινίες   (Karazisis and Marmarinos 2008: 53)

Well, that's why I like theatre You know why? Because you can always kill someone whenever you want [...] And what else? Because you can always grow old whenever you wish and however you wish That's why we stay up late and we drink and we watch films.

Finally, politicians as invited guests to opening nights become the target of satire:

(13) Στα παρασκήνια μετά την παράσταση η Μαρία Δαμανάκη χαιρετάει τους ηθοποιούς Η χειραψία της σαν ψόφιο ψάρι
                                                        (Karazisis and Marmarinos 2008: 50)

After the performance at the wings Maria Damanaki [i.e. an ex left-wing now Socialist MP] congratulates the actors Her handshake feels like a dead fish

Some of the intertexts discussed above draw an analogy between Stalinism and the Greek theatre in that both systems are oppressive and use censorship. Another perceived comparison is that both systems can deny acceptance and/or positive evaluation to those who displease them. Non-conformist citizens and unconventional artists may be executed: the former literally, the latter figuratively or on the performance level (see the repeated "Bang" noise in Examples (7), (8), and (11)). In a broader context, the production's parallelism with politics is that both Stalinist politics and the Modern Greek theatre are based on an incongruous reality. The production assumes that Greek theatre adopts an arbitrary ideological stance

---

12. Hungarian film director highly praised by and regarded as a major influence on the remodernist film movement. His film work is characterized by raw close-ups, abstract mediums, long shots, and a metaphysical outlook.

towards its values, symbols, and people, comparable to the manipulation and violence of the Stalinist regime.

The linguistic analysis so far has suggested that humour in this episode is related to metatheatrical parody realised through intertextual allusions and a range of formal and informal registers,[13] as well as heavy use of media discourses. Theatrically, parody is realised through the representation of dramatic action in a farcical mode: one of the Representatives takes up the role of the narrator who kills the assumed targets of criticism, as noted in the previous examples, whose stage representation is supposedly the Student. The execution is performed each time the phrase Έχετε πει "You have been reported to say…" is uttered. After that, the Representative shoots fire to the Student, who drops dead and then quickly rises on upright seated position on the stage floor only to drop dead again at a subsequent shot. The analogy with Stalinism is that arbitrary decisions about whom to kill or not were common to Stalin and his people. Also the implied meaning is that, in totalitarian systems such as Stalinism (and the Greek theatre), freedom of expression is curtailed and can put somebody under threat. The combination of the farcical repetition on text and performance level enhances parody.

Apart from such theatrical codes pertinent to acting (here kinesics), parody is signified through musical and paralinguistic codes. Here I am specifically referring to the musical score played at the piano by the second Representative and Mary. The score parodically imitates the tone of requiems. In addition, Mary's idiolect when pronouncing the list of names of critics imitates scary voices from thriller films.

Consequently, my discussion illustrates that humour in this episode too is activated because of the interaction of different textual and performative signs and codes, making the extract an instance of *hyperdetermined humour* (Attardo 2001:100–101).

I will now discuss another instance of hyperdetermined parody in the episode "Considerations about reality", namely a parodic imitation of the well-known Greek film song Ηθοποιός σημαίνει φως ("Actor Means Light"):

(14) Ηθοποιός σημαίνει φως. Είναι καημός πολύ πικρός και στεναγμός πολύ μικρός. Μίλησε, κλαις; Όχι, δε λες. Μήπως πεινάς; Και τι να φας. Όλο γυρνάς, πες μου πού πας; Σ' αναζητώ στο χώρο αυτό, γιατί είμ' εγώ πολύ μικρός και θλιβερός ηθοποιός. Θα παίξεις μια, θα παίξω δυο. Θα κλάψεις μια, θα κλάψω δυο. Σαν καλαμιά, σαν καλαμιά θα σ' αρνηθώ, θα σκεπαστώ, θα τυλιχτώ μ' άσπρο πανί κι ένα πουλί, άσπρο πουλί που καλεί τ' άλλο πουλί, το μαύρο

---

13. Cf. Manteli (2008a), where intertextual allusions and register clash as recurrent verbal humour mechanisms in the translation of Aristophanes' *Acharnians* are discussed.

πουλί. Παρηγοριά στη λυγαριά, υπομονή. Αχ πώς πονεί. Κι ύστερα λες για
δυο τρελές που μ' αγαπούν γιατί σιωπούν, γιατί σιωπούν.

(Karazisis and Marmarinos (2008: 51–52)

Actor means light. It is a very bitter sorrow and a very little sigh. Speak, are
you crying? You don't deny it. Maybe you're hungry? Nothing to eat! Always
on the run, tell me where are you going? I'm looking for you in this space,
because I'm very petty and a pathetic actor. You'll act once, I'll act twice. You'll
cry once, I'll cry twice. Like the stubble, like the stubble I'll reject you, I'll
cover myself, I'll wrap myself in a white cloth and a bird, a white bird calling
another bird, the black bird. Comfort to the wicker, be patient. Oh, how it
hurts. And then you talk about two crazy women who love me why are they
silent, why are they silent.

The song is exploited parodically on the performance level, while its layout,
overall organization, and content are not parodied at all. It is worth mentioning
that the song has been associated with the actor who first performed it, namely
D. Horn, an acclaimed Greek actor of the older generation (see above). D. Horn
became popular among the Greek audience of 1940s–1960s for his excellent acting style which nonetheless reflected the principles and the forms of traditional
Greek theatre. Moreover, D. Horn's idiosyncratic paralinguistic and rhetorical
codes have typified him as an actor and identified him with this specific song.
Parody works effectively at the performance level since one of the Representatives
imitates D. Horn's acting codes with an overemphasis on voice projection, articulation, intonation, etc., as he performs the song himself. Moreover, the particular
speech delivery highlights the absurdity of the lyrics which can be attributed to
the punning effect realised through a rhyming pattern, and to metaphors which
establish incongruity. The musical score can be easily appreciated by the audience
who recognize its rhyming pattern and rhythm played at the piano by a Representative and Mary. In addition, one may also assume that the lyrics enhance the
metatheatrical qualities of the episode since the topic centers on the art of actors,
the difficulties of their profession, the painful procedure of choosing roles or not
being chosen to play at all, and the relationship with the audience.

Parody becomes more explicit since the Greek audience may establish more
intertextual allusions: first, D. Horn was one of the leading actors of the National
Theatre of Greece and later one of the most popular theatre people of the independent Greek theatre; second, the song was composed and its lyrics were written by
Manos Hatzidakis, one of the most celebrated Greek composers. These allusions
can end up triggering the actualization of a second script, namely the respect to
Greek artists of an older generation whose aesthetics contrast with modern and
postmodern aesthetics. It becomes then clear that the targets of parody in this

particular extract are the symbols of the older generation as well as the norms of the theatre and art system of Greece.

From all the above analysis, one might argue that the visual, musical, para-linguistic, and intertextual sings or clues of parody make the extract an instance of *hyperdetermined humour* (Attardo 2001: 100–101) so regularly present that it forms a strand.

6. "Send me some nature…" or the "Siberia" episode: Irony and hyperdetermination

I will now turn to a discussion of the "Siberia" episode which, in my view, is typical of the political discourse of the performance. The episode functions as a metaphor of the history of Modern Greek theatre supposedly suffering from conservatism and ironically compared to Soviet history in the era of Stalinist propaganda. The perceived analogy is that, in both histories (i.e. the Greek and the Soviet one), modernist movements, groups, and individuals have been repressed.[14] As Karazisis and Marmarinos claim in their interview to Dimadi (2008), the basic concept underlying the performance is that Stalinism and the Modern Greek the-atre are "relative ideological systems with an inherent theatricality recognized in their ability to ascribe roles and decide what is real or not".[15] In relation to the function of the performance's political discourse, the performance suggests that political discourse constructs reality, symbols, and norms, as well as manufac-tures stereotyped roles (cf. Tsakona and Popa this volume).

Irony underlines the "Siberia" episode since Siberia is not represented as a vast land historically identified as a faraway labour camp for millions of Soviet dissidents in the era of Stalin, thus a symbol of totalitarianism, but as an ideal spot for holidays preferred by people:

---

14. However, I should stress that the analogy is grim enough if one considers that, in fact in So-viet history non-conformist artists were driven into Siberian exile for offending the standards of Soviet realism, and were physically extinguished.

15. Cf. also the following lines from the dramatic text (episode "Proposal"):

Μου λες: Το θέατρο είναι σαν τον Στάλιν. Έχει τη δύναμη να μετατρέπει τον αφηρη-μένο στοχασμό σε βίωμα.   (Karazisis and Marmarinos 2008: 65)

You claim: Theatre is like Stalin. It has the power to convert an abstract reflection into experience.

(15)   ναι, έτσι μυριάδες όχι χιλιάδες- ανθρώπων θέλησαν να την επισκεφθούν [...]
       Η ωραιότερη συλλογή από καπέλα γυναικών και ανδρών. Ανθρώπων δηλαδή
       που έζησαν εκεί ή οδηγήθηκαν να κάνουν εκεί τις διακοπές τους
                                            (Karazisis and Marmarinos 2008: 39)

       not just thousands but myriads of people wished to visit Siberia [...] The most
       beautiful collection of men's and women's hats. That means, hats of people
       who lived there or were driven there on their holidays

The dramatic text is a blend of figures of speech and genres, such as metaphors
(e.g. Siberia as a frozen princess, a sleeping beauty, a window filled with water en-
closed in a frozen glass wonderfully lit; Karazisis and Marmarinos 2008: 38, 39),
catalogues of names of certain Russian dissidents sent to exile during the 1930s
and 1940s (Karazisis and Marmarinos 2008: 37–38), detailed anecdotal accounts
and biographies of dissidents (e.g. Fedor Raskolnikov and Lallie's mother, an unknown Soviet dissident; Karazisis and Marmarinos 2008: 38), historical evidence
(e.g. the number of people sent to exile during the "soft decade(s)"), and geographical information about Siberia, its inhabitants, and its economy (Karazisis
and Marmarinos 2008: 40).

Apparently, discourse in the "Siberia" episode is politically and historically
based and foregrounds historical memory. Within this heavy political discourse,
humour is attested as register clash in the extract of dissidents' biographies. Specifically, a formal reference to a male dissident (i.e. via his last name) plus a historical report about his exile is contrasted with a casual reference to a female
dissident (i.e. Επίσης, τη μητέρα της Lallie – να, ξέχασα το πλήρες όνομα "Lallie's
mother, too – see, I forgot her full name"; Karazisis and Marmarinos 2008: 38). In
addition, a narrative with details of a more private nature (i.e. the toilet conditions
on the female's train journey to Siberia; Karazisis and Marmarinos 2008: 38) enhances the irony of the episode and diffuses a tongue-in-cheek tone in an extract
of particularly loaded political discourse.

On the theatrical level, the political context of the performance is signified through video screening of extracts from A. Dovzhenko's (1930) Earth (see
"Film 3" and "Film 4"; Karazisis and Marmarinos n.d.). A. Dovzhenko was a most
important early Soviet film-maker whose film work was vilified by contemporary Soviet critics who considered its realism as counter-revolutionary. Moreover,
irony may be realised through a range of theatrical signs: extra-theatrical information, for example a reference to the light designer of the production and his
excellent work (Karazisis and Marmarinos 2008: 38); didactic theatrical asides
whose moral intent is humorously subverted in the text, for example puns, rhyming effect, register clash, and intertextual allusions to children's songs (Karazisis
and Marmarinos 2008: 40; see also Example (16) below). On the performance

level, irony is signified through a pseudo-educative tone adopted by the leading performer in his speech delivery, a video clip featuring a collection of hats (supposed to be worn by the men and women who "went on holiday" in Siberia), and an off-stage audio-recording narrating an ill-treatment episode with a dog.

I will now focus on a more detailed discussion of the verbal humour of the theatrical asides in the "Siberia" episode:

(16) Πλειστηριασμοί επί πλειστηριασμών για μία εικόνα.
Όχι του Θεού ή κανενός αγίου
αλλά για ένα ποταμάκι με νερό
μια αγελάδα
άλογα σε βοσκή
ξέρω γω... έλατα
μία βαρκούλα του ψαρά
Βρέστη – το λιμάνι
Και όχι ζωγραφική, ποτέ ζωγραφική, αλλά την αλήθεια
– ήγουν – φωτογραφία. Πραγματικές απεικονίσεις είναι
το μέλημα.
Να στέλνουμε λοιπόν εκεί που 'χουν ανάγκη τα
απαραίτητα:
Στην Αφρική νερό – γιατί διψάνε
Στο Μπαγκλαντές λεφτά – γιατί πεινάνε
Κάνα ποτό στη Λαπωνία – που μεθάνε
Στη Σιβηρία card-postalle – γιατί ζητάνε
(Karazisis and Marmarinos 2008: 40)

Auctions upon auctions for an icon.
Not of God or any saint
but of a stream of water
a cow
grazing horses
I don't know... maybe Christmas-trees
a small fisherman's boat
Brest – the port
And not painting, never painting, but the truth
– videlicet – a photograph. The concern is about
real images.
Let us send then to people what they need:
Water to Africa – because people are thirsty
Money to Bangladesh – because people are hungry
A little booze to Lapland – where people get drunk
Postcards to Siberia – because people ask for them.

Humour in these asides rests first on a pun based on polysemy: the Greek polyse-mous word εικόνα "icon, picture" refers either to pictures of Christ, Virgin Mary, and Saints, or to any picture of something or someone. Parody stems from the incongruity between the didactic and politically-correct tone of voice (speech de-livery) in some lines (Στην Αφρική νερό... γιατί ζητάνε "Water to Africa... because people ask for them"), combined with the punning and rhyming effect of these phrases in the original Greek text, thus creating a genre clash between a play-ful children's poem and serious political discourse. Parallelism foregrounds the incongruity among such syntactically and rhythmically similar phrases. Further-more, the phrase μία βαρκούλα του ψαρά "a small fisherman's boat" constitutes a parodic allusion to an old well-known Greek children's song. Register clash also occurs in the form of an old high mode preposition επί "upon" and the archaic discourse marker ήγουν "videlicet".[16]

Some of the above examples of verbal humour are instances of hyperdeter-mined irony since they are enhanced on the performance level. First, the incon-gruous collocation of the polysemous εικόνα "icon" with ένα ποταμάκι με νερό "a stream of water", μια αγελάδα "a cow", and άλογα σε βοσκή "grazing horses" is enhanced by a video clip featuring landscapes. Secondly, the parodic allusion to a children's poem is delivered by the Representative in an ironic tone inducing mockery, while a video clip is screened featuring a collection of hats supposed to be worn by the Soviet dissidents in exile. At the end of the episode an off-stage audio-recording narrating an ill-treatment episode with a dog adds to the script of oppression, which underlies the Siberia episode.

It then becomes obvious that, as in the previous cases examined in this chap-ter, in this episode, too, irony may be realised through a range of active sources (i.e. register, visual, and acoustic codes). This interaction of different active sourc-es of humour on the performance level may be seen as an extension to Attardo's theoretical framework of *hyperdetermined humour,* in the sense of "the presence of more than one active source of humour at the same time, or as the simultane-ous activity of a given source of humour in different contexts" (Attardo 2001: 100–101). Arguably, such a look to an already existing theoretical construct may be

---

16. The humour mechanisms identified here have been extensively discussed in the linguistic literature on humour: polysemy and rhyming have been classified as typical wordplay mecha-nisms (see among others Attardo et al. 1994; Delabastita 1996; Attardo 2001; Antonopoulou 2004); intertextuality is related to the recycling and recontextualisation of fixed expressions and allusive phrases (see among others Redfern 1997; Antonopoulou 2004); register clash fore-grounds incongruity and is usually pertinent to diglossic humour in Greek, in particular to the use of old high mode *katharevousa* with its formal and learned lexis and structures in inappro-priate, ordinary, or banal situations (Canakis 1994, 2008; Antonopoulou 2002, 2004; Tsakona 2004; Manteli 2008a).

particularly useful when discussing the humour of more complex texts, such as performance texts. Overall, my discussion of the National Theatre's production shows that humour in the dramatic text and the performance is not only simultaneously activated through different codes, but it is mostly realised as hyperdetermined instances of parody and irony.

7.   Concluding remarks

The starting point of my work was to explore how the genre of postmodern theatre relates to humour and therefore to discuss what particular comic mechanisms are activated and how humour is signified, both verbally and on the performance level. As humour is not classified as a prototypical feature of postmodern theatre, I hope that my work has added emphasis to the discussion of the comic mechanisms and the humour of postmodern theatre, an aspect that has not received particular attention either from humour or theatre scholars.

Through the production *Stalin: A Discussion about Greek Theatre*, I discussed how political discourse can be exploited in drama (text) and theatre (performance). More specifically I showed how political allegory can become a symbol of the theatre. In the National Theatre of Greece production *Stalin: A Discussion about Greek Theatre*, a political system (i.e. Stalinism) is compared to the system of Modern Greek theatre as a paradigm of power politics. I argued that the political humour is mostly related to an ironic and parodic approach to Greek post-war politics as well as the Soviet history. Its targets are the long established myths, norms, symbols, and key ideas of both political cultures. Consequently, political humour is used in a theatre performance to address totalitarian ideologies and systems and expose their potential to distort political reality and historical memory. What is more, it is used as a vehicle to draw analogies between Stalin's regime and Modern Greek theatre on the basis that both systems are (or have been) manipulative and oppressive.

On the linguistic level, my discussion of *Stalin: A Discussion about Greek Theatre* suggests that postmodern Greek parodic drama should also consider intertextual relations with oral genres and media discourses. Additionally, it has been shown that the narrative of the drama abounds with metatheatrical discourse often targeted against the Greek theatre and its people, past and present symbols and myths. Through this kind of ironic self-referential discourse, the production *Stalin: A Discussion about Greek Theatre* not only invites the audience to reflect on Modern Greek theatre, but also experiments with the audience-stage relationship effectively. Consequently, it is through humour that the National Theatre production intends to deconstruct the audience's criteria of viewing theatre performance as a cultural practice and their understanding of the mythologies of Modern Greek theatre overall. This strategy could be compared to Guzzanti's satirical impersonation which invites the public to recognise Berlusconi's theatrical image and review their attitude to politics and power (Watters this volume). It also exhibits remarkable similarities to *The Animated Planet Show* whose metalanguage provides a tool for the audience to reflect on present political conditions (Popa this volume).

   In my discussion of humour, parody, and irony I applied the incongruity theory and the basics of the GTVH to a genre (i.e. postmodern drama) which the theory has not exploited so far.[17] The overall argument was that mechanisms of humour, parody, and irony in the National Theatre of Greece production are activated through the use of different media, aesthetic forms, and theatrical codes, genres and discourses. Such a co-occurrence of different codes and signs forms *strands*, while the visual, musical, paralinguistic, and intertextual signs of clues of parody and irony make some extracts of the performance text instances of hyperdetermined *humour*. On this basis, I propose that the interaction of different active sources of humour on the performance level may be seen as an extension to Attardo's theoretical framework of *hyperdetermined humour* (Attardo 2001: 100–101, 109–110, 122–125), which may help us discuss the humour of more complex, multimodal texts, such as performance texts. Therefore, I contend that my work may enrich both humour and theatre theories. It shows how a linguistic theory can receive a wider applicability in theatre/performance studies since it applies what has been recognised by the GTVH, but has not yet been part of theatre research. It also shows how humour theory can be enriched by the analysis of theatre texts.

Acknowledgments

The author would like to thank Michael Marmarinos for granting her permission to view the DVD of the recorded production (March 31, 2008).

References

Allain, Paul and Harvie, Jen. 2006. *The Routledge Companion to Theatre and Performance.* London/New York: Routledge.

---

17. Cf. Antonopoulou's research (2003: 21–25) into text types (i.e. comic dialogues in a film script and a sitcom) that the GTVH has hardly discussed; also Balirano and Corduas' (2008: 227–251) semiotic approach based on the multimodal script analysis of a TV show implementing Attardo's (2001) taxonomy of line positions.

Antonopoulou, Eleni. 2002. "A cognitive approach to literary humour devices: Translating Raymond Chandler." *The Translator* 8: 195–220.

Antonopoulou, Eleni. 2003. "Parody and perverted logic in humorous film and sitcom scripts: A GTVH based account for humorous devices." *Antares* VI: 21–25.

Antonopoulou, Eleni. 2004. *Humour in Interlingual Transference* [Parousia Journal Monograph Series 57]. Athens: Parousia.

Attardo, Salvatore. 2001. *Humorous Texts: A Semantic and Pragmatic Analysis* [Humour Research 6]. Berlin/New York: Mouton de Gruyter.

Attardo, Salvatore, Hughes Attardo, Donalee, Baltes, Paul and Petray, Marnie Jo. 1994. "The linear organisation of jokes: Statistical analysis of two thousand texts." *Humour: International Journal of Humour Research* 7: 27–54.

Balirano, Guiseppe and Corduas, Marcella. 2008. "Detecting semiotically-expressed humor in diasporic TV productions." *Humour: International Journal of Humour Research* 21: 227–251.

Bergson, Henri. 1901/1997. *Le Rire. Essai sur la Signification du Comique*. Paris: Presses Universitaires de France.

Canakis, Costas. 1994. "Diglossia as an agent of humour in the writings of Helena Akrita." *Journal of Modern Greek Studies* 12: 221–237.

Canakis, Costas. 2008. "Η στρατηγική χρήση κοινωνιογλωσσικών παραμέτρων στο ευθυμογράφημα της Έλενας Ακρίτα τη δεκαετία του 1980 και σήμερα" (The strategic use of sociolinguistic parameters in the humorous writings of Helena Akrita in the 1980s and today). In *Ο Λόγος της Μαζικής Επικοινωνίας: Το Ελληνικό Παράδειγμα* (The Discourse of Mass Communication: The Greek Example), Periklis Politis (ed.), 350–380. Thessaloniki: Centre of Greek Language. [in Greek]

Casa di Goethe. 2010. The official website. http://www.casadigoethe.it/en/standing-exhibitions/collection.html (accessed March 19, 2011).

Chasapi-Christodoulou, Efsevia. 2002. *Η Ελληνική Μυθολογία στο Νεοελληνικό Δράμα. Από την Εποχή του Κρητικού Θεάτρου έως το Τέλος του 20ού Αιώνα* (Greek Mythology in Modern Greek Drama. From the Era of Cretan Theatre to the End of 20th Century), 2 vols. Thessaloniki: University Studio Press. [in Greek]

Chatzipantazis, Theodoros. 2004. *Η Ελληνική Κωμωδία και τα Πρότυπά της στο 19ο Αιώνα* (Greek Comedy and its Models in 19th Century). Heraklion: Panepistimiakes Ekdosis Kritis. [in Greek]

Chlopicki, Wladyslaw. 2003. Book review of Attardo (2001). *Journal of Pragmatics* 35: 155–159.

Christidis, Minas. 2006. "Αλαλούμ και μαύρο σκοτάδι" (Stir and black darkness). *Eleftherotypia*, July 3. [in Greek]

Delabastita, Dirk. 1996. "Introduction." *The Translator* 2: 127–137.

Diamantakou-Agathou, Keti. 2007. *Περί Τραγωδίας και Τρυγωδίας: Οκτώ Διαδρομές στο Τραγικό και το Κωμικό Θέατρο* (On Tragedy and Trygody: Eight Routes to Tragic and Comic Theatre). Athena: Papazisis. [in Greek]

Dimadi, Iliana. 2008. "Ο Στάλιν και το θέατρο συναντώνται στην ουτοπία" (Stalin and theatre meet at utopia). Interview with Michael Marmarinos and Akilas Karazisis. *Athinorama*, February 28. http://www.athinorama.gr/theatre/articles/?id=4926 (accessed July 22, 2011). [in Greek]

Dovzhenko, Alexander (writer, producer and director). 1930. *Zemlya* (Earth) (motion picture). Soviet Union: VUFKU.

Karazisis, Akilas and Marmarinos, Michael. 2008. *Στάλιν: Μια Συζήτηση για το Ελληνικό Θέατρο* (Stalin: A Discussion about Greek Theatre). Athens: Aigokeros. [in Greek]

Karazisis, Akilas and Marmarinos, Michael. n.d. *Στάλιν: Μια Συζήτηση για το Ελληνικό Θέατρο* (Stalin: A Discussion about Greek Theatre). Performance's DVD.

Kleftogianni, Ioanna. 2008. "Δεν εμπιστευόμαστε ιστορικούς και θεατρολόγους" (We don't trust historians and theatrologists). Interview with Michael Marmarinos and Akilas Karazisis. *Eleftherotypia*, February 22. http://archive.enet.gr/online/ss3?q=&a=%CA%EB%E5%F6%F4%EF%E3%E9%DC%ED%ED%E7&pb=0&dt1=01/01/2008&dt2=01/04/2008&r=6&p=0&id=45503400 (accessed March 26, 2011). [in Greek]

Kölner Theatre Festival. 2008. The official website. http://www.bpb.de/presse/55RQGG,0,ECHT%21_is_a_resounding_success.html (accessed March 18, 2009).

Kotthoff, Helga. 1995. "The social semiotics of Georgian toast performances: Oral genre as cultural activity." *Journal of Pragmatics* 24: 353–380.

Kraounakis, Stamatis. 2007. "Ρώτα μια αλογόμυγα και θα σου πει πού είναι το σκατό" (Ask a horsefly and it'll tell you where the dung is). *Athens Voice*, December 13. [in Greek]

Manteli, Vicky. 2008a. *Η Απόδοση των Αχαρνέων στη Νεοελληνική Σκηνή: Μετάφραση και Παράσταση* (The *Acharnians'* Revival on Modern Greek Stage: Translation and Performance). Unpublished PhD thesis, University of Athens, Greece. [in Greek]

Manteli, Vicky. 2008b. "Greece." In *The World of Theatre 2008 Edition. An Account of the World's Theatre Seasons 2005–2006 and 2006–2007*, Ramendu Majumdar and Mofidul Hoque (eds), 142–148. Bangladesh: Kamala Printers.

Manteli, Vicky. 2010. "Humour and… Zorbas in a National Theatre of Greece production. *Zorbas: The True Story*". Paper presented at the Interdisciplinary Humour Conference "San Zen che ride", San Zeno di Montagna, Italy, 25–28 August 2010.

Marinou, Efi. 2008. "Στάλιν από καρδιάς…" (Stalin with love…). Interview with Michael Marmarinos and Akilas Karazisis. *7 (Kyriakatiki Eleftherotypia)*, February 7–14. http://archive.enet.gr/online/ss3?q=&a=%CC%E1%F1%DF%ED%EF%F5&pb=75&dt1=02/01/2008&dt2=31/03/2008&r=0&p=0&id=33943432 (accessed March 31, 2011). [in Greek]

Matziri, Sotiria. 2008. "Το φετίχ του ακατανόητου" (The fetish of the incomprehensible). *Eleftherotypia*, March 15. http://archive.enet.gr/online/online_text/c=113,dt=15.03.2008,id=33625192 (accessed July 22, 2011). [in Greek]

Μικρή Εγκυκλοπαίδεια. Στάλιν: Μια Συζήτηση για το Ελληνικό Θέατρο. Πρόγραμμα της παράστασης (Concise Encyclopaedia: Stalin. A Discussion about Greek Theatre. Theatre bill). 2007–2008. Athens: The National Theatre of Greece. [in Greek]

Pavis, Patrice. 1998. *Dictionary of the Theatre: Terms, Concepts, and Analysis*. Transl. Christine Shantz. Toronto/Buffalo: University of Toronto Press.

Redfern, Walter D. 1997. "Traduction, puns, clichés, plagiat." In *Essays on Punning and Translation*, Dirk Delabastita (ed.), 261–270. Manchester/Namur: St. Jerome and Presses Universitaires de Namur.

Tsakona, Villy. 2004. *Το Χιούμορ στον Γραπτό Αφηγηματικό Λόγο: Γλωσσολογική Προσέγγιση* (Humour in Written Narratives: A Linguistic Approach). Unpublished PhD Thesis, University of Athens, Greece. http://thesis.ekt.gr/thesisBookReader/id/17786?id=17786&lang=el#page/1/mode/2up (accessed March 5, 2011). [in Greek]

CHAPTER 11

Postscript

A final (?) note on political humour

Diana Elena Popa and Villy Tsakona
Dunărea de Jos University of Galați, Romania /
Democritus University of Thrace, Greece

Political humour is employed to define the boundaries between opposing political groups and to express discontent against politicians and political acts. The sociopolitical context of its production and circulation not only influences its form, content, functions, and targets, but also determines whether it will be accepted, banned, or manipulated to serve the political agendas of certain groups. In this context, political humour becomes a ritual site where political identities are constantly constructed and (re)negotiated. Drawing on studies coming from different sociocultural communities, the authors underline the variety of humorous genres and communicative functions related to political humour, while they point out that humour research needs to look beyond the metapragmatic stereotype often surrounding the use of humour in politics.

The present collection of essays has attempted to offer an overview of some of the main issues concerning contemporary political humour research. Given that the data analysed come from different languages and countries (Estonia, Germany, Greece, Italy, Poland, and Romania) and the methodologies adopted originate in different fields (discourse analysis, folklore and cultural studies, media studies, sociolinguistics, sociology, theatre semiotics), a variety of topics have been discussed and different dimensions of political humour have become the focus of analysis.

The first part of the volume was dedicated to politicians' humour as a means of public positioning, deliberation, and eventually attack against political adversaries. Such humour is exploited to undermine and exclude those who are not with "us" and to bring closer those who are with "us", "us" referring to other politicians and/or the wider voting audience. Hence, incongruity as the core of humour is identified in the political views, acts, and decisions of the "others", which happen to deviate from those of "ours" or from how "we" think they ought to be.

Politicians' humour usually attracts media attention or is performed on air for the sake of the wider audience, thus political debates often turn into a more or less institutionalised competition for the most memorable, funny, quoted, irritating, etc. punch line or jab line.

The second part of the volume involved political satire as realised in different genres: animation, impersonation, and cartoons. In all cases, the deconstruction of the public image of prominent political figures motivates and inspires satirists. The criticism expressed against politicians and their acts appears to be reflecting and reinforcing more or less widespread views on politics. In order to convey their criticism, satirists draw on topics, themes, values, cultural references in general which are expected to be easily accessible to the wider audience. However, the case studies presented here show that political reform as a consequence of humour is hardly the case: satirists are often faced with different kinds of censorship (i.e. banning of the TV animation show in Romania, lawsuits in contemporary Italy, and deprivation of civil rights in Fascist Italy) and they may be forced to adjust their means of expression or even to put an end to their satire.

The third part of the volume pointed to more complicated, but not less interesting, aspects of the politics of humour. Political humour can first be manipulated in public debates on national(istic) issues. In particular, ethnic jokes targeting minorities can be reframed by a minority group as an accusation of oppression and abuse by the majority. Such conflicts are becoming more common in contemporary globalised societies, where the internet plays a central role in hosting and circulating different opinions, thus allowing citizens to participate in public debates along with politicians and journalists. On the other hand, humour based on political references becomes an integral part of postmodern art and gives artists the opportunity to express their views and criticism against not necessarily political targets – at least not in the narrow sense of the word *political*. In such cases, political humour draws on a variety of texts, semiotic resources, and modes, and assumes a sophisticated and at the same time creative and open-minded audience.

As mentioned in the introduction of the volume, the common thread linking all the cases of political humour investigated here is *criticism*: politicians and politics are not as (each humorist thinks) they (ideally) should be and this is highlighted and framed via the humorous mode. The present collection would also like to suggest that humour is not only a means of critique and a rhetorical weapon against the political adversary, but *a symbol over which the struggle for political power takes place*. Politicians, media people, artists, common people, all engage in political humour in their effort to symbolically control the discourse produced on politics: how politics should be and how they believe it would/could be if they were in power. In this symbolic battle, those who can laugh at the expense of their opponents are commonly conceived to be closer to winning them over.

Especially institutionalised humorous genres (such as TV satire, cartoons, and artistic performances) could be described as *ritual sites* where political values and standpoints are more or less freely represented, contested, and defended, and specific political identities are constructed. Such identities are ascribed to the targeted politicians and constructed by the participating ones (see Coleman et al. 2009), as well as constructed by the satirists, cartoonists, etc. for themselves (cf. Tsakona 2011). In public settings where the prevailing mode of interaction is the serious one, but humour is not sanctioned either (such as parliamentary debates, TV political debates, and online fora), the struggle over political humour and the meanings conveyed by it, is more salient and straightforward, while it also involves identity construction via the juxtaposition of humorous and serious messages. The same could be suggested for more private and informal contexts, such as informal conversations among peers, although research on political humour in such settings is – to the best of our knowledge – non-existent.

In general, it could be suggested that the analyses conducted in the present volume bring to the fore both the transmission and ritual dimensions of (humorous) communication. In Carey's (1992: 15–18) and Kadmon Sella's (2007: 104–107) perspective, the transmission view considers communication to be a means of achieving control over distance and people via the dissemination of knowledge, ideas, and information, hence this view is utilitarian and message-oriented. The ritual view perceives communication as communal, participatory, and experiential, hence it sees communication as culture, that is, as a representation of shared beliefs: "[w]hile the ritual perspective finds in communication the fundamental symbolic order in which we live, the transmission view reveals [...] the inner workings of communication as an apparatus of persuasion" (Kadmon Sella 2007: 107). Needless to say, "the ritual view and the transmission view are not mutually exclusive: [j]ust as ritual communication transmits information, transmissive communication has a ritualistic dimension" (Kadmon Sella 2007: 107). Communication in the form of political humour serves persuasive and sometimes even informative functions (at least in the sense of transmitting the humorist's opinion on politics), while at the same time it unites people by reflecting and reproducing shared political meanings and values.

The context of humour has been shown to play a significant role in shaping humorists' production and the audience's understanding. First, the immediate *institutional* context influences the political humour produced therein. In both the German and the Greek parliaments, humour is not considered common practice due to the restrictions on parliamentarians' verbal (or other) conduct. Nevertheless, the increased aggressiveness and competitiveness of a polarised parliamentary system, such as the Greek one, may lead to more numerous and/or more hostile humorous exchanges among parliamentarians, especially during a "no confidence" debate, where the stability of the government and its impression to the voting citizens are at stake. On the other hand, the rules of interaction in TV political debates prompt politicians to resort to verbal aggression, which is simultaneously interpreted as humour by recipients who are not actively involved in the political dialogue. Moreover, the way the media selects and reproduces politicians' humorous sound bites provides the latter the opportunity to appear as participating in fictional dialogues with their colleagues, although they actually do not. Finally, state legislation and respective practices allow for governmental and/or media control over political satire, even in Western democracies: satirical shows can be reformed and satirists can be persecuted.

Cultural and *historical* parameters seem to be equally significant to institutional ones. In Greece, the cultural preference for oral narratives as means of argumentation and identity construction is transferred from informal communicative settings (e.g. everyday interactions with peers) to formal parliamentary ones. Furthermore, the social turmoil surrounding the Greek riots in December 2008 incited politicians to launch intense humorous attacks against their opponents in an effort to make a good impression by supporting or rejecting the persons who were considered responsible for these riots. On the other hand, due to state censorship experiences in their recent past, ex-Communist states, such as Estonia and Romania, are still sensitive to issues regarding freedom of speech, hence the right to joke freely surfaces in the public discourse produced by Estonians and Romanians as directly related to the freedom of speech. Furthermore, due to persisting implicit restrictions on the transmission of political or other information, political satire in such states may sometimes be used to transmit political messages and information that the "serious" media would still not dare to. Finally, in contemporary multicultural environments, jokes may trigger fierce ethno-political debates where minority groups protest against majority repression.

Given the variety of genres and sociocultural contexts examined here, no strict categorisations could be easily made concerning the functions and effects of political humour in relation to the specific social, political, and cultural contexts of its production. However, we hope that the chapters of the present volume managed not only to offer some insights on the main trends in political humour research, but also to bring to the fore the aforementioned variety and the importance of various contextual parameters in shaping interpretations of, and reactions to, political humour. What is more, there currently seems to be a redefinition and further elaboration of the forms and functions of political humour. For instance, political humour is already employed against non political targets in postmodern performances, the Greek case study presented here being indicative of such a trend. Needless to say, more research is required along these lines.

A recent trend in political discourse analysis adopts (or aspires to) a more ethnographic approach, which would take into consideration what citizens appear to understand, and think of, politicians' political discourse, and how they position themselves towards political ideas and stances (Okulska and Cap 2010: 6; see also Janoschka 2010). Such an approach would be equally beneficial for future research projects on political humour. So far, the analysis has concentrated on what (the analyst claims) the humorist means and intends to achieve. Instead, actual audience reactions and positioning towards political humour need to be investigated so as to reveal the real (and not just intended or assumed as intended) effects of political humour. For example, Kramer (2011) explores what speakers think of (rape) jokes, how they position themselves towards them, thus constructing their situated identities, and why they choose to participate in highly controversial debates on the meaning of jokes in the first place. Kramer's perspective sheds light on the specific moral assumptions underlying speakers' argumentation as well as on the ideologies surrounding the content and use of humour.

Such an approach could be adopted to also identify and analyse politicians' actual motives for using humour or participating in humorous TV shows. As Coleman et al. (2009) suggest, politicians participate in satirical TV shows not only to communicate with the wider audience and project a memorable, pleasant, and attractive image of themselves (as is often assumed in relevant studies), but also to *amuse themselves*. Interestingly, Coleman et al.'s study also reveals that at least some politicians consider such shows to be more suitable contexts for expressing their views than "serious" political shows, where they would have to face incompetent or biased journalists or where they would not be given enough time to present their political standpoints.

Cross-cultural and diachronic studies comparing the functions and connotations of political humour usage as well as the ideologies surrounding it in different cultural settings and historical eras could constitute a step further in political humour research. Humor usage and respective ideologies seem to depend on, and interact with, political ideologies, hence what speakers think can or cannot be achieved via humour is strongly influenced by the sociopolitical environment they live in. The two following extracts are illustrative of this connection. First, a number of studies referring to parliamentary humour in former Communist states (Ilie 2010: 210–211; Madzharova Bruteig 2010: 280; Ornatowski 2010: 250–260) agree on the fact that parliamentary humour constitutes a reliable index of the (degree of) democratisation of parliamentary procedures. Focusing on Polish parliamentary humour in particular, Ornatowski (2010: 252) suggests that

> [h]umour and laughter were notably absent from the Socialist-era parliament, since *the official representation of parliament* was one of serious "deputies of the working people" building Socialism in grim toil (Kaminska-Szmaj 2001). Levity would have been out of keeping with the noble earnestness of the enterprise. Humour, including political humour, was of course rife in other venues in public and private life, but was notably absent from public political contexts. Hence, outbursts of merriment in the Sejm [i.e. the lower Chamber of Deputies in the Polish bicameral parliamentary system] following the transition were widely noted as one of the most visible signs of change in the tenor of political life.
>
> (our emphasis)

In other words, humour was evaluated as incompatible with the "serious" political tasks that had to be performed in Communist political and parliamentary settings, thus it was ostracised from them and re-emerged in them after 1989. The change in dominant political ideologies (and conditions) eventually allowed for more and different uses of humour.

On the other hand, in contemporary Western societies, different ideologies are invested in humour: humour is often perceived as a powerful means of rebellion against authority and repression (see Tsakona and Popa this volume). Billig (2005), however, claims that, in late capitalism, there is hardly any relation between humour and rebelliousness: humour has become an entertainment product of the media and cannot be considered "dangerous" for the political status quo. More specifically, he notes that

> there are difficulties with an equation between rebelliousness and humour. A feeling of rebellion and an enjoyment of humour that transgresses social demands do not necessarily equate with a politics of rebellion. The conditions in late capitalism illustrate this. *The position of the joking rebel is a valued one.* It is much celebrated in the entertainment products of the media. These products do not encourage their audiences to become rebels in an absolute sense, for the rebelliousness conforms to the standards of the times. At the flick of a switch (and after the proper payment by credit card), we can enjoy regular programmes of fun and mockery. Dutiful consumption encourages us to mock apparent authority, enabling us to enjoy the feeling of constant rebelliousness in economic conditions that demand continual dissatisfaction with yesterday's products.
>
> (Billig 2005: 209; our emphasis)

In this context, contemporary humorous politicians, cartoonists, satirists, etc. may present themselves (and often be perceived by the wider public) as messengers of a continuous disappointment from the ways politics is conducted, while mostly aiming at promoting and (literally or metaphorically) selling their public and/or political personas. Humour thus becomes a more or less profitable means for financial gain and political power. The ideology of humour as a means of active resistance to, or even rebellion against, political oppression and social injustice cannot be easily (if at all) supported by its current forms and uses in capitalist media environments.

Both extracts above reveal that what speakers think about the essence and/or functions of humour may be shaped by wider ideological frames (i.e. Communist ideology, humour-as-rebellious ideology). Speakers' attitudes and ideas about pragmatic phenomena, such as humour, form the basis of what Agha (1998, 2007) calls a *metapragmatic stereotype*. A metapragmatic stereotype consists of a set of value judgments about pragmatic phenomena, aiming at fixing their variability into static, easily recognizable entities, which will in turn help them understand and handle such phenomena "properly" in everyday interaction. However, as is the case with all kinds of stereotypes, metapragmatic ones, while reflecting and shaping speakers' view and conceptualisations of language use, may not necessarily coincide with what actually happens in discourse: "Such stereotypes of social indexicality have the character of positional metapragmatic norms which do not, in general, reflect the actual behaviours of all speakers" (Agha 2007: 289). The present volume points to that direction: what speakers, politicians, professional humorists, etc. think political humour is about (e.g. an improper distraction from serious endeavours in Communist regimes, a means of resistance and revolt in late capitalism) may not necessarily be supported by its mere use in real life situations.

A final comment concerns the hotly debated issue among humour researchers of whether humour can influence politics and to what extent. The essays included here indicate that humour usually do not influence politics, but rather politics influences the forms, content, and functions of political humour. If political humour could initiate political reform, then we would most probably inhabit a world without it: political reality would be as it "should" have been and no incongruities would be detected to ponder on and laugh at. Political humour is a creative, entertaining, and symbolically powerful means of political deliberation, which is typically used to convey criticism against figures, decisions, and practices, whether political or not. At least this is what this volume would like to suggest until further research reveals that this is just another metapragmatic stereotype.

References

Agha, Asif. 1998. "Stereotypes and registers of honorific language." *Language in Society* 27: 153–193.

Agha, Asif. 2007. *Language and Social Relations* [Studies in the Social and Cultural Foundations of Language]. Cambridge: Cambridge University Press.

Billig, Michael. 2005. *Laughter and Ridicule. Towards a Social Critique of Humour* [Theory, Culture and Society]. London: Sage.

Carey, James W. 1992. *Communication as Culture: Essays on Media and Society* [Media and Pop Culture 1]. London: Routledge.

Coleman, Stephen, Kuik, Anke and van Zoonen, Liesbet. 2009. "Laughter and liability: The politics of British and Dutch television satire." *The British Journal of Politics and International Relations* 11: 652–665.

Ilie, Cornelia. 2010. "Managing dissent and interpersonal relations in the Romanian parliamentary discourse." In *European Parliaments under Scrutiny* [Discourse Approaches to Politics, Culture and Society 38], Cornelia Ilie (ed.), 193–221. Amsterdam/Philadelphia: John Benjamins.

Janoschka, Anja. 2010. "Direct e-communication: Linguistic weapons in a political weblog." In *Perspectives in Politics and Discourse* [Discourse Approaches to Politics, Culture and Society 36], Urszula Okulska and Piotr Cap (eds), 215–236. Amsterdam/Philadelphia: John Benjamins.

Kadmon Sella, Zohar. 2007. "The journey of ritual communication." *Studies in Communication Sciences* 7: 103–124.

Kaminska-Szmaj, Irena. 2001. *Slowa na Wolnosci: Jezyk Polityki po 1989 Roku* (Words in Freedom: The Language of Politics after 1989). Wroclaw: Europa. [in Polish]

Kramer, Elise. 2011. "The playful is political: The metapragmatics of internet rape-joke arguments." *Language in Society* 40: 137–168.

Madzharova Bruteig, Yordanka. 2010. "Czech parliamentary discourse: Parliamentary interactions and the construction of the addressee." In *European Parliaments under Scrutiny* [Discourse Approaches to Politics, Culture and Society 38], Cornelia Ilie (ed.), 265–302. Amsterdam/Philadelphia: John Benjamins.

Okulska, Urszula and Cap, Piotr. 2010. "Analysis of political discourse: Landmarks, challenges and prospects." In *Perspectives in Politics and Discourse* [Discourse Approaches to Politics, Culture and Society 36], Urszula Okulska and Piotr Cap (eds), 3–20. Amsterdam/Philadelphia: John Benjamins.

Ornatowski, Cezar M. 2010. "Parliamentary discourse and political transition: Polish parliament after 1989." In *European Parliaments under Scrutiny* [Discourse Approaches to Politics, Culture and Society 38], Cornelia Ilie (ed.), 223–264. Amsterdam/Philadelphia: John Benjamins.

Tsakona, Villy. 2011. "Humour, religion, and politics in Greek cartoons: Symbiosis or conflict?" In *Humour and Religion: Challenges and Ambiguities*, Hans Geybels and Walter Van Herck (eds), 248–267. London: Continuum.

Contributors

Argiris Archakis is Associate Professor in Discourse Analysis and Sociolinguistics in the Department of Philology, University of Patras, Greece. His research focuses on Discourse Analysis, Sociolinguistics, and Pragmatics. His publications in these areas include articles in *Journal of Pragmatics, Narrative Inquiry, Humor: International Journal of Humor Research, Journal of Sociolinguistics, Pragmatics, Discourse & Society*, and *Journal of Greek Linguistics*. He has recently co-authored a book with Villy Tsakona titled *Identities, Narratives, and Language Education* (in Greek, Patakis Publications, 2011).

Contact address: University of Patras, Department of Philology,
                   265 00 Patra –Rio, Greece
                   archakis@upatras.gr

Marta Dynel, Ph.D., is Assistant Professor (adiunkt) in the Department of Pragmatics in the Institute of English, University of Łódź, Poland, where she completed her doctoral thesis (2006) devoted to the pragmatics of conversational humour. Her research interests are primarily in pragmatic, cognitive, and sociolinguistic mechanisms of humour, as well as the methodology of pragmatic research on film discourse (notably: participation framework, impoliteness, the Gricean model of communication, and deception). Her publications include a monograph: *Humorous Garden-Paths: A Pragmatic-Cognitive Study* (Cambridge Scholars Publishing, 2009), and an edited volume: *The Pragmatics of Humour across Discourse Domains* (John Benjamins, P&BNS, 2011).

Contact address: Instytut Anglistyki, Al. Kosciuszki 65, 90-514 Lodz, Poland
                   marta.dynel@yahoo.com

Marianthi Georgalidou is Assistant Professor in Discourse Analysis in the University of the Aegean, Greece, where she teaches Discourse Analysis, Pragmatics and Sociolinguistics. She has presented papers and published articles on the pragmatics of code-switching and minority discourse, on child discourse, gender and politeness.

Contact address: Volou 2, Rhodes 851 00, Greece
                   georgalidou@rhodes.aegean.gr

Liisi Laineste, Ph.D., has been researching ethnic and political jokes since 2000 and is currently Senior Researcher at the Estonian Literary Museum. She received her MA in 2005 in folkloristics at the University of Tartu, Estonia (*Characters in Estonian Ethnic Jokes*) and her Ph.D. on the same field in 2008 (*Post-Socialist Jokes in Estonia: Continuity and Change*). Working at the Estonian Literary Museum since 2001, she has been involved in two grant projects of Estonian Science Foundation dealing with (ethnic) humour. Her research interests involve ethnic and political humour, cultural studies, post-Socialism, and internet studies. She has published 14 articles on humour.
Contact address: Kastani 16–3, Tartu 50409, Estonia
liisi@haldjas.folklore.ee, liispet@gmail.com

Vicky Manteli is Adjunct Lecturer at the Hellenic Open University where she teaches Classical Greek Theatre. She has also taught Theory and Theatre Semiotics and Theatre Terminology and English Language at the Department of Theatre Studies, University of the Peloponnese, Greece. She has presented papers on humour, modern theatre, and the reception of Aristophanes' theatre in Greek and international conferences. She has published articles on humour and comedy, classical Greek comedy translation, the performance and the semiotics of classical and modern Greek theatre and drama. She has co-translated J. M. Walton's *Living Greek Theatre. A Handbook of Classical Performance and Modern Production* (in Greek, Ellinika Grammata, 2006). Her study on Aristophanes' religious humour interlingual transference was recently published by Continuum Books.
Contact address: 53, Sarantapihou str., Athens 114 71, Greece
manteliv@enl.uoa.gr

Efharis Mascha is Adjunct Lecturer at the Hellenic Open University. She did her BA in Sociology at Panteion University of Athens. Then, she did a Master of Arts in Sociology and Ph.D. in Ideology and Discourse Analysis at the University of Essex. Following that, she did a post-doc at the Advanced Cultural Studies Institute of Linkoping University, Sweden. Her work consists of an array of articles in Greek and international journals on sociology, humour, political cartooning, and popular culture.
Contact address: 28th October street 37, Nea Pendeli 152 36, Athens, Greece
evimascha@hotmail.com

Ralph Müller is Associate Professor in German literature at the University of Fribourg, Switzerland. He studied German literature and history at the Universities of Fribourg and Hamburg. He received his Ph.D. from the University Fribourg in 2003. His dissertation investigated punch line structures in German literature, and his post-doctoral fellowship in Lancaster, Amsterdam, and Munich was based on a study of creative metaphors in political discourse.

Contact address: Dept. Germanistik, Av. de l'Europe 20, 1700 Fribourg, Switzerland
ralph.mueller@unifr.ch

Diana Elena Popa is Senior Lecturer at Dunărea de Jos University of Galați, Romania. She teaches Media and Communication and British Culture and Civilisation to undergraduate students. Her main research interests are in the field of humor studies, media and communication studies, political studies, in which she has published a number of papers. She was the local organiser of the *8th International Summer School and Symposium on Humor and Laughter: Theory and Applications in 2008* and the organiser of the *1st International Conference on Humor in Conventional and Unconventional Politics* in 2009, which took place at Dunărea de Jos University of Galați and were endorsed by the International Society for Humor Studies.

Contact address: Department of English, Dunarea de Jos University of Galati, 111 Domnească St.,
Galați 800201, Romania
helen_anaid@hotmail.com

Villy Tsakona is Assistant Professor (ministerial approval pending) in Sociolinguistics and Discourse Analysis at the Department of Education Sciences in Pre-School Ages, Democritus University of Thrace, Greece. She has presented papers and published articles on the pragmatic, text and conversation analysis of humorous texts, while she has been working on a post-doc research project on parliamentary discourse analysis. She has edited the bilingualised English-Greek versions of P. Trudgill's *A Glossary of Sociolinguistics* (2007, University of Athens) and A. Cruse's *A Glossary of Semantics and Pragmatics* (2008, University of Athens) and has recently co-authored a book with Argiris Archakis titled *Identities, Narratives, and Language Education* (in Greek, Patakis Publications, 2011).

Contact address: Salaminas 48, 116 74 Glyfada, Greece
villytsa@otenet.gr

Clare Watters is Ph.D. candidate in the Department of Italian Studies, University of Birmingham, United Kingdom, where she is also General Editor of the *Birmingham Journal for Europe* and teaches on twentieth century Italian history, media, and society. Her doctoral thesis focuses on the work of Italian political comedians during the Berlusconi era and her research interests include European film, media, and performance with relation to humour. Her work has been published in *Comedy Studies* and the *New York Times* online.

Contact address: Department of Italian Studies, University of Birmingham, Edgbaston, Birmingham, B15 2TT, United Kingdom
cxw723@bham.ac.uk

Name index

Subject index